Reauthoring *Savage Inequalities*

SUNY series, Critical Race Studies in Education
───────────
Derrick R. Brooms, editor

Reauthoring *Savage Inequalities*
Narratives of Community Cultural Wealth in
Urban Educational Environments

Edited by
Lori D. Patton, Ishwanzya D. Rivers,
Raquel L. Farmer-Hinton, and Joi D. Lewis

Cover photo by Stephen Harlan on Unsplash.

Published by State University of New York Press, Albany

© 2023 State University of New York

All rights reserved

Printed in the United States of America

No part of this book may be used or reproduced in any manner whatsoever without written permission. No part of this book may be stored in a retrieval system or transmitted in any form or by any means including electronic, electrostatic, magnetic tape, mechanical, photocopying, recording, or otherwise without the prior permission in writing of the publisher.

For information, contact State University of New York Press, Albany, NY
www.sunypress.edu

Library of Congress Cataloging-in-Publication Data

Names: Patton, Lori D., editor. | Rivers, Ishwanzya D., editor. | Farmer-Hinton, Raquel L., editor. | Lewis, Joi D., editor.
Title: Reauthoring savage inequalities : narratives of community cultural wealth in urban educational environments / edited by Lori D. Patton, Ishwanzya D. Rivers, Raquel L. Farmer-Hinton, and Joi D. Lewis.
Description: Albany : State University of New York Press, [2023] | Series: SUNY series, Critical Race Studies in Education | Includes bibliographical references and index.
Identifiers: LCCN 2022035456 | ISBN 9781438492902 (hardcover : alk. paper) | ISBN 9781438492926 (ebook) | ISBN 9781438492919 (pbk. : alk. paper)
Subjects: LCSH: Education, Urban—Social aspects—United States. | Children of minorities—Education—United States. | Community and school—United States. | Kozol, Jonathan. Savage inequalities.
Classification: LCC LC5131 .R42 2023 | DDC 370.9173/20973—dc23/eng/20221228
LC record available at https://lccn.loc.gov/2022035456

10 9 8 7 6 5 4 3 2 1

To our 89 Blocks . . .
and all the teachers who nurtured and taught us

A 2 minute pause . . .
an offering by Dr. Joi Lewis

Oh Say can you see me
The Land of the free and the home of the SLAVE
2 minutes, 2 minutes 120 seconds.
I have 2 minutes—120 seconds to tell you that Public Education was not built for the masses
And that
Filling up our classes
with
the Nation's elite ensures that
the whole thing is just going to blow

I have 100 seconds and counting and the access and equity gap is mounting
And poverty just gets reproduced and the world acts like we just don't know
what to do
we can start by realizing that
providing free healthcare and affordable housing
Are
Important steps toward making sure that
NO CHILD IS LEFT BEHIND-
But thanks for the reminder that that the policy does not even include those students who have to SIGN
And whose first language may be Spanish,
Or might have almost vanished
Like the Anishinaabe people who are victims of genocide
I have 60 seconds to tell us
That

all of our issues are all related
and that no matter how we state it
the isolation bomb must be detonated
Can't you hear it ticking
You see
Capitalism is tricking
Us into consuming our own destruction
And buying into racism
An evil social construction
I have 30 seconds of information
To stop the bomb of inequity and degradation
By Transforming Urban Education
in East St. Louis and in this Nation
We can start by offering free and equitable education
And interrupt meritocracy
That we call a democracy
But is really affirmative action for the rich
I have 20 seconds to tell you that the SAT
Was not designed for
people who look like me
And that it is not the only indicator of success
My last seconds to say that the system is a mess
Oh my goodness I'm almost out of time
But if we work together
The system can be more than better
So I want to put my 2 minutes with your 2 minutes
And multiply it by 1619
to increase all of our time
Now we have 3,238 minutes to change the world.
And that should give us plenty of time.

Reauthoring *Savage Inequalities*
Narratives of Community Cultural Wealth in Urban Educational Environments

Edited by
Lori D. Patton, Ishwanzya D. Rivers,
Raquel L. Farmer-Hinton, and Joi D. Lewis

Cover photo by Stephen Harlan on Unsplash.

Published by State University of New York Press, Albany

© 2023 State University of New York

All rights reserved

Printed in the United States of America

No part of this book may be used or reproduced in any manner whatsoever without written permission. No part of this book may be stored in a retrieval system or transmitted in any form or by any means including electronic, electrostatic, magnetic tape, mechanical, photocopying, recording, or otherwise without the prior permission in writing of the publisher.

For information, contact State University of New York Press, Albany, NY
www.sunypress.edu

Library of Congress Cataloging-in-Publication Data

Names: Patton, Lori D., editor. | Rivers, Ishwanzya D., editor. | Farmer-Hinton, Raquel L., editor. | Lewis, Joi D., editor.
Title: Reauthoring savage inequalities : narratives of community cultural wealth in urban educational environments / edited by Lori D. Patton, Ishwanzya D. Rivers, Raquel L. Farmer-Hinton, and Joi D. Lewis.
Description: Albany : State University of New York Press, [2023] | Series: SUNY series, Critical Race Studies in Education | Includes bibliographical references and index.
Identifiers: LCCN 2022035456 | ISBN 9781438492902 (hardcover : alk. paper) | ISBN 9781438492926 (ebook) | ISBN 9781438492919 (pbk. : alk. paper)
Subjects: LCSH: Education, Urban—Social aspects—United States. | Children of minorities—Education—United States. | Community and school—United States. | Kozol, Jonathan. Savage inequalities.
Classification: LCC LC5131 .R42 2023 | DDC 370.9173/20973—dc23/eng/20221228
LC record available at https://lccn.loc.gov/2022035456

10 9 8 7 6 5 4 3 2 1

*To our 89 Blocks . . .
and all the teachers who nurtured and taught us*

A 2 minute pause . . .
an offering by Dr. Joi Lewis

Oh Say can you see me
The Land of the free and the home of the SLAVE
2 minutes, 2 minutes 120 seconds.
I have 2 minutes—120 seconds to tell you that Public Education was not built for the masses
And that
Filling up our classes
with
the Nation's elite ensures that
the whole thing is just going to blow

I have 100 seconds and counting and the access and equity gap is mounting
And poverty just gets reproduced and the world acts like we just don't know
what to do
we can start by realizing that
providing free healthcare and affordable housing
Are
Important steps toward making sure that
NO CHILD IS LEFT BEHIND-
But thanks for the reminder that that the policy does not even include those students who have to SIGN
And whose first language may be Spanish,
Or might have almost vanished
Like the Anishinaabe people who are victims of genocide
I have 60 seconds to tell us
That

all of our issues are all related
and that no matter how we state it
the isolation bomb must be detonated
Can't you hear it ticking
You see
Capitalism is tricking
Us into consuming our own destruction
And buying into racism
An evil social construction
I have 30 seconds of information
To stop the bomb of inequity and degradation
By Transforming Urban Education
in East St. Louis and in this Nation
We can start by offering free and equitable education
And interrupt meritocracy
That we call a democracy
But is really affirmative action for the rich
I have 20 seconds to tell you that the SAT
Was not designed for
people who look like me
And that it is not the only indicator of success
My last seconds to say that the system is a mess
Oh my goodness I'm almost out of time
But if we work together
The system can be more than better
So I want to put my 2 minutes with your 2 minutes
And multiply it by 1619
to increase all of our time
Now we have 3,238 minutes to change the world.
And that should give us plenty of time.

Contents

Foreword   xiii
   William T. Trent

Introduction   1
   Lori D. Patton, Ishwanzya D. Rivers, Raquel L. Farmer-Hinton, and Joi D. Lewis

Part 1.
Resilience, Wholeness, and Thriving in Urban Schools (Self)

Chapter 1
Peering Back in a Press Forward: Critiques of Educational
Equality that Protect White Innocence   9
   Chayla Haynes

Chapter 2
Displaced Equalities: Exploring the Impact of Place on
Urban Students   23
   Jada Renee Koushik

Chapter 3
Persisting through Life as a Result of My Urban Education:
The Making of a Black Male Professor   35
   Omari Jackson

Guest Commentary and Reflection: We Know Best What Tools
and Resources Will Sustain Us   49
   Dorinda J. Carter Andrews

Part 2.
The Urban Community as Educator (Community)

Chapter 4
Chicago's Other Children 57
Mirelsie Velazquez

Chapter 5
Far from Savage: (Re)Turning to My Village and Revealing
the "Two Worlds of Washington" 67
Steve D. Mobley Jr.

Chapter 6
A Third-World City: An Autoethnography on Growing Up in
Detroit, Michigan, and Becoming a Teacher 79
Amber C. Bryant

Guest Commentary and Reflection: The Complexity and Nuances
of Origin Stories 93
Marvin Lynn

Part 3.
Centering Students in Teaching and Learning (Students)

Chapter 7
"People Don't *Really* Know Camden High": Student Perspectives
on their Negatively Viewed High School 103
   *Keith Benson with help from Deliyah Whetstone, Tina Q. Baker,
Merv Ragsdale, T'emon'et Elliot, Joel Tarte, Dwyane Cooke,
Naima Battie, Ajianna Bailey, Joselyn Chevere, Rasheed Pollard,
Ijshanna Martin, and Brene' Troutman*

Chapter 8
No Excuses: Believing and Achieving 119
   Jane Bean-Folkes, Susan Browne, and Chanelle Rose

Chapter 9
Avenues to Organic Engagement: One Counselor-Educator's
Experiences Working with Community Agencies to Promote
Educational Success in an Urban Community 141
   Ahmad R. Washington

Contents | ix

Guest Commentary and Reflection: There's More to the Story:
Counter-Narrating Urban Failure and Success   161
  Noelle W. Arnold

Part 4.
Reflections on Educator and
Institutional Influences (Educators)

Chapter 10
Fictive Kin as Driving Forces for Academic Success in Detroit:
Black Women's Narratives on Successfully Navigating through
College   171
  Diane Fuselier-Thompson, Ezella McPherson,
  and Carly Braxton

Chapter 11
"Old School" Urban Education: How Friends, Families,
Communities, and Teachers Support Success in Early Childhood   191
  Theresa J. Canada

Chapter 12
"I Have Seen the Mountaintop": Intersectionality and the
Auto-ethnography of a Mediocre Student at a Gifted School   201
  Heather Moore Roberson

Chapter 13
Dispelling the Myth of Despair and Hopelessness:
How Ethical Leadership Creates a Counter-Narrative to
Kozol's Leadership Caricature   211
  Lonnie R. Morris Jr. and Maceo A. Cooper-Jenkins

Guest Commentary and Reflection: Same Place, Different Race
  H. Rich Milner IV

Part 5.
Renarrativizing "Home" (Place)

Chapter 14
And Still We Made It: Counter-Narratives of Success,
Educational Attainment, and Opportunity in Atlanta   231
  Brittany M. Williams and Lyntoria Newton

Chapter 15
In Search of Oz: Culture, Education, and Counter-Narratives of Inequity in Southern Colored Schools 245
Toby S. Jenkins

Chapter 16
Bringing the Love Back Home: An Ode to the Wiz and Growing Up in East St. Louis 267
Jodi L. Jordan, Deborah J. Patton, and Lori D. Patton

Guest Commentary and Reflection: Emerald City, Oz, and *Savage Inequalities* in Education: Centering the Ruby Slippers 277
Theodorea Berry

Part 6.
Sunday Dinners with Love

Chapter 17
The Meaning of Sunday Dinners 283
Raquel L. Farmer-Hinton

Chapter 18
East St Louis: Where Our Black Lives Always Mattered 289
Dallas Jewell Watson and Joi D. Lewis

Chapter 19
We Were Always a Community: Cooking, Eating, and Living in the John DeShields Housing Project 303
Ishwanzya D. Rivers

Guest Commentary and Reflection: "You Can't Keep Telling Us What We Already Know": A Fugitive End to Educational Narratives of Tragedy 309
David Stovall

Afterword 313
Tara Yosso

Contributors 317

Index 329

Foreword

WILLIAM TRENT

The opportunity to contribute the foreword to this edited volume of critically necessary and well-executed scholarship evokes a deep sense of gratitude and humility. The gratitude is easy to explain as this work is quite personal. I have had the privilege of getting to know each of the coeditors of this book. Doctors Raquel Farmer-Hinton and Ishwanzya Rivers were graduate students in my department. I met Doctor Joi Lewis while a Fellow in Residence at the Spencer Foundation. These three introduced me to Doctor Lori Patton. It was then that I began to encourage Doctors Farmer-Hinton and Rivers to convince their two fellow East St. Louis African American women scholars to collaborate on an article about their educational experiences in the East St. Louis schools and how they managed to eventually earn their doctorate. In my mind, such an article, lecture, or book would be natural for them. They collectively and individually possessed every ingredient needed to tell the story. They certainly showed the talent and knowledge. These four African American women are quite gifted with impressive career accomplishments. Importantly, they have great love and passion for their home, the community, the schools, their friends, and their village.

Doctors Farmer-Hinton and Rivers embraced the idea of developing the paper and invited Doctors Lewis and Patton to join the effort. The result of that collaboration is now clear. The AERA panel they developed and presented has grown from that presentation where much of the audience had hallway seats, into this well-conceived and developed collection.

The challenge they mount in this edited book to the deficit-driven master narrative of the deficiencies in Black learners P-20 and in urban education in particular, is timely and valuable, arriving as it does with the nation in the throes of a tsunami of ills. Importantly, the book is well conceptualized and built intentionally on a structure anchored in critical race theory and emphasizing the centrality of community cultural wealth. This conceptual structure of the book is carried through each of the chapters. The counter-stories collected here are capable of carrying readers into spaces and circumstances about which they have huge misconceptions. Therein lies a major contribution of this book.

The master narrative being challenged is an old and difficult adversary. Major contributions to this master narrative of Black intellectual inferiority and imperfect socialization are decades old in the academic community and emanate from some of the most well-known scholars at prestigious universities. Early on we had the studies of cranial size and shape; the *Mis-measurement of Man* (1981) and *From Neurons to Neighborhoods* (2000) challenge that earlier body of work. Patrick Moynihan (1965) gave us the *Negro Family* and later advised then President Nixon in 1972 that Black participation in higher education was at a point where benign neglect could be an appropriate political strategy. James Coleman et al. authored the 1965 equal opportunity report that revisited and was interpreted in ways that reinforced the master narrative on the failures of the Black family.

This book, *Reauthoring Savage Inequalities: Narratives of Community Cultural Wealth in Urban Educational Environments*, is an important contribution to the ongoing scholarship that embraces and endorses a very different narrative of sacrifice, striving, achievement, and accomplishment; of families and neighbors who were invested in the successes of their neighbors' children, and they let those children know that they were. It is a narrative about educators who heard words misspoken or incorrectly arranged in a sentence but who knew that those speakers did not lack the ability to learn and that they could teach the student how to master language use and why it was important to do so.

This volume will be useful in preservice teacher education and for in-service professional development supports offered to teachers who cannot or would not live in the community where the children they teach live; postsecondary educators and program administrators will find it useful because it will provide the reason for "taking a second or third look" at an applicant from "one of those schools." The understanding of structural and systemic racism and its consequences, made real by COVID, will have readers of this book finding reasons and insights that will help correct the sometimes frequent "ecological fallacy" in assessing their students' aspirations, skills, competencies, and character. They will begin to think "that's where she/he is from," not who she/he is. A book that does that for the reader is a substantial gift. Providing a narrative that correctly presents the motivations, aspirations, talents, and capabilities of urban students and their teachers can go a long way toward disrupting the school-to-prison pipeline. The authenticity and honesty of the stories in this volume will encourage a much richer investment in these learners.

Introduction

LORI D. PATTON, ISHWANZYA D. RIVERS,
RAQUEL FARMER-HINTON, AND JOI D. LEWIS

Jonathon Kozol's *Savage Inequalities: Children in America's Schools* is among the most well-known and highly regarded works in urban education studies. Published in 1991, *Savage Inequalities* was the result of Kozol's research on the persistent inequities in urban schools. His book brought these issues to the forefront and ushered in the need for greater attention to the challenges, politics, and conditions that prohibit students, administrators, and communities from realizing the promise of educational democracy. So powerful was *Savage Inequalities* that not only did it cast a spotlight on schooling inequities and disparities, this *New York Times* bestseller became the default framing for how broad audiences, educators, policymakers, and school leaders would understand urban schooling.

While we value Kozol's scholarship, we also contend that his work created a dominant narrative about urban schooling that did not fully incorporate the voices of individuals from those communities and in some ways offered an incomplete depiction. In our 2013 article published in *Teachers College Record*, "Dear Mr. Kozol: Four African American Women Scholars and the Re-authoring of Savage Inequalities" we share our experiences of growing up and being educated in East St. Louis, Illinois. We followed with a 2021 article in *Urban Education* titled, "That Wasn't My Reality: Counter-Narratives of Educational Success as East St. Louis' Educators "Reimagine" *Savage Inequalities*." Through the aforementioned articles, we shared the disconnect that exists between our lived experiences and

Kozol's characterization of East St. Louis. We stated, "We found it difficult to merge his outsider views with our insider experiences. . . . Individually, we knew that our backgrounds included many unnamed human and structural resources, valuable beyond a dominant and patriarchal framework" (p. 3). Although a critique of Kozol's single storytelling was our starting point, stopping there was insufficient. Rather, we were collectively interested in the often-unnamed sources of support that ensured our success and the success of so many of our peers and family members. We wanted to center those who were responsible not only for our survival but also our capacity to thrive along our educational pathways and life trajectories. As a result, we applied Yosso's (2005) community cultural wealth framework, situated in critical race theory, to reflect on our experiences with growing up in East Saint Louis. By using Yosso's scholarship, we had language to restory our experiences in a way that resisted the dominant narrative that *Savage Inequalities* has become.

Our restorying process led us to produce this edited volume as a space for scholars to engage in the same iterative process of counter-storytelling and highlighting those within their communities who embodied love, care, compassion, pride, and an arsenal of community cultural wealth that is rarely centered in educational discourse, particularly with regard to notions of success. This volume includes contributions from a range of individuals including scholars, educators, and practitioners, each of whom engage in re-storying their experiences in urban educational environments. The counter-narratives they share represent diverse perspectives, ways of knowing, and the creation of knowledge by students, teachers, and administrators who not only grapple with some of the themes highlighted in *Savage Inequalities* but also offer a counter-narrative that presents the lived experiences of being educated and educating in schools and communities that have been systemically isolated and disenfranchised.

The counter-narratives in this volume illuminate the nuances of unjust, dominating, or hegemonic depictions of teaching and learning in urban areas. Solórzano and Yosso (2002) argue that counter-stories can serve as sources of survival and sources of political and cultural resistance for socially marginalized individuals and groups; second, counter-stories challenge master narratives of race and other intersectional markers of identity that promote stereotypical and deficit-oriented representations of people of color (Delgado, 1989; Solórzano & Yosso, 2002). In the latter sense, counter-stories can be understood as a form of talking back, by which marginalized groups can speak truth to power and, in so doing, begin the task of moving from silence and marginalization to speech and liberation (hooks, 1989). Collectively, the compilation of diverse narratives in this book center the voices of minoritized populations in urban educational and community contexts. The contributors present critical and engaging narratives of schooling in urban educational and community contexts including some of the areas highlighted in *Savage Inequalities* (e.g., Camden, East St. Louis, Detroit, and New York).

The contributors provoke readers to think critically about the value of narrative as a strategy to disrupt dominant discourses and challenge conventional knowledges regarding education in urban contexts. They also grapple with and complicate Kozol's interpretation of urban educational environments by juxtaposing it with their own experiences. In doing so, they disrupt and resist wholesale applications of hopelessness and despair, so frequently placed upon teachers, students, families, and communities in urban settings. These narratives can be a resource for future educators to gain a deeper understanding of the inequities present in urban educational contexts and the strategies that teachers, families, students, and communities employ in the face of these challenges. Moreover, the narratives can re-educate those who misunderstand urban students and families as subjects who need to be saved or strategically avoid urban teaching placements.

Overall, this book serves a threefold purpose. First, it is a venue through which the lived experiences and realities of those in urban educational contexts are foregrounded and framed through community cultural wealth. Second, the book serves as a valuable educational resource for educators and students to engage in critical dialogue about *Savage Inequalities* and the power relations and hegemony that shape larger discourses on urban education (e.g., who tells the stories, how they get told, and ultimately who listens). Lastly, this book exists as a counter-narrative to current political and media discourses that fuel clear misunderstandings and master narratives of urban schools and their stakeholders. Instead of accepting narratives that characterize urban school communities as trapped and wallowing in despair, this book explores the diversity in the urban experience where students, staff, parents, and community members continue to work hard despite the purposeful divestment in urban communities of color in cities across this nation.

The book is divided into six sections. The foreword by William Trent provides rich context for this book, particularly how Trent encouraged us to pursue this work and to share our counternarrative, which he insisted was both valuable and necessary. Each section is centered around a theme we identified as editors that captured the essence of the narratives contained therein. In Part 1, "Resilience, Wholeness, and Thriving in Urban Schools," Chayla Haynes, Jada Renee Koushik, and Omari Jackson's narratives remind readers of how self and sensemaking is situated in urban communities and urban education. In Part 2, "The Urban Community as Educator," Mirelsie Velazquez, Steve D. Mobley, and Amber C. Bryant share narratives that illustrate how urban communities often provide an education for life lessons that expand beyond school. In Part 3, "Centering Students in Teaching and Learning," Keith Benson and students from Camden City Schools, Jane Bean-Folkes, Susan Brown and Chanelle Rose, and Ahmad Washington provide a collection of narratives that center students voices, as well as the community organizations that serve these students and invest in them. In Part 4, "Reflections on Educator and Institutional Influences," Diane Fuselier-Thompson, Ezella McPherson and Carly Braxton, Theresa J. Canada, Heather Moore Roberson, Lonnie Morris Jr. and Maceo Cooper-Jenkins discuss stories of how institutional leaders and educators shaped their schooling experiences. In Part 5, "Re-Narrativizing 'Home,'" Brittany Williams and Lyntoria Newton, Toby Jenkins, Jodi Jordan, Deborah Patton and Lori Patton describe conceptions of home and reminisce about the role of place in urban schools and communities. In Part 6, "Sunday Dinners with Love," Raquel Farmer-Hinton, Dallas Jewell Watson, Joi Lewis, and Ishwanzya Rivers reflect on Sunday dinners and shared meals as an educative space in urban environments. The book concludes with an afterword by Tara Yosso, who provides readers with further thoughts on community cultural wealth and the values and resources minoritized communities possess and rely upon to navigate within and beyond urban schooling contexts.

In order to promote readers' sensemaking of and connection to the narratives, we invited guest responses from leading scholars in urban education. Dorinda Carter Andrews (Part 1), Marvin Lynn (Part 2), Noelle Arnold (Part 3), Rich Milner IV (Part 4), Theodorea Berry (Part 5), and David Stovall (Part 6) review, respond to, and complicate the narratives within their respective sections while also reflecting on their own experiences and perspectives on urban schooling. Further, they each offer a set of thought-provoking questions and readings for additional discussion.

We hope readers will engage with this book in a way that not only recognizes the importance of naming existing savage inequalities that plague many urban schools and communities but goes further to illuminate the community cultural wealth that exists and is by far the most valuable perspective for understanding educational success. The narratives contained in this volume consider the ecological complexities inherent in urban school systems and surrounding communities, connecting them to the participants' stories, and extending the discourse on teaching and learning in urban school districts to revise what it means to work and live in these communities.

References

Delgado, R. (1989). Storytelling for oppositionists and others: A plea for narrative. *Michigan Law Review, 87,* 2411–2441.

Farmer-Hinton, R., Lewis, J. D., Patton, L. D., & Rivers, I. D. (2013). Dear Mr. Kozol . . . Four African American women scholars and the re-authoring of *Savage Inequalities*. *Teachers College Record, 115*(5), 1–38.

hooks, b. (1989). *Talking back: Thinking feminist, thinking black.* South End Press.

Rivers, I. D., Patton, L. D., Farmer-Hinton, R. L., & Lewis, J. D. (2021). That wasn't my reality: Counter-narratives of educational success as East St. Louis' educators "reimagine" *Savage Inequalities*. *Urban Education*, 0042085920987283.

Solórzano, D., & Yosso, T. (2002). Critical race methodology: Counter-storytelling as an analytical framework for education research. *Qualitative Inquiry, 8*(1), 23–44.

Yosso, T. J. (2005). Whose culture has capital? A critical race theory discussion of community cultural wealth. *Race Ethnicity and Education, 8*(1), 69–91.

Yosso, T. J. (2006). *Critical race counterstories along the Chicana/Chicano educational pipeline.* Routledge.

Part 1

Resilience, Wholeness, and Thriving in Urban Schools (Self)

Chapter 1

Peering Back in a Press Forward

Critiques of Educational Equality that
Protect White Innocence

CHAYLA HAYNES

Introduction

I picked up Jonathan Kozol's *Savage Inequalities* (1991) ready to give it another try. I was introduced to the book as a first-year master's student at Bowling Green State University. As you might imagine, I was the only Black woman and Student of Color both in my cohort and in the course in which this book was assigned. From what I recall, it was also the first time that material referencing anything remotely relevant to my lived experience was centered in the classroom. I could barely get through the book the first time I read it. I remember repeatedly setting it down and experiencing a sort of disbelief because little of what I read captured what I or my family and friends (quick shout-out to my brother from another mother, G. Alverez Reid) experienced growing up and going to school in Washington, DC, and later Maryland. I had a similar experience in reading *Savage Inequalities* for a second time but believe I am better able to explain why. Instead of affirming the sense of pride I have in my city and my people, I still find Jonathan Kozol's characterization of the District of Columbia and its schools, as well as those in other urban cities, to be monocular and deficient in nature. I was surprised to also learn how few colleagues shared my opinion; perhaps, because they as children, according to Kozol (1991), attended schools in districts "where they were educated to be governors and not to be governed" (p. 176).

But like Farmer-Hinton et al. (2013), who challenged Kozol's depiction of their hometown of East St. Louis, I also felt that the narratives presented in *Savage Inequalities* were "actually only one side of a much more diverse story" (p. 7). Kozol's chapter on Washington, DC, in particular, which includes some discussion about schools and neighborhoods in Maryland and Virginia, tells a familiar story about the haves (i.e., White middle- and upper-class families and the well-resourced schools they attended, seemingly because only those parents wanted the best for their children) and the have nots (i.e., Black and Brown poor and working-class families and the derelict schools they attended, presumably the best those parents could do for their children). By situating his critique of public education on this sort of binary, Kozol constructs a narrative about Washington, DC that *essentializes* (Hobbel & Chapman, 2009) Black and Brown peoples' experiences, conceivably to tap into White peoples' guilt without fully calling into question how structural inequality maintains the economic inequity that concerns him, in a chapter he called "the Innocence of Equality." With this chapter, I use my own lived experience to complicate notions of equality that reinforce Whiteness or White normalcy (Harris, 1993): this is something I believe Kozol might have achieved if only he approached his analysis about Washington, DC schools more critically and from a community cultural wealth perspective (Yosso, 2005). What follows is a discussion of Yosso's (2005) community cultural wealth framework. Then, I use the framework to present my own narrative as a means to resituate Jonathan Kozol's portrayal of the DC Metro area and its schools as places where no students, least of all Black students, can thrive.

Community Cultural Wealth

Informed by critical race theory, Yosso's (2005) conceptualization of community cultural wealth problematizes dominant discourses about cultural capital, which by in large emphasizes meritocracy and embraces deficit narratives about Communities of Color. Accordingly, such deficit narratives are master narratives that act as a hegemonic device, teaching minoritized and White families how to devalue Blackness and Brownness

(Haynes et al., 2016). Kozol (1991) provides readers with illustrations of this very phenomenon, in his chapter about Washington, DC. Kozol begins by describing the circumstances by which parents whose children attend affluent (largely White) schools feel as though "other people's children are of inherently lesser value" (p. 177), as to suggest that they believe money or disproportions in school resources across districts, in effect, are not *the problem*. He continues stating,

> In these ways, [White parents] fend off dangers of disturbing introspection; and this, in turn, enables them to give their children something far more precious than the simple gift of pedagogic privilege. They give them uncontaminated satisfaction in their victories. Their children learn to shut from mind the possibility that they are winners in an unfair race, and seldom let themselves lose sleep about the losers.

Without application of a critical lens, like Yosso's community cultural wealth framework, Kozol's (1991) portrayal of families and children in Washington, DC schools, like the other cities in *Savage Inequalities*, is a one-dimensional story about the *losers*. Though likely unintended, the narrative Kozol constructs ignites a master script (Haynes et al., 2016) that places Black and Brown people in dreadful conditions, presumably of their own making. As a result, the stories and analysis presented in *Savage Inequalities* do not permit the complexity of Black humanity of hope, struggle, and resistance that undergirds my (and many other People of Color's) lived experience to be told.

Using critical race theory as a frame, Yosso's (2005) community cultural wealth framework exposes how racism contributes to often distorted and disparaging depictions about People of Color. The traditional Bourdieusian view of cultural capital often renders communities of color as culturally poor because the cultural knowledge they possess tends to hold little value in a society that has White middle-class culture as its norm (Yosso, 2005). Kozol (1991), to illustrate, tells a story about a visit with a mother and child (named Harper) in a housing project in Anacostia, a neighborhood in southeast Washington, DC. He describes the neighborhood and the surroundings, from his point of view, recalling men loitering, a six-year-old holding a baby, "perhaps his sister, in his arms," public drug deals, and outdoor dice games, imaginably to illustrate Harper's mother's feeling of being in a "battle zone" (p. 187). After spending the day with Harper and her mother, Kozol (1991) concludes that Black people's deformity has become entertainment in American media, while the story about "poor children's lifelong deformation by their own society and government" goes untold (p. 191). He continues, "The story that we do not hear is of the aggressive marketing of these commodities [i.e., sneakers, liquor, drugs] in neighborhoods where very poor [B]lack people live; neighborhoods where appetites for purchasable mediocrity are easily inflamed because there sometimes is so little that is rich and beautiful to offer competition."

Characterizations, like these, that cast Black (and Brown) folks, and their children, as culturally poor and thus sometimes "moral-less" and "reckless," but continual "victims" are frequent throughout Kozol's *Savage Inequalities*.

Yosso (2005) argues that some communities will always be treated as culturally poor, while others are treated as culturally wealthy, when interpretations of cultural capital are associated with knowledge, skills, and abilities that only White middle-class people possess or inherit. Centering the lived experience and life histories of Communities of Color, Yosso's (2005) community cultural wealth framework outlines six forms of cultural capital that highlight accumulated resources and assets that People of Color utilize to survive and resist micro- and macro-forms of oppression.

Aspirational capital can be described as the ability to maintain a hope for the future in the face of hardship and structural racism (Yosso, 2005). Yosso (2005) also asserts that aspirational capital is demonstrated often by families who encourage their children to envision and pursue lives beyond their present circumstances. *Linguistic capital* captures the multitude of skills that students of color, in particular, have in the areas of language and communication. Developed in bilingual households and/or through cultural traditions of storytelling, dance, art, and song, these children tend to understand oral histories, possess real-world literacy skills, and demonstrate social maturity (Yosso, 2005). Kinship ties, or *familial capital*, recognize the role of extended family in nurturing not only a commitment to community but also an emotional, educational, moral, and occupational consciousness among children of color (Yosso, 2005). Referred to as pedagogies of the home, these understandings of kinship, family, and community, along with their importance, are taught formally (e.g., churches and community gatherings) and informally (family-to-family interactions) through lessons that reflect the sociopolitical context of the world (Yosso, 2005). *Social capital*, from a community cultural wealth point of view, underscores the significance of collectivism. Yosso (2005) asserts that Communities of Color engage the "each one, teach one" principle, as they use and share resources and emotional support gained navigating social institutions (e.g., the legal system, the education system, and the medical system) to help members of their social networks overcome them, as well. The ability of Children of Color to negotiate social institutions (settings and environments) not created with them in mind is attributed to *navigational capital*. Navigational capital also captures the psychological and social skills that People of Color develop when they encounter, survive, and/or recover from hostile racial conditions both in and outside of the classroom (Yosso, 2005). Finally, *resistant capital* illuminates the knowledge and skills that People of Color learn through engaging in oppositional behaviors to challenge structural racism and inequality. Moreover, Yosso (2005) posits that maintaining and passing on the multiple forms of community cultural wealth in itself is a form of resistant capital. For example, my decision to use my lived experience to present a counternarrative that reflects Black families and their children as hopeful, hardworking, and committed to academic excellence is in itself a form of resistant capital because I aim to resituate Kozol's depiction of Washington, DC in *Savage Inequalities*.

Peering Back: Cultural Wealth Building

I was born and raised in northwest Washington, DC, and was taught early to appreciate where I came from. Washington, DC, the nation's capital—home to Georgetown University, Howard University, and the epicenter of art, history, politics, and culture—was far from the DC that I knew. My DC was church, Bible study, and secret devotions; block parties, Georgia Avenue Day, the Emory Park hydrant on hot summer days, and Go-Go (Chuck, Rare Essence, Junkyard, and Northeast Groovers to be exact); home cooking, the corner store and neighbors waving from their stoop; laughter, family, and coming home smelling like "outdoors" from playing outside all day. Everything about it filled my mind and my world. The five city blocks I traveled each day between grandma's house, school, and church were formative learning experiences in my development of *resistant and navigational capital*, making the twenty-minute drive across the DC line and over the Anacostia River Bridge into Forestville, MD, where I lived as an adult, feel somewhat light years away. Being a Black woman was not so much about the color of my skin as it was about my way of life. My Black womanhood is what I refer to when describing my ancestry, my culture, and my identity. My Black womanhood continues to shape the everyday dynamics of my life.

Illustrative of *familial capital*, I come from a large but close-knit family with deep communal bonds, although I am an only child (Yosso, 2005). The maternal side of my family, of which I am the closest, spans over 100 years and seven generations, all still residing in the DC Metro area or the DMV (DC, Maryland, and Virginia) to area natives. My grandparents were working-poor people, with 10 children. My mother was their fifth child. Between them, my aunts and uncles have eighteen children, all relatively close in age. This made mundane activities, such as going to school, having Sunday dinner, or attending church feel like family reunions because they brought my immediate and extended family together. As was common at the time, a few of my mom's siblings (and their children) lived with my grandmother, after her husband (my grandfather) passed away. I was raised by a single mother, who by her own account did not see a college education, in her youth, as a necessity. However, her mother (my grandmother) did. At that time, most of my family believed that getting a job within the Federal Government was the best way to go after high school. But my mom, at the insistence of my grandmother, enrolled in Mount Union College in Ohio on an academic scholarship. Surprisingly, my mom was reluctant to go. The way she tells the story, she only filled out the college application and applied for the scholarship because a friend of hers did. One afternoon, a group of girls on her cheerleading squad were going to a college informational for high school juniors at Cardoza High School, where my mom was enrolled at the time. Mom said to me, "The other kids were going to the meeting, so I went too." My mom apparently forgot all about it, until notification came that she was accepted and awarded the scholarship. She had no plans to leave home. But, she said, "When your grandmother heard about it, she turned to me and said, 'lil girl, you going.' Before I knew it, your grandmother had bought me a plane ticket and shipped my belongings to Ohio. I had never even been on a plane before." As I listen to my mom tell me this story, I can imagine grandma doing just that. Hop, as my grandmother was lovingly called by her children (Hop could leap across the room in a single bound to get her kids and grandkids back in line, if need be), was a no-nonsense woman.

So, my mom grudgingly went away to college. She was a first-generation college student and the only one of her siblings to attend college and graduate. After two years, she transferred to Syracuse University to study nursing. I found an old photo of her from back in the day. She was the only Black woman and Person of Color in her cohort. Shortly after my mother graduated, I was born, and she raised me, just as her mother raised her, to believe that who I was in spirit and in likeness (my Black womanhood, my family, my inner strength, and my abilities) were God-given gifts.

The first time I asked my mom to tell me about what it was like for her raising a child, as a single mother, she said, placing emphasis on *aspirational capital*, "The decisions I made were not driven so much by what it was I could afford. I wanted for you what every parent wants for their child; that is, what is in their best interests. As your mother, I wanted to provide you and expose you to learning opportunities that would help you become a well-rounded person. I was invested in that and felt that was my responsibility, as your mother, to achieve that in the best ways that I could." I never asked my mom, but I suppose that is exactly what my grandmother wanted for her. Perhaps that is why she put my mother on that plane to Ohio in the first place.

Grade School

Shortly before the events Kozol (1991) presents in *Savage Inequalities*, I was attending Truesdell Elementary, a public school in northwest Washington, DC. Because the school was located in my neighborhood, I attended school with students and was cared for by teachers, like Mrs. Mason, my second grade teacher. I still hold memories of Mrs. Mason in my heart and mind. Mrs. Mason was a Black woman educator who treated her students like we were her children. She held me to the highest academic standards, not uncommon among Black teachers who taught Black children (Milner, 2006). Her not-so-hidden curriculum reinforced the message that I received at home: education is important. She spoke to my life with her pedagogy, impressing upon me that what I was learning now would prepare me for the bright future that was ahead, one that, according to her, included college. She was my first model of a Black woman pedagogue but thankfully not my last (thank you Mrs. McGee and Ms. Spruill from high school and Dr. Wilhelmina Boyd and Dr. Lori Patton Davis from college and graduate school). Mrs. Mason, like other teachers at Truesdell Elementary, provided students the *navigational capital* they knew we would need, as they were people from the community who faced similar types of socioeconomic challenges as my family. I am aware that some people hear "DC" and think "drugs and death, decay and destitution" (Kozol, 1991, p. 187), particularly among low-income Black families. But for me, growing up in DC fostered my sense of belonging and security, characteristics that I would look for later in my postsecondary education.

School zoning in the District of Columbia provided most students with a choice to walk to school. I walked to school each day with other kids from the neighborhood, including my school-aged cousins. Like many schools in DC at the time, Truesdell was under-resourced. Though I did not notice this until I was enrolled in Maryland public schools. My new surroundings were quite different. Neighborhoods in Maryland had shopping malls instead of local corner stores. I also noted that houses were detached, as opposed to in a row, side by side. Those are some of the major differences that stayed with me at the time. Most people also seemed to travel by car and not by foot or public transportation like I was familiar with. The move to Maryland took place when I was in third grade. My mom's job took us just outside of the city, to Prince George's County, Maryland. The apartment we lived in required that I be bused to school. I did appreciate not having to walk, especially in the cold months. Although I did not understand why I had to commute nearly 40 minutes from home to attend Calverton Elementary, while Ridgecrest Elementary was less than a 10-minute bus ride away. The transition to a new school was difficult. I was separated from the familial kinships (with blood relatives and Black families from my neighborhood) that provided me with so much support. My anxiety intensified when the school district rezoned. I was then bused to Hollywood Elementary to start and complete the sixth grade. I now know what was so difficult for me to comprehend back then. Mandatory school busing from racially diverse, low-income school districts was (and is) done to desegregate largely White and middle-class school districts. No longer were my classrooms filled with children or teachers from my neighborhood who shared my heritage and lived experience; factors that contributed significantly to my ability to thrive. In this regard, Kozol makes a valid point in his chapter on Washington, DC. This experience served as a catalyst in my development of resistant capital mandatory busing, like other forms of compensatory justice (Tyack, 1993), in most every case, advantages the privileged in pursuit of equality (Kozol, 1991). Over the next ten years of schooling that I had in Maryland, I did not remember many White children being bused to my neighborhood.

High School

It was the fall of 1990, and I was doing everything I could to just make it through the first day of high school unscathed. The whole experience seemed a bit overwhelming. Moving from mods to periods, from cubbies to lockers, and from one teacher to six in one day, was a lot of pressure. I struggled to "relax, relate and release," a coping strategy I learned watching Whitley Gilbert on the *A Different World* navigate college life at the fictional Hillman College, an HBCU. My high school stood on a hilltop in Beltsville, Maryland, and seemed enormous to me. It housed over 1,900 students and educated ninth through twelfth graders, later expanding to add eighth graders. I sensed the importance of high school in terms of academic achievement and the bearing it would have on my future. But that was not my top priority at the time. My mother expected me to be productive. That meant I was supposed to maintain an afterschool job (which I began at 15 and nine months) and be a good student. As a nurse, my single mom worked a lot. But the emphasis she placed on school taught me that she felt an education would prepare me for a fulfilling future.

My academic experiences in high school were somewhat reflective of the misguided goals of public education being the great equalizer (Kinloch et al., 2017). But in reality, my high school, like many others at the time, maintained academic norms that promoted racial stratification among students through school tracking (Darling-Hammond, 1995). In a tracking system, the type of preparation provided is presumed to coincide with the occupational track that best matches the student's academic potential and aptitude. Students could be placed on an academic, general, or vocational track (Oakes & Lipton Martin, 1985). Students in academically advanced tracks studied higher mathematics, more foreign languages, and literature.

During my freshman year, I remember having to take courses that taught vocational skills, like typing and cosmetology, perhaps in preparation for a vocational career. I remember back then being rather bored by school. And my mediocre grades, my mom thought, did not reflect my potential. The "spare the rod, spoil the child" attitude my mom had about discipline motivated me to refine my study habits and place more of a focus on my schoolwork. By the fourth quarter of my freshman year, I was earning straight As on my report card. My grades drew the attention of my high school guidance counselor. And just like that, my mom and I were informed that I would start my sophomore year in something my school referred to as the Academic Center. I could not conceive it then, but my mom was outraged by the thought of a dual system (Kozol, 1991) existing inside a public high school.

Some of my new courses included honors history, Spanish, computer applications, and scholastic leadership, where I actually received course credit for serving in the Student Government Association. This was also one of the first times that I shared a classroom with students of different nationalities. Even though the Academic Center was located in the same building, the classroom climates and the available resources (e.g., the computer lab and books) I encountered seemed much different than the school year before. I liken my transition to the Academic Center to that referenced in the movie *Class Act* with Kid 'n Play (to date the best pop culture interpretation of school tracking). Just like in the movie, there were seemingly two different systems of education operating in the same school. The coursework and activities I was being exposed to as a student in the Academic Center ultimately taught me a valuable new language of sorts: Whiteness (Harris, 1993), a form of *linguistic capital* that would prove useful in my ability to perform in White academic spaces. "Whiteness as normal describes the beliefs and self-reinforcing, institutionalized practices that privileges White ways" (Haynes et al., 2019, p. 1149).

College

My mom was adamant that upon graduation from high school I should be able to support myself and my lifestyle, either by getting a full-time job or going to college. She kindly explained that "supporting myself" involved getting my own place, my own car, and my own landline. It was the 1990s, and the world was not yet dependent on cell phones. She preferred that I go to college and did what she could to cultivate that desire within me. It was her hope that I would go away to school; she encouraged going south. When asked why, she replied, "Black people are not all the same. I want you to go out and learn that for yourself." Upon my mother's advice, I narrowed my college choices down to four schools. Three of the schools were in North Carolina, and each focused on liberal arts education, including one historically Black college (or HBCU). My safety school option was a public university in Maryland, and I preferred to go away to school. That so-called safety school was the one institution that did not accept me. I recall my rejection letter indicated that they had met their quota of qualified applicants. My mom and I were unsure about what they meant by that but concluded that school was not the best one for me. My mom took a day off work, and we drove down to North Carolina to visit each campus. As soon as I stepped out of the car at Elon College (now a university and private institution), I felt it was the place for me. Their public and lived motto was "What a College Should Be," and I bought right into it. Looking back on it, I am sure I was not the only prospective student who fell in love with the picturesque setting, ivy-covered buildings, and country-club inspired amenities (I mean facilities). Aside from my anecdotal understanding of college that I learned from watching *A Different World* and *The Cosby Show*, I had little awareness about what a college was about.

I can remember only visiting a college campus once or twice while participating in high school cheerleading competitions in Maryland. Even though I grew up just down the road from Howard University, I had never been there. My mom told me that might be a result of something she experienced during her youth. She recollected, "Black children from working-class families knew better than to walk on the same side of the street as Howard University. Back then, the Black students who went to Howard came from well-to-do families; I did not fit the bill." Much like anyone would imagine about a private liberal arts school in the South, racial and ethnic diversity were limited at Elon. I enrolled the same year Nelson Mandela had become the first Black African elected president of South Africa. Our world was embracing the idea of global diversity, and Elon, like many most institutions I suspect, was not about to be left out of the national dialogue. As a freshman, I participated in a required reading program and a subsequent diversity seminar course. We were assigned *Things Fall Apart*, a 1958 English-language novel by Nigerian author Chinua Achebe, in the summer before freshman year. The book was later to serve as a basis for learning and discussion in the diversity seminar that I was enrolled in. However, I did not feel as though the instructor incorporated the book into the course in any meaningful way. Educational norms and practices, like these, that engage diversity as benign variation (Mohanty, 1990) can contribute to the invisibility that racially and ethnically minoritized students feel in White academic spaces because they often do not permit a critique of the role of power, privilege, and difference in shaping lived experience, particularly among majoritized populations (Haynes & Joseph, 2016). My experience in that course (see Haynes et al., 2016) foreshadowed much of what learning conditions were like for me going forward as a Black woman studying in the Ivory Tower. Those classroom learning experiences gave me the *resistant capital* that I now leverage in my own research and classroom as a faculty member who illustrates how academic norms advance and/or undermine racial justice in higher education broadly but particularly at predominantly White institutions (PWIs).

A Press Forward

In sharing my story, I aimed to resituate Kozol's *Savage Inequalities* by illustrating how community cultural wealth (Yosso, 2005), aided my ability to learn in Black classrooms of the Washington, DC area and later in White academic spaces. After looking back, I am forced to acknowledge just how much influence these educational experiences have had on shaping my scholar and educator identity. What I hope my story reveals is how complicit we as educators can be in the oppression of others when we fail to recognize how structural inequality that reinforces White normalcy can affect the Black family and educational pathways of Black children. The cultural wealth (Yosso, 2005) that I have accumulated along my educational journey helps me to *press forward toward the goal* (Philippians 3:14) of racial justice in higher education, and P-20 education broadly. I close with a narrative describing how I *press forward* (Phil 3:14).

Pressing Forward Toward the Goal

In my press forward, I make a commitment to myself to fully acknowledge in form, function, and consciousness just how urgent and personal this business of education is to me because "my spirit is a part of this. [T]hat is why I get spiritual" (J-IVY on Kanye West's *Never Let Me Down*).

In my press forward, I will not only seek shelter in safe, yet hidden spaces of the academy, where only people who know my struggle and feel my pain surround me. Disrupting Whiteness and the legacy of exclusion that guides much of the work we do in higher education cannot be done in a vacuum. It is a life's work for me; one likely to involve much emotional labor.

I will *press forward* knowing that our outrage is not bound by one understanding of inequality but by the shared feelings of intolerance for the status quo. I acknowledge that I need you in order to teach in ways that transgress. I see you as instrumental to the (un)learning process and I will not discount your ability to labor in the struggle because of our differing backgrounds and lived experiences.

I *press forward* knowing that this is only the beginning of my story and acknowledging that I will continually be shaped by my participation in the P-20 educational system. I commit to press forward in an effort to make my students' tomorrow better than my yesterday.

References

Cooper, C. J. (1986). Coercive remedies paradox, the. *Harvard Journal of Law and Public Policy, 9*, 77–82.

Chubb, J., & Moe, T. (1988). Politics, markets, and the organizations of schools. In A. H. Halsey, H. Lauder., P. Brown, & A. S. Wells (Eds.), *Education: Culture, economy society* (pp. 332–337). Oxford University Press.

Darling-Hammond, L. (1995). Restructuring schools for student success. In A. H. Halsey, H. Lauder, P. Brown, & A. S. Wells (Eds.), *Education: Culture, economy society* (pp. 332–337). Oxford University Press.

Farmer-Hinton, R. L., Lewis, J. D., Patton, L. D., & Rivers, I. D. (2013). Dear Mr. Kozol. . . . Four African American women scholars and the re-authoring of *Savage Inequalities*. *Teachers College Record, 115*(5), 1–38.

Freire, P. (1996). *Pedagogy of the oppressed* (revised). Continuum.

Harris, C. I. (1993). Whiteness as property. *Harvard Law Review, 106*(8), 1707–1791.

Haynes, C., Allen, E., & Stewart, S. (2016). Three paths, one struggle: Black women and girls battling invisibility in U.S. classrooms. *Journal of Negro Education, 85*(3), 380–391.

Haynes, C., & Bazner, K. J. (2019). A message for faculty from the present-day movement for Black lives. *International Journal of Qualitative Studies in Education, 32*(9), 1146–1161.

Haynes, C., & Joseph, N. M. (2016). Transforming the STEM system: Teaching that disrupts White institutional space. In N. M. Joseph, C. Haynes, & F. Cobb (Eds.), *Interrogating whiteness and relinquishing power: White faculty's commitment to racial consciousness in STEM classrooms* (pp. 1–12). Peter Lang.

Hobbel, N., & Chapman, T. K. (2009). Beyond the sole category of race: Using a CRT intersectional framework to map identity projects. *Journal of Curriculum Theorizing, 25*(2), 76–89.

hooks, bell (1994). *Teaching to transgress: Education as the practice of freedom*. Routledge.

Kinloch, V., Burkhard, T., & Penn, C. (2017). When school is not enough: Understanding the lives and literacies of Black youth. *Research in the Teaching of English, 52*(1), 34–54.

Kozol, J. (1991). *Savage inequalities: Children in America's schools.* Harper Perennial.

Milner IV, H. R. (2006). The promise of Black teachers' success with Black students. *Educational Foundations, 20,* 89–104.

Mohanty, C. T. (1990). On race and voice: Challenges for liberal education in the 1990s. In A. H. Halsey, H. Lauder., P. Brown, & A. S. Wells (Eds.), *Education: Culture, economy society* (pp. 557–571). Oxford University Press.

Oakes, J., & Lipton, M. (1990). Tracking and ability grouping: A structural barrier to access and achievement. In J. Goodlad & P. Keating (Eds.), *Access to knowledge* (pp. 187–204). New York College Entrance Examination Board.

Tyack, D. (1993). Constructing difference: Historical reflections on schooling and social diversity. *Teachers College Record, 95,* 8–34.

West, K., Jay-Z, & J-Ivy. (2004). Never let you down. In *The College Dropout.*

Yosso, T. J. (2005). Whose culture has capital? A critical race theory discussion of community cultural wealth. *Race Ethnicity and Education, 8*(1), 69–91.

Chapter 2

Displaced Equalities

Exploring the Impact of Place on Urban Students

JADA RENEE KOUSHIK

Jonathan Kozol's (1991) book, *Savage Inequalities*, illustrated the "good school" versus "bad school" stock story. Specifically, Kozol explored the flagrant financial, physical, and pedagogical contrasts in learning environments between poor urban communities and those found in middle- to upper-class communities. In this chapter, I begin by situating myself and reflecting upon identity, place, and my unexpected educational experiences while growing up in Detroit, Michigan. I argue that the "good school" stock story masks the complexities of class and race that I experienced as an urban student trying to find a sense of place and identity in a wealthy, private, suburban school setting. I offer my counter-narrative to illustrate the impact of place on displaced urban students, including how *Savage Inequalities* can be further unpacked in light of dominant discourses surrounding Whiteness, privilege, and meritocracy.

An Urban Student Displaced: "You Talk Like a White Girl!"

I vividly recall the awkwardness and shame when confronted with this statement—one that was usually accompanied by an accusatory scowl. I was only eight years old. Yet I already understood that I was different and that this difference was not appreciated among the children that lived in my community. I often wondered: What can I do to fit in with the neighborhood kids? How can I behave more like them? How can I sound *more* Black?

My mother had the best of intentions when, in the third grade, she sent me to an affluent private school in Grosse Pointe Farms, Michigan. She wanted me to have opportunities that were not available in the Detroit Public Schools; she wanted me to pursue my dreams without limitations. With all of her love, and a substantial portion of her income, my mother placed me in a school where I was a racial, economic, and social minority. Magnificent homes and expansive estates (Figure 2.1) surrounded my new school, and, for the first time in my young life, I understood what it meant to be an outsider. Within a few months, I realized that I would need to drastically change the way that I talked, dressed, and how I wore my hair—just in order to thrive.

I hastily enrolled in cheerleading, track, softball, and forensics, and after a while my transformation became quite easy. I even enjoyed playing the part of a wealthy Black girl at a private suburban school. Yet, every night, I had to return to my home (Figure 2.2) in Detroit, and the neighborhood kids were not impressed by my newfound persona.

Figure 2.1. A typical house near my elementary school (Grosse Pointe Farms, MI). Photo credit: Stephanie V. Fulks.

Figure 2.2. The home that I grew up in was demolished in 1996 to build a shopping plaza, but this house closely resembles my childhood home (Detroit, MI). Photo credit: Stephanie V. Fulks.

I was labeled a "sellout," and my peers confronted me on numerous occasions because they thought that I considered myself better than them. Eventually I learned to code switch, where I changed my dialect and behaviors based upon my surroundings and social situation. But, sometimes, I still cannot help but wonder . . . am I *Black* enough?

I am currently a PhD candidate at the University of Saskatchewan, which is a public research university located in the midwestern prairies of Canada. Some people may say that I have come a long way from inner-city Detroit, but it has been a fairly easy adjustment for me. I suppose that I have always been trained to adapt, urged to morph, and encouraged to hide my true colors. You may wonder why I am contributing to a volume that strives to reauthor *Savage Inequalities* by offering counter-narratives of striving and success in urban education. What does a highly educated Black woman who grew up attending wealthy, private, suburban schools know about urban education and the experiences of inner-city students? I argue that, as an urban youth growing up on Detroit's East Side, I was displaced in Grosse Pointe Farms and ill-equipped to grapple with the complexities of class and race that I experienced in a suburban setting. I am writing this narrative because I adorned "Whiteness" in order to succeed in the suburbs, and I wonder how many other urban students have struggled to find a sense of place and identity in nonurban educational settings?

My narrative explores the relationship between place and identity, and I use an intersectional analysis to unpack some of the unanticipated issues that I faced as a displaced urban student. Intersectionality reflects the ways that multiple oppressions including (but not limited to) race, class, and gender are experienced (Crenshaw, 1989). Furthermore, I use the term "intersectionality" to depict the relatedness and fluidity of social constructs (e.g., race, sex, gender, class) and place. My aim is not to dispute or reconcile issues highlighted in *Savage Inequalities* but to walk alongside Mr. Kozol as he unearths these disparities in America's public school systems and offer an alternative, intersectional narrative that centers the community cultural wealth of place (see Yosso, 2005).

Place (Still) Matters

Savage Inequalities paints a stark picture of public schools in places such as Detroit, and Kozol (1991) primarily argues for the desegregation of schools in these regions as a solution to downtrodden school buildings, abysmal student retention rates, underpaid teaching staff, and meager educational budgets. Growing up, I remember the kids on my street complaining about not having textbooks or school supplies until December or January of the school year. Even as a young child, I felt anger and frustration toward the Detroit Board of Education for leaving our neighborhood schools in constant financial turmoil. It seemed like every few weeks the news media reported threats of teacher strikes or educational budget cuts and staff layoffs. Many parents were desperate to provide their children with the stable, equitable learning environment that seemed ubiquitous in the suburbs.

However, the sort of mass desegregation that Kozol (1991) suggested would involve a substantial amount of student movement within cities and between urban and suburban areas. I contend that *Savage Inequalities* diminishes the importance of place and connections to community cultural wealth (see Yosso, 2005) by uncritically promoting the placement of urban students into suburban settings. I vividly remember the daily drive from my quaint, beloved home in Detroit to my lavishly landscaped elementary school in Grosse Pointe Farms (Figure 2.3).

With each passing street, I felt more and more disconnected from my family, friends, and community. Traversing between Detroit and Grosse Pointe Farms helped me to recognize place as space that is "invested with meaning in the context of power" (Cresswell, 2004, p. 12). This power is expressed in various contextual and material ways; however, at

Figure 2.3. My affluent elementary school (Grosse Pointe Farms, MI). Photo credit: Stephanie V. Fulks.

the margins of Detroit, it included the erection of semiporous borders, the redlining of poorer sections of town, and the unequal funding of school systems. This is readily seen in areas that appear at the periphery of Detroit, where a few prominent neighborhoods have successfully petitioned to segregate from Detroit and adopt a more palatable name and identity (e.g., Eastpointe, East English Village).

Kozol (1991) fails to recognize any community cultural wealth such as local knowledge, cultural resistance, and social connections in the classrooms that he visited. Instead, he posits that the urban students in many of the schools he visited appeared to be both physically and mentally separated from the outside world. Kozol describes a conversation with a sixth-grade teacher in New York:

I ask her, "Do the children ever comment on the building?"

"They don't say," she answers, "but they know."

I ask her if they see it as a racial message.

"All these children see TV," she says. "They know what suburban schools are like. Then they look around them at their school. This was a roller-rink, you know . . . They don't comment on it but you see it in their eyes. They understand." (p. 88)

The racial and social implications of a school being placed in a roller rink must not be diminished. However, this statement highlights the various ways that these urban students interact with the wider world and implies that they are not ignorant of the disparities that they see on television and more poignantly in their everyday lives. Even in my own experiences, I recall an overabundance of geographical content and world history in my classes, and the omission of Black History and African American literature. This omission always left me with a sense of unease, as I constantly felt like my history (and identity) was being omitted from the story of our country and effectively erased from existence.

Taking the concept of place a bit further, a sense of place encompasses "psychological being, social community, cultural symbols, bio-physical territory, and political and economic systems" (Ardoin, 2006, p. 121). This is meaningful because contested places are the "loci of past, ongoing, and potential future conflicts and displacements" (Semken & Brandt, 2010, p. 287). I believe that education that remains emplaced can offer a range of unique benefits for troubled communities in contested places (Semken & Brandt, 2010), and that engendering a sense of place in students can disrupt dominant discourses surrounding urban areas. This is especially true for the City of Detroit, which is persistently depicted in the media as dangerous, unsavory, and corrupt. Why are stories of community cultural wealth and individual success and resilience rarely portrayed in the media, and which groups are harmed by or benefit from maintaining the "stock story" of Detroit?

Emplaced Racism and Privilege

In the seventh grade, my American history teacher introduced us to the Civil War, which she described as a bloody battle that pitted brother against brother and effectively "freed" the slaves. When one of my classmates asked her for more details about slavery, she mentioned that Black people were bought and sold to work on plantations, but thanks to President Lincoln, African Americans are now free. She glanced at me (the only Black person in the room) when she made this statement, which triggered my classmates to stare at me expectantly as I prayed to God that I would melt into the floor and disappear. I was personally embarrassed, culturally ashamed, and utterly confused by her dismissive explanation of slavery. What about the savage abuse and mistreatment of slaves by their "owners" and the blatant disregard for human life exemplified through murder, rape, and the constant separation of families? What about the abolition movement, and the history of courageous African American leaders, activists, and social reformers such as Frederick Douglass and Harriet Tubman? That day was the first day that I truly felt the weight of my "race" on my shoulders.

The historical, cultural, and social features of arguably all of the schools that Kozol (1991) visited in the writing of *Savage Inequalities* were heavily steeped in long-standing histories of racism and oppression. In appreciating the impact of oppression on places, one must note that "racism is political; it facilitates and justifies socioeconomic mobility for one group at the expense of the other" (Larocque, 1991, p. 75; see also Yosso, 2005). Racism is also depicted as a redistribution of resources, whereas resources are somewhat equally collected from everyone in society and then the majority of those resources are given back to people with the most social, political, and economic capital. Kozol (1991) seems to corroborate this politically emplaced conception of racism with the following observation:

> With more efficient local governance, East St. Louis might become a better-managed ghetto, a less ravaged racial settlement, but the soil would remain contaminated and the schools would still resemble relics of the South post-reconstruction. They might be a trifle cleaner and they might perhaps provide their children with a dozen more computers or typewriters, better stoves for cooking classes, or a better shop for training future gas-station mechanics; but the children would still be poisoned in their bodies and disfigured in their spirits. (pp. 38–39)

This passage paints East St. Louis as such a bleak, desolate, and hopeless place that it is impossible to decouple Kozol's (1991) imagery of the city from the people that live there.

Relatedly, I lived in New Orleans for two years during graduate school, and people were shocked to learn that I was born and raised in Detroit. I received a lot of amusing questions regarding murder rates, whether I had ever been car-jacked, or if I carried a razor blade for protection. However, I was mortified when, during a fairly large social gathering, a White female colleague pointedly asked if I had ever been raped in Detroit. It saddened me to realize how poorly outsiders viewed my hometown, but statements such as Kozol's (1991) marking children in East St. Louis as having poisoned bodies and disfigured spirits can paint a universal picture of a place.

Kozol is passionate in his messaging surrounding the injustices and class-based inequities that he witnessed, and he asserts that sooner or later academic studies of school finance ask, "How can we achieve more equity in education in America?" (Kozol, 1991, p. 175). He laments that these statements do not really mean equity and that the true intention is to prescribe "something close enough to equity to silence criticism by approximating justice, but far enough from equity to guarantee the benefits enjoyed by privilege" (p. 175). Even though Kozol (1991) does not label it as such, privilege is also at play when he describes the need for both generals and soldiers in society: "Societies cannot be all generals, no soldiers. But, by our schooling patterns, we assure that all soldiers' children are more likely to be soldiers and that the offspring of generals will have at least the option to be generals" (p. 176). While I appreciate this assessment, I feel compelled to share a story of resilience that disrupts this narrative by recognizing the influence of familial capital and community cultural wealth (see Farmer-Hinton, Lewis, Patton, & Rivers, 2013; Yosso, 2005).

Although I attended private schools from kindergarten through twelfth grade (which I suppose provided me with the option to become a "general"), my elder sister Stephanie attended a combination of private and public schools (Figure 2.4) in Detroit.

Figure 2.4. My sister attended Cartens Elementary School, now abandoned (Detroit, MI). Photo credit: Stephanie V. Fulks.

The schools differed in teacher-student ratios and access to school supplies (i.e., in public schools, they had to share textbooks), but Stephanie felt that many of the teachers in both the public and private school systems taught with passion and a sense of student care. Furthermore, our mother, grandmother, aunts, and uncles served as a foundation on which my sister and I could stand and reach for the stars. Our family members, or familial capital, contributed to our formal, informal, and nonformal learning environments to inspire and encourage us to become artists, educators, authors, and so forth. So it was not only the school system that shaped our futures and opportunities but also the support and love from the community cultural wealth that surrounded us.

Savage Inequalities sporadically touches upon the notion of meritocracy but does not truly explore the implications of this dominant discourse in our society. The myth of meritocracy rests on the belief that democratic choice is available for all (MacIntosh, 1998) and that each person, no matter from what racial, social, or economic background, can "pull himself up by the bootstraps" and attain the American Dream. Kozol (1991) describes the fallacy of magnet schools in that they attract the brightest students who are selected by race, income, and academic attainment. He argues that such schools are further segregating in nature by skimming off the best students and teachers and placing them in a separate learning environment, safely away from students that are often from poorer, less educated families. Kozol (1991) reflects that the magnet school "system has the surface aspects of meritocracy, but merit in this case is predetermined by conditions that are closely tied to class and race" (p. 60). This intersectional view of race, class, and education illustrates the complexities associated with social constructs and place.

The myth of meritocracy is often evoked when urban students like myself are positioned on pedestals for their academic and professional achievements that set them apart from the "places" of community cultural wealth in which they were raised. I frequently hear comments that echo this myth and avidly tout my accomplishments: "Look at you! You're a Black woman from inner city Detroit and you did it! You worked hard, you went to college, and now you're getting a doctoral degree. See, if you can do it, then these lazy kids running around the streets can do it too!" I actively resist these types of accolades, by explaining that I am the exception as opposed to the rule. I was able to "talk White," to adapt to the demands of private school and standardized tests and to politely acquiesce in the face of racism, classism, and even sexism. Exceptions such as myself are few and far between and should not be portrayed as the rule for all disadvantaged and/or displaced students.

Conclusion

During my first semester of doctoral study at the University of Saskatchewan, I enrolled in an antiracist education course, which formally introduced me to the concepts of privilege, Whiteness, and meritocracy. I found this experience to be uncomfortable, enlightening, and truly transformative, as each lesson unearthed the discrepancies between the ways in which students are (mis)educated based upon societal, political, and economic hierarchies (see Anyon, 1994). Each night I called home crying to my sister, realizing my complicity in hegemonic practices and the internalized racism that I had never perceived.

Evolution marks my varied educational experiences, and in the almost 30 years following the publication of *Savage Inequalities* the American education system has evolved to include a massive infusion of charter schools, the widely adopted and highly criticized Common Core State Standards, and the election of Betsy DeVos as the secretary of education. Inequalities based upon class and race (among others) are still witnessed today, ranging from the disparities found in schools, to disparities in health care, to inequities in access to clean drinking water (e.g., Detroit mass water shut-off in 2014; Flint lead poisoning water crises in 2015).

Kozol (1991) concludes with a reflection of himself standing by the Ohio River, relishing the beauty of nature and pondering the inherent goodness and limitless potential of America. He ends the novel in a place set away from the hustle and bustle of city life, one that he contends can "render life rewarding and the spirit clean" (Kozol, 1991, p. 233). While this conjures quite a romantic image, I argue that beauty and "goodness" also rest in urban places such as Detroit and that beauty transpires between neighbors and binds communities. Place matters, and the voices of individuals that reside in the communities depicted in *Savage Inequalities* should be privileged regarding the emplaced or displaced education of their children.

References

Anyon, J. (1994). Social class and hidden curriculum of work. In J. Kretovics & E. J. Nussel (Eds.), *Transforming urban education* (pp. 253–276). Allyn & Bacon.

Ardoin, N. (2006). Towards an interdisciplinary understanding of place: Lessons for environmental education. *Canadian Journal of Environmental Education, 11*(1), 112–126.

Cook, V. A., & Hemming, P. J. (2011). Education spaces: Embodied dimensions and dynamics. *Social & Cultural Geography, 12*(1), 1–8.

Crenshaw, K. (1989). Demarginalizing the intersection of race and sex: A Black feminist critique of antidiscrimination doctrine, feminist theory and antiracist politics. *University of Chicago Legal Forum*, pp. 139–167.

Cresswell, T. (2004). *Place: A short introduction*. Blackwell.

Farmer-Hinton, R. L., Lewis, J. D., Patton, L. D., & Rivers, I. D. (2013). Dear Mr. Kozol. . . . Four African American women scholars and the re-authoring of *Savage Inequalities*. *Teachers College Record, 115*(5), 1–38.

Kozol, J. (1991). *Savage inequalities: Children in America's schools*. Crown.

Larocque, E. (1991). Racism runs through Canadian society. In O. McKague (Ed.), *Racism in Canada* (pp. 73–76). Fifth House.

MacIntosh, P. (1998). White privilege: Unpacking the invisible knapsack. In P. Rothenberg (Ed.), *Race, class, and gender in the United States: An integrated study* (pp. 165–169). Worth.

Semken, S., & Brandt, E. (2010). Implications of sense of place and place-based education for ecological integrity and cultural sustainability in diverse places. *Cultural Studies of Science Education, 3*, 287–302.

Yosso, T. J. 2005. Whose culture has capital? A critical race theory discussion of community cultural wealth. *Race Ethnicity and Education, 8*(1), 69–91.

Chapter 3

Persisting through Life as a Result of My Urban Education

The Making of a Black Male Professor

OMARI JACKSON

Savage Inequalities chronicles the structural challenges in inner cities without recognizing the cultural wealth that exists in each city. Detroit, much like East St. Louis, has suffered from the economic transformation—industrial workforce to service workforce—displacing once gainfully employed citizens. As all social institutions are connected, there is an association between the decline of the economy and the decline of the education system. However, significant cultural wealth exists. This chapter highlights the human capital and cultural advantages (which are abundant in inner-city communities) and challenges the existing canon of knowledge on urban education in such works as Kozol's *Savage Inequalities*. Three premises guide my need to counter Kozol's and others' characterization of inner cities: (1) There is a large body of literature highlighting the challenges of urban school districts, yet there is a dearth of information on the positives of urban education; (2) urban citizens are sensitive to people from the outside examining us and casting hopelessness on our communities; and (3) most urban educational research is conducted by White scholars who have no firsthand experience learning in urban schools. These scholars use dominant logic, variables, and methods to study minoritized populations (Zuberi & Bonilla-Silva, 2008).

Like many Black children, I completed my primary and secondary education in an urban school district. The goal of this chapter is to give voice to minoritized individuals attending urban schools and to provide insight that is not traditionally solicited. After all, most education researchers enter challenged communities and highlight the problems in those communities, essentially replicating the nightly news. This chapter counters such narratives by highlighting the lessons I learned in Detroit's Public School system and how these lessons inform my responsibilities as a professor. To situate my experiences within an established theoretical framework, I apply Yosso's (2005) model of community cultural wealth to explore my educational and professional achievements as well as my scholarly activities.

Background

I grew up in the 1980s, a time when the American economy was shifting from a semiskilled labor market to a skilled labor market (Berman, Bound, & Griliches, 1994). America has always experienced shifts in the economy; and technology has always altered the ways products are produced and services deployed. Although technological advances always shift the labor market, the shift that occurred during my childhood had a more deleterious impact on semiskilled workers. During the shift from an industrial to service labor market, many manual laborers found themselves unemployed and lacking the credentials (i.e., a college degree) to survive in a new economy (Kasarda, 1989). For Detroit, and a few other urban centers, the transition was especially rough because the economy was not diversified. Other than the automobile industry, there were no other major employers. Additionally, the transition was rough for Detroit because it impacted the Black middle class. Detroit's sizable Black middle class was a result of Blacks moving north from various southern states as a part of the Great Migration. These southern migrants expanded Detroit's Black middle class due to the wages and benefits of a semiskilled labor market.

My father was a part of this generation who left rural towns in the South for urban cities in the North. My father moved to Detroit in the early 1970s. As a part of the last wave of the Great Migration, his generation was the last to fully benefit from stable, well-paying jobs as manual laborers. In fact, it is important to note Blacks only made significant progress in the labor market for a short period—the mid-1960s to mid-1970s (Bound & Freeman, 1992). Anyone who came of age just a decade after his generation had a lesser likelihood of attaining stable, well-paying jobs as manual laborers.

Much of the poverty during my childhood could be attributed to the lack of jobs in the automobile industry for the generation that was born just a decade after my father. Detroit was once a city where citizens could thrive with a high school diploma or less. However, eventually a college degree became necessary to thrive in Detroit, and those who lack such were left out of the labor market. Furthermore, without structural changes in laws and policies, it became difficult to change the trajectory of minoritized youth. As a majority Black, working-class city, Detroit was hit hard. As a result, Detroit saw increases in crime, decreases in home-ownership, and fewer resources for the school system.

From 1971 to 2012, my father worked for Ford Motor Company, which enabled him to provide a stable middle-class living for me, my siblings, and my mother. It turns out my father's tenure with Ford was a shared experience for Black men in Detroit because Ford had a history of providing work opportunities for Black men when other automobile companies were resistant to such hiring practices (Maloney & Whatley, 1995). It is important to note my mother worked as well in various pink-collar[1] roles. While my mother's income may have seemed negligible in comparison to my father's, her salary was "icing on the cake," meaning any income in addition to the middle-class salaries of automobile workers was a bonus for my family. As such, in terms of financial resources, I came from a high-resourced household. In fact, I would argue our finances paralleled those of the upper middle class.

My parents could have afforded to live in most metropolitan Detroit suburbs. However, my father liked the city. He felt there was something authentic about the city for Black folks. Although residing in the inner city was my father's personal preference, this preference was likely based on historical patterns dictated by formal segregation and psychological comfort of living near people with similar backgrounds. Though Cutler and Glaeser (1997) suggest Blacks residing in segregated areas are worse off because they lack the resources of the Black middle class, they also suggest *if* middle-class Blacks are present, then Blacks with fewer resources benefit from the presence of the Black middle class. Literature covering the Black middle class also notes the close spatial proximity between middle-class Blacks and poorer Blacks (Pattillo, 1999). While we did not have many poor families in our immediate community (i.e., within a half-mile radius), poorer families did live in our school zone. Accordingly, my elementary school was even more diverse than my immediate community. Furthermore, middle-class Blacks recognize their relative privilege and feel responsible for enhancing the quality of life for Blacks with fewer resources (Heflin & Pattillo, 2006; Sampson & Milam, 1975). This is important to note because Blacks have been portrayed in the media as individuals who lack unity (i.e., media narratives of Black-on-Black crime).

My parents certainly felt responsible for other children; they included our friends in extracurricular activities. For instance, my parents invited our friends to go to local amusement parks, carnivals, local beaches, the YMCA, and many other activities that would have likely been nonexistent in our friends' lives. My parents' desire to enhance the quality of life for other children likely stemmed from the fact they were first-generation members of the middle class as most middle-class Black people are first-generation members of the middle class (Lacy, 2007; Oliver & Shapiro, 2006). Accordingly, my parents felt connected to Black people with fewer resources because they themselves grew up with limited financial resources; they knew, firsthand, the resources needed to improve anyone's quality of life.

My neighborhood was incredibly diverse in terms of social class. Within my immediate community, there were Black teachers, principals, engineers, police officers, and nurses. I remember these individuals driving home, pulling into their driveways, and getting out of their cars in business casual attire. They looked "cool." In my young years, I determined I did not want to go to work and get dirty. Although I did not have conversations with college-educated citizens in my neighborhood, these daily and visual representations showed me a range of career possibilities. The lack of interaction with such individuals has influenced my interest in speaking with potential first-generation college students about the limitless opportunities that result from attending college.

Most of our community members were gainfully employed and such economic resources were evidenced in neighborhood aesthetics. I can only recollect one house that, from time to time, was uninhabited. However, the other homes were all inhabited by homeowners. Neighbors maintained their lawns and decorated the exterior of their homes during holidays such as Christmas and Halloween. Most notably, I remember the flags that represented the seasons: fall, winter, spring, and summer. It was the kind of effort, care, and detail that seems more common among homeowners/community members who took pride in the beautification of their home and neighborhood.

My interest in eradicating social challenges within the Black community is directly tied to my parents' decision to live in the city and to educate me in the public school system. Such a decision is the foundation for my life's work as a professor. While many researchers are interested in studying the Black community, few work to eradicate social ills. They simply write papers and books to receive promotion/tenure without creating change. I care deeply about creating change because it is *my* community. While I succeeded because of intentional and consistent support from family and teachers, I recognize many of my classmates lacked such support systems. In every position I have ever held, my ambition has been to show students of color their strengths and how these strengths can be used to counteract their weaknesses. For instance, I was a good student in K–12. I generally earned B+/A– grades. While I did not have "good"[2] standardized test scores, I was admitted to a selective university: The University of Michigan. Michigan likely accepted me because of my commitment to my community, demonstrated through various extracurricular activity involvement.

Narrative

Kozol's *Savage Inequalities* as well as the aforementioned literature provide insight about resources Blacks lack; these resources are important for optimum standardized test scores, grade point averages, and college success (Sawyer, 2013; Westrick, Le, Robbins, Radunzel & Schmidt, 2015). However, there is a dearth of studies that examine the community cultural wealth developed while attending urban K–12 schools: the cultural wealth that prepares us for collegiate and postcollegiate pursuits. Yosso's (2005) model of community cultural wealth is valuable when explaining the minoritized experience because it highlights the importance of nonfinancial capital. As a result of historical institutional racism, African Americans[3] generally do not have financial wealth. However, African Americans are wealthy in terms of other forms of capital such as aspirational, familial, social, navigational, resistant, and linguistic capital (see Yosso, 2005), each of which contributes to one's overall cultural capital and the knowledge people need to advance. Though Yosso's model includes six types of capital, five of these explain my educational and professional achievements as well as my scholarly activities.

Aspirational Capital

Aspirational capital enabled me to dream. Though my parents did not have college degrees, I knew I would attain a college degree. Because my parents knew the importance of college (yet nothing about the college preparation process), they encouraged me to apply for admission to a magnet school. My teachers, at all levels, were instrumental in creating hopes and dreams. They told me I could be anything (as opposed to the commonly perceived notion that inner-city teachers give up on students). I remember my high school principal, Dr. George Cohen, saying each of us will go to college. Instead of asking if we want to attend college, teachers asked us *which* college we want to attend; it was a given that we would all attend college. Additionally, I vividly remember Dr. Cohen's extensive vocabulary. As students, we would say he used "big" words. In true Dr. Cohen fashion, I now refer to his choice of words as "polysyllabic." Though we made fun of him, many of us wanted to speak in that fashion and saw college as a way to become what he embodied—intelligence and class. When knowing the importance of inspiring students to dream, it is not surprising that approximately 90% of my graduating class attended college.

Aspirational capital also speaks to my ability to persist despite barriers. Unfortunately, many Black college students are insecure about their place in college and suffer from low levels of psychological well-being (Peteet, Montgomery, & Weeks, 2015). While I had moments of insecurity, like any college student, I never felt like college was not for me. My K–12 teachers instilled confidence in my academic potential and abilities. Though not generally highlighted in the literature as a trait developed in inner-city public schools, my confidence in my academic abilities was developed in Detroit's public school system. My teachers were well aware of the role confidence plays as a noncognitive factor correlated with collegiate academic success (Stankov, Morony, & Lee, 2014). They would tell me things like I would become the first Black president. While President Barack Obama beat me to this, I saw the world as my oyster. Becoming president, a teacher, a doctor, or a lawyer was within my reach.

To whom much is given, much is required. This paraphrased Bible verse is widely used in the Black community. For children growing up in Black communities, this message is conveyed throughout social institutions such as the church, the family, and school. Accordingly, it is part of the socialization process. It means I must not squander my talent and influence, and I must strive to enhance the quality of life in the Black community. From personal experiences and research, I know education is the great equalizer. Therefore, I worked with precollege programs at Wayne State University (WSU). I also worked with summer bridge programs at WSU and The University of Michigan. Students in these programs often had the academic potential, but they were at risk of failing to use their social and cultural capital to successfully navigate college. Our teachers taught us to work hard, yet they never taught us that we did not face significant disadvantages. I interpret the aforementioned Bible verse, as not everyone is given all they need; therefore, those who are given resources and experiences must help others.

Familial Capital and Social Capital

My commitment to improve the Black community is a result of my experience in an urban environment. Yosso's ideas of familial and social capital situate my experience. She defines familial capital as a sense of community that is nurtured by the family. Through the family, one learns that one's family is not simply the nuclear family or blood relatives; rather, family is extended and inclusive of others who share common experiences. Yosso defines social capital as networks and community resources but broader than the traditional social capital that is operationalized for upward mobility. While I am not deemphasizing the importance of material (or instrumental) resources for upward mobility, I want to stress the nonmaterial (or emotional) resources that facilitated my upward mobility. Though Yosso's model separates the familial and social capital that contribute to the overall cultural capital of minoritized students, my experience couples the two capitals such that a particular experience can be both familial and social capital concomitantly. Despite the challenges that persist in Black communities, people support each other. Parents develop and nurture relationships with each other. If a neighborhood is in need, people gather to help. As a child, I remember neighbors barbecuing and offering food to children. These experiences taught me to rely on my community in times of need; however, even more importantly, it taught me to be available for others to rely upon me.

During a previous faculty appointment, I worked at a small liberal arts college in a rural northern New England town. Though I knew it was important to work with underrepresented students to succeed in college, I was not aware of how grateful I should be for my experience growing up in an urban environment. For the first time, I met a sizable population of Black students who were educated in various K–12 systems in New England. Many of my Black students were never taught by a Black teacher and did not grow up around other Blacks. As a result, they were detached from Black culture/history, spoke negatively about Blacks, and were disinterested in uplifting the Black community. Unfortunately, they saw college as an opportunity to assimilate into White culture. After attaining their degrees, they will potentially leave the Black community behind. Observing my students' lack of racial pride forced me to think forward into my then four-year-old son's future, growing up in northern New England; attending schools with few Black students, teachers, and administrators. I was isolating him from the Black community experience that provided me with cultural wealth, and he would not receive the same positive edifications I received. To satisfy my personal goals as a father, and my professional/moral goals as a professor, I relocated to an HBCU[4] in an urban, inner-city area. This change enables me to give my son the Black community that I had as a youth as well as an opportunity to uplift the Black community.

NAVIGATIONAL CAPITAL

Many Black children, educated in urban schools, remember teachers saying, "While others may walk, you must run." This meant Whites often have the luxury of doing simply what is required while Blacks must go above and beyond. In Yosso's model, navigational capital is a resource that helps one build resilience[5] and navigate social institutions. Resilience is a mindset that enables a person to persist through stressful experiences. In addition to simply persisting, this individual *thrives* and enhances the manner in which they navigate future stressful experiences. My teachers instituted navigational capital. During my time in K–12, their advice about "running" was simply kept in my proverbial back pocket and largely had no application in my daily life as the vast majority of my classmates and teachers were Black. After experiencing racism at the hands of a college academic advisor and college classmates, I considered transferring to an HBCU during my first semester in college. I called my father, and he gave me a pep talk. He largely said he did not send me to college to feel intimidated and to give up. This advice might seem trite, but he could have easily supported my decision to transfer. This bit of advice was monumental, and coupled with the years of advice from my teachers, navigational capital from my community was responsible for me remaining in college and thriving. Any higher education professional can likely think of an underrepresented student who had potential but lacked confidence in their fit for college and, as a result, left school. I was fortunate to have navigational capital reinforced by two social institutions—family and education.

As previously mentioned, Yosso's model suggests individuals with navigational capital do not simply persist: they thrive and enhance their ability to deal with challenging situations. The aforementioned navigational messages continue to inform my responsibilities as a professor in two capacities—it informs my work ethic, *and* I impart this wisdom to my students. As a faculty member at a predominantly White institution, my qualifications were always questioned. I once gave students a story in hopes of inspiring them to persist. Many of the students received unfavorable grades on an exam. I shared a personal story about failing chemistry, but persisting. My students contacted my department chair and asked if I was qualified to teach. At the time, it had been sixteen years since I failed chemistry; and I had taught sociology for nine years. They were enrolled in an introductory sociology class. My bachelor's, master's, and doctoral degrees are in sociology. Questions about my qualifications to teach were ludicrous. My chair recommended I refrain from telling students about my failures and that I should show students a copy of my curriculum vitae at the start of the semester. Though I did neither of these, such a recommendation evidenced the need to go above and beyond. In this instance, above and beyond meant making sure I was using effective teaching methods and having stronger service and research experience than my White counterparts. When one knows it is raining, they carry an umbrella. I successfully navigated college, graduate school, and a faculty appointment at a conservative, predominantly White institution because my teachers equipped me with an umbrella for the rain.

RESISTANT CAPITAL

Failure was not an option. In high school, we did not have enough books to take home for study, classrooms were overcrowded, and we had few technological advancements. Despite these circumstances, our teachers taught us success was important. Such challenges provided me with the ability to succeed despite unfavorable conditions—even when I was a college student. There were times when I could not purchase my textbooks and course materials immediately because a check, mailed[6] by my mother, was lost in the mail. I asked professors to place a copy of the book on reserve in the library, asked to borrow friends' books or course materials, and occasionally made copies of course materials (of course honoring all copyright laws). Large class sizes in high school prepared me for large classes in college (though I am not arguing large class sizes are desirable). Lower levels of technology socialized us to learn despite the mode of teaching. In college, some of my professors utilized technology when lecturing, while others did not. I was prepared to learn in the fashion of the professor. As a student in a school system with few material resources, I learned to find a way (or make a way) as opposed to failing due to a lack of systemic support. Yosso's (2005) model speaks about resistant capital as a conscious effort to instruct "children to engage in behaviours and maintain attitudes that challenge the status quo" (p. 81). Because Blacks are commonly portrayed as lazy and "full" of excuses, our teachers taught us to never use excuses because to do so would support racist narratives about Blacks' work ethic.

Yosso's resistant capital also purports cultural knowledge enables one to resist oppressive structures. By refraining from giving excuses, our teachers were teaching us to reject such propaganda the media and other social institutions promulgate about Blacks. Accordingly, I always associated Blackness with resilience as opposed to the negative images. My teachers taught us to recognize the progress Blacks have made. I vividly remember learning about the Harlem Renaissance, reading *I Know Why the Caged Bird Sings*, and writing reports on Lewis Latimer and other inventors. Having Black teachers, and non-Black teachers who were passionate about the Black community, I was given books and assignments that reflected my cultural heritage. As a result of being required to learn about my heritage, I now teach courses and create scholarship on the Black community. Furthermore, the foundation of my career efforts is not centered on the challenges of our community—rather the successes and strategies for enhancing our community.

Conclusion

My success is a result of abundant cultural wealth that exists in the inner city but is largely unexamined by scholars. When reflecting on my road to success, my teachers and family played important roles in my character development. They instilled confidence, which made me feel I could accomplish all aspirations despite barriers. They also taught me to believe in myself and my community. Furthermore, they instilled social responsibility, which translated into a commitment to serve my community.

I am certain Blacks, and likely other groups of color, will read this chapter and feel a sense of connection to the aforementioned lessons. Accordingly, this is a reminder "to whom much is given, much is required." We must recognize support systems that facilitated our successes. Conversely, we must recognize many minoritized brothers and sisters lack such support; as a result, we must recommit ourselves to the uplifting of our communities and choose some way to give back.

I also wrote this chapter in hopes educational research can move in the direction of studying what works for Black children's educational success. Scholars often only identify challenges in the public school system and Black community, yet fail to recognize the cultural wealth that exists. When cultural wealth is minimized, there exists a hegemonic relationship between dominant White culture and the culture of minoritized groups, thereby "othering" the cultural experience of minoritized groups. A redirection of academic scholarship changes the narrative of urban public schools and communities and casts these communities as spaces with tremendous cultural and social capitals in need of financial capital.

This chapter should instill hope in K–12 teachers and administrators. Hope starts from the top and trickles down. I had hope because my parents and teachers had hope. You must have hope to wake up each day and work with children whose backgrounds come with fewer resources. You must have hope to teach in an environment where you are not given all the material resources needed. Know the nonmaterial resources you provide will take children farther than most think. Teach our children to aspire and persist, despite barriers. After all, cultural wealth facilitates the attainment of material culture.

Lastly, I encourage higher education professionals who admit students and award financial support at the undergraduate and graduate levels to inquire about underrepresented students' work in their communities. When looking for underrepresented students to contribute to the diversity of your campus, strongly consider students from urban public schools with interests in uplifting their communities. These students will share their community cultural wealth with others.

Notes

1. Positions that are white collar in nature (i.e., receptionist, personal assistant, medical assistant, etc.), but pay less than white-collar and blue-collar positions.
2. Based on mean/median scores at Michigan.
3. African American and Black are used interchangeably.
4. Historically Black College or University—an institution founded before 1964, with the mission to educate Black Americans.
5. That members of underrepresented groups are expected to be resilient places the blame and correction on them for circumstances they did not create, but are forced to navigate with resilience.
6. Before most forms of electronic transfer.

References

Babbie, E. (2010). *The practice of social research* (12th ed.). Wadsworth.
Bonilla-Silva, E. (2013). *Racism without racists: Color-blind racism and the persistence of racial inequality in America* (4th ed.). Rowman & Littlefield.
Berman, B., Bound, J., & Griliches, Z. (1994). Changes in the demand for skilled labor within U.S. manufacturing: Evidence from the annual survey of manufacturers. *The Quarterly Journal of Economics, 109*(2), 367–397. https://doi.org/10.2307/2118467
Bound, J. & Freeman, R. B. (1992). What went wrong? The erosion of relative earnings and employment among young Black men in the 1980s. *The Quarterly Journal of Economics, 107*(1), 201–232. https://doi.org/10.2307/2118327
Cutler, D. M., & Glaeser, E. L. (1997). Are ghettos good or bad? *The Quarterly Journal of Economics, 112*(3), 827–872. https://doi.org/10.1162/003355397555361
Heflin, C. M., & Pattillo, M. (2006). Poverty in the family: Race, siblings, and socioeconomic heterogeneity. *Social Science Research, 35*(4), 804–822.
Kasarda, J. D. (1989). Urban industrial transition and the underclass. *The Annals of the American Academy of Political and Social Science, 501*, 26–47. https://doi.org/10.1177/0002716289501001002
Kozol, J. (1991). *Savage inequalities: Children in America's schools*. Crown.
Lacy, K. (2007). *Blue-chip black*. University of California Press.
Maloney, T. N., & Whatley, W. C. Making the effort: The contours of racial discrimination in Detroit's labor markets, 1920–1940. *The Journal of Economic History, 55*(3), 465–493. doi:10.1017/S0022050700041607
Ogbu, J. U. (2009). *Black American students in an affluent suburb: A study of academic disengagement*. Routledge.

Oliver, M. L., & Shapiro, T. M. (2006). *Black wealth/white wealth* (10th Anniversary ed.). Routledge.
Pattillo, M. E. (1999). *Black picket fences: Privilege and peril among the black middle class*. University of Chicago Press.
Peteet, B. J., Montgomery, L., & Weekes, J. C. (2015). Predictors of Imposter phenomenon among talented ethnic minority undergraduate students. *The Journal of Negro Education, 84*(2), 175–186.
Sampson, W. A., & Milam, V. (1975). The intraracial attitudes of the black middle class: Have they changed? *Social Problems, 23*(2), 153–165.
Sawyer, R. (2013). Beyond correlations: Usefulness of high school GPA and test scores in making college admissions decisions. *Applied Measurement in Education, 26*(2), 89–112.
Stankov, L., Morony, S., & Lee, Y. P. (2014). Confidence: The best non-cognitive predictor of academic achievement? *Educational Psychology 34*(1), 9–28.
Westrick, P. A., Le, H., Robbins, S. B., Radunzel, J. M. R., & Schmidt, F. (2015). College performance and retention: A Meta-analysis of the predictive validities of ACT scores, high school grades, and SES. *Educational Assessment, 20*(1), 23–45.
Yosso, T. J. (2005). Whose culture has capital? A critical race theory discussion of community cultural wealth. *Race Ethnicity and Education, 8*(1), 69–91.
Zuberi, T., & Bonilla-Silva, E. (2008). *White logic, white methods*. Rowman & Littlefield.

Guest Commentary and Reflection

We Know Best What Tools and Resources Will Sustain Us

DORINDA J. CARTER ANDREWS

As a Black woman educator, scholar, researcher, and mother, I have long been convinced that Black people (we) must tell their (our) own stories and that research-based, data-driven decisions about the educational well-being of our children must draw from the community cultural knowledge and wealth (Yosso, 2005) of Black peoples. Having a fundamental understanding that Black people know best what tools and resources are needed to sustain their children's cultural identities and foster their academic identities in schools can help ensure that Pre-K–12 school leaders are able to develop educational policies, implement programs, and enact practices that allow Black youth to discover and demonstrate their brilliance.

The counternarratives of Chayla Haynes, Omari Jackson, and Jada Renee Koushik remind us that there are still essentialist "stock stories" in educational research that depict urban, predominantly Black, economically disenfranchised schools as "bad schools" and suburban, predominantly white, economically advantaged schools as "good schools." While we know not all urban schools and communities are Black, many of them across the nation are densely populated with people of African descent; this is true for the schools and cities described in Kozol's (1991) *Savage Inequalities* (e.g., East St. Louis, Chicago, New York, DC) and in communities where Haynes, Jackson, and Koushik grew up (in Detroit and DC). Several themes are illuminated in their writings that nuance less critical examinations of racial and class inequalities/inequities between well-resourced schools in high-economic, predominantly white communities and inadequately resourced schools in high-poverty, predominantly Black communities.

First, we need narratives and educational research about People of Color (POC) living and learning in urban centers that are written and conducted by people who are native to those communities. There is danger in any single story about a cultural group of POC and their communities, particularly if it is narrated through the white gaze and/or by white people. Further, there is a danger in having researchers with multiple privileged identities utilize the educational experiences of youth living in high-poverty and high-need conditions to expose/highlight systemic racial, class, funding, and other types of inequities in the absence of a critical sociocultural and humanizing approach to the research and writing. In these instances, the work is often damage centered (Tuck, 2009) and renders Communities of Color as culturally deficient. Even with the purest and most socially just intentions, white researchers, writers, and scholars must understand that their immersion in whiteness as a cultural norm and advantages of racial privilege under white supremacy prevent them from being able to present "findings" about urban schools and communities outside of colonial and white supremacist logics, ideologies, and research methodologies. When POC native to urban communities assist in narrating the educational stories, there is greater likelihood that a strengths-based approach to understanding urban schools and ways to maximize youth academic success and life outcomes in these educational settings will be lifted up.

Secondly, urban schools and communities are resource-rich and complex places; they are simultaneously spaces of struggle, survival, wholeness, and thriving. And Black life in urban contexts is complex yet beautiful. As these scholars highlight, much of the research on the experiences of urban youth and schools, including that of Kozol in *Savage Inequalities*, perpetuates narratives of community deficiency, dehumanization, and essentialism while trying to illuminate racial and class inequities. There is a dearth of literature that illuminates the ways that, despite structural and systemic inadequate resource allocation for schooling, the community cultural wealth of urban and Black communities provides a sense of belonging, joy, positive racial identity development, and cultural security for youth of color. When research about urban schooling is done well, one can make a critical argument about the ways that systematic racial discrimination and segregation displace Black and Brown people living in urban centers and simultaneously speak to the various forms of community cultural wealth that reside in those communities and schools despite youth's daily susceptibility to the environmental and educational injustices experienced in an imperialist white supremacist capitalist patriarchal (hooks, 2004) educational system. Educational researchers and practitioners must consider the various forms of capital that exist in urban communities—such as familial, aspirational, cultural, navigational, resistance, and social capital—that provide valuable resources to youth of color for traversing inadequately resourced schools. These assets and resources are critical levers to reforming colonial schooling policies and practices that systematically oppress youth of color.

A third theme that illuminates from these scholars' counternarratives is the utility of having classroom teachers and school leaders who enact culturally responsive and sustaining practices (Foster, 1998; Gay, 2018; Ladson-Billings, 1995; Paris & Alim, 2017) in urban schools and suburban schools that urban youth attend. These authors also highlight the significance of practitioners and community members serving as othermothers and otherfathers in ways that foster their positive racial and academic identities. These practices further resilience, wholeness and thriving in urban and suburban schools where Black students attend. Kozol fails to highlight these forms of capital for Black youth and paints a broad stroke of these "bad [urban] schools" as lacking any value to the cultural and academic identities of Black youth in economically disenfranchised contexts. Further, in his depiction of suburban schools as "good schools," Kozol does not account for the lived experiences of Black youth (not native to those communities) who utilize their community cultural wealth to navigate the environmentally toxic and unsafe terrain of those predominantly white, economically advantaged schools. Thus, these schools' "goodness" is relative depending on the racialized-classed framing one utilizes for examination.

Through their counternarratives, Haynes, Koushik, and Jackson challenge educational researchers and practitioners to (re)consider what they glean from Kozol's *Savage Inequalities* that helps them provide better educational policies, programs, and practices for urban youth. I offer a few questions to consider for educational research and practice moving forward. I also provide a list of reading suggestions that can promote richer discussion of a critical analysis of systematic inequity and injustice in urban schools and communities. These readings can assist educational researchers and practitioners in engaging decolonial research and praxis as they identify ways to eradicate injustices in order to maximize urban youth wholeness and thriving in educational settings and beyond.

Discussion Questions

1. How might future research in urban schools and communities resist taking a damage-centered approach to justice-centered research, by collaborating *with* community members, students, families, and administrators in eradicating systemic educational inequities?

2. In what ways can educational researchers and school practitioners integrate the cultural epistemologies of People of Color in urban communities to advance the school and life outcomes of urban youth?

3. What are ways to ensure that educational researchers take decolonizing and humanizing approaches to their research and writing that do not perpetuate uplifting white supremacy and a lack of structural analysis of oppression in urban education?

4. How can teachers partner with families and youth to provide culturally sustaining and responsive classroom practices that integrate community cultural wealth?

Additional Readings

Duncan-Andrade, J. M. R., & Morrell, E. (2008). (2nd ed.). *The art of critical pedagogy: Possibilities of moving from theory to practice in urban schools.* Peter Lang.

Love, B. (2020). *We want to do more than survive: Abolitionist teaching and the pursuit of educational freedom.* Beacon Press.

Milner, H. R., & Lomotey, K. (2013). (Ed.). *Handbook of urban education.* Routledge.

Tuck, E. (2009). Suspending damage: A letter to communities. *Harvard Educational Review, 79*(3), 409–427.

References

Foster, M. (1998). *Black teachers on teaching.* New Press.

Gay, G. (2018). *Culturally responsive teaching: Theory, research, and practice* (2nd ed.). Teachers College Press.

hooks, b. (2004). *The will to change: Men, masculinity, and love*. Atria Books.
Kozol, J. (1991). *Savage inequalities: Children in America's schools*. Crown.
Ladson-Billings, G. (1995). Toward a theory of culturally relevant pedagogy. *American Educational Research Journal, 32*(3), 465–491.
Paris, D., & Alim, H. S. (2017). *Culturally sustaining pedagogies: Teaching and learning for justice in a changing world*. Teachers College Press.
Tuck, E. (2009). Suspending damage: A letter to communities. *Harvard Educational Review, 79*(3), 409–427.
Yosso, T. J. (2005). Whose culture has capital? A critical race theory discussion of community cultural wealth. *Race Ethnicity and Education, 8*(1), 69–91.

Part 2

The Urban Community as Educator (Community)

Chapter 4

Chicago's Other Children

MIRELSIE VELÁZQUEZ

In the spring of 1980 my family relocated from the warm familiarity of Puerto Rico to the cold reality of life in Chicago. Entering kindergarten during the fall of 1980 to Chicago's Puerto Rican Humboldt Park community inadvertently set the stage for my lifelong work on the history of schooling inequality of Puerto Ricans in the city. By the age of four, my life and education were intricately linked to a larger history marked by decades of community struggles for affirmation. I encountered this history from the moment I entered kindergarten, as I was confronted by an English-speaking world, far removed from the warmth I left thousands of miles away until I moved on to seek higher education at a predominately white institution. My stepfather still reminds me of my initial unwillingness to embrace my new school environment, even my inability to walk through inches of snow to reach the school, insisting my stepfather carry me and my winter gear. Once I got to school, it was a daily battle against the mispronunciation of my name, hoping to be understood. Additionally, there were outdated textbooks, overcrowded and underfunded schools; nonetheless, this was my new home. Jonathan Kozol's *Savage Inequalities* (1991) chapter "Other People's Children" chronicles the lived reality of Chicago's poor and underserved students of color in the city's South Side. My life as a poor, migrant, monolingual, child in Chicago's Near North Side mirrored that reality. Attending schools ill-equipped to teach in a city uninterested in educating me: that was my reality from 1980 until I graduated from high school in 1993. It was a high school that had improved a decade later to "only" a 22% dropout rate (Miller, Luppsescu, & Correa, 2003).

The castelike system of education in Chicago that Kozol writes about, however, is only part of the story. The Chicago of my childhood and schooling history told another story. In this chapter I will contextualize the lived reality of my own educational experiences as a working-class, Puerto Rican migrant in Chicago schools, some of which mirrored the narrative shared in Kozol's work, through both my own personal accounts and historical data. My experience as a student in Chicago amidst economic, political, and racial turmoil through the administration of the first female mayor of the city (Jane Byrne), the first African-American mayor of Chicago (Harold Washington), and the administration of a second Mayor Daley, framed my schooling life. Similarly, the community activism that also frames the history of Chicago's Puerto Rican community was one that laid the groundwork for my own intellectual trajectory, rejecting notions regarding the perceived disinterest of the community in the schooling lives of their children. Instead of hopelessness and despair in the schooling lives of their children, the Chicago I inherited was one of struggle, yes, but a struggle to confront the unjust education of their children, not one of defeat as Kozol presents.

Schooling Inequity in the Lives of Chicago's Children

Kozol (1991) reminds us that economic disinvestment is just one of the caveats that helps us understand the plight of many inner-city children's educational experiences. When I entered high school in 1989 Chicago spent approximately $5,500 for each secondary student, compared to up to $9,000 in some neighboring suburbs (Kozol, 1991, p. 54). But as Kozol himself recognized, money is only part of the problem. However, as students we too recognized the discrepancies in the financial investment in our education when we traveled to neighboring communities for sports or academic events and to schools without metal detectors but with green fields instead. The discrepancies became even more profound for those of us who navigated our way out of city schools and moved on to higher education, becoming aware of the education money could offer as we listened to the experiences of our new classmates who attended these affluent schools. That disinvestment along with the history of race and racism in the United States has created a castelike system of education in cities such as Chicago that marginalizes the education of Black and Brown children. The history of housing segregation across the city relegated the average Latina/o/x and African American student to segregated schools, where they tended to represent the majority of students.

When I entered Chicago schools in 1980 Latina/o students comprised 18.4% of the public school population, with African Americans constituting 60.8% (Danns, 2014, p. 8). The city entered a Consent Decree in September of 1980 acknowledging "the existence of substantial racial isolation" reaffirming "that racial isolation is educationally disadvantageous to all students" (Green, 1981, p. 3). With the white population in Chicago schools dropping from 47.7% in 1965 to 18.6% in 1980, students of color were increasingly attending isolated, segregated, and underserved schools in larger numbers (Danns, 2014, p. 8). By the time I graduated in 1993, Latina/o/x students were over 27% of the student population, with those numbers almost doubling by 2011 (Danns, 2014, p. 8). Our isolation within Chicago Public Schools became more obvious when we moved on to institutions of higher learning, where Latina/os would constitute less than 6% of the student population at the state's flagship institution: the University of Illinois at Urbana-Champaign (Chancellor's Committee on Latina/o Issues, 2003, p. 11).

But for the few that moved on to higher education, we took our communities with us as the struggle for educational justice and the investment that our communities had in us—as demonstrated through their battles for educational justice—filled us with hope. Kozol (1991) reminds us, "But to ask an individual to break down doors that we have chained and bolted in advance of his arrival is unfair" (p. 62). But when we think of them as "other people's children" we can detach ourselves from the responsibility of ensuring justice. Chicago's most underserved populations have taken this responsibility seriously, as is evident in their history of organizing around schooling concerns. Decade after decade Chicago's most vulnerable worked tirelessly to break down doors in order to dismantle the system of inequality within city schools. Danns (2014) reminds us that "while adults disagree, the nation's school children were used by its government as harbingers of social change and were being tasked with the responsibility of overcoming years of segregation and discrimination they had no hand in creating" (p. 192).

Resisting, Rethinking, Readjusting Schooling in Chicago to Meet Students' Needs

The Chicago of Jonathan Kozol's *Savage Inequalities* (1991) vividly portrays the everyday lives of thousands of the city's poorest children, disproportionately Brown and Black children, whose schooling lives are marked by economic, political, and racial injustices. As Kozol (1991) contends, "About injustice, most poor children in America cannot be fooled," yet we treat African American children in districts such as Chicago as if they have no understanding of their own reality and of the systemic injustices that continue to affect their community (p. 57). Chicago Public Schools have been constant sites of struggle and resistance for communities of color. From the organizing and mobilization of African Americans against segregation and lack of adequate resources for their children beginning in the postwar years, the Puerto Rican community's struggle to claim space and representation beginning in the 1960s, to the Mexican American community's hunger strike for the building of a new school in the early 21st century. Chicago's "Other" children have been at the forefront of an education civil rights movement in the city since their relocation to Chicago in large numbers in the early to mid-20th century. The "City of Big Shoulders" has shouldered a big responsibility regarding its most vulnerable and marginalized populations, but it's the communities themselves that have acted to ensure a promise of simple justice for their children. In Dionne Danns's pivotal work, the history of African American activism in Chicago, both for desegregation and community control of schools, is well documented. As Danns (2014) reminds us, "The most popular way for people to show their discontentment, whether in support or opposition of desegregation, was in the form of protest" (p. 7). With a growing population of African American and Latino residents, Chicago schools, beginning in the 1960s, became contested spaces in which justice would be denied at times, but justice would also be fought for, demanded, and found. In Chicago's Near North side, Puerto Rican students and community members organized for both the building of a new school for their growing community, but also to remove administrators and teachers who the community saw as ill-fitted and disinterested in caring for their children (Velázquez, 2016, 2022). As the Puerto Rican community engaged in their own struggle for educational justice, they linked their own experiences within both the city of Chicago and city schools with the struggles faced by the African American and Mexican communities.

Living in the Puerto Rican community in Chicago, it's true I inherited a history of economic and political disinvestment in our community schools; however, the history of community organizing and survival created a much-needed bridge for my educational trajectory. I lived and learned in the same community that in 1966 confronted the police brutality, displacement, and health and education discrepancies faced by the community—all in a multiday community uprising (see Padilla, 1987; Fernandez, 2012; and Perez, 2003). I was part of a community that sought to create educational opportunities for their youth with the creation of community-led initiatives and representation in Chicago's board of education in the late 1960s (Velázquez, 2016, 2022). My siblings entered Clemente High School a few years after the community fought for and demanded a new school to replace the aging Tuley High School but further fought to have the school named in honor of their Puerto Rican heritage. There are additional stories of affirmation and important narratives that can help us not only recognize the failures of the past but also how to move forward to ensure a sense of justice for future generations. These narratives offer us a more layered understanding of the everyday lives of community children in Chicago, beyond the stories shared by Jonathan Kozol. Further, it expands the limited statistical information that does not highlight the success students may have experienced but only emphasizes their failures. As Steven Winter (1989) reminds us: "In its prototypical sense as storytelling, narrative too proceeds from the ground up. In narrative, we take the experience and configure it in a conventional and comprehensive form. This is what gives narrative its communicative power; it is what makes narrative a powerful tool of persuasion and therefore, a potential transformative device for the disempowered" (p. 2228). The story of our lives should not be taken for granted, and it's in those stories where we can begin to deconstruct how to better connect schools with the lived experiences and reality of the children we as a society hope to educate.

Recognizing and Historicizing Black and Brown School Activism

In the 1960s and 1970s student-led walkouts and organizing created a lens through which to examine the culpability of the city in further marginalizing their population of African American and Latinx students, although the decades that followed found the population contending with the very same issues earlier generations faced and fought against. Kozol's Chicago did not look very different from earlier decades, however, despite the fact that Chicago's African American and Latinx communities have historically fought for (and continue to fight for) a sense of educational justice: from the increase in the hiring of staff and teachers of color, inclusive curriculum that reflects the communities present within Chicago schools and adequate resources, to fighting against the crippling segregation practices that continue to keep Black and Brown children from the city's best schools. The Chicago I remember is not one marked by apathy and defeat but a city that has always been at the forefront of the battles surrounding schools and schooling in the city. But as much as communities wanted something better for their children, the disinvestment (financial and political) in our schools by those in power tells a different story and, for many, created a different path. It is the stories of the communities who lived these experiences that are critical in understanding the educational injustices examined by Jonathan Kozol, so as to view these communities not as in need of saving but as spaces in which community members will always be confronting the reality of their daily lives. For Chicago's Latina/o/x and African American communities, the familial and social capital that students walked into schools with every day facilitated their relationships with a school system that worked against them. According to Yosso (2005), familial capital is "those cultural knowledges nurtured among family (kin) that carry a sense of community history, memory and cultural intuition" that "engages a commitment to community well-being" (p. 79). Further, through social capital, communities and community children build on the networks of people and community resources that serve to empower and facilitate their attempts at seeking a sense of justice in their schooling lives (Yosso, 2005). Chicago's Latina/o/x and African American communities have historically engaged in the creation and maintenance of community and school-based organizations that served to bridge them with educational spaces, despite continued attempts at discrediting their attempts (Danns, 2014; Stovall, 2016).

I entered Chicago schools in 1980 and graduated high school in 1993. During that time Chicago schools saw three major teacher strikes (1983, 1984, 1987, along with a two-day walkout in 1985). Although the strikes were a disruption to my education, they also served as sites of resistance for confronting the inequities within city schools. My ability to use the navigational capital, Yosso (2005) discusses, to move through city schools and move on to higher education is due in large part to many of the educators who were fighting their own battles against the very system that sought to miseducate or under-educate me. Many of us who traversed Chicago schools had our own Coral Hawkins, who became a beacon of light to some of the children in *Savage Inequalities*; teachers who were not only exemplary educators but whose care ethics allowed them to love the children they were entrusted with not only as their charges but as part of the community family from which they too emerged. My second, third, and fourth grade teacher, Ms. Rosa Navarro, was one of those educators invested in the children in her own Puerto Rican community. She knew our families, and set us up on an educational path that taught us to expect more from our teachers and schools. Ms. Navarro and Ms. Hawkins were not anomalies but rather examples of exceptional teachers who aligned their own educational experiences and relationship with the community and had a commitment to offer valuable educational opportunities to their children. Kozol (1991) states, "It is tempting to focus on these teachers and, by doing this, to paint a hopeful portrait of the good things that go on under adverse conditions." He further states that these stories are consoling (p. 5). However, I argue that we should not shy away from highlighting these stories as Kozol does by not highlighting the liberatory narratives that complement those stories of hopelessness faced by many of the city's children. These liberatory narratives should be central to educational stories, even if juxtaposed with the grim realities of urban education. The hope and love that creates familial and social capital (Yosso, 2005), shared from both teachers and communities working toward it, creates change. This change, specifically in communities across cities such as Chicago, seeks to transcend the unjust educational experiences of thousands of children, many times at the hands of the community. Other people's children are, in fact, our children too.

Conclusion: A Promise of Simple Justice in the Schooling Lives of Chicago's Children

A 1983 report on the current status of school desegregation in Chicago was interestingly titled "A Promise of Simple Justice in the Education of Chicago School Children." As the report stated, the quality of life for Chicagoans should not merely be measured by its economic, crime, housing, or transportation status; more importantly, "Chicago's future must also be measured by the achievement of its public school children" (Davidson, 1983,

p. vi). Chicago public schools have long been characterized by their racial isolation, and because its schools grew out of the idea of neighborhood schools, as neighborhoods became marked by racial and ethnic segregation, their schools followed suit. According to one account, "Official restrictive covenants, and neighborhood school policies established to be consistent with them, worked to contain blacks and other minorities in specified areas of the city" leading to 91% of elementary schools and 71% of high schools to be single race by 1956 (Green, 1981, p. 2). White flight out of Chicago neighborhoods and its public schools has led to an increase in school segregation despite policies initiated by the Chicago Board of Education following the Hauser Committee Report of 1964 (Green, 1981, p. 3). The school uprisings of the 1960s and the 1970s were clear indicators of not only the hopelessness felt across Chicago schools by students, teachers, and community members but their communities' commitment to ensuring a sense of justice for their children in a city that continues to devalue their educational aspirations. Chicago's Puerto Ricans' sense of hope stemmed from the community's resistance to merely comply with the structures that limited their participation and sense of justice within labor, housing, and educational spaces. Borrowing from David Tyack (1992), "Schools have continued to shape the core of our national identity," moreover, they have consistently served as a political arena for citizens (or communities) to contend with one another (p. 1).

It was this very simple act of justice sought by not only Puerto Rican students but also African American and Mexican American students, that inspired a decade if not a generation of school-centered activism in Chicago. This history has also inspired a host of academic work by the very children that these schools sought to educate. The narratives shared by scholars such as Angelica Rivera (2008), Gabriel Cortez (2008), Erica Davila (2005), and others, were very much linked to experiences they shared as schoolchildren. Although they had the opportunity to move on to further their educational aspirations, their work was influenced in many ways by the contentious relationship between the city and its community members, especially around schooling concerns. Schools did more than just educate (or miseducate) its children; schools in Chicago similarly created meaningful spaces in which communities could articulate their positions within a larger movement in a city that was furthering their marginalization. The narratives collected by scholars like myself and others such as Rivera, Davila, and Cortez, offer a glimpse into how generations of Latina/os and

African Americans in Chicago have negotiated their own lives in order to create meaningful spaces for their children. Further, the navigational capital (Yosso, 2005) that students of color employ in order to maneuver through institutions of higher learning historically not meant for them, and their resilience within these spaces, further links them to their home communities. It is these narratives that allow us a different reading than what's offered in Kozol's framing of the city. Although Kozol's work is very much needed, there must be room for communities to both name their own reality and highlight the many ways they work to facilitate change that will allow educators and students the space to imagine and engage in transformative change. That is the Chicago I remember and the one many of us want others to know about.

References

Chancellor's Committee on Latina/o Issues. (2003). *Latinas/os at the University of Illinois: A history of neglect and strategies for improvement, 1992–2002.* University of Illinois at Urbana-Champaign.

Cortez, G. (2008). *Education, politics, and a hunger strike: A popular movement's struggle for education in Chicago's Little Village Community.* [Unpublished doctoral dissertation]. University of Illinois at Urbana-Champaign.

Danns, D. (2014). *Desegregating Chicago's public schools: Policy implementation, politics, and protest, 1965–1985.* Palgrave Macmillan.

Davidson, M. (1983). *An interim report: A promise of simple justice in the education of Chicago children?* Prepared for Monitoring Commission for Desegregation Implementation. Retrieved from Chicago History Museum.

Davila, E. (2005). *Educational policies and practices in lived context: Puerto Ricans schooled in Chicago.* [Unpublished doctoral dissertation]. University of Illinois at Urbana-Champaign.

Fernandez, L. (2012). *Brown in the windy city: Mexicans and Puerto Ricans in postwar Chicago.* University of Chicago.

Green, R. L. (1981). *Consultants research report, student desegregation plan for the Chicago Public Schools, Part I: Educational components:* Prepared for the Board of Education of the City of Chicago. Retrieved from Chicago History Museum.

Kozol, J. (1992). *Savage Inequalities: Children in America's schools.* Harper Perennial.

Padilla, F. (1988). *Puerto Rican Chicago.* University of Notre Dame Press.

Perez, G. (2004). *The near Northwest side story: Migration, displacement, and Puerto Rican families.* University of California Press.

Rivera, A. (2008). *Re-inserting Mexican-American women's voices into 1950s Chicago educational history*. [Unpublished doctoral dissertation]. University of Illinois at Urbana-Champaign.

Stovall, D. (2016). *Born out of struggle: Critical race theory, school creation, and the politics of interruption*. State University of New York Press.

Tyack, D. (1992). Introduction. In S. Mondale (Ed.), *Schools: The story of American public education* (pp. 1–10). Beacon Press.

Velazquez, M. (2016). Looking forward, working for change: Puerto Rican women and the quest for educational justice in Chicago. *Centro Journal, 28*(2).

Velázquez, M. (2022). *Puerto Rican Chicago: Schooling the city, 1940–1977*. University of Illinois Press.

Winter, S. L. (1989). The cognitive dimension of the Agon between legal power and narrative meaning. *Michigan Law Review, 87*, 2225–2279.

Yosso, T. J. (2005). Whose culture has capital? A critical race theory discussion of community cultural wealth. *Race Ethnicity and Education, 8*(1), 69–91.

Chapter 5

Far from Savage

(Re)Turning to My Village and Revealing the "Two Worlds of Washington"

STEVE D. MOBLEY JR.

(Re)Turning Home

There are "two worlds of Washington," . . . One is the Washington of cherry blossoms, the sparkling white monuments, the magisterial buildings of government . . . of politics and power . . . Just over a mile away, the other world is Anacostia.

—Jonathan Kozol

Savage Inequalities: Children in America's Schools (1991) featured the narratives of myriad urban educational stakeholders and quickly became a prominent work heralded for bringing to light the vast disparities that exist in U.S. public schools. The author, Jonathan Kozol, underscored over and over again throughout his book that urban classrooms were overcrowded, dilapidated structures and that parents were fearful their children were not receiving an adequate education. While the narratives were provocative, critical perspectives were lost. Kozol's portrayals of the students, parents, and teachers that he chose to feature were void of the nuances that recognize the significance of many unnamed human and structural resources that are deemed valuable beyond dominant and patriarchal frameworks (Farmer-Hinton, Lewis, Patton, & Rivers, 2013). Furthermore, with regard to urban education, Kozol's work sends the covert message that "if it's urban, then it must be bad" (Milner, 2008). To imply that all or even most urban schools, neighborhoods, and their community members are inferior or deficient is woefully inaccurate (Ford, 2010; Morris, 2004). The much-needed holistic portrayals of the underrepresented communities that *should* have been exemplified in *Savage Inequalities* were simply not (re)presented. Where was the hope? Where was the success?

Education research has and continues to adopt deficit perspectives and use the negative stereotypes inherent in society about minority populations to glean resonance and produce knowledge that continues to "other" and further pathologize these populations. Historically and contemporarily, two divergent discourses exist. On one extreme, it has been espoused that urban communities create their own problems due to deviant behavior, individual inadequacy, and dysfunctional families. Other rationalizations take the form of victimization debates, where urban communities are socially relegated to the margins due to forces beyond their control (i.e., economic exploitation, class discrimination, social ostracization) (Valenica, 2010). Contemporary research exploring urban schools and the communities in which they are situated must continue to move beyond the detrimental one-dimensional stereotypical tropes (i.e. destitute students, "inner city" life, powerless parents, etc.) that have saturated educational discourses. Contrary to the popular deficit-based perspectives that are embedded within debates that surround urban education, there is a significant body of work that originates with the notion that urban communities *and* their schools are places with myriad strengths. There are a number of scholars who have sought to disrupt and challenge the skewed discourses that portray urban school cultures as inferior or "lacking" (e.g., Baldridge, 2014; Carey, 2016; Howard, 2014; Ladson-Billings, 2000). This scholarship shifts research lenses away from previous assessments that view urban teachers, students, and their families as entities merely burdened with disadvantage. Instead, they focus on these communities and their members as sites that are rich with cultural assets and resilience systems that are ripe with lessons that can be imparted to broader educational conversations (Yosso, 2005). My hope is that this chapter extends these critical dialogues.

I was born and raised in Washington, DC, and am extremely proud of my hometown. DC is a complex city. Like many other urban communities across the nation, there are extremes present. I was a student in the Washington, DC Public School system (DCPS) during the time Kozol debuted *Savage Inequalities*. His portrayal of DC revealed two worlds: one filled with museums, historic monuments, and our nation's government structure and the other riddled with crime and urban blight. I was educated in the latter reality he chose to highlight. Though I was educated in DC during the *Savage Inequalities* era, when it was deemed the "murder capital" of the nation, there is more to my lived experiences and others who came of age with me in the nation's capital. Washington, DC, is a storied community that is enriched by its residents and the many facets that make up its rich communal fabric—to me, it is *home*. It will always be a part of me.

This chapter is a "homecoming" of sorts, and features Washington, DC, and its educational successes and shows how my community thrived and was at the forefront of my educational achievement. As I bring forth my counter-narrative, my hope is that this chapter and its much-needed narratives shall be used as an educational resource to further show how the challenges that are apparent in urban education can be overcome with strategic educational interventions. Familial involvement, community partnerships, mentorship, and focused advocacy are *key*. Overall, the goal of this chapter is to disrupt the master narrative. I will use my counter-story as a scholarly space to highlight how my K–12 educational experiences directly confront those that are featured in *Savage Inequalities*. The (un)told shall be revealed.

Dismantling "A Single Story"

> Stories matter. Many stories matter. Stories have been used to dispossess and to malign. But stories can also be used to empower, and to humanize. Stories can break the dignity of a people. But stories can also repair that broken dignity.
>
> —Chimamanda Ngozi Adichie, 2009

During my engagement with *Savage Inequalities*, what was most distressing was that as I absorbed its contents, I became well aware that Kozol's portrayals were marred with stereotypes—*especially* Black stereotypes. A *single* story was ever-present. Unfortunately, Kozol depicted DC, its public schools, and the people of color who live there as hopeless and helpless.

There are numerous instances in *Savage Inequalities* where deficit-laden accounts of urban education are featured. For example, in the following passage, Kozol states: "I look into the faces of these children. At this moment they seem full of hope and innocence and expectation. . . . By the time they are 14, a certain rawness and vulgarity may have set in. Many will be hostile and embittered by that time. Others will coarsen, partly the result of diet, partly self-neglect and self-dislike" (1991, pp. 182–183).

The above quote conveys a shallow and deceptive characterization regarding urban students and their lived experiences. This description of DC public school students hints at the potential for these students to be hopeful and promising but only to a certain extent. He alludes to promise but then goes on to label these students as "vulgar," "hostile," and "embittered" with little explanation (or at least in-depth explanation). Kozol's accounts of students who are "disadvantaged" and "marginalized" places the blame on *them*. Within this work it is constantly reiterated that urban communities and their students are somehow at fault, rather than recognizing the institutional and systemic forces that impact their daily lives both inside and outside of their urban educational contexts (Milner, 2008; Weiner, 2003).

The major problem that often arises when researchers "study" minoritized and underrepresented communities is their failure to understand and provide a sense of humanity to these populations. "One might think that such an error could easily be alleviated by merely studying [African-Americans] as human beings" (Gordon, 2000, p. 71). Why aren't Black educational communities explored honestly and respectfully? Is their humanity always lost? Is it easier to be led by destructive assumptions when engaging Black issues in education research? "If I didn't define myself for myself, I would be crunched into other people's fantasies for me and eaten alive" (Lorde, 2007, p. 137). Lorde's words call to action and empower education scholars who study minority communities to champion counter-stories that have the power to (re)right *and* (re)write the deficit narratives that have dominated, diminished, and constrained numerous minority educational contexts.

The Washington, DC school system where I was educated transcends Kozol's provocative and "vivid images about poverty and pollution that likely engendered discomfort among readers, who were unaware that people lived and were educated in such conditions" (Farmer-Hinton, Lewis, Patton, & Rivers, 2013, p. 3). Some of Kozol's stories I lived, but not all of them. Being raised and reared in the heart of the nation's capital was interesting to say the least. The nationwide crack cocaine epidemic of the 1980s and 1990s plagued the city, and as a result crime and murder riddled my hometown. During this time, it was routine for my friends and I to find discarded drug needles while on the jungle gym, or immediately following recess we were often forced to hide under our desks due to gang activity and gunfire occurring on our school playground. This was my environment, but I always yearned for more.

The portrayals of urban blight that were brought to the forefront in *Savage Inequalities* were a part of my experiences growing up in DC, but they were certainly not the whole picture. Assumptions that may make these images generalizable to the entire Washington, DC community are unfair. When unraveling the nuances present within urban schools and the communities they are situated in, it is negligent to place these learning spaces and their community contexts into two separate categories. The environmental conditions that surround students and their families have a profound impact on their lived experiences. Many of the turbulent systemic environmental factors, especially when considering urban contexts extend far beyond the control of urban communities (Milner, Murray, Farinde, & Delale-O'Connor, 2015). There is a nuanced duality present that deserves recognition of the internal and external forces that impact urban schools, their students, families, and the surrounding communities.

During my youth I was not able to appropriately name the societal ills that are often used to oppress urban communities and keep people of color in substandard conditions. However, I was made very aware that I could use my intellect to transcend these very spaces that I dwelled in every day. It was communicated to me by my village—my mother, my family, my teachers, and community that there were eminent possibilities in my future horizons. The messages were deliberate and action oriented. In both overt and covert ways I was told that I was smart, worthy, and did not have to be confined nor relegated to the block where I was raised. A pivotal foundation was put into place for me early on.

Evoking *My* Counter-story

The utilization of master narratives to represent groups with oppressed identities rids them of their richness and complexity (Montecinos, 1995). Due to the use of pervasive monovocal accounts, counter-storytelling has been enacted within educational research as a method to free the voices of people of color to enact change within K–12 and higher education spaces. Derrick Bell (1992) and Solórzano and Yosso (2002) define this research act as a method to convey the stories of people of color who are often overlooked and dismissed within scholarly inquiry. It is also "a means by which to examine, critique, and counter majoritarian stories (or master narratives) composed about people of color" (Harper, 2009, p. 701). There is immense utility in this method. Counter-stories are *sought* out as a means to unravel master narratives and to "expose deficit-informed research that silences and distorts [the] epistemologies of people of color" (Harper, 2009, p. 702). As I convey my counter-story, I use my educational experiences in Washington, DC, to challenge and confront the problematic portrayals in *Savage Inequalities*.

I Was Different

I was privileged to learn in various educational spaces in Washington, DC. The many lessons imparted to me from the schools Kozol considered to be "broken," my familial foundations, and neighborhood community encompassed the many faces and voices that were and are representative of the rich Black diaspora that I was exposed to. I was surrounded by excellent teachers and many community members who were invested in my success. This recognition was not made apparent in *Savage Inequalities*. The stories that Kozol chose to highlight are actually one extreme of a complex story. His narratives further generated monolithic views that are consistently (re)produced and contribute to the overwhelmingly toxic fallacies that are often used to depict the identity and meaning of urban communities and their schools (Farmer-Hinton, Lewis, Patton, & Rivers, 2013). There is much more to the contrary.

Growing up I found solace in books rather than sports. I chose to stay after school and compete in science fairs and the "Odyssey of the Mind," rather than try out for flag football. I reveled in coming home with honor roll status and being placed in gifted and talented programs throughout my K–12 years. My childhood heroes were Levar Burton from *Reading Rainbow* and Big Bird from *Sesame Street*, as opposed to the basketball star Magic Johnson or the rapper Tupac Shakur. *I was different*. This difference was praised by my family, many of my peers, and my teachers. "In the larger social milieu, Black [men] are often portrayed and stereotyped as criminals, gang members, athletes, and entertainers" (Fries-Britt & Griffin, 2007, p. 511). The aforementioned anchors my counter-story. Even in my difference, I was celebrated and not forced to fit into any stereotype that awaited me in the broader societal context. I now know that from a young age I was being equipped to defend my existence in this world, a world that would constantly question me and I it.

During my adolescence, school was a refuge for me. The DC public school system was my first scholarly educational space. It was there, in those schools where my talents and educational interests were honed and highly encouraged. My kindergarten teacher, Ms. Hughes, recognized my intellect and recommended me for the Scott-Montgomery Elementary School Gifted and Talented program. That program was responsible for exposing me to the very museums and monuments that Kozol deemed as untouchable or foreign to many DC families. In junior high, Ms. Hilbert told me to read *Black Boy* by Richard Wright and awakened my curiosity in the Harlem Renaissance and those who would for me become models of Black excellence and success. In high school, Ms. Bradshaw, my 12th grade English teacher, taught me the wonders of Chaucer, Hurston, and Shakespeare. Each of these teachers and many others took an interest in me. Together in these "broken" buildings I was celebrated for being *Steve* and cultivated in many ways.

A Mother's Love

I grew up working class. A product of a single-parent household, my mother utilized the parenting style associated with the *accomplishment of natural growth* (Laureau, 2003). "The commitment among working class parents [is to] provide comfort, food, shelter, safety and other basic support given economic challenges and the formidable demands of child rearing" (Laureau, 2003, p. 5). I was what you would call "the quintessential latch key kid." My mother worked evening and midnight shifts throughout my adolescence. When I was dismissed from school my mother was headed to work. Due to her "alternative" work schedule, she put many rules into place to ensure that I would not fall prey to a perilous lifestyle associated with sex, drugs, and incarceration to which many of my friends and peers fell victim. Each day I was required to call her at work by 4 p.m. so that she knew I was safe.

There were also many instances when she would summon me to her workplace. I often spent the night with her at Howard University Hospital where we would complete algebra homework, rehearse lines for school plays, and even drill vocabulary words for spelling bees. My mother was one of my fiercest advocates. She ensured that I was highly involved in both in-school activities and those outside the classroom. During the academic year *and* summer months she enrolled me in numerous enrichment programs, DC arts initiatives, and Upward Bound. Her expectations were high. It was my mother who first told me, "Little Steve, you are smart, you are going to go to college." Her guidance and encouragement were integral to my bourgeoning academic self-image. Because of her, I was unashamed of being smart, especially during the time in my adolescence when I most susceptible to peer pressure. To her, excellence was the standard and not an option.

Motivational parental encouragement is critical in maintaining high expectations for low-income students. Support for postsecondary education is positively associated with college participation (Hossler, Braxton, & Coopersmith, 1989; Cabrera & La Nasa, 2000). Though my mother did not graduate from college, her expectations for me were not inhibited due to her educational attainment. Her formidable influence on me contradicts the stance that the level of parental education is the best predictor of their expectations for their children (Hossler et al., 1989). My mother's involvement in my educational trajectory also counters discourses that assert that urban parents are disengaged, apathetic, and simply not present in their students' lives. What is also intriguing about her influence and guidance was that she ensured that an extended network of caring individuals who were invested in my future surrounded me. She knew that she could not always be physically present but guaranteed that a village was near when she was not.

It Takes A Village: My "Big Brothers" and "Big Sisters"

I was raised as an only child, thus, those who became a part of my extended family were invaluable to me as I moved through my educational journey in Washington, DC. As I reflect on the many mentors that came into my life during my K–12 experiences, those who stand out most are the group of college students who volunteered in my neighborhood recreation center. Their guidance and friendship became an indispensable part of my life, especially when I began my college search process. Even though I did not attend a high school with a strong college-going culture, they provided me with examples of successful college students and made a sincere investment in my overall growth and well-being. They were the big brothers and big sisters that I did not have by birth.

Among Americans of African descent there are powerful connections that are formed that extend beyond blood familial ties. "Fictive kinships"[1] are often established and used to expand the networks of Black students as they confront life-changing events that occur during their development within K–12 and postsecondary contexts (Fordham, 1996). Within Black communities, there is an ideal that there is a presence of brotherhood and sisterhood among all African Americans. This collective identity is evident in the various kinship terms that Black Americans may use to refer to each other, such as "brother," or "sister" (Chatters, Taylor, & Jayakody, 1994). "In this light, one might think of a fictive kin group as a tightly bonded group of individuals who have come together for a specific purpose" (Tierney & Venegas, 2006, p. 1691).

Over time Turrick, Desmond, Melantha, Jerrah, Mbili, Moja, Pabvon, and Nairobi truly became my brothers and sisters. At the time, they were students at Howard University. Their lives intrigued me, especially because I had decided to apply to and attend a Historically Black College (HBCU). Each of them pushed and expanded my Black consciousness and were the first to introduce me to W. E. B. Du Bois, the beauty of the Swahili language, and the allure of Black fraternities and sororities. As a group their impact was indelible, but Turrick went above and beyond. He truly extended himself to me outside of his duties as the director of youth services for my neighborhood recreation center. He was fiercely protective of me and exposed me to a world that extended beyond my DC block. Whether it was transporting me throughout the city to take the standardized tests required for college admission, attending school assemblies where I was being featured, or simply lending a sympathetic ear as I endured stressful situations, he was there. I am still baffled that he was able to maintain his own college life and take me on as his "little brother."

My "fictive kinships" were established so that I could both survive and attain social resilience within my urban environment. Black communities share their cultural capital and then develop their social capital for survival and success in a society where the forces of racism and discrimination are pervasive (Yosso, 2005). These pivotal relationships I was afforded provided support and a sense of overall community belonging that was absolutely necessary. The kinship ties that I was afforded reiterate the importance of how I was able to obtain a vital connection to the DC community and its valuable resources. My "big brothers" and "big sisters" modeled lessons of caring, tenacity, and provided me with a moral, educational, and occupational consciousness (Yosso, 2005). These relationships reaffirm that fictive kin can be as important as those related by blood (Dillworth-Anderson, 2001).

To Care: (Re)Turning to Resilience

If stories come to you, care for them. And learn to give them away where they are needed. Sometimes a person needs a story more than food to stay alive. That is why we put stories into each other's memory. This is how people care for themselves. . . . Never forget these obligations (Lopez, 1990, p. 60).

While my story reveals the many systemic issues that are apparent in urban schools, there is an undercurrent of resilience that is also present. I intentionally have signaled a critical need for educational stakeholders to strongly consider making a bold and concerted effort to (re)turn to urban educational environments so that effective change may occur. These spaces have the innate ability and have served as forums to enact and empower underserved communities so that they may show how they have, will, and shall continue to empower and resist the status quo. It must be asserted that students educated in urban schools *still* demonstrate resilience in the face of racism, poverty, and environments with few resources (Griffin & Allen, 2006). Continued conversations surrounding the systemic issues that impact urban K–12 schools are absolutely necessary. My hope is that this chapter calls education scholars, scholar-practitioners, students, and their families to action to know that their voices matter and are needed in the discourses that affect them.

Note

1. The term "fictive kinship" refers to people within a given context where they are not related by birth but share a close "familial" relationship (Fordham, 1996; Ogbu, 1991).

References

Adichie, C. N. (2009). *The danger of a single story*. TEDGlobal. http://b.3cdn.net/ascend/2029fab7aa68da3f31_jqm6bn6lz.pdf

Baldridge, B. J. (2014). Relocating the deficit: Reimagining Black youth in neoliberal times. *American Educational Research Journal, 51*(3), 440–472.

Bell, D. (1992). *Faces at the bottom of the well: The permanence of racism.* Basic Books.

Cabrera, A. F., & La Nasa, S. M. (2000). Understanding the college-choice process. *New Directions for Institutional Research, 2000* (107), 5–22.

Carey, R. L. (2016). "Keep that in mind . . . you're gonna go to college": Family influence on the college going processes of Black and Latino high school boys. *The Urban Review, 48*(5), 718–742.

Chatters, L. M., Taylor, R. J., & Jayakody, R. (1994). Fictive kinship relations in black extended families. *Journal of Comparative Family Studies, 25*(3), 297–312.

Dilworth-Anderson, P. (2001). Extended kin networks in black families. In A. J. Walker, M. Manoogian-O'Dell, L. A. McGraw, & D. L. G. White (Eds.), *Families in later life: Connections and transitions* (pp. 104–106). Pine Forge Press.

Farmer-Hinton, R. L., Lewis, J. D., Patton, L. D., & Rivers, I. D. (2013). Dear Mr. Kozol . . . Four African American women scholars and the re-authoring of Savage Inequalities. *Teachers College Record, 115*(5), 1–38.

Ford, D. (2010). *Reversing underachievement among gifted Black students: Promising practices and programs.* Teachers College Press.

Fordham, S. (1996). *Blacked out: Dilemmas of race, identity, and success at Capital High.* University of Chicago Press.

Fries-Britt, S., & Griffin, K. A. (2007). The Black box: How high-achieving Blacks resist stereotypes about Black Americans. *Journal of College Student Development, 48*(5), 509–524.

Gibson & J. U. Ogbu (Eds.), *Minority status and schooling: A comparative study of immigrant and involuntary minorities* (pp. 3–33). Garland Press.

Gordon, L. R. (2000). *Existentia Africana: Understanding Africana existential thought.* Routledge.

Griffin, K., & Allen, W. (2006). Mo'money, mo'problems? High-achieving Black high school students' experiences with resources, racial climate, and resilience. *The Journal of Negro Education,* 478–494.

Harper, S. R. (2009). Niggers no more: A critical race counternarrative on Black male student achievement at predominantly White colleges and universities. *International Journal of Qualitative Studies in Education, 22*(6), 697–712.

Hossler, D., Braxton, J., & Coopersmith, G. (1989). Understanding student college choice. *Higher Education: Handbook of Theory and Research, 5,* 231–288.

Howard, T. C. (2014). *Black male(d): Peril and promise in the education of African American males.* Teachers College Press.

Kozol, J. (2012). *Savage inequalities: Children in America's schools.* Crown.

Ladson-Billings, G. (2000). Fighting for our lives preparing teachers to teach African American students. *Journal of Teacher Education, 51*(3), 206–214.

Lareau, A. (2003). *Unequal childhoods: Class, race, and family life*. University of California Press.

Lopez, B. (1990). *Crow and weasel*. North Point Press.

Lorde, A. (2007) *Sister Outsider: Essays and speeches*. Crossing Press.

Milner, H. R. (2008). Disrupting deficit notions of difference: Counter-narratives of teachers and community in urban education. *Teaching and Teacher Education, 24*(6), 1573–1598.

Milner IV, H. R., Murray, I. E., Farinde, A. A., & Delale-O'Connor, L. (2015). Outside of school matters: What we need to know in urban environments. *Equity & Excellence in Education, 48*(4), 529–548.

Montecinos, C. (1995). Culture as an ongoing dialogue: Implications for multicultural teacher education. In C. Sleeter & P. McLaren (Eds.), *Multicultural education, critical pedagogy, and the politics of difference* (pp. 269–308). State University of New York Press.

Morris, J. E. (2004). Can anything good come from Nazareth? Race, class, and African American schooling and community in the urban South and Midwest. *American Educational Research Journal, 41*(1), 69–112.

Ogbu, J. U. (1991). Immigrant and involuntary minorities in comparative perspective. In M. A. Gibson & J. U. Ogbu (Eds.), *Minority status and schooling: A comparative study of immigrant and involuntary minorities* (pp. 3–33). Garland Press.

Solórzano, D. G., & T. J. Yosso. 2002. Critical race methodology: Counter-storytelling as an analytical framework for education research. *Qualitative Inquiry, 8*(1), 23–44.

Tierney, W. G., & Venegas, K. M. (2006). Fictive kin and social capital: The role of peer groups in applying and paying for college. *American Behavioral Scientist, 49*(12), 1687–1702.

Valencia, R. R. (2010). *Dismantling contemporary deficit thinking: Educational thought and practice*. Routledge.

Weiner, L. (2003). Why is classroom management so vexing to urban teachers? *Theory Into Practice, 42*(4), 305–312.

Yosso, T. J. (2005). Whose culture has capital? A critical race theory discussion of community cultural wealth. *Race Ethnicity and Education, 8*(1), 69–91.

Chapter 6

A Third-World City

An Autoethnography on Growing Up in Detroit, Michigan, and Becoming a Teacher

AMBER C. BRYANT

Poverty is man's worst form of violence.

—Mahatma Gandhi

In 2014, news stations reported the massive water shut-off policy affecting thousands of families and children in Detroit, Michigan; the water shut-off crisis was accompanied by Detroit's largest municipal bankruptcy ($20 billion) in American history (Kurt, 2016). The United Nations (UN) expressed strong concerns about the human rights issues related to the living conditions of Detroit's residents and attempted to get involved to reduce the impact of the residential water shutoffs. The UN argued that the lack of water, a basic human necessity, plunged Detroit into third-world living conditions (Kurth, 2016). The massive water shut-off and the city's bankruptcy only begin to describe the city's mounting political problems and complex (and often contradictory) means for response and recovery. While currently bleak, this narrative has not always been the story for Detroit. In this chapter, I offer my personal counter-narrative of growing up in Detroit influenced both by its bustling economic years as well as its deindustrialized decline. Though this narrative is largely situated around

Jonathon Kozol's (1991) *Savage Inequalities*, autoethnographic methods and critical theory allowed me to investigate school inequities by analyzing my experiences as a youth, then teacher, in Detroit. I conclude this chapter by sharing four tenets about my teaching philosophy: teaching with intentionality, implementing an explicit curriculum, knowing the power of empathy, and understanding the necessity of dedication.

Background

From 1900 to 1930, Detroit was the fastest-growing city in the world due to the economic boom of the emerging car industries (F.Y., 2012; Sansone, 2012). As a city, its illustrious character drew many diverse families from all over the country with hopes of finding socioeconomic stability in the factory industries. The emergence of the "Big Three" auto companies (Ford, Chrysler, and General Motors) also attracted masses of laborers seeking middle-class wages and benefits for semiskilled jobs. My family was part of this migration; my family moved from Alabama in the early 1900s and settled on Detroit's Westside. Eventually, we bought homes and several family members retired from Chrysler, GM, and American Axle plants.

In the early 1900s, Detroit was made up of approximately 99% White Americans; yet, by the turn of the 21st century, Detroit's population was approximately 80% African American (Gibson & Jung, 2005). The surrounding suburban cities of Detroit stayed demographically White for nearly a century while Detroit became densely populated with African Americans (see Table 6.1) (Gibson & Jung, 2005).

Table 6.1. Racial Demographics of Detroit and Surrounding Cities (1860–1990)

	1860		1990	
City	% of African American	% of Whites	% of African American	% of Whites
Ann Arbor	2.1%	97.9%	9%	82%
Detroit	3.1%	96.9%	21.6%	75.7%
Flint	0.8%	99.2%	47.9%	49.6%
Lansing	0.9%	99.1%	18.6%	73.9%
Grand Rapids	0.7%	99.2%	18.5%	76.4%

Source: Gibson and Jung (2005).

The dense population of African Americans in Detroit, who were already marginalized by racialized laws and policies, became economically isolated as the larger economic boom shifted downward (see Table 6.2). As Wilson (2012) points out,

> Long periods of racial oppression can result in a system of inequality that may persist for indefinite periods of time even after racial barriers are removed. This is because the most disadvantaged member of racial minority groups who suffer the cumulative effects of both race and class subjugation (including those effects passed on from generation to generation), are disproportionately represented among the segment of the general population that has been denied the resources to compete effectively in a free and open market. (pp. 146–147)

Here, Wilson explains the perpetuation of poverty within marginalized communities, even among African Americans living in a post–civil rights era. For example, in 2009, with Detroit's population over 80% African American, over 50% of its children lived in poverty, and over 50% of its adults were considered functionally illiterate (F.Y., 2012). In 2014, the United Way compared the cost of living to income and determined that 67% of Detroit's residents lived under the federal poverty line (Abbey-Lambertz, 2014). After being dubbed the "fastest growing city in the world" in 1930, less than a century later in 2013, *Forbes* magazine named Detroit the "most miserable city" in America (Badenhausen, 2013). Additionally, for decades, Detroit has been labeled one of the most dangerous cities

Table 6.2. Average Detroit Economic Demographics Compared to Michigan and US

	Detroit	**Michigan**	**U.S.**
Median household income	$26,000/yr.	$49,000/yr.	$53,000/yr.
Per capita income	$15,000/yr.	$26,000/yr.	$29,000/yr.
Persons in poverty	40%	16%	14%
African American/White populations	*83%* 11%	*13%* 80%	*13%* 77%

Source: U.S. Census Bureau (2015a, 2015b, 2015c).

in America, often times taking the number-one position (Fisher, 2015). Although not recovering from a natural disaster, Detroit's decline and slow comeback sadly resembles the disaster-relief area of post-Katrina New Orleans—widespread urban decay, extreme poverty, slow economic development, socioeconomic, and racial disparities as well as little insight for what to do next.

Detroit is seeking a road to recovery, and I argue that the city's initial efforts should include adequately educating its children. An educated society creates stronger economic gains among its citizenry and benefits individuals and communities in holistic ways (Darling-Hammond, 2010; OECD, 2013, Shannon, 2014; Wilson, 2012). Below, I utilize autoethnographic methods and critical theory to analyze my counter-narrative of growing up in and teaching in Detroit; and my position is largely situated around Jonathon Kozol's (1991) educational investigations in *Savage Inequalities*. This chapter supports Kozol's understanding of racial inequities in schools and presupposes that the solutions lie with the community's cultural wealth (Yosso, 2005) as well as with the policies that affect said community. As my narrative will show, there are four tenets important to teaching and learning in urban districts with high-minority, high-poverty student populations such as Detroit: teaching with intentionality, implementing an explicit curriculum, knowing the power of empathy, and understanding the necessity of dedication. This narrative seeks to explain and support the development of these tenets based on two significant incidents in my teaching career.

Reading Kozol

On a crisp fall afternoon, as I walked through the University of Michigan's (U of M) campus to my undergraduate English course, my mind raced, and my heart pounded. I could feel anger and insecurity growing with every step toward class. My professor had assigned the reading of Jonathan Kozol's *Savage Inequalities*, and I was prepared to speak my mind, unapologetically, about the racial and economic injustices in our country that Kozol so provocatively recollects. I walked into that English class that afternoon and shared my feelings of disappointment and rage that the truths discussed in Kozol's book had been hidden from our country's most advantaged and politically active citizens. U of M is a predominantly White institution with rigid academic standards for admittance. What I found to be phenomenal then still confounds me today: the allowance, protection, and perpetuation of ignorance for privileged young White Americans. I do not intend to position this chapter from a deficit ideology of White Americans, yet I will honestly reflect on my observations as the autoethnographic genre of writing mandates. Anton Chekhov once said that the task of the writer is not to solve the problem but to state it correctly; this accurately and critically describes the autoethnographic process. Nevertheless, as a first-generation college student listening to my White counterparts discuss their ignorance and astonishment of urban school environments, I realized that it was this disconnection between minority students' realities and their White peers' realities that allow for the systemic failures of our nation's school systems to remain hidden. Not surprisingly, the eager Michigan students expressed their desire to want to change "the system" and to make equality a reality in America. This dialogue was the beginning of what would lead to my career in higher education.

Narrative: Growing Up and Teaching in Detroit

While growing up in Detroit in the 1990s, I was surrounded by community cultural wealth (see Yosso, 2005) of Black people every day: the majority of my teachers were Black, all of our neighbors were Black, and Detroit even had a Black mayor working through his second decade as municipal leader. I felt safe every day of my life as a child (as much as I can remember at least). My life was "normal" and, some would even argue, "privileged." In retrospect, gunshots were heard almost nightly, three family members under the age of 30 were shot and killed before I turned 10 years old, the majority of my family members were single-parent women with limited education, and homeless people were as prominent and constant as the city's structural fixtures and landmarks. Yet my sisters and I played outside after school every day, and we attended church regularly in a proud "mega-church," built from the pockets and hopes of its poverty-stricken congregation. (Note: the "mega church" was distinctive because it was not one of the innumerable storefront churches that existed alongside privately owned liquor stores, barbershops, daycares, and small boutiques.) Detroit was bustling and alive when I was growing up, having benefited from the economic boom that accompanied President Clinton's administration as well as the unprecedented technological advancements that marked the decade. The 1990s were good.

During the early-to-mid-2000s, I attended the University of Michigan and was blessed to have a daughter during those years. The class that required the reading of Kozol also required class activities at an offsite community center (either a high school or a Michigan state prison) where, as students, we facilitated creative writing and theater workshops. The objective was to expose separate and isolated communities to one another and to provide a service to underserved citizens. My major at the time was English language and literature; my goals quickly shifted to the field of education upon graduation in 2009. This dedication came only after my exposure to urban teaching as an undergraduate student.

In Fall 2007, as a junior at U of M, I walked into Cooley High School on Detroit's Westside with few to no expectations. All I knew was that I was going to be at this school every Friday to facilitate writing workshops for 11th graders. Upon entering, I was troubled by the *savage inequality* of the building: the lockers were hanging by the hinges, tiles were missing from the floors, and the classroom windows were barred. I barely noticed the scarce amount of high school students. I had incorrectly assumed that schools were inherently safe places, but the barred windows and metal detectors at the entryways suggested otherwise. The first bell rang at 8 a.m., yet the halls stayed occupied with students showing no regard for the ring's intended authority. This was the tone set by my first moments in Detroit's public schools after leaving a Detroit high school as a student only six years earlier. Below, I will recount two specifically memorable incidents throughout my two years working in Detroit's public high schools that speak to four principles, all based in community cultural wealth (see Yosso, 2005): teaching with intentionality, explicitness in curricula, the power of empathy, and the necessity of dedication.

Incident 1: "They Need to Know!"

In 2007, during my undergraduate career, I was so removed from the state of public education that I had not realized how much the country was failing to provide an adequate education to all of its children. While in Detroit's public schools, I witnessed an army of teachers and leaders trying to motivate and educate a community out of its poverty. One lesson learned from my reimmersion into K–12 education in Detroit, as a teacher, was the need to acknowledge and appreciate the power of one's perspective.

I was attempting to teach a creative writing lesson in a class that had a roster of over 35 students despite me never seeing more than 16 students at a time. One afternoon, my perspective was challenged by my class and, consequently, shaped me in a way that has changed my teaching philosophy. On this day, the constant, complacent attitudes and demeanors of my students ushered me into a "teacher moment" of feeling unappreciated, undervalued, and disrespected. I stopped passing out papers and walked up the aisle to the front of the room. "I don't need this education! You do!" After slamming both hands down on the front desk and looking intensely around the room at the class, I said: "I already have a high school diploma." Out of frustration, I continued: "You complain so much about the way your school is, but what are you doing for yourself to make things better for *you*."

These remarks, however misplaced and emotional, accurately expressed my discontentment with my students' attitudes at the moment. "We do our best. You can't compare us to other kids," said one student sitting in the front desk near the door. "I can and people surely will," I said matter-of-factly. I knew exactly what this student was referring to: the recent media comparisons (fueled by the Bush administration's No Child Left Behind program) of Black school performance to White school performance, and thus, comparisons of Black student success to White student success. These high school students often vocalized their discontentment with racial disparities seen between the city of Detroit and its wealthy neighboring communities. These students knew they were less fortunate, and that was a truth that they easily accepted. The cause behind their misfortunes, as to why they believed their lives were less advantaged, however, was my area of concern. I realized that my students felt that their misfortune was due to their lack of effort, willpower, and abilities. The students unknowingly attributed privileges, experienced by White children, to a perceived inherent superiority instead of to the reality that these advantages are merely a result of having access to a history of beneficial policies and systems as that of White Americans (see Yosso, 2005).

It all made sense from there. My background growing up in Detroit, my undergraduate reading of and dialogue about Kozol's *Savage Inequalities*, and my experiences teaching in an under-resourced school. When teachers' working conditions allow for "teacher moments" of frustration, teachers then, internally or externally, question their students' dedication to their education. This leads teachers to simultaneously place the cause of the disengagement on the children while removing the responsibility of adults to provide equally supportive learning environments for all children. When schools disregard the proven negative effects of over-surveillance in schools, irrelevant school curricula, and teacher/administrator deficit ideologies, scholar identities are disturbed, and community cultural wealth is not shared (Landsman & Lewis, 2011; Losen, 2014; Moore & Lewis, 2012; Yosso, 2005).

Systemic barriers were unknown to the high school students sitting in my classroom feeling responsible for the shortcomings of adults. For example, it has been reported that Black children in urban schools with majority-minority student populations receive a lower quality education from less qualified teachers. Teachers who tend to have fewer years of experience are often unqualified to teach their assigned subject areas (i.e., long-term substitute teachers) (Darling-Hammond, 2010). Incidentally and chronically, Black students perform poorly on state and national standardized tests perpetuating systems of academic inferiority (Darling-Hammond, 2010; Landsman & Lewis, 2011; Moore & Lewis, 2012).

Additionally, systemic barriers are also racial biases that lead to differential treatment of students by teachers. Casteel (1998) shares that "African American students are given less attention, ignored more, praised less, and reprimanded more than their Caucasian American counterparts by Caucasian American teachers in integrated classes" and that "approximately 9 out of 10 teachers in integrated school settings tend to be overwhelmingly Caucasian and female" (p. 115; see also NCES, 2013). Systemic barriers and racial bias were unknown to the high school students sitting in my classroom.

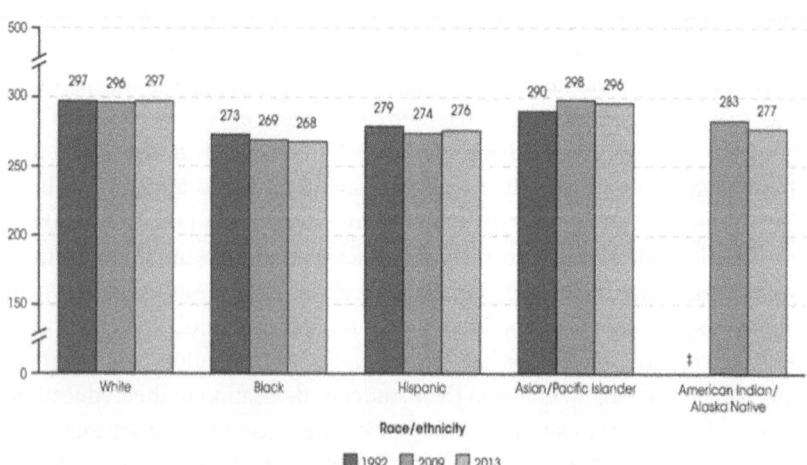

Figure 6.1. Average reading scale scores for 12th grade students by race (1992, 2009, 2013). Source: NCES 2016.

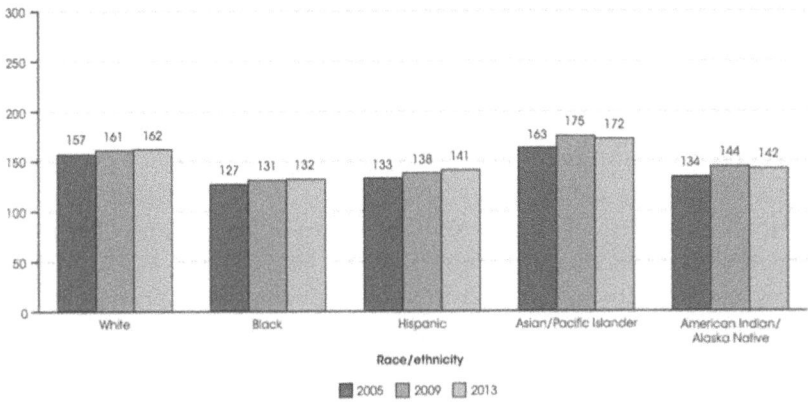

Figure 6.2. Average math scale scores for 12th grade students by race (1992, 2009, 2013). Source: NCES 2016.

Holding government and school systems accountable for inequitable distribution of resources does not negate the necessity of motivation and self-efficacy in students when it comes to academic success and achievement. However, my intention in highlighting the systemic weaknesses in the public school system is to further the claim that providing a high-quality education to the nation's children is the responsibility of all citizens. In order to better prepare our children to be leaders of tomorrow, it is essential to use our community cultural wealth (see Yosso, 2005) to make explicit the economic and social obstacles that are preventing today's students from creating a more sustainable economic future.

I spent the next two weeks at Cooley High School explaining the lessons of *Plessy v. Ferguson*, *Brown v. Board of Education*, *Milliken v. Bradley*, and the ongoing fight for equal education for all, explicitly encouraging my students to be critical and to challenge systems and stereotypes (see Yosso, 2005). Most importantly, I wanted my students to seek more knowledge for their own understandings. Educators in the classroom have a responsibility to own the four tenets I shared: teach with intentionality, implement an explicit curriculum, know the power of empathy, and understand the necessity of dedication. Educators must prepare children for the world in which they live with a relevant and appropriate curriculum and a political agenda to create a positively progressive future. This must be done with intentionality toward a more equitable future.

Incident 2: "If We Don't, Who Will?"

At another school on the city's West Side, I walked out into the parking lot, elated from the day's lesson, to an empty space with broken glass marking where my gold Chrysler 2001 Sebring was parked. My car had been stolen from the school parking lot. The feeling of disbelief was so overwhelming that I struggled to think of what to do next. I walked back into the school and reported the incident to the tiny police station housed at the end of the main hall. They filled out the complaint appropriately, yet with little disbelief. My car was to be recovered six months later stripped down to just the frame. I rented a car the next week and returned to the classroom that Friday. The students were astonished that I returned, but I explained to them that I was here for them. By embodying community cultural wealth, I shared that they are not responsible for what happened while we were learning together, and they will not be punished because of it. To me, they were worth fighting for, and they learned that about me that day.

There were many bitter days at the high school where the ugliness of poverty, ignorance, and violence was rampant. In those moments, the reason for low teacher retention was obvious: content was hard to teach because of high absenteeism, mobility of students between schools and classes, and the aggression and disengagement of students. I had lost my car and my confidence, and now I was receiving only minimal effort from my class. On one of the rougher days, I turned to the cooperating teacher and said, "I don't want to do this." Then, I continued somberly, "I don't want to teach." She looked at me with a jerk of her neck, as if she was surprised and a bit taken aback. "*I* don't want to do this," she said, "but if we don't, who will?" In that moment, I was reminded that the students were not to blame and, although the school conditions affected them, the conditions were not their fault. The empathy that I felt toward the hopelessness of students in schools with underfunded resources and dilapidated facilities was now my strongest emotion. I teach because if everyone decides to "forget" or walk away from so many of our children (our nation's most vulnerable population) then our future is lost. I teach with a political agenda. I teach to emancipate oppressed communities. Ultimately, I teach to combat poverty and help to reduce human suffering worldwide. In line with my shared four tenets, this empathy and dedication are vital to teaching effectively in urban communities with high-poverty populations.

Conclusion

These are innocent children, after all. They have done nothing wrong. They have committed no crime. They are too young to have offended us in any way at all. One searches for some way to understand why a society as rich and, frequently, as generous as ours would leave these children in their penury and squadron for so long—and with little public indignation.

—Jonathan Kozol

Unfortunately, I have learned that fairness and equity are relative concepts. The lack of acknowledgment of inner-city learning environments that Kozol mentions is still true today. *Savage Inequalities* brought to light social inequities many minorities have felt all their lives, knowingly and unknowingly. Despite what we have learned through *Savage Inequalities* close to three decades ago, racial and regional educational disparities are continuously perpetuated by ill-informed policy and practices. Working in the public school system allows me to fully realize society's worst problems and to understand the impact of these problems on students' lives. Kozol's *Savage Inequalities* captures the rawness of inequitable teaching and learning. Through my narrative, I sought to highlight how community cultural wealth dictates the dedication and resiliency that is necessary to educate children in low-income areas (Yosso, 2005). Children are created equal in regard to intellectual and academic ability, yet not all childhoods are equal in fostering academic excellence. Until we, as a nation, decide to address issues of political and systemic oppression, we will continue to house a nation of children who are waiting for adults to get things right.

References

Abbey-Lambertz, K. (2014). Most Detroit families can't afford their basic needs: Report. *The Huffington Post.* https://www.huffpost.com/entry/detroit-poverty-alice-report_n_5760602

Badenhausen, K. (2013). Detroit tops 2013 list of America's most miserable cities. *Forbes.* https://www.forbes.com/sites/kurtbadenhausen/2013/02/21/detroit-tops-2013-list-of-americas-most-miserable-cities/#104b58e455f3

Casteel, C. A. (1998). Teacher-student interactions and race in integrated classrooms. *The Journal of Educational Research, 92*(2), 115–120.

Darling-Hammond, L. (2010). *The flat world and education: How America's commitment to equity will determine our future.* Teachers College Press.

Fisher, D. (2015). America's most dangerous cities: Detroit can't shake no. 1 spot. *Forbes.* https://www.forbes.com/sites/danielfisher/2015/10/29/americas-most-dangerous-cities-detroit-cant-shake-no-1-spot/#3d4d3649467d

F. Y. (2012). Detroit metaphoropolis. *The Economist.* https://www.economist.com/prospero/2012/10/05/metaphoropolis

Gibson, C., & Jung, K. (2005). Table 23. Michigan-race and Hispanic origin for selected large cities and other places: earliest census to 1990. *United States Census Bureau.* https://www.census.gov/population/www/documentation/twps0076/twps0076.html

Kozol, J. (1991). *Savage inequalities: Children in America's schools.* Harper Perennial.

Kurth, J. (2016). United Nations to hear about Detroit, Flint water woes. *The Detroit News.* https://www.detroitnews.com/story/news/michigan/flint-water-crisis/2016/01/26/un-water/79349514/

Landsman, J., & Lewis, C. (2011). *White teachers/diverse classrooms: Creating inclusive schools, building on students' diversity and providing educational equity* (2nd ed.). Stylus.

Losen, D. J. (Ed.). (2014). *Closing the school discipline gap: Equitable remedies for excessive exclusion.* Teachers College Press.

Moore, J. L., and Lewis, C. (2012). *African American students in urban schools: Critical issues and solutions for achievement.* Peter Lang.

National Center for Education Statistics. (2016). *Status and trends in the education of racial and ethnic groups 2016.* https://nces.ed.gov/pubs2016/2016007.pdf

National Center for Education Statistics. (2013). *Public school teacher data file, 1987–88 through 2011–12.* https://nces.ed.gov/programs/digest/d17/tables/dt17_209.10.asp

Organization for Economic and Co-operative Development. (2013). *Education indicators in focus.* http://www.oecd.org/education/skills-beyond school/educationindicatorsinfocus.htm

Sansone, C. (2012). "Perspectives on Detroit" panel kicks off MLaw Detroit Month. *University of Michigan Law School.* https://www.law.umich.edu/newsandinfo/features/Pages/perspectives_on_detroit.aspx

Shannon, P. (2014). *Reading poverty in America.* Routledge.

Wilson, W. J. (2012). *The truly disadvantaged: The inner city, the underclass and public policy* (2nd ed.). University of Chicago Press.

U.S. Bureau of Labor Statistics. (2016). Employment projections. https://www.bls.gov/emp/

U.S. Census Bureau. (2015a). *Quick facts: Detroit.* https://www.census.gov/quickfacts/detroitcitymichigan

U.S. Census Bureau. (2015b). *Quick facts: Michigan.* https://www.census.gov/quickfacts/MI

U.S. Census Bureau. (2015c). *Quick facts: United States.* https://www.census.gov/quickfacts/fact/table/US/PST045218

Yosso, T. J. (2005). Whose culture has capital? A critical race theory discussion of community cultural wealth. *Race Ethnicity and Education* 8(1), 69–91.

Guest Commentary and Reflection

The Complexity and Nuances of Origin Stories

MARVIN LYNN

Re-Authoring Savage Inequalities is an important and timely book. In this book, scholars of color draw on Yosso's (2005) community cultural wealth concept to offer a rich counternarrative on portions of Jonathan Kozol's seminal work, *Savage Inequalities*. These important scholars have origin stories that, in one way or another, begin in urbanized and often demonized "inner" cities such as Chicago, Detroit, Washington, DC, and East St. Louis. They skillfully draw on Yosso's community cultural wealth framework to offer strong counternarratives to Kozol's legendary book, *Savage Inequalities*, in which he recounts a series of devastating truths about several "inner cities" and their broken, dilapidated, and sometimes unusable school buildings. His words are vivid, honest, but hurtful. While his accounts are accurate, they reflect and as these authors argue, a limited, one-dimensional, and deficit-based frame through which to see both the cities and their schools. By contrast, the beautifully constructed counter-narratives written by the scholars in this edited book draw out "goodness," as discussed in Sara Lawrence-Lightfoot's (1983, 1994; & Davis, 1997) work, while also speaking to the harsh realities faced in urban schools and communities. I will offer my reflections on the themes across these counter-narratives while discussing the possible implications for research, teaching, policy, and practice in urban schools. As a scholar and administrator, with his own urban origin story, who has spent more than two decades in public urban or urbanized universities, I will offer a few critical questions and point to additional resources that will further expand this important conversation.

In my commentary, I will be exploring three chapters written by diverse scholars who hail from Chicago, Washington, DC, and Detroit respectively. The authors in this section of the volume add layers of complexity and nuance to our understanding of their cities and schools. This complexity was reflected well in Farmer-Hinton, Lewis, Patton Davis, & Rivers (2013):

> I lived in the projects, a housing complex surrounded by great people and not-so-great people. . . . I saw men and women get up every day and go to work, come home, and spend time with their families. . . . I also remember gunshots and police kicking down our back door looking for our next-door neighbors. I remember drug wars and seeing the effects of drugs on families and children . . . I remember lots of trees and green grass, lawns that neighbors took care of. I remember being able to run up and down the street playing or jumping rope. I can see the existence of both good things and bad things in my neighborhood. (p. 28)

While they don't deny the realities that Kozol describes in his book, they also have fond memories of the people who cared for them in these cities. The authors use narrative inquiry as an approach to offering powerful counter-narratives about their hometown of East St. Louis that bring human agency, resilience, and perseverance into view in ways previously not seen. They also provide a rich historical analysis of conditions that undergird the complex economic conditions facing East St. Louis. Their meticulous attention to the economic, social, and political history of the city along with their counter-narratives create a rich, multilayered, and impactful rendering of this misunderstood city. Their work also provides a wonderful backdrop for the three narratives in this section.

Velazquez's work humanizes Kozol's *Savage Inequalities* by highlighting the perspectives and experiences of a Latina scholar who attended Chicago Public Schools. She illustrates skillfully her expert knowledge of Chicago education history, politics, and school policy. Her stories about the resilience of the Puerto Rican community and the selflessness of some of her teachers is further testament to why scholars like Velazquez, or Marvin Lynn for that matter, exist in the first place. As a Chicago Public School alumnus who graduated from high school just four years before the author, I also have fond memories of teachers who were committed to my success. In fact I attribute my career to them. These stories are missing from Kozol's work. Velazquez emphasizes an important point about human agency in her work. She importantly writes, "Instead of hopelessness and despair in the schooling lives of their children, the Chicago I inherited was one of struggle, yes, but a struggle to confront the unjust education of their children, not one of defeat as Kozol presents." In her view, Kozol's work represents the denial of human agency: particularly for communities of color that are twice victimized, first by the inequitable conditions in which they live and go to school in and then again by Kozol's disempowering and invisibilizing criticisms of their schools and communities.

Mobley's work also speaks back to Kozol's "deficit-based" framing of poor African American children and families in DC. He writes, "Where was the hope? Where was the success?" He recognizes inherent truths in Kozol's discussions about the inequalities experienced by poor Black and Brown people but also recognizes that these "stock stories," in isolation, are insufficient. He focuses on the familial relationships, both real and fictive, that propelled his success. This undermines the narrative that poor Black communities are spaces where adults prey on children and fail to support their academic success. Like previously mentioned scholars, Mobley is able to draw on his scholarly background as a way to situate his life experience as a member of the complicated DC community Kozol wrote about. He reveals a level of complexity inherent in the community that is not evident in Kozol's work. Again, Mobley makes it clear why we need poor and working-class scholars of color who can bring both experience and expertise to the table. Through Mobley's counter-story, we come to recognize that DC is, at times, unsafe and scary (I recall his mention of the needles in the playground), but it is also a refuge. Here, Mobley sums it up well: "This scholarship shifts research lenses away from previous assessments that view urban teachers, students, and their families as entities merely burdened with disadvantage. Instead, they focus on these communities and their members as sites that are rich with cultural assets and resilience systems that are ripe with lessons that can be imparted to broader educational conversations."

Bryant's essay balances the realities that Kozol's book revealed and the community cultural wealth that Black families cultivated in order to resist the challenges they faced. Bryant reflects on memories of growing up in Detroit and ultimately becoming a teacher guided by four key principles she found to be critical in supporting the teaching and learning of children in predominantly minoritized in terms of race and income. Bryant shares the historical backdrop of an up-and-coming Detroit with a booming economy. Situated in the midst of this growth due to the auto industry was the migration of families from the south to Detroit and other urban cities in the North. Bryant reminds us that a once all-white city, experienced a complete demographic shift to one that became 80% Black. Alongside this shift were racist laws, policies, and structures that would ultimately change Detroit from one of the fastest-growing cities to one of the most miserable cities in which to live. It was these types of realities that traveled with Bryant to college at the University of Michigan as she and classmates were assigned to read *Savage Inequalities*. Nestled between Detroit's decline and Bryant's rise as an educator were the stories of community cultural wealth she experienced during childhood and that she ultimately modeled for students in the Detroit public schools where she taught.

Many scholars of color who have experienced poverty and lived in communities that have been historically underserved are necessarily led to use their platform and the power that comes with it to tell different stories about the communities they know and love. For that reason, this work resonates with me. Like these scholars, I too hail from a poor/working-class Black community in a large city: Chicago. As a scholar, I too have made it part of my professional mission to tell stories about urban communities that humanize urban folks of color and the spaces in which they work and live. Earlier in my career, I focused some attention on the work of Jean Anyon whose work in poor schools in New Jersey portrayed Black male teachers as disrespectful, rude, and abusive to Black children (Lynn, 2002). While I did not doubt that Anyon's stories were, in fact, true, I did express major concerns about what Adiche, quoted in Mobley's work, refers to as "a single story." Like the authors, I was frustrated by the many one-sided narratives that demonized poor communities and educators of color. I have also written elsewhere about the conflation of culture with behaviors and attitudes that are merely a response to depraved social and economic conditions (Lynn, 2006b).

In my early qualitative research on the work and lives of African American male teachers, I drew principally on the work of Sara Lawrence-Lightfoot (1983, 1994, 1997) to help me think more clearly about how to render narratives that intentionally focus on representing "goodness" found in communities, schools, and the work and lives of the subjects I studied. In my dissertation (Lynn, 2001), I attempt to tell stories about inequality while also empowering Black men to speak on their own behalf and on behalf of their schools and communities. Besides my dissertation, it was most evident in a piece I wrote called "Dancing between Two Worlds" published in the *International Journal of Qualitative Studies in Education* (Lynn, 2006).

While I have not formally studied schools and communities in my hometown of Chicago, as the editors of this volume have done, I believe my mission has been similar. As working-class and poor scholars of color who study urban schools and communities, we bring a depth of personal knowledge and experience that enhances the professional knowledge we acquire through careful and systematic investigation of these environments. We bring a specific type of subjectivity to the process that humanizes those whom we study and adds greater complexity to our narratives about the nature of inequality in schools and communities. While we are not afraid to reveal ugly truths about the urban spaces we love, we also have a commitment to ensuring that we illuminate the nature and function of structural inequalities such as racism in these environments. In fact, we are committed to not only explicating the way White supremacy has structured these environments but also to revealing the ways in which racism shapes the current outcomes in the environments we write about.

IMPLICATIONS

The one clear implication here is that universities must do more to recruit PhDs of color across a range of disciplines but especially in education. In addition, doctoral candidates of color must be equipped with the theoretical and methodological tools to conduct excellent research in urban spaces, particularly those they are familiar with. This is unconventional because it contradicts existing, and perhaps unwritten, rules about the need for researcher impartiality. What if universities required emerging researchers to have extensive background knowledge about the research context prior to engaging in careful study of it?

In the field of teacher education, we work hard to help teacher candidates build awareness about and hopefully eradicate the existence of a deficit lens. There is also a great deal of research that explores how and why this is necessary and important for classroom teachers. In fact, tools that are designed to assess teachers' readiness for the classroom, such as the edTPA, also assess whether or not a teacher candidate is relying heavily on deficit-thinking as a way to understand who their students are

(Lynn, 2014). While the assessment tool cannot eliminate the existence of deficit-thinking, it certainly gives teachers a clear indication that is not appropriate and that is likely to hinder their teaching, particularly with Black, Indigenous, and People of Color (BIPOC, 2020). Researchers should also be required to, first of all, study Richard Valencia's (1997a) work on the "Evolution of Deficit Thinking." This would significantly improve educational research and practice. In addition, white researchers must interrogate their own racist assumptions about Black, Indigenous, and People of Color and bring a critical lens of self-critique to their research. They should be required to read this work in their methods courses and apply this lens to their understanding of the "worlds" they intend to study. Their research should be evaluated on the basis of whether or not it contributes to, promotes, or advances deficit-thinking or promotes stereotypical understandings about the people, the schools, or the communities they seek to study.

What additional readings might I suggest? I talked earlier about Sara Lawrence-Lightfoot's seminal work in the area of "portraiture." There is more to say. An entire special issue on portraiture in education was published in the journal *Qualitative Inquiry* (Dixson & Chapman, 2005). There are scores more recent research articles that draw on portraiture as a tool to frame educational research, mostly based in schools. For example, Donaldson (2020) uses portraiture to write about the developmental processes for early learning educators. A Google Scholar search reveals that scholars, particularly in the field of education, have continued to draw on Lightfoot's methods as a tool to illuminate "goodness" in their work. I encourage a greater pursuit of this area of study.

I appreciate the exploration of critical race theory (CRT), a theory near and dear to my heart. I would recommend that readers more fully explore the CRT in education literature. Farmer-Hinton and colleagues draw on critical race theory as a way to call attention to their efforts to restory East St. Louis. They explain the elements of CRT and focus attention on counter-storytelling as a method of challenging majoritarian stories that misrepresent the lives of Black, Indigenous, and People of Color. Solórzano and Yosso (2002) articulate a critical race method and explicate the process for constructing a counter-story. This work could prove useful for scholars of color attempting to offer more complex renderings of stories that focus on the schooling and lives of communities of color. Additionally, the work of Richard Delgado (1989, 1995) and Derrick Bell (1987, 1992) who originated counter-stories in CRT would prove beneficial. Lynn, Jennings, and Hughes (2013) offer an analysis of Bell's counter-storytelling method. There are numerous other resources that help bring a greater focus on race and racism to scholarship that seeks to reexamine the results of research that is focused on schools and communities primarily inhabited by Black, Indigenous, and/or People of Color.

Discussion Questions

1. In what ways can educators use the curriculum to balance "goodness" while also acknowledging the harsh realities of some urban educational environments?
2. Create a list of deficit narratives that have been used to describe urban environments. For each deficit narrative, what are two to three counternarratives to disrupt deficit thinking?

Additional Readings

Bell, D. A. (1987). *And we are not saved: The elusive quest for racial justice.* Basic Books.
Bell, D. A. (1992). *Faces at the bottom of the well: The permanence of racism.* Basic Books.
Delgado, R. (1989). Storytelling for oppositionists and others: A plea for narrative. *Michigan Law Review, 87*(8), 2411–2441.
Delgado, R. (1995). *The Rodrigo chronicles: Conversations about America and race.* NYU Press.
Dixson, A. D., Chapman, T. K., & Hill, D. A. (2005). Research as an aesthetic process: extending the portraiture methodology. *Qualitative Inquiry, 11,* 16–26.
Donaldson, M. (2000). Everything go upside down: Navigating mistakes in early learning and teaching. *Schools, 17*(1), 70–91.
Farmer-Hinton, R. L., Lewis, J. D., Patton, L. D., & Rivers, I. D. (2013). Dear Mr. Kozol. . . . Four African American women scholars and the re-authoring of *Savage Inequalities. Teachers College Record, 115*(5), 1–38.
Lawrence-Lightfoot, S. (1983). *The good high school: Portraits of character and culture.* Basic Books.
Lynn, M., Jennings, M. E., & Hughes, S. (2013). Critical race pedagogy 2.0: Lessons from Derrick Bell. *Race Ethnicity and Education, 16*(4), 603–628.
Solórzano, D. G., & Yosso, T. J. (2002). Critical race methodology: counter-storytelling as an analytical framework for education research. *Qualitative Inquiry, 8*(1), 23–44.

References

Lawrence-Lightfoot, S. (1983). *The good high school: Portraits of character and culture*. Basic Books.

Lightfoot-Lawrence, S. (1994). *I've known rivers: Lives of loss and liberation*. Addison-Wesley.

Lawrence-Lightfoot, S., & Davis, J. H. (1997). *The art and science of portraiture*. Jossey-Bass.

Lynn, M. (2001). *Portraits in Black: Storying the lives and pedagogies of Black men educators* (Unpublished doctoral dissertation, University of California, Los Angeles, 2001). ProQuest Dissertations and Theses, 319.

Lynn, M. (2002). Critical race theory and the perspectives of Black men teachers in the Los Angeles public schools. *Equity & Excellence in Education, 35*(2), 119–130.

Lynn, M. (2006a). Dancing between two worlds: A portrait of the life of a black male teacher in South Central LA. *International Journal of Qualitative Studies in Education, 19*(2), 221–242.

Lynn, M. (2006b). Race, culture, and the education of African Americans. *Educational Theory, 56*(1), pp. 107–119.

Lynn, M. (2014, March 19). Making culturally relevant pedagogy relevant to aspiring teachers. *Diverse Issues in Higher Education.* https://diverseeducation.com/article/61280/

The BIPOC Project. (n.d.). https://www.thebipocproject.org/.

Valencia, R. R. (1997). *The evolution of deficit thinking: Educational thought and practice*. Routledge.

Valencia, R. R., & Solórzano, D. G. (1997). Contemporary deficit thinking. In R. Valencia (Ed.), *The evolution of deficit thinking: Educational thought and practice* (pp. 160–210). The Falmer Press/Taylor & Francis.

Part 3

Centering Students in Teaching and Learning (Students)

Chapter 7

"People Don't *Really* Know Camden High"

Student Perspectives on their
Negatively Viewed High School

KEITH E. BENSON *with help from*
DELIYAII WHETSTONE, TINA Q. BAKER, MERV RAGSDALE,
T'EMON'ET ELLIOT, JOEL TARTE, DWYANE COOKE,
NAIMA BATTIE, AJIANNA BAILEY, JOSELYN CHEVERE,
RASHEED POLLARD, IJSHANNA MARTIN, and BRENÉ TROUTMAN

Introduction

Today's urban public schools are often viewed pejoratively by the American public. Images of aging buildings, crumbling facilities, apathetic teachers, and troubled minority youth wholly disinterested in education capture society's limited perspective. Collective assumptions and biases concerning urban public education have been captured in speeches from politicians and modern-day education reformists, as well as popular media through films like *Lean on Me* (1989), *Dangerous Minds* (1995), and *Waiting for Superman* (2010).

Contemporary popular views of urban schools are laced with comparative assumptions: urban schools lack *this*, while suburban schools have *that*. Though critical to the urban education canon, Jonathan Kozol's

Savage Inequalities (1991) reflects this perspective in an effort to illuminate educational and social inequities in public schools to a larger audience. Kozol highlighted disparities in facilities, staff quality and experience, as well as in economic resources between urban and suburban districts. Though eye-opening for many, little has changed to ensure equity since the book's original publication 30 years ago. Urban schools' facilities are still old and in varying stages of decay, urban students are still likely to be taught by teachers with far less experience, and there still exists a resource divide manifested in shortage of available supplies and technology with urban students often not having books to take home or sufficient computer access. And due to budget cuts in urban districts across the country, essential support staff disparities between urban and suburban schools are amplified with the reduction of librarians, guidance counselors, and school nurses.

Additionally, there exists an inequality in curriculum between poor minority urban districts like the ones visited by Kozol and their suburban counterparts. While suburban students have easy access to the arts, technology, and the social sciences in their course offerings, urban public school students are exposed to endless test prep and a streamlining of creative electives like music, journalism, and even career training education (CTE). Urban schools still suffer from funding disparities caused primarily by austere education budget cuts at the federal, state, and local levels, in addition to the proliferation of budget-siphoning charter schools in urban America.

Further, suburban school districts typically have more opportunity for direct democratic participation than urban districts. While in suburban America, residents often publicly elect their representatives on local school boards, attend and speak out at board meetings for extended periods, and use their sociopolitical agency to influence education decisions regarding curriculum, hiring, and the general direction of the district. In urban districts across the country, democratic rights have eroded with an increasing number of urban districts consolidating power through state takeovers or imposing appointed, unelected school board members dictating decisions to residents. Lastly, urban school districts are increasingly likely to be staffed at the highest levels by individuals with business and policy backgrounds who, seemingly uniformly, impose a business-model approach to education. These often-inexperienced district leaders are usually not educators by trade and yet are tasked with turning around some of the nation's most challenged schools in America's most disenfranchised communities. Indeed, the "savage inequalities" Kozol documented over two decades ago still exist.

While confronting the stark inequities targeting urban education, then and now, it is easy to view urban public education from a deficit perspective. What is less common, however, are examinations of urban public schools through the lens of their students and recognizing that amid inequality, oft-maligned urban schools offer what Yosso (2005) described as a community cultural wealth where communities work to ensure students' academic and social progress despite deliberate inequity and oppression.

Typically, the conversation concerning urban education is manipulated by those furthest removed from the experience. Adults, often from privileged positions, pontificate on the matter, yet they too often neglect to authentically engage students (Friend & Caruthers, 2012). Categorizations of urban public schools as insufficient, or spaces worthy of collective pity, aren't solely affixed to urban public school buildings, as students attending these schools bear similar residual labeling and prejudice.

Rather than sustaining this common trajectory of deficit discourse pertaining to urban schools that empowers the voices of disconnected, privileged adults (Spring, 1997; Ladson-Billings, 2001), it is necessary to include the views of the young people attending these urban public schools. I use this chapter as a space of opportunity for students to assert their voices and more completely convey their perspectives on attending unequal, "failing" urban schools. While noting their frustrations in bearing the brunt of educational inequity as detailed in *Savage Inequalities*, the students express much more of what is right within their schools than is acknowledged in the urban public school narrative. Their perspectives help form a more complete conceptualization of urban educative spaces, not of deficit, but community cultural wealth. (Friend & Caruthers, 2012; Yosso, 2005).

In this chapter, I will center the voices of students attending Camden High School (CHS) in New Jersey where I teach. Jonathan Kozol visited this high school in the original *Savage Inequalities*. Today, CHS and the Camden City School District (CCSD) are overwhelmingly subject to negative depictions in local media and referenced as a "human catastrophe" by Governor Chris Christie (Christie, 2016), a "sewer" and "prison pipeline" by a New Jersey Democratic powerbroker George Norcross (Mooney, 2011), in the "worst school district in America" (Epstein, 2015).

The students featured here, much like the thousands of other public school students in Camden, are aware of and understand the common narrative concerning their city's public schools. They are all too familiar with the concept that they currently attend a high school labeled "failing," much like most of the primary schools they attended prior to their arrival at Camden High School. This narrative centers perspectives of Camden High School students as they describe what Kozol and countless others miss when looking exclusively at their schools' comparative deficiencies. Through their perspectives, we all can develop a more complete and nuanced understanding of what these educational spaces mean to the students who experience them (Mitra, 2005).

Theoretical Framework

Standpoint theory, which frames this study, seeks to put forward subjugated groups' voices, interpretations, and critiques concerning how dominant groups exert authority upon them (Barnett, 2009; Creedon, 2007; Collins, 1990). While standpoint theory in past research was primarily exhibited in feminist studies generally (Wood, 2005; Harding, 2009; Harstock, 1983), and subsequently the experiences of Black feminists (Collins, 1990) and Hispanic feminists (Pompper, 2007) more specifically, standpoint theory seeks to highlight the perceptions of any nondominant group whose views are often disregarded or ignored altogether yet are grounded in their own lived experiences as a marginalized group.

While standpoint theory shares similarities with other modern critical theories such as critical race theory (Delgado & Stefancic, 2006; Ladson-Billings & Tate 1995; Ladson-Billings, 2012), critical feminist theory (Geisinger, 2001; Rhodes, 1990), critical queer theory (Sullivan, 2003; Jagose, 1996) and neo-Marxist theory (Burris, 1987) as they present counter-narratives to dominant hegemonic White, capitalist, *hetero-patriarchal* values (hooks, 2004), standpoint theory uses the perspectives and lived experiences of the marginalized as the central unit of analysis. Where other theories emerge from the exclusionary processes and traditions of established disciplines (Harding, 2009), standpoint theory's priority is uplifting and including the voices of the oppressed rather than adhering to rigid academic research traditions (Ortega, 2015).

This chapter highlights the perspectives of a silenced Camden High School student body who attend a school cast as deficient in Kozol's *Savage Inequalities* and is still today often deemed "failing" in public discourse and media outlets. While public perception of Camden High School, and urban public high schools like it across the country, has been cemented in the local public consciousness as deficient, to students attending Camden High School, the school is so much more. The low-income and minority student voices included here represent the silenced and disregarded.

Yosso's Community Cultural Wealth Framework

In attempts to research how postsecondary institutions can best attract and retain under-represented populations to their institutions, namely minorities from low SES backgrounds, Tara Yosso (2005) challenged institutions to reframe their perspectives of traditionally marginalized students. Yosso suggested that institutions of higher learning, when engaging nontraditional students, ought not do so from a deficient perspective, obsessing over what such students lack in the form of traditional academic success metrics but instead recognize traditionally marginalized students bring with them a unique, yet valuable form of capital, dubbed community cultural wealth.

In describing community cultural wealth, Yosso identified six manifestations of such capital: aspirational, social, navigational, resistant, familial, and linguistic. Aspirational capital refers to the "hopes and dreams" students from disadvantaged backgrounds cling to despite experiencing educational and societal marginalization and oppression. Social capital, on the other hand, is described as the ways in which nontraditional students use "who they know" and form relationships with, to make useful connections and maximize personal success in environments where they are underrepresented.

Yosso describes navigational capital as students' abilities to effectively adapt and adhere to institutions and their norms for their survival: much like Du Bois's (1903) conception of African Americans' adaptive cultural dualism and double consciousness. Resistance capital refers to minority students' connection to racial and social struggle that is tied to their cultural histories and legacies; the idea that traditionally under-represented students have a responsibility to be successful for the benefit of people from similar racial, ethnic, and cultural backgrounds.

Familial capital relates to the personal and organizational connections nontraditional students arrive to campuses with. Students know how to tap into and lean on their long-standing relationships with their communities, family members, churches, and other social organizations for support and guidance to help optimize their success. And finally, Yosso explains that linguistic capital refers to the way students from low

SES, minority students, communicate with primarily one another and, secondarily, college classmates.

Applying elements of Yosso's community cultural wealth model, initially conveyed as a means by which colleges could recognize the enormous capital nontraditional students bring with them to universities despite lacking in traditional academic success metrics, can also be applied to correcting the deficit framing applied to urban public schools. Utilizing standpoint theory to capture and highlight the voices of the ignored urban minority student, coupled with the community cultural wealth model to help describe the various forms of capital that exist in such institutions, provides us with theoretical lens that enables us to more fully grasp what maligned urban public schools are to the young people who attend them.

Camden Context and Study Participants

Camden, New Jersey, is a northeastern city directly east of Philadelphia that has long been plagued by poverty, unemployment, and violence (Epstein, 2015). Much like other Camden public services that fell into disrepair over the city's sixty-year depression, its public schools were not immune to the impact of unyielding multigenerational poverty and decades of federal and state urban divestment. The CCSD is categorized socioeconomically by the New Jersey Department of Education (NJDOE) as a District Factor Group A, meaning that CCSD serves one of the poorest areas in New Jersey. Indeed, Camden has long been the poorest city in the state. According to *USA Today* (2013), over 83% of CPS students qualify for free or reduced lunch.

CCSD schools are under state takeover resulting from a 2012 NJDOE Quality Single Accountability Continuum assessment that rated 20 of 23 CCSD as "failing" due to the District's persistently low graduation and promotion rates, poor performance on state standardized tests, poor curriculum, and a host of other metrics. Camden residents have been forbidden from voting for a fully publicly elected school board since 2002 with the passage of the *New Jersey Municipal Redevelopment Act (2001)*.

Today, all members of the CCSD school board are directly appointed by Mayor Dana Redd. Additionally, in 2013, acting on a request by Mayor Redd, Governor Christie and the state took over controls and operations of the Camden public school system. Later that same year, Christie stripped away the right of the Camden's Advisory School Board to appoint a new superintendent to lead the CCSD, and instead Christie appointed a former

Teach for America staffer to fill the post of superintendent despite having less than two full years teaching experience, lacking a master's degree, and requisite certification to fill the post. Of New Jersey's 586 independently operated school districts, CCSD is the only district in New Jersey with an all-appointed board of education, under state takeover, and a state-appointed superintendent.

Districtwide, during the 2014–2015 academic year, CPS had a graduation rate of 64%. Further, CCSD's enrollment is dwindling annually due to the ever-increasing proliferation of charter schools. This academic year, there are about 14,000 K–12 students in Camden with about 5,000 students enrolled in charters (Laday, 2015).

In the years since Kozol's visit, policymakers and powerbrokers have implemented various district and state interventions in hopes of improving educational outcomes in Camden's public schools that have yielded little statistical progress, if any. Camden's public schools, despite diversifying teaching practices, regularly turning over school and district leadership, are still considered by many unaffiliated with the schools to be among the worst schools in New Jersey.

STUDY PARTICIPANTS AND METHODOLOGY

The twelve youths (eight girls; four boys) whose stories are centered are juniors or seniors and identify as African American or Hispanic. The students range in age from 16 to 18. All of them attend a class called Jobs for America's Graduates (JAG). The course is designed to prepare students for life beyond high school whether they opt to pursue postsecondary education or employment opportunities. I engage the students in a conversation about their perceptions of CHS, often the local exemplar of urban school failure. As voices of urban youth are virtually nonexistent in the popular narrative concerning unequal, failing urban schools, these students' voices contributed a more complete understanding of what it is to be educated in a school long viewed to be deficient as well as offer perspectives as to how such spaces can be communities of cultural wealth (Payne, Starks & Gibson, 2009; Yosso, 2005; Burton, Obeidallah, & Allison, 1996).

CHS Students Speak

The students communicated an oppositional view to the prevailing deficit assumptions attributed to their school and themselves. They readily acknowledged the aspects of CHS they wanted to see improve but generally expressed a positive emotional connection to their school, a sincere appreciation for their teachers and fellow students, and feelings of optimism regarding their future that many credited to their years at CHS. Finally, students generally held a strong sense of skepticism concerning the motives and accuracy of people who attach negative viewpoints to their school and their larger Camden community.

People Don't *Really* Know about Camden High School

Although the commonly held reputation of CHS, both locally and throughout New Jersey, is formed by traditional school success indicators such as standardized test scores, graduation rates, and college attendance, hearsay from individuals external to CHS reinforce a negative narrative. Conversely, students attending CHS relied on the "paradigm of the personal" (Britzman, 1990), and much less from what outside people reported or statistics. As such, students who contributed to this chapter roundly reported that their school is much more than what statistics represent, or what people say about it.

Tina, a senior and Rutgers Future Scholar said:

> People talk a lot about our school. They say it's easy and stuff like that, but we learn here. We earn a lot here actually. A lot of what we learn is how to grow up and be adults. They think we [CHS students] are stupid . . . that all we care about is dropping out, having babies, smoking weed or whatever. But not only the school, whenever someone outside talks about our city, it's to always focus on the negative, never on the good stuff . . . we have a lot of students who have close to a 4.0, we have honors classes, and caring guidance counselors who get us ready to graduate and get ready for college.

Deliyah, a junior in CHS said:

> People don't know about all the good things that help us out. . . . They don't know about School Based Youth Services and the LYNK office people who are in the D-building . . . They are so important because they are there for us to talk to when we need it. Some kids don't have that. So to have people who care and right there for us is good . . . they keep us from mak-

ing mistakes that could get us into trouble. . . . Also we have a partnership with an outside group called Women of the Dream where these local black businesswomen and entrepreneurs take us on trips, talk to us, and mentor us [girls]. . . . They don't know about our Jobs for America's Graduates program that helps us learn about the work world, how to get jobs, and prepares us for college. . . . There's a lot people don't know about Camden High.

Tina and Deliyah corrected misconceptions about CHS by tapping in their respective aspirational and social capital. Tina refuted the idea that CHS is attended by ambivalent urban teens intent on abusing drugs and having sex, by referencing the many students in the school who succeed academically yet remain largely unrecognized. Deliyah on the other hand, exhibited the schools' provision of social capital for students in offering a bevy of wraparound resources that assist in guiding and counseling the schools' students toward success. Interestingly, when I asked them, "What is it that people don't know about CHS?," each student stated popular assumptions made about their school and the students within it, then pivoted to highlight the lesser-known positive aspects of attending their school. Joselyn, a 12th grade student, varsity cheerleader, and JROTC lieutenant, commented on the negative views of CHS and corrected an incomplete characterization of her school and schooling experience:

> People just base their opinions off statistics and simply listen to people who have never been here or went to school here. They don't see all the extra-curricular activities offered here. They don't see how our debate teams travel to Trenton, and win and beat these other schools, those other White schools that are supposed to be way smarter than us . . . If they're so much smarter, how come we're the team that wins? . . . We win a lot here, in sports, in JROTC competitions. . . . All that stuff we do here in Camden and no one knows, they just pay attention to the bad stuff.

More Than Just a School Building

While much research points to feelings of alienation, marginalization, and cultural mismatch between low SES urban youth and their schools (Dance, 2002), less literature is dedicated to emotional attachments developed and fostered between these students and their school. Aware of the relative deficiencies between Camden High School and neighboring suburban schools, Camden High School students communicated a strong emotional connection to their school that extended beyond academics (Antrop-Gonzalez, 2002). Brené Troutman, a junior commented:

> When I leave Camden High School, I'm gonna miss it, I know I am. . . . I remember taking the tour of Camden High when I was in middle school at Bonsall. . . . I remember wanting to come here because everyone in my family went here . . . my mom, my sister, everyone . . . I'm gonna miss everything about this school, the nasty lunches, the hallways, the teachers. . . . Right now really, I like the unity our students have. . . . Yeah we argue and may fight sometimes, but overall, we really do support each other. . . . At the basketball games and football games, even in assemblies, we really have fun being together.

Ijshanna, a senior added:

> I'm gonna miss this school when I graduate because this is the school that made me . . . my parents both went here, and all my brothers graduated from here, and now it's my turn . . . I been here for four years . . . I feel like I came in here a little kid and am going to leave a grown woman . . . I got my first job at Maximum Research using things I learned here at this school, and now I'm going to college next year . . . I feel like I matured here over my years here but I don't really wanna leave the nest just yet.

The students' affinity for their school was apparent in their responses even as they acknowledged challenges. The students exhibited Yosso's conception of familial capital within and emotional connection to CHS. What they shared is reminiscent of ancestral and community bonds that are not necessarily tied to academics. Their familial traditions and neighborhood identities were inextricably linked to urban public schools such as CHS that have been identified as "deficient" or "failing." The relationships between CHS, the community, and its students are more visceral and emotional, and thus less measurable. Lenaami, a junior and state champion track athlete volunteered: "Camden High School has tradition. Look how long this school has been here. My mom and dad both went here, and here I am, right here too. . . . There never was a doubt as to where I wanted to go. . . . Tradition is real here, and especially as far as sports. Reppin' [Representing] Camden High means something."

People Who Don't Go Here Don't Know What They're Talking About

Constant connectivity and direct experience were the only conditions under which anyone could accurately speak about their high school. Students expressed sentiments of frustration, disappointment, and suspicion of those critiquing their school. Further, students expressed both anger and determination when asked about the likelihood that they are stereotyped and prejudged because of where attend school. Naima Battie, a senior explained: "The bias and comments people have against my school, like the Governor calling Camden schools a 'failure factory,' and saying only three people in Camden schools were college-ready or whatever, I feel like they are talking about me . . . and I care." Naima's comments communicate the stigma students feel when confronting prejudices about their school, an environment where they spend a considerable amount of time learning, working, and growing. From her perspective, not only are the pejorative comments and deficit framing attached to the school building itself, but, by extension, unfairly affixed to the students attending CHS themselves. T'emon'et added: "They talk about us like we're not even human, like we don't have feelings . . . I think they categorize us and our schools like this as a way to try to keep us caged in. . . . They don't really want to give any credit that good comes out of Camden and Camden High." Joselyn, regarding the comments and assumptions made about her school, contributed: "I get defensive (laughs) . . . I really do . . . Sometimes if I actually hear people talking trash about my school, I'll correct them and tell them all the reasons they are wrong, sometimes I won't. . . . Their comments stereotype us but I know I'm just as good as anyone else. . . . They think lower of me because I say I'm from Camden High. . . . But that only make me want to succeed more to show them what we can do."

Comments made by both Joselyn and Te'mon'et exhibit resistance capital in their awareness of how Camden High School students are negatively portrayed and prejudged based primarily on the school's deficit reputation, and in response, use it as fuel and motivation to succeed.

Optimism toward the Future (Aspirational Capital)

As the concept of students being "college-and-career ready" increasingly permeates our secondary education lexicon, causal assumptions are often made regarding a student's potential for future success based on the high school they attended. Simply put, the assumption is that students who graduate from "good" high schools, coded language for suburban schools with mostly White students, are most likely to succeed in comparison to their counterparts in urban, predominantly minority, local public high school who seemingly have no chance at achieving success.

Counter to that collective assumption, CHS students, exhibiting what Yosso would describe as resistance and aspirational capital, are determined to succeed despite the stigma cast on their school. The students were roundly optimistic about their futures and believed CHS prepared them well for life beyond the high school setting. Te'mon'et, a senior explained:

> I had people in my life tell me I wasn't gonna be shit. . . . They say I wouldn't be anything or amount to anything. . . . But here I am, a senior, about to graduate. I have acceptance letters to college on my dresser, and also starting my own business . . . How many high school students can say that? Here I had a lot of help and support. I mean a lot of support from a lot of my teachers and counselors . . . I enjoyed my experience here at Camden High . . . That's not to say it was perfect because there were some teachers I could not stand . . . But no place is perfect.

Joel, a senior added:

> A lot of rumors and lies get spread about our school and the kids that go here. They'll say "look at how kids cut school" or "look at their test scores." But what they aren't considering is that many kids here have to go through things kids at this age they really shouldn't have to go through . . . Some people out here struggle, and maybe we may have moments when we struggle, and I think this school exposes us to the real world . . . But look at me, I live in Camden. I go to Camden High. I don't hustle. I'm working at Smashburger and I'm going to college . . . I think I would have been successful no

matter where I went to high school, but I think Camden High prepared me for the world.

Camden High School students like Joel and Te'mon'et recognize the reputation of their school is not ideal and that some things could be improved upon. That, however, from the viewpoint of these students does not take away from the positive aspects of their "failing" school enveloped by inequity, from being a place that nurtures and affirms students, and ultimately equips them with the Cultural Community Wealth to prepare them for the next phase of their lives.

Conclusion

In 1991 Kozol's *Savage Inequalities* highlighted the fact that American schools in urban and suburban areas were far from being equal educational settings. Kozol's book was groundbreaking in its detailed description of the extent to which urban students were being systematically shortchanged in their educational experience compared to their suburban counterparts. Subsequently, in the eras of No Child Left Behind (2001) and Race to the Top (2008), which stress reliance on standardization and accountability, coupled with sensationalized media depictions of urban schools and endless news coverage on "failing schools," it has been easy for the American public to caricature urban public schools as wastelands of failure. While some may arrive at the irrational conclusion that urban public schools ought to be wholly dismantled, and others may feel pity for the urban student "trapped in failing schools," the narrative around urban schools gets altered once the voices of students attending these schools is added to the discourse.

Despite the challenges, students in urban environments and schools are extraordinarily resilient and capable of recognizing authentically meaningful, positive qualities in the very educational setting many associated with the school are quick to castigate as deficient. In engaging the students to share their narratives, I did not intend to imply that disparities in funding, staff quality, and adequate school supplies do not matter to urban students in urban schools, or that our society does not have a moral and legal responsibility to achieve equality in the delivery of education to urban students. What is important, however, is that in our quest to achieve educational equality (which yet remains elusive), we understand that in the midst of such disparities, urban students do experience and achieve success. And too often ignored is the fact that these urban students often credit their own frequently maligned schools for helping them get there. I am grateful to them for their willingness to share their narratives with me and their trust in me as a teacher in CHS to articulate their narratives in this space.

References

Antrop-Gonzalez, R. (2003). This school is my sanctuary: The Dr. Pedro Albizu Campos Alternative High School. *CENTRO Journal, XV*(2), 232–255.

Britzman, D. (1990). *Practice makes perfect: A critical study of learning to teach.* State University of New York Press.

Barnett, B. (2009). Inverting the inverted pyramid: Using feminist theories to teach journalism. *Feminist Teacher*, 1–20.

Burris, V. (n.d.). *The neo-Marxist synthesis of Marx and Weber on class.* Wiley.

Burton, L., Obeidallah, D., & Allison, K. (1996). Ethnographic insights on the social context and adolescent development among inner-city African-American teens. In R. Jessor, A. Colby, & R. Shewder (Eds.), *Ethnography and human development: Context and meaning in social inquiry.* University of Chicago Press.

Collins, P. (1990). *Feminist thought: Knowledge, consciousness and the politics of empowerment.* Routledge.

Creedon, P. (2007). *Women in mass communication.* SAGE.

Dance, L. J. (2002). *Tough fronts: The impact of street culture on schooling.* RoutledgeFalmer.

Delgado, R., & Stefancic, J. (2012). *Critical race theory: An introduction.* New York University Press.

Dixson, A., Buras, K., & Jeffers, E. (2015). The color of reform: Race, education reform and charter schools in post-Katrina New Orleans. *Qualitative Inquiry, 31*(3), 288–299.

Du Bois, W. E. B. (1903). *The souls of Black folk.* Dover Thrift.

Friend, J., & Caruthers, L. (2012). Reconstructing the cultural context of urban schools: Listening to the voices of high school students. *Educational Studies, 48*, 366–388.

Geisinger, B. (n.d.). *Critical feminist theory, rape, and hooking up.* Iowa State University. ISU Graduate Theses and Dissertations.

Harding, S. (2009). Standpoint theories: Productively controversial. *Hypatia, 24*(4), 192–200.

Hartstock, N. (1983). The feminist standpoint: Developing the ground for a specifically historical materialism. In S. Harding, & M. Hintikka (Eds.), *Discovering reality: Feminist perspectives on epistemology, metaphysics, methodology, and philosophy of science* (pp. 283–310). Kluwer Academic.

hooks, b. (2004). *The will to change: Men, masculinity, and love*. Washington Square Press.

Jagose, A. (1996). *Queer theory: An introduction*. New York University Press.

Kozol, J. (1991). *Savage inequalities: Children in America's schools*. Broadway Books.

Laday, J. (2015, April 21). NJEA files motion to stop Camden's transfer of public schools to Renaissance. *South Jersey Times*.

Ladson-Billings, G. (2006). From the achievement gap to the education debt: Understanding achievement in U.S. Schools. *Educational Researcher, 35*(7), 3–12.

Ladson-Billings, G., & Tate, W. (1995, Fall). Toward a critical race theory. *Teachers College Record, 97*(1), 47–68.

Mitra, D. (2005). Adults advising youth: Leading while getting out of the way. *Education Administration Quarterly, 41*, 520–553. https://doi.org/10.1177/0013161X04269620

NBC News. (2013, March 7). What's the matter with Camden?

New Jersey Economic Development Authority. (2013). *Redevelopment practice: Regulatory update, tax incentives overhaul legislation; Economic Opportunity Act of 2013*. NJEDA.

Ortega, M. (2016). *In-between: Latina feminist phenomenology, multiplicity, and the self*. State University of New York Press.

Payne, Y. A., Starks, B. C., & Gibson, L. (2009). Contextualizing Black boys' use of a street identity in high school. *New Directions for Youth Development 123*, 35–51.

Pompper, D. (2007). The gender-ethnicity construct in public relation organizations: Using feminist standpoint theory to discover Latinas' realities. *The Howard Journal of Communications, 18*(4), 291–311.

Rhode, D. (1990). *Theoretical perspectives on sexual difference*. Yale University Press.

Spring, J. (1997). *Deculturalism and the struggle for equality: A brief history in education of dominated cultures in the United States*. McGraw-Hill.

Sullivan, N. (2003). *A critical introduction to queer theory*. New York University Press.

Wood, J. (2005). *Gendered lives: Communication, gender and culture*. Wadsworth.

Yosso, T. J. (2005). Whose culture has capital? A critical race theory discussion of community cultural wealth. *Race Ethnicity and Education, 8*(10), 69–91.

Chapter 8

No Excuses

Believing and Achieving

JANE BEAN-FOLKES, SUSAN BROWNE, CHANELLE ROSE

In Jonathan Kozol's (1991) *Savage Inequalities: Children in America's Schools*, the author documented the inequities in Camden, New Jersey's public schools, as compared to those in nearby suburban communities such as Cherry Hill. The schools he described were 95% to 99% non-White and dominated by poor reading scores, poor motivation, and high dropout rates. Using information gathered from administrators, teachers, students, and families, he argued that despite the *Brown v. Board of Education* decision of 1954, New Jersey schools remained segregated and unequal. In this chapter, authored by three university professors of color who work in Camden preparing future teachers to work in similar cities, we revisit Kozol's depiction of poor and/or underserved students in urban cities between 1980 and 1990, including Camden, Baltimore, Washington, Detroit, Chicago, and New York. This process left us with the impression that students in these areas continue to receive their education in segregated communities with poor conditions and ill-prepared teachers. However, in preparing this chapter, we highlight a different possibility for Camden's communities and schools through the eyes of four former students. In fact, this chapter reenvisions *Savage Inequalities* by offering a much different view of Camden. The chapter's goal is twofold. First, we aim to enable readers to engage in the lived experiences of the city's students. Second, we hope to help future educators gain a deeper understanding of the inequities present in Camden and to reeducate those who misunderstand the challenges faced by urban students, teachers, and families.

This chapter is a tale of two competing stories that clash with one another with regard to the cultural assumptions, values, and beliefs of urban cities (Bell, 2003; Sue, 2015). We also believe it is important for pre- and in-service teachers to be responsive to the instructional context of students in their classrooms. As Gay (2000) states, "Teaching is a contextual and situational process. As such, it is most effective when ecological factors, such as prior experiences, community settings, cultural backgrounds, and ethnic identities of teachers and students are included in its implementation" (p. 21). Similarly, Yosso's (2005) framework is used to highlight individual factors that contribute to the success of students like those from Camden. In fact, we framed the narratives using Yosso's (2005) community cultural wealth model (CCWM) to provide clarity about the family and community structures of Camden that provide forms of capital (i.e., aspirational, navigational, social, linguistic, familial, and resistant capital) (Farmer-Hinton, Lewis, Patton, & Rivers, 2013). Our work illuminates how the different forms of capital reflected in Yosso's CCWM framework can enable students to succeed. Highlighted in this counter-narrative are the voices of four educators who attended school in Camden thirty years ago, their impressions of growing up and going to school in a racially segregated community, and how it has shaped their current lives.

Setting a Historical Background

On May 5, 2014, hundreds of students from Camden High—one of the city's oldest high schools, and one that carries a stigma as the "worst" school in the district—marched from their school to the administration building in downtown Camden to protest the dismissal of teachers due to deep budget cuts. Creative arts student Samir Nichols told the crowd of frustrated students: "If we don't stand up now, we will never get our teachers back" (personal communication, May 5, 2014). The student protests at Camden High demonstrate the passion and dedication of the city's often-derided youth while also highlighting the current state of the educational crisis thirty years after Kozol's piercing 1991 analysis.

Since the publication of *Savage Inequalities*, multiple narratives about Camden have developed, including its current one of rapid revitalization (Oakley & Tsao, 2016; Wiig, 2018). Unfortunately, however, much of that revitalization has occurred in Camden's most popular attraction: the city's waterfront property (Morgia & Vicino, 2013). Additionally, new investment in the neighborhood around Cooper Hospital—including the $50 million health sciences center for Rutgers–Camden, the Cooper Medical School of Rowan University, and the Kroc Recreational Center in East Camden—are designed to attract more taxpayers to the community and foster economic growth. However, many critics argue that the waterfront facilities have failed to address the economic plight of most residents because they brought few local jobs or training opportunities, and they primarily catered to people living outside the community (Katz, 2009; Morgia & Vicino, 2013).

Despite the revitalization trope of Camden often touted by Mayor Dana Reed and other civic leaders, its infamous reputation as one of the most dangerous, impoverished, and crime-ridden cities in America remains etched in people's minds (Guy, 2013; Kurdzuk, 2012; Seligsohn & Mazelis, 2015; Simon, 2013). Even though New Jersey has one of the highest median household incomes in America, it is also home to four of the country's largest impoverished urban communities: Camden, Trenton, Paterson, and Newark. In fact, Camden's population has continued to decline from 79,904 in 2000, to 77,344 in 2012, and approximately two out of every five residents are living below the national poverty line. In 2013, the U.S. Bureau of Labor Statistics reported that Camden's unemployment rate was nearly twice the state average (8.4%), reaching 16.6%. During the same year, Camden's City Police Force was dismantled amidst broad community protest and petitions signed by over 9,000 residents who requested a vote on the issue (Rudolf, 2012). The city has been designated as a food desert by the USDA, and environmental racism continues to plague its residents despite the notable advances of the Camden County Municipal Utilities Authority under the dynamic leadership of Andy Kricun.

Against this backdrop, Camden's educational crisis looms large, and many of the problems addressed in *Savage Inequalities* continue to disproportionately impact poor students of color. Many of the schools suffer from overcrowding, high dropout rates, declining enrollment, low test scores, and inadequate resources (David, Hesla, & Pendergrass, 2017). In 1985, the New Jersey Supreme Court issued what became known as the first Abbot decision (*Abbot v. Burke*), which transferred to an administrative law judge for an initial hearing of the class-action lawsuit filed by school children's parents in East Orange, Camden, Irvington, and Jersey City, which challenged New Jersey's system of financing public education. In Abbot II in 1990, the Court upheld the administrative law judge's decision, deeming the state's method of funding in 28 "poor urban" school districts unconstitutional because it created significant expenditure disparities between them and wealthy suburban school districts (Lichtenstein, 1991). Between 1990 and 2011, the Court issued a series of Abbot Rulings designed to achieve school equity in a variety of areas ranging from per-pupil foundation funding and school facility improvements to teacher qualifications and class size. In addition, the Abbot rulings administered the implementation of significant improvements that included adequate K–12 foundational funding and universal preschool for all three- and four-year-old children (Lenihan, 2009). However, with the exception of a few ostensible success stories in Union City, Elizabeth, Vineland, and Millville, many schools in the Abbot districts still fail to adequately meet the educational needs of their students. Although the reasons for this are multilayered and beyond the scope of this section, the shift toward closing neighborhood schools and opening corporate-run charter schools has become the solution for Camden as well as many communities across the country, despite the potentially divisive possibilities (David, Hesla, & Pendergrass, 2017).

Echoing the sentiments of the *Wall Street Journal* in Kozol's discussion of Camden schools, many proponents of charter schools and public charter hybrids argue that more money does not always equal better education, since per-pupil school expenditures in the state of New Jersey are seemingly among the highest in the country. In 2012, the New Jersey Legislature passed the "Urban Hope Act," a bipartisan school choice bill sponsored by Senator Donald Norcross, which authorizes the Camden school district to partner with private, nonprofit organizations to operate charter-style public schools or "renaissance schools," as long as the schools are located in "newly constructed" or "substantially renovated" facilities (Camden County Democratic Committee, 2012; Katz, 2012; Hester, 2012). The following year, the state's Department of Education took over the school system in Camden at the request of Mayor Reed and Governor Chris Christie, who relinquished the board of education's right to select a superintendent (Katz & Vargas, 2013a; Katz & Vargas, 2013b). While some members of the community view this as a necessity to address the city's "failing" schools, others ask the question: would this happen in more affluent white suburban areas like Cherry Hill? This question has little significance to those parents who view charter schools like LEAP

Academy, located in downtown Camden, as a viable alternative to the failing school districts they left behind. Opponents, however, see this shift to hybrid charter schools as an attack on public schools because they not only divert funds away from the latter, but they also limit the number of admitted children with special education needs. Moreover, they contend that closing neighborhood schools destabilizes communities, puts children at greater risk because they have to travel farther, and ultimately serves as a death knell for future public schools (Tegekar & Potter, 2016).

Despite the apparent challenges confronting Camden's school district, the student protests at Camden High and the silenced voices of those who demand better but still treasure the sense of community found in these "failing schools" raise serious questions about the legacy of the *Brown* decision. The majority of Camden's Black and Brown schools are definitely separate, but they are not equal; the student, family, and community voices that speak to these inequities represent the ways in which cultural capital can empower individuals and situate their voices in strength-based perspectives (Yosso, 2005). Ladson-Billings (1998) points to these counter-narratives as the "deconstruction of oppressive structures and discourses, reconstruction of human agency, and construction of equitable and socially just relations of power" (p. 9).

Critical Race Theory, Culturally Relevant Pedagogy, Community and Cultural Wealth to Story Map

Critical race theory (CRT) in education is framed by the study of power and oppression that draws from multiple disciplines that include law, sociology, history, ethnic studies, and women's studies to examine issues around schooling. Among the vast issues addressed by CRT are deficit perspectives, Euro-centered curricula, limited resources, and standardized testing. Yosso (2005) explains that as a framework, CRT "can be used to theorize, examine and challenge the ways race and racism implicitly and explicitly impact school structures, practices and discourse" (p. 70). According to Solórzano and Yosso (2002), critical race researchers speak to the ways schools at all levels contradictorily oppress and marginalize in the midst of potential for liberatory and transformational pedagogies.

CRT offers a practical and relevant lens through which to analyze and interpret the teachers' voices embedded in this work. A major tenet of CRT centers the experiences and voices of the marginalized and oppressed

(Delgado Bernal 2002; Delgado & Stefancic, 2000; Solórzano & Yosso, 2002). These *counter-stories* are spaces for resistance and reframing thinking by addressing dominant ideologies that fail to acknowledge systemic realties routinely faced by people of color. Solórzano and Yosso (2002) "define the counter-story as a method of telling the stories of those people whose experiences are not often told (i.e., those on the margins of society)" (p. 32). These stories are also often corrective in their challenges to "majoritarian" white perspectives. Counter-stories comprise voices that speak to and validate life circumstances. Similarly, Ladson-Billings & Tate (1995) point to these stories as a form of "psychic preservation."

Frameworks such as *culturally relevant pedagogy* (Au & Jordan, 1981; Ladson-Billings, 1995) call for an affirmation of cultural experiences, identity, and relevance for students. *Culturally relevant teaching* (Ladson-Billings, 1994) explores how students are empowered academically, socially, emotionally, and politically, and *culturally sustaining practices* (Paris, 2012) capitalize on the sustainment of a "linguistic, literate, and cultural pluralism as part of the democratic project of schooling" (p. 93). However, as Black educators, there is more that needs to be addressed than Kozol's description of the Camden school district. We have personally observed too often how White pre- and in-service teachers in our classrooms want to embrace these frameworks and address true student achievement within this population, but many of them have reduced the frameworks to checklists rather than a truly developed understanding of communities in which students from the Camden area live. In order to understand, teach, and embrace students' cultures, learning needs, experiences, and languages, it is important for teachers to explore the narrative accounts given by members of color from the community. Thus, we argue for an awareness of the need to reshape White teacher candidates' education through effective teacher preparation that addresses diversity issues and opens dialogues about the kinds of literature and practices needed for educational advancement (Bean-Folkes, 2012, 2015).

In order to capture former students' counternarratives, we initially began with Bourdieu's (1977) theory of cultural capital to provide an explanation for the students' success. Cultural capital examines the "class-based socialization of culturally relevant skills, abilities, tastes, preferences, or norms that act as a form of currency in the social realm" (Winkle-Wagner, 2010, p. 5). We know that parents provide cultural capital to their children, which can lead to a child's educational success (Dumais, 2002; Lee & Brown, 2006; Martin & Spenner, 2009). According to Bourdieu, cultural capital refers to an accumulation of cultural knowledge, skills, and abilities possessed and inherited by privileged groups in society. Bourdieu asserts that cultural capital (i.e., education and language), social capital (i.e., social networks and connections) and economic capital (i.e., money and other material possessions) can be acquired two ways: from one's family, and/or through formal schooling. The dominant groups within society are able to maintain power because of their access to acquiring and learning strategies to use these forms of capital for social mobility (Yosso, 2005, p. 76). However, we found the traditional perspective of cultural capital too narrowly defined as white, middle-class values, hence our decision to employ Yosso's (2005) community cultural wealth (CCW) framework to examine the six alternative forms of capital.

To further clarify our point, Yosso (2005) adds:

> In addressing the debate over knowledge within the context of social inequality, Pierre Bourdieu argued that the knowledges of the upper and middle classes are considered capital valuable to a hierarchical society. If one is not born into a family whose knowledge is already deemed valuable, one could then access the knowledge of the middle and upper class and the potential for social mobility through formal schooling. Bourdieu's theoretical insight about how a hierarchical society reproduces itself has often been interpreted as a way to explain why the academic and social outcomes of People of Color are significantly lower than the outcomes of Whites. The assumption follows that People of Color "lack" the social and cultural capital required for social mobility. As a result, schools most often work from this assumption in structuring ways to help 'disadvantaged' students whose race and class background has left them lacking necessary knowledge, social skills, abilities and cultural capital. (p. 70)

We drew upon Yosso's (2005) community cultural wealth model (CCWM) to understand and map lived experiences in the narratives from four former Camden residents and students. Yosso's model shifts our lens away from a deficit view of communities of color as places full of cultural poverty and other disadvantages, and focuses instead on "the array of cultural knowledge, skills, abilities, and contacts possessed by socially marginalized groups that often go unrecognized and unacknowledged" (p. 69).

The CCWM comprises six forms of capital, which Yosso purposefully distances from dominant and economic barometers of capital, merit, and value in order to give the often-missed intrinsic and communal merits of communities of color precedence and privilege (Yosso & Garciá, 2007). The first form is *"aspirational capital,"* or "the ability to maintain hopes and dreams for the future, even in the face of real and perceived barriers" (p. 77). The second form is *"linguistic capital,"* which refers to "the intellectual and social skills attained through communication experiences in more than one language and/or style" (p. 78). *"Familial capital"* relates to the knowledge that is produced and nurtured through kinship that extends beyond traditional notions of what "family" means, accounting for historical and communal bonds with others. The fourth form is *"social capital,"* which refers to "networks of people and community resources" that exist to help communities of color navigate social systems" (p. 79). *"Navigational capital"* is a cultural form that represents the possession of skills and knowledge to strategically move through systems and structures neither originally designed nor intended for people of color. The last form is *"resistant capital,"* which relates to the increasing competence and skills that are accessed and enacted through persistent stances against the systemic inequality experienced by people of color (Yosso, 2005).

Other scholars (Farmer-Hinton, Lewis, Patton, & Rivers, 2013) have also found CCWM appropriate because of its capacity to provide space for us to name racism as a key determining factor that has and continues to influence the policies and processes that negatively affect schooling in communities across the country. Yosso's model is useful in addressing inequitable schooling in Camden as part of a larger dominant script that promotes a cultural difference that blames people of color for the educational inequities they face rather than acknowledging racial disparity. This model is also valuable for allowing us to engage in acts of agency and self-empowerment, to bring these stories to the center, to resist dominant and deficit ideologies, to insert perspectives that defend and give voice to former residents, and to tap into the cultural wealth they attained through their educational upbringing and schooling in Camden (Yosso, 2005).

Methodology

This narrative inquiry, which is qualitative in nature, unfolds using critical race methodology (Solórzano & Yosso, 2002). The counter-story is our method of telling the stories and experiences of living and going to school in Camden, New Jersey. We began by searching for participants who lived and attended the public schools in Camden during the time of Kozol's visits. We polled former students, colleagues, and community members for participants, whom we interviewed by phone and via email. We explained that our purpose was to speak with them about their experiences growing up and attending schools in Camden, and we constructed a narrative protocol that was used to capture the respective narratives. Each of the participants responded to an inquiry that stated: "We are very interested in hearing from you regarding your schooling. Would you take a few minutes to answer these questions to share with us? Please feel free to include in an email or as a Word.doc."

The questionnaire and interviews were collected over a six-week period after which time the narratives were transcribed. Once the interviews were completed, we read and reread for the counter-narrative themes. As we coded the narratives, we saw common threads in each participant's experience. Further analysis of the transcripts was also conducted using the six characteristics of CCWM. Each of the lived experiences provided a nondeficit view of life in Camden during this time. Through additional analysis, we discovered that four of the six models served as themes for

Table 8.1

Questions Asked of Each Participant
1. Tell us about your school.
2. How did it impact your life?
3. When did you attend the Camden public schools?
4. What should people know about the Camden Schools?
5. What was the role of the community in your experiences growing up in Camden?
6. What was it like growing up when you did?
7. Do you feel that you did well in school? What would have helped you to do better?
8. Was it emphasized that you do well in school? What was more important than going to school?
9. What were the schools like?
10. Tell us about your favorite or most important school moment.
11. Did you explore higher education alone? Who helped to inform you?
12. How do you feel about the Camden school system today? We are interested in learning more about your experiences. What would be a good time for us to meet?

Credit: Jane Bean-Folkes, Susan Browne and Chanelle Rose.

Table 8.2

Participants (African American Women, ages 40s–50s)			
Dana grew up in the Parkside neighborhood of Camden and went to school in the city from grades K-12. Dana was raised by her mother. The youngest of three children, Dana grew up with two older brothers. Her oldest brother was 21 years older and the second brother was 10 years older. She completed an Educational Leadership doctorate as part of a Camden cohort enrolled at a South Jersey University where the authors teach.	Laticia was born and raised in Camden. Laticia was raised by her mother. She pointed out that she had many male role models. She is married with three children. Laticia began her college career at Kean University in Early Childhood and received two master's degrees from in Pennsylvania.	Yasmine was born and raised in the Parkside neighborhood of Camden. She is the oldest of three children who were also raised in Camden. Her father retired as an Academic Dean of Camden County College, and her mother was a "stay at home mom" until her youngest brother was school age. Her mother, now deceased, retired as a Cafeteria Manager of a Camden Middle School. Her father continues to live in Camden. Laticia has a BA from Hampton Institute with a minor in Communication Disorders and a MA in Special Education from Trinity University.	Robin was born in Philadelphia during the beginning of the gang war era near the high rises that were attached to the Richard Allen housing projects. When her father went overseas to serve in the Vietnam war, the family moved to Camden. Robin has one brother. She is married with two children. She and her husband, who is a pastor, are building a new church in South Jersey. She attended Temple University and transferred to Rutgers, where she majored in social work. Robin later went back to her elementary education major at the urging of her husband.

Credit: Jane Bean-Folkes, Susan Browne and Chanelle Rose.

this work. During this process, we contacted and shared our transcripts with participants as well as with each other through email and phone conversations in order to maintain trustworthiness.

Introducing the Voices

Familial Capital

> All of the teachers that taught us lived in our neighborhood, and so we grew up with our teachers and teacher's kids and so it was [a] village concept.
>
> —Robin

The voices we hear are of four former Camden students who grew up in neighborhoods such as Parkside and have family currently living in Camden. Their stories reflect a closely bound urban community where evidence of Yosso's (2005) CCWM is vibrantly present. Robin's description of a village speaks to *familial capital* that is evident through strong communal bonds. Parents, extended family, church, and school were constant reminders of education as progress and progress as power. Community expectations were nurtured through kinship connections that extended to teachers. As Dana explained: "There was crime and violence, gangs, but also a community. . . . teachers that were very nurturing, so they treated you as if they were your children and they had high expectations for you like they had for their own children."

In thinking about her teachers, Robin remarked: "If you are familiar with the movie *Crooklyn* by Spike Lee, that personified how we grew up in Camden. You didn't do too much cause your teachers lived down the street; you couldn't get away with too much, but that built character, and not only [in] academics but that we were well-rounded citizens." Leticia, Dana, and Yasmine all attended neighborhood schools for grades K-12, as did Robin, whose family moved from high-rise projects in Philadelphia in the mid-1960s to escape the developing gang war era. Each of these women went on to receive master's degrees, and Dana was the first to receive her doctorate among a cohort of Camden graduate students in an Educational Leadership program.

Majoritarian perspectives exit from positions of racial privilege. Inherent in this way of knowing, "the majoritarian story tells us that darker skin and poverty correlate with bad neighborhoods and bad schools" (Solórzano & Yosso, 2002, p. 29). However, the counter-narratives of the four teacher voices corroborate the existence of communities of color and poverty as places possessing strong cultural resources. Together these teacher voices offer insights into a strong community connected by shared hopes and aspirations. In one memory, Dana recalled her graduation day and walking down the street in her cap and gown while neighbors applauded her from their porches. She described a community that looked out for one another, one whose individuals were not afraid to get involved.

Social, Aspirational, and Navigational Capital

These counter-narratives are rich with elements of Yosso's (2005) CCWM. The narratives embody social and aspirational capital as well as navigational capital, which emerges through examples of the knowledge needed to strategically move through systems and structures neither originally designed nor intended for people of color. Many of the women also pointed to high school counselors and teachers playing a significant role in their pursuit of higher education. Two names, Mrs. Cream and Mr. Jenkins, frequently surface across their narratives as powerful examples of inspiration and support that translated into *aspirational, social, and navigational capital*. Leticia:

> It was all about the teachers. Teachers. Teachers. Teachers. . . . [My mom] wanted you to go every day. She really didn't understand. . . . The part that impacted me the most was the actual teachers, because they invested in you outside of school hours and so as long as you were involved, you got that extra support. If you think about the teachers that had the biggest impact on you, it was either the teachers that went above and beyond after school or those teachers that really took pride in teaching. You know they would try and keep you interested and you could tell they knew their craft.

Yasmine:

> All of my teachers at the "High" had so much faith in us and us in them. Those four years [of high school] were some of the

best years I had as a student. Ms. Cream, Mr. Jenkins, and Mr. Madden knew our families and knew all of us by name and face. We knew they loved us without question. We knew that the administration, teachers, parents, and fellow students all wanted the best. People were so envious of us that they would lie about their address, just to attend the "High." We had so many options back then: check out the yearbooks from those years. Academically, you were either college-bound, business or vocational. We had a fantastic music/theatre department that offered summer band. Our athletes were some of the best in the country.

Robin: "So we were the first class to come in with Mrs. Cream and we were her first graduating class in 1976. All of my teachers at the "High" had so much faith in us and us in them. Those 4 years were some of the best years I had as a student. Mrs. Cream, Mr. Jenkins and Mr., Madden knew our families and knew all of us by name and face." Indeed, far from the grim and often deficit-centered environment that Kozol speaks, Laticia, Yasmine, and Robin offer descriptions of educators who wanted the best for them and who had a positive impact on their lives. School and family interactions were built on what Noddings (2005) describes as ongoing relationships of care and trust. The precursors to understanding issues of access and maneuvering multiple environments (Yosso, 2005) were being established. Words like 'love' and 'pride' are associated with what teachers provided along with knowledge. Kozol spoke to a Camden high school principal who described teachers as "straitjacketed" because of testing. The principal went on to say, "As a result, they [students] can be given no electives, nothing wonderful or fanciful or beautiful, nothing that touches the spirit or the soul" (p. 143). Yasmine's story differs significantly with memories of academic or vocational options and music, theater, and athletics. Robin describes her high school experience as the best years she ever had. The voices of these women offer salient counter-narratives for teachers who saw schools as sites linked to community and were able to nurture social change.

Life in Camden and in School: Then

In the community, you know as you get up in the morning and you stop at the store if you don't stop [at the store] the owner the next day will be like where were you yesterday, did you go to school? So even the store owners knew you didn't come in and they are checking on you if you went to school.

—Dana

During the early part of the 1970s, Camden was described as an uninviting place, especially if you were from outside the community. However, many of the participants described it as just the opposite. The social network provided a safety net for the youth of the community. This *social capital* gave students a set of resources that extended beyond the family and provided students with a set of social principles to navigate the system.

As Dana recalls: "People looked out for one another. [The] majority of my neighbors were elderly, meaning they were in their 70s/80s, and if you did something, they went right across the street and told your mom and you got in trouble, and if something was going on or something was bothering you, they would come off their porch and they would say something." Children understood that this urban community was centered on the people who lived and worked there. School was important and so was the community in which they lived. Children in the neighborhood played together and worked together to sustain the look of their community.

The love for life and learning in these Camden neighborhoods was abundant in the stories told. The school buildings were described as extremely old and fairly historical. In fact, many were named after famous individuals who hailed from Camden. Central air and elevators, however, were far from the norm: "You had to physically walk up the steps, but the classrooms were fairly well, fairly good at the time," remarked Dana.

Dana remembered that the faculty during the 1970s and 1980s was comprised of diverse young teachers who helped students navigate the system by providing knowledge and strategies of success. These faculty members also provided *aspirational capital* as a model for what can be achieved despite the barriers. According to Dana, "some of those teachers are currently still teaching. The ones who taught me are still there. The teachers in the school were 80% African American and 20% Caucasian, and during this time growing up, the teachers treated the students like their own children." Indeed, teachers were committed, and despite the lack of materials, students felt like they were dedicated to using creative strategies to help them succeed.

Life in Camden and in School: Now

In 2013, the state took over the Camden schools and the schools in Camden became charter or charter/hybrid. There was significant turmoil in the loss of jobs and the restructuring of Camden's public schools. The change from a community-based staff to largely a staff that lives outside the community has meant a reduction in the connection between the school, families, and the community. Today, charter schools are viewed by the New Jersey Department of Education Commissioner, David Hespe, as part of a mission to expand choice for parents in the state's struggling urban centers, who are seeking the best educational experiences for their children. They are an option and perhaps one way to address the needs of urban students. However, others would argue that this comes at a direct cost to traditional neighborhood schooling. The wealth of community cultural capital the participants documented in their narratives has been significantly lost, and these changes offer a sense of longing for communities of old in an effort to transform Camden's educational trajectories. As documented, the growth in charters has led to a growth in teacher loss and nonacademic programs for some of the state's lowest academic performers. This, in turn, has reduced the amount of navigational capital that would support students with skills and knowledge to strategically move through educational and social systems.

What we can gather from participants' narratives is that the approval of charter schools has meant the decline of the traditional public school as well as the breakdown of communities. We might argue it is mainly the loss of "social capital," but it has also meant the drastic increase in teachers who are not connected to the lives of students who live in Camden. It has also meant a loss of *resistant capital*, which relates to the increasing competence and skills that are accessed and enacted through persistent stances against the systemic inequality that people of color experience from faculty of color. The participants told us repeatedly that the single most powerful impact on their education careers was the impact of their teachers. These teachers lived, worked, shopped, and worshiped in the community, and their presence contributed to its growth. These teachers were conscious of the fact that they had obtained a level of success because their own teachers had pushed them to succeed, and they felt their students needed to do the same. Forty years later, one cannot help but ponder what impact the current lack of commitment has on the education of Camden's students?

Currently, teachers of color in New Jersey represent only 18% of the 125,200 K-12 public school teachers, yet students of color constitute 82% of the pupil population. This lack of role models can have a vital impact on the decrease in the minority teaching workforce because it is the people who stand behind the students who make them great, not an institution. It is the people who really care and are involved in the lives of the students—these are the individuals the students respect: someone who serves as a surrogate big brother or sister, who cares enough to want to know when they do good or bad things, and who is aware of a student's talents and gifts and understands their personal responsibility to shape lives.

The four former students to whom we spoke voiced concern about today's Camden schools, including their low-test scores, the state's district takeover (which was based on low test scores), politics, and nepotism. Three of the former students we interviewed have moved away from Camden. One individual lives and works in Camden and all still have family and friends who still live in the area. They voiced additional concern that educators like the ones they encountered are now retiring, and young new teachers from the suburbs come to Camden to simply reduce their student loans and then leave. In analyzing their narratives, we are able to see a shift in the sources of capital for today's students. Leticia:

> For the new teachers coming in, their retention rate is not that high because they have a hard time connecting with the students. Students in the city need to have a connection with their teachers; if they feel like you just come to school every day and you just try to teach a lesson, they won't respond to you, so they have to know that you are invested in them holistically . . . high turnover rate . . . children taking care of themselves.

Furthermore, the participants expressed concern for the influx of teachers from outside the Camden area. The issue is not simply the charter schools but the loss of faculty connected to the community that has caused a loss of the *navigational capital* that once benefited the four participants. Yasmine:

> They [teachers from outside of Camden] work in the charter schools because what happens, you got student loans, you are a young white girl [and] you get into one of the inner-city schools and they pay your student loans off. Now you come

out here in [the suburbs] and think that you understand the Black child but you don't have your student loans anymore because you gave 3–5 years to Camden because that is the inner city. That is what they do.

The idea that, when children are challenged, there is something wrong with them, I can't get it out of my mind that it could be something in my teaching practice, not that saying you're wrong, but something that I can do in my teaching practice [is] to change the response of the students.

Lastly, there was concern for recognizing a variety of talents, and the *navigational capital* of being a member of this type of organization supported student growth. As Robin reminisced: "The fine arts [in the Camden public schools] were seen as very important because if you didn't succeed academically they gave you another avenue to succeed to become successful. So maybe you weren't the brightest, the sharpest knives in the drawer, but you were a phenomenal musician and they tapped into that. Now, the fine arts department really doesn't exist at the magnitude that it used to." So, what have we learned? Interestingly, Kozol (1991) describes the educational inequities in the schools he visited as unacceptable by many standards. He stated that, while there were wonderful teachers such as Mrs. Carla Hawkins in urban schools, and sometimes several such teachers in a single school, it was inaccurate to focus on a few teachers to paint a hopeful portrait of the good things that occur under adverse conditions. Furthermore, he wrote that it is not what these exceptional teachers do, it is who they are, and it is hard to replicate or write into a standardized curriculum. Adding this pedagogy would be an easy fix to education. However, what Kozol (1991) did not take into account was the sources of capital that existed for students in the Camden community. Though the problems in the schools today are more systemic and not as easy to correct, the most striking observation from the participants' stories is the current lack of capital—*aspirational, social, & navigational*. They are most concerned about the challenges new students face in school paradigms that currently lack these resources which give as Yosso and Garciá (2007) stated, the often-missed intrinsic and communal merits of communities of color precedence and privilege.

Although schools of education produce a large number of pre-service teachers to work in urban districts, these teachers are ill-prepared to teach and mentor students when they know little about their backgrounds, and have often had little meaningful exposure to anyone outside their own social class. For them, misunderstood urban students and families are often viewed as subjects who need to be saved. This leads us to consider how significant it is to privilege the narratives of Dana, Laticia, Yasmine, and Robin in challenging majoritarian deficit perspectives that fail to recognize and acknowledge the lived experiences of students in communities of color.

The influx of charter schools is not a cause, but a contribution to the issue of educating students in urban settings. In a blog, Gloria Ladson-Billings wrote:

> I do know the experience of walking into schools (especially elementary and middle schools) where Black students ask me with eagerness, 'Are you a teacher here?' And I recognize the disappointment that falls over those same faces when I shake my head, 'No.' Their longing for a teacher that "looks like them" is palpable. The current statistics indicate that class after class of children—Black, Native American, Latino, and Asian—go through entire school careers without ever having a teacher of their same race or ethnicity.

But, continues Ladson-Billings:

> I want to suggest that there is something that may be even more important than Black students having Black teachers, and that is White students having Black teachers! It is important for White students to encounter Black people who are knowledgeable and hold some level of authority over them. Black students ALREADY know that Black people have a wide range of capabilities. They see them in their homes, their neighborhoods, and their churches. They are the Sunday School teachers, their Scout Leaders, their coaches, and family members. But what opportunities do White students have to see and experience Black competence?

All students need a diverse teaching force to prepare them for global society. The challenge begins with educators and future educators training good teachers, and educating them for diversity. Good teachers need to gain a thorough understanding of the inequities present in urban educational contexts and the strategies that teachers, families, students, and communities employ in the face of these challenges. What Kozol (1991) did not identify and address, and what we aimed to address in this chapter is the wealth of capital from which these students benefited *through* their teachers. It is important to consider the triangulation of family, school, and community to ensure that students in underserved urban environments become successful through more engaged involvement in their schools, their communities, and the world.

References

Bean-Folkes, J. (2012). Schools of hope: Teaching literacy in the Obama era. In E. Thomas (Ed.) *Reading the African American experience in the Obama era: A handbook for teaching, learning, and activism*. Peter Lang.

Bean-Folkes, J. (2015). A tale of words: Perspectives and provocations. *NCTE-Early Childhood Education Assembly*, 2(2), 1–6.

Bell, L. (2003). Telling tales: What stories can teach us about racism. *Race Ethnicity and Education*, 6, 3–28.

Bourdieu, P. (1977). Cultural reproduction and social reproduction. In J. Karabel & A. H. Halsey (Eds.), *Power and ideology in education* (pp. 487–511). Oxford University Press.

Bullard, R. (2005). *The Quest for environmental justice: Human rights and the politics of pollution*. Sierra Club Books.

Camden County Democratic Committee. (2012, January 3). Norcross sponsored 'Urban Hope Act' now law.

David, R., Hesla, K., & Pendergrass, S. A. (2017). *A growing movement: America's largest public charter school communities*. National Alliance for Public Charter Schools.

Delgado Bernal, D. (2002). Critical race theory, Latino critical theory, and critical race-gendered epistemologies: Recognizing students of color as holders and creators of knowledge. *Qualitative Inquiry*, 8(1), 105–126.

Delgado R., & Stefancic, J. (2000). Introduction. In R. Delgado & J. Stefancic (Eds.), *Critical race theory: The cutting edge* (2nd ed.; pp. xv–xix). Temple University Press.

Dumais, S. A. (2002). Cultural capital, gender, and school success: The role of habitus. *Sociology of Education*, 75, 44–68. http://dx.doi.org/10.2307/3090253

Dunn, P. (2014, May 16). Camden student protest draws praise, attention. *Courier Post*. http://www.courierpostonline.com/story/news/local/south-jersey/2014/05/14/camden-students-rally-staff-cuts/9097417/

Education Law Center. (2016). *The history of Abbott v. Burke*. http://www.edlawcenter.org/cases/abbott-v-burke/abbott-history.html.

Gillette, H. (2005). *Camden after the fall: Decline and renewal in a post-industrial City*. University of Pennsylvania Press.

Guy, S. (2013, March 7). America's 'invincible' city brought to its knees by poverty, violence. *NBCNews*. http://www.nbcnews.com/feature/in-plain-sight

Hester, T. (2012, June 12). Christie signs Urban Hope Act allowing nonprofit-run schools in Camden, Newark, and Trenton. *NJTV News*. https://www.njtvonline.org/news/uncategorized/governor-christie-signs-urban-hope-act/

Ingersoll, R., Merrill, L., & Stuckey, D. (2014). *Seven trends: The transformation of the teaching force, updated April 2014. CPRE report (#RR-80)*. Consortium for Policy Research in Education, University of Pennsylvania.

Katz, M. (2009, November 9). Camden's waterfront and its woes: N.J. vowed to revitalize the city. Today, job numbers are largely unchanged, but millions have gone to such "anchors" as Cooper, Campbell's, and the aquarium. *Philadelphia Inquirer*, p. 1A.

Katz, M., & Vargas, C. (2013a, March 26). Christie to announce state takeover of Camden schools. *Philadelphia Inquirer*, p. 1A.

Katz, M., & Vargas, C. (2013b, March 25). NJ governor Christie to announce state takeover of Camden schools. *Philadelphia Inquirer*.

Kozol, J. (1991). *Savage inequalities: Children in America's schools*. Harper Perennial.

Kurdzuk, T. (2012, December 5). Say something nice about Camden, after the city actually improves: Editorial. *The Star-Ledger*. http://blog.nj.com/njv_editorial_page/2012/12/say_something_nice_about_camde.html#comments.

Ladson-Billings, G. (1998). Just what is critical race theory and what's it doing in a nice field like education? *International Journal of Qualitative Studies in Education, 11*(1), 7–24.

Ladson-Billings, G. (2015, January 19). What if we had more Black teachers? *The University of Wisconsin-Madison School of Education News*. https://news.education.wisc.edu/news/2015/01/19/ladson-billings-examines---what-if-we-had-more-black-teachers-

Lee, J. S. & Bowen, N. K. (2006). Parent involvement, cultural capital, and the achievement gap among elementary school children. *American Educational Research Journal, 43*, 193–218. http://dx.doi.org/10.3102/00028312043002193

Lenihan, J. (2009). Lurking behind the shadow of enduring reform school funding and New Jersey's school funding reform act of 2008. *Seton Legislative Journal, 34*(1), 119–156.

Lichtenstein, J. (1991). Abbott v. Burke: Reaffirming New Jersey's constitutional commitment to equal educational opportunity. *Hofstra Law Review, 20*(2), 429–494.

Martin, N. D., & Spenner, K. L. (2009). Capital conversion and accumulation: A social portrait of legacies at an elite university. *Research in Higher Education, 50*, 623–648. http://dx.doi.org/10.1007/s11162-009-9136-9

Morgia, L, & Vicino, T. J. (2013). Waterfront politics: Revisiting the case of Camden, New Jersey's redevelopment. *Urban Research & Practice*, *6*(3), 329–345.

Noddings, N. (2005) 'Caring in education', *the encyclopedia of informal education*, www.infed.org/biblio/noddings_caring_in_education.htm.

Oakley, D., & Tsao, H-S. (2016). A new way of revitalizing distressed urban communities? Assessing the impact of the federal empowerment zone program. *Journal of Urban Affairs*, *28*(5), 443–471.

Rudolf, J. (2012, November 19). Chris Christie pushes Camden police force to disband, despite questions over new plan's finances. *Huffington Post*. http://www.huffingtonpost.com/2012/11/19/chris-christie-camden-police_n_2025372.html

Seligsohn, A., & Mazelis, J. M. (2015). Deindustrialized small cities and poverty: The view from Camden. In Haymes, S. N., de Haymes, M. V., & Miller, R. J. (Eds.), *The Routledge handbook of poverty in the United States*. Routledge.

Simon, D. (2013, March 1). Camden homicide is the third this week. *Philadelphia Inquirer*. Retrieved from http://articles.philly.com/2013-03-01/news/37354710_1_camdenhomicide-ninth-homicide-twitter-darransimon

Solórzano, D., & Yosso, T. (2002). Critical race methodology: Counterstorytelling as an analytical framework for education research. *Qualitative Inquiry*, *8*(1), 23–44.

Sue, D. W. (2015). *Race talk and the conspiracy of silence: Understanding and facilitating difficult dialogues on race*. Wiley.

Taibi, M. (2013, December 11). Apocalypse, New Jersey: A dispatch from America's most desperate town. *Rolling Stone*. http://www.rollingstone.com/culture/news/apocalypse-new-jersey-a-dispatch-from-americas-most-desperate-town-20131211

Tegekar, P., & Potter, H. (2016). *Charter schools, gentrification, and weighted lotteries*. National Housing Institute.

Wiig, A. (2018). Secure the city, revitalize the zone: Smart urbanization in Camden, New Jersey. *Environment and Planning C: Politics and Space*, *36*(3), 403–422.

Winkle-Wagner, R. (2010). Cultural capital: The promises and pitfalls in educational research. *ASHE Higher Education Report Series*, *36*, 1.

Yosso, T. J. (2005). Whose culture has capital? A critical race theory discussion of community cultural wealth. *Race Ethnicity and Education*, *8*(1), 69–91. doi:10.1080/1361332052000341006

Yosso, T., & Garciá, D. G. (2007). "This is no slum!": A critical race theory analysis of community cultural wealth in Culture Clash's *Chavez Ravine*. *Aztlan: A Journal of Chicano Studies*, *32*(1), 145–177.

Chapter 9

Avenues to Organic Engagement

One Counselor-Educator's Experiences Working with Community Agencies to Promote Educational Success in an Urban Community

AHMAD R. WASHINGTON

Introduction

> We have got this tailspin of culture, in our inner cities in particular, of men not working and just generations of men not even thinking about working or learning the value and the culture of work, and so there is a real culture problem here that has to be dealt with.
>
> —Former House Budget Chairman, Paul Ryan

In the news media, popular culture, and educational discourse, the word "urban," over time, has come to symbolize more than large, densely populated metropolitan areas across the country. Rather than merely spatial locations or enclaves saturated by civilians who, of their own volition, choose to reside there, the term "urban" and its seemingly interchangeable companion "inner city," is imbued with negative images and unflattering connotations. These negative images and messages emanate from a deeply entrenched and pervasive narrative that is steeped in a discourse of Black cultural pathology and depravity (Anderson, 2004). This predominant narrative portrays urban environments as overwhelmingly crime-ridden and unsafe, and places to be generally avoided, especially by White patrons and pedestrians. Since the early 20th century, the rhetorical and visual associations between the word "urban" and mass hysteria about epidemic criminal behavior has occurred, in lockstep, with an increased presence of racial and ethnic minorities, particularly Blacks and Latinos from poor and working-class backgrounds (Farmer-Hinton, Lewis, Patton, & Rivers, 2013).

The notion that many of the larger metropolitan urban communities are incubators for lawlessness, where scourges of violent criminal offenses occur unabatedly was propagated, with particular fervor, during the mid-to-late 1960s, a period where a series of massive civil upheavals of justifiable Black rage erupted occurred across the country (Alexander, 2012; Anderson, 2016; Embrick, 2015). Black residents in Detroit, Chicago, Newark, and Watts initiated uprisings in response to unrelenting violence that included but was not limited to: the intentional and malicious mischaracterizations of Black Liberation organizations (i.e., Black Panthers) as clandestine threats initiated unprovoked violence against government agencies to destabilize the country—mischaracterizations used to justify the hypersurveillance, hyperincarceration, and killing of prominent movement leaders; police brutality and shootings of unarmed Black people; the sluggish implementation of school desegregation post-*Brown*; and a paucity of employment opportunities that offered decent, livable wages during a period of accelerating deindustrialization (National Advisory Commission on Civil Disorders, 1968; Tibbs, 2012).

Politicians pounced on the opportunity to misconstrue and disconnect these civil uprisings from American institutional racism and economic oppression, presumably to generate tangible scientific evidence to support a preexisting myth and assumption about Black communities: an unwillingness of Black communities, particularly Black parents, to assume greater responsibility for the fate of its own collective future (Alexander, 2012; Anderson, 2015). Narrow racial scripts and tropes, including the irresponsible, chronically unemployed, absentee Black father; the sexually promiscuous Black single mother; the opportunistic, swindling Black welfare queen; and the unconscionable and unpredictably violent young Black male criminal teetering precariously on the verge of supposed extinction (a.k.a. thug, super-predator) were just some of the most sensationalized images and narratives circulating during the 1960s, 1970s, 1980s, and

1990s and well into the contemporary moment (Brown, 2002; Hall, 1981; Hamer, 2001; Hancock, 2004; Hill Collins, 2004; Moynihan, 1965; Omi & Winant, 2014). Circulating these images through dominant socializing institutions like the media reinforces hegemonic discourses that portray urban Black communities as spaces of perpetual disarray. Thus, as Forman (2002) cogently asserts, "Seen as a social product, space is also more easily understood as political and ideological, and the interrelationship forged within space are, accordingly, political or ideologically laden" (p. 4). Paul Ryan's comments at the outset of this chapter, a not-so-veiled attempt to engender disdain for socially excluded Black people in urban communities by invoking the dog-whistle inner-city Black male trope, stand as evidence buttressing Forman's insightful analysis.

As a consequence of this framing, Black youth have come to represent the dregs of society who unceasingly leech resources from honest, hardworking, taxpaying Americans. Rather than promoting an ethos of compassion and empathy or, at the very least, sympathy for people in inner cities, these caricatures of the inner city have been used, strategically, to intensify preexisting racial animus, antipathy, and vitriol among White Americans, particularly White men who have been manipulated into believing they have been alienated and displaced by racial minorities they perceive as lazy and undeserving (Anderson, 2015; Day, 2015).

What is often omitted from this discourse, obviously, is any discussion about how the urban context is the culmination of meticulously crafted, anti-Black state and federal policies that had their genesis in the early 20th century (Hacker, 2003; Massey & Denton, 1993). Countless critical sociologists, social and cultural theorists, representing various fields and vocations, have relentlessly interrogated this inherently racist, decontextualized, and ahistorical conceptualization of urban cities, as well as the resultant victim-blaming ideology it proffers in social discourse and public policy (King Jr., 1968; Macedo, 2006; Rose, 1994, 2008; Shakur, 1987). For these scholars, the spaces historically designated "urban," particularly as "urban" is now situated in the White American psyche and imagination as a rogue and lawless sociocultural space for Blacks and Latinos, were orchestrated through racially exclusionary policies that prioritized the psychological, sociopolitical, and economic needs and desires of White Americans without extending the same courtesies and considerations to Black people (Anderson, 2015; Feagin, 1999).

This discourse of Black pathology and the policies they buttress are germane to urban education, and the educational experiences of Black children in particular, for several critical reasons. First, as Keisch and Scott (2015) astutely point out, "Education and housing policy have been closely linked in the structural landscape of racial apartheid in the U.S, and schools have long been a major selling point in terms of housing markets in specific neighborhoods" (p. 11). Second, regardless of where they attend school, Black children are constantly having to negotiate classrooms designed to continually "reproduce the dominant ideology through a web of lies that distort and transfigure reality. Central to this cultural reproduction mechanism is the overcelebration of myths that inculcate us with beliefs about the supremacy of Western heritage at the same time as the dominant ideology creates other instruments that degrade and devalue other cultural narratives along the lines of race, ethnicity, language, and gender" (Macedo, 2006, p. 37). This hegemonic ideology and its attendant aspirational ideals (e.g., espoused ideals of freedom, democracy, meritocracy, rugged individualism, and a deferential Protestant work ethic), Lipman (2004) writes, indoctrinates "the vast majority of people to accept massive social inequality and unequal power relations" and consequently, "social inequality and unequal relations of power are legitimized, normalized, and perceived as inevitable" (p. 14).

In many ways, Johnathan Kozol's (1991) widely cited critical ethnographic text *Savage Inequalities* has been understood as an incisive and progressive socio-educational counternarrative to the cultural hegemony alluded to in Lipman's (2004) foregoing quote. *Savage Inequality* portrays, in sharp relief, how social and economic policies generated by local and state government further stratified preexisting lines of racial and economic inequality and reverberated within urban social affairs and public education to the detriment of poor and working-class people and students of color, Black students most especially. For example, the construction of major highways and interstates, directly through Black inner-city enclaves, helped expedite commutes from the city for White suburban residents (Coates, 2015). *Savage Inequalities* unpacks how the decisions to finance public education through commercial and residential property taxes reproduces massive qualitative differences between the school experiences children and families in urban and suburban communities receive (Kozol, 1991).

Savage Inequalities was generally lauded for its graphic portrayals of racial inequality and the visceral reactions it was able to generate among readers, especially White readers unfamiliar with the sheer scope and scale of educational injustices. For those indoctrinated with the belief that a postracial America had arrived, *Savage Inequalities* served as a harsh and jolting reminder "that despite *Brown v. Board of Education* (1954) and subsequent civil rights legislation and remedies, the education system remained segregated and inherently unequal" (Farmer-Hinton, Lewis, Patton, & Rivers, 2013, p. 2). Further, because it was generally perceived as a progressive clarion call from a White ally for desperately needed, responsive state and federal services to improve the deplorable condition of urban education, Kozol's work is considered part of the urban teacher education canon (Farmer-Hinton, Lewis, Patton & Rivers).

Despite the fact that Kozol's work offered scathing critiques that implicated local and state officials for the decisions they made that repeatedly imperiled the lives of Blacks in various U.S. cities, a major criticism of *Savage Inequalities* is how it overlooked, even if unintentionally, the resilience, perseverance, and self-determination of Black residents and how they leveraged the community cultural knowledge and resources they possessed (Farmer-Hinton, Lewis, Patton, & Rivers, 2013). Intent aside, such an omission reproduces deeply entrenched deficit narratives about Black communities being hapless and incapable of strategizing and implementing solutions to the intersecting axes of institutional power that conspire to constrain Black actualization (Farmer-Hinton, Lewis, Patton, & Rivers, 2013). On its own, this deficit narrative is dehumanizing and paternalistic; however, what makes these narratives even more pernicious is how they become fodder for not only culturally encapsulated White middle-class teachers but also culturally encapsulated White middle-class urban school counselors. Being culturally encapsulated and disconnected from these communities leaves urban school counselors too far removed to see the robust number of resources that exist there. To see these resources requires turning away from deficit narratives and toward embracing a social justice school counseling orientation that values and centers a community's cultural wealth.

Urban School Counseling

School counselors must courageously raise their voices to highlight social and educational injustice while simultaneously catalyzing social justice and social change on the ground (ASCA, 2019; Bemak & Chung, 2008, 2005; Dixon, Tucker, & Clark, 2010). This expectation is predicated on the belief that the existing social and educational structures, like those discussed in *Savage Inequalities*, perpetuate the status quo and circumscribe the long-range socioeconomic life opportunities for Black students (Griffin & Steen, 2011; Hipolito-Delgado & Lee, 2007; Ratts, DeKruyf, & Chen-Hayes, 2007).

Urban school counselors' roles in disrupting the status quo, through social justice advocacy, are germane to this discussion about *Savage Inequalities* because of the many institutional barriers endemic to the contemporary urban school context. Counseling and educational literature are replete with examples of the pervasive educational inequities in urban school settings, including massive teacher turnover, school closures, excessive suspensions and expulsions, and students' limited access to more rigorous academic content. These are just a few of the very tangible impediments urban school counselors must eliminate as they work with Black students (Day-Vines & Day-Hairston, 2005; Washington, 2018).

Eschewing the deficit narratives that could be inferred from Kozol's (1991) text is extremely vital to school counseling in general and to urban school counseling, in particular, for two very obvious reasons. First, much like the teaching profession, the school counseling profession is overwhelmingly racially homogeneous, dominated numerically by White practitioners (Bridgeland & Bruce, 2011). Second, these demographic trends in the school counseling profession are occurring at a time when data indicate American K–12 schools are becoming increasingly more racially, ethnically, and linguistically diverse (Kena, Musu-Gillette, Robinson, Wang, Rathbun, Zhang, Wilkinson-Flicker, Barmer, & Dunlop Velez, 2015). Thus, it is far from unreasonable to ask: how will White school counselors fight the injustice confronting students of color when these students' lived experiences are in such stark contrast to their own? The ability to connect with these students is usurped entirely when school counselors are not challenged to examine how they have been socialized to Black students and the communities they come from through a lens of deficiency and deprivation (Holcomb-McCoy, 2004; Booth & Washington, 2015; Dale & Daniel, 2013). This is an important consideration because the failure to see Black students and their communities as resourceful and possessing their own cultural history and knowledge, skills, abilities, and contacts can thwart constructive school-family-community partnerships, which are vitally important in helping Black students thrive (Bryant & Henry, 2010; Yosso, 2005).

School-Family-Community Collaborations

School-family-community collaborations are partnerships initiated at the behest of school counselors to connect educators, families, and community stakeholders in meaningful dialogue about strategies that nurture student progress (Bryant & Henry, 2010). Because it would be arduous and ineffective for school counselors to work independently to promote all students' school-community collaborations, there are more comprehensive and efficient alternatives for addressing the countless responsibilities school counselors assume in relation to student outcomes (Bryan & Henry, 2010). As such, school counselors are strongly encouraged to foster collaborations between their schools and the communities in which they are immersed and to periodically evaluate the effectiveness of these collaborations (ASCA, 2019).

To cultivate constructive school-community collaborations in Black school contexts, it is important for school counselors to confront racist narratives of cultural deficiency that depict Black students as flawed and uninterested in achieving educational success and Black families and communities as devoid of the resources necessary to promote educational success. Seeing Black students, families, and communities through the lens of these pathologizing tropes, urban school counselors can begin to pity, detest, or fetishize Black students and operate from the erroneous and self-serving assumption that they, alone, have the Herculean responsibility and quasi-divine capability of rescuing Black students from their assumed imminent failure (Hughey, 2010).

To combat this, school counselor educators must continually implore school counseling students to recognize how they have been indoctrinated to see Black people as flawed and to employ a strengths-based approach when collaborating with community-based organizations serving and supporting Black students. By envisaging Black communities and organizations as beacons of promise and not apathetic onlookers, urban school counseling students concretize in their mind the idea that Black communities are self-sufficient and indispensable partners (Bryan & Henry, 2010). Instead of places to be pitied, school counseling students are, ideally, instructed to establish respectful relationships with urban communities that are viewed as asset-rich and not asset-depleted (Farmer-Hinton, Lewis, Patton, & Rivers, 2013).

Yosso's (2005) Community Cultural Framework

I contend that school counselor educators—as they engage in their own service-oriented, university-community collaborations—should model school-community collaboration frameworks for urban school counseling students to study and emulate in their own practice. As school counselor educators attempt to forge these partnerships, it is imperative that they recognize that Black families' pursuits of educational justice represent the continuation of an enduring legacy of organized resistance to the racial dehumanization endemic to this country (Yosso, 2005). Grounding school-community collaboration practices in this knowledge and awareness reflects an expressed mandate within counselor education and school counseling specifically to center the dispossessed in our practice as we are charged to work intentionally to eradicate dehumanizing social practices that precipitate disorder (Ratts, DeKruyf, & Chen-Hayes, 2007; Ratts, Singh, Nassar-McMillan, Butler, & McCullough, 2016). In education, supplanting the deficit-laden jargon that pathologizes Black children with an antiracist framework—one that accentuates the varied forms of cultural capital communities of color are continually reimagining—is an essential prerequisite to a transformative pedagogy that promotes the holistic development of children of color (Yosso, 2005).

Community cultural wealth, as theorized by Yosso (2005), encompasses aspirational capital, linguistic capital, familial capital, social capital, navigational capital, and resistant capital. Aspirational capital describes a persistence and refusal to relinquish one's ambitions despite having to continually traverse obstacles that can occasionally seem insurmountable. Linguistic capital entails the ability to use multiple languages and modes of veiled and subversive expression to articulate information without arousing suspicion. Familial capital refers to the information people of color derive from the complex interpersonal connections they establish and maintain with people who may or may not be biologically related. Social capital denotes the valuable information communities of color obtain through social and organizational affiliations: information that they then circulate through wider professional and community networks. Navigational capital signifies the ability to display composure, tremendous skill, and stealth "to maneuver through institutions not created with Communities of Color in mind" (Yosso, 2005, p. 80). Lastly, resistant capital reflects the corpus of radical thought and dissenting behavior communities of color have utilized to fight injustice. Yosso's (2005) community cultural wealth is premised on the belief that centering communities of color's cultural wealth helps reclaim liberatory pedagogical traditions meant to usurp the violent Anglonormative precepts that undergird how American education functions. This cloak of Anglonormative precepts, imposed from above and outside with the support and consent of the dominant White cultural group in this country, is detrimental to students of color because they devalue "all characteristics belonging to subordinated groups, characteristics that deviate from the decreed patterns" (Freire & Macedo, 2005, p. 35).

I focus on my experiences transitioning to an urban Midwestern city after accepting a tenure-track faculty position at a major flagship institution. I describe my experiences interacting with local agencies and elaborate on the various services these organizations render to better the lives of Black students and their families. I connect these experiences to my own professional identity as an urban school counselor educator who prioritizes community-based scholarship that focuses on sociopolitical power and how it is wielded to marginalize and oppress people of color, Black Americans in particular (Henfield, Washington, Bersevic, & De La Rue, 2019; Henfield, Washington, Rue, & Byrd, 2017; Washington, Goings, & Henfield, 2020).

Through this first-person narrative I disrupt and dislodge stock, deficit-laden representations of urban communities as blighted through an affirming strengths-based counternarrative that highlights the exceptional work being done in these communities. Initiating this process of disruption is also something I do inside the classroom with my school counseling students and outside the classroom with current school counselors because "many professional school counselors are of the majority race and presumably have been socialized in the same American, ethnocentric curricula and school system that disserves marginalized students" (Mitcham-Smith, 2007, p. 341).

Personal Narrative of Organic Engagement

From the very beginning of my career, community-engaged scholarship rooted in the ideals of Black consciousness and racial social justice has been integral to my school counselor educator identity. In the academy, particularly at research institutions where the quantity of publications generated determines success, purpose-driven, community-engaged scholarship is often discouraged because it requires an emic perspective achieved through community immersion and struggle (Harding, 1974). This identity, grounded in an African-centered orientation towards education and Black children, is described eloquently here by Dr. Wade Nobles (1998): "The role of culture in education means that education must be consciously guided by an awareness, understanding, and utilization of the historical conditions and cultural experiences which shape and give meaning to Black children's reality . . . Hence, placing children or centering them within the context of familiar cultural and social references, from their own historical setting, is key to fostering educational excellence" (pp. xv–xvi). Nobles's definition of education is consistent with a long-held belief that education in this country was not designed with noble or benevolent intentions to facilitate the upward advancement of dispossessed Black people who, through the processes of enslavement and legal segregation, had been systematically disallowed from participating in every conceivable facet of social and civic life (Watkins, 2001). Therefore, education in the traditional sense could not possibly function as a great equalizer as it is often romanticized because, as Carter G. Woodson poignantly stated in 1933: "The same education process which inspires and stimulates the oppressor with the thought that he is everything and has accomplished everything worthwhile, depresses and crushes at the same time the spark of genius in the Negro by making him feel that his race does not amount to much and never will measure up to the standards of other peoples. The Negro thus educated is a hopeless liability of the race" (p. 5). Black counselor educators have assigned tremendous importance to how they use their membership within the counseling profession to align themselves with Black communities. In their qualitative research study on the experiences of African American male counselor educators (AAMCE), Brooks and Steen (2010) learned that part of the appeal of becoming a counselor educator was that it afforded "many chances to perform duties that are meaningful to the individual faculty member and the community at large" (p. 147) to compensate for a general "disconnect between the academy and the community" (p. 146).

Part of my transition to my current institution involved deliberately initiating community-engaged service/research projects that were personally and professionally fulfilling, and, hopefully, socially transformative. This is something that I articulated during my initial and on-campus interviews and reiterate to graduate students post-hire.

"Don't Go West of Ninth Street . . ."

The University of Louisville is one of the major flagship institutions in the state of Kentucky. In many of the printed advertisements dispersed across campus and throughout the community, the University of Louisville is touted as a research-intensive university nestled in the heart of a large major metropolitan city. Publicly, the University of Louisville embraces the idea of being an urban university committed to ameliorating inequality in the local community through social justice community-engaged scholarship. However, as I was witnessing academic departments and programs, as well as University of Louisville faculty members, endorsing the ideals of social justice and community empowerment in their research, teaching, and service, I noticed blatant racialized and class stereotypes circulating in the larger Louisville community about the residents of West Louisville. This is exemplified in the local colloquialism "Don't go west of Ninth Street" that I heard weeks after arriving in the community.

What I have since come to learn is that "Don't go west of Ninth Street" refers to the intersection of Ninth and Broadway in Louisville's West End. Broadway is a major artery running east-west through the heart of Louisville. "Don't go west of Ninth . . ." acts as a signifier that communicates a belief that venturing west of the intersection of Ninth and Broadway might expose one to violence and other forms of "street crime." More specifically, "Don't go west of Ninth" acts as a discursive primer, or what Omi and Winant (2014) refer to as a racial project, for Whites that reinforces preexisting cognitions and emotions about biological notions of race and the relationship between race and social problems, especially the presupposed criminality and deviance that has been historically tethered to Blackness. Louisville writer Dan Cruther makes the point this way: "Most white Louisvillians know it because they've heard some variation of the warning, 'Don't go west of Ninth Street.' They might have heard it when they moved to town and were looking for a place to live, or from parents or friends concerned about their safety. Or they might have absorbed it osmotically from watching local TV news, where the lead story is too often 'another shooting in the West End'" (p. 25). Early in my first semester, one of the counselor education doctoral students, a White woman, spoke with me about traveling west of Ninth, and how she had come to learn and understand the phrase. She found the phrase sensational, degrading, and wholly inconsistent with her experiences on the West End of Louisville. Together we unpacked its meaning. We discussed how the phrase is meant to buttress essentialized racial myths about Blackness and Whiteness and stabilize preexisting lines of demarcation between the purportedly law-abiding citizens who work and live east of Ninth Street, and the residents of west Louisville who are, overwhelmingly, people of color and perpetually stigmatized as lawless, irredeemable, and, therefore, patently disposable.

This rigid bifurcation helps confer immeasurable material sociopolitical and economic benefits and advantages onto Whiteness that exacerbate social inequalities between Whites and Blacks that are a consequence of chattel enslavement, political disenfranchisement, educational segregation, job discrimination, blatant racial violence, and other forms of repression (Bell, 1992; Harris, 1993; Omi & Winant, 2014). Unbeknownst to me at the time, many of the individuals and organizations I would eventually partner with existed west of the Ninth Street divide.

Reaching Out to Community Organizations

A number of Signature Partnerships have been forged between academic programs in the College of Education at the University of Louisville and local Louisville schools and agencies. For instance, in my department the Signature Partnerships include a free mental health clinic in West Louisville (the Cardinal Success Program), and a holistic mental health delivery system that operates in a nearby high school (the Academy @Shawnee). Master's and doctoral students majoring in counseling psychology, clinical mental health, school counseling, art therapy, and counselor education obtain their training at these sites and receive supervision from faculty in the department. Additionally, throughout the academic semester, several members of the department faculty, myself included, are scheduled to teach classes at these locations on Louisville's West End. Below I highlight some of the tireless advocates working in the greater Louisville community to affirm Black children. After my arrival to the University of Louisville in 2015, I have had the pleasure of engaging with all of these individuals and their organizations to develop new programs or to revise programs already in existence.

Diversity, Equity, and Poverty Programs in Jefferson County Public Schools

Dr. John Marshall is the chief equity officer in Jefferson County Public School District. Dr. Marshall champions inclusion and educational equity for racially, ethnically, culturally, and linguistically diverse students in Louisville. I first had the pleasure of meeting John at the Louisville Urban League just a few months after getting to Louisville. John discussed his role with the district and how he works closely with teachers, administrators, school counselors, students, families, and community stakeholders to create intellectually stimulating educational environments for all students. John's passion was evident from the minute we began conversing. John spoke candidly about the work he has been doing within the district and community to bring awareness to issues of educational inequity and how these inequities can drastically alter the life outcomes for students. John talked about his deep connections to the community and his desire to see African American students thrive.

Dr. Marshall attended high school in Louisville, and his commitment to this community is apparent in his advocacy work within the district. I have heard him be a staunch critic of school disciplinary practices that, when disaggregating district data, reveal disproportionate impacts on Black students. John has presented to school board members, teachers, parents, and other community stakeholders decrying existing polities and demanding that revisions be made immediately. John's aesthetic and rhetorical styles, and frequent references to preeminent Black scholars from the past (e.g., W. E. B. Dubois and Carter G. Woodson) characterize resistant cultural capital (Yosso, 2005). Additionally, the fact he, too, attended school in Louisville and ascended to a position within the district despite racial barriers epitomizes aspirational capital (Yosso, 2005). These forms of capital are not peripheral or contrived; they are the bedrock of John's administrative and pedagogical praxis. John reminds me of how critically important it is to anchor strategies for educational equity for Black children in the insightful words and indomitable spirit of our foremothers and forefathers (Harding, 1974).

Since that initial encounter, John and I have conceptualized various projects; some we have initiated, and others are still on the horizon. John connected me with educators and school counselors to discuss critical hip-hop pedagogy (Akom, 2009) and its relevance to the contemporary K–12 environment. With John's assistance, I have been able to facilitate professional development seminars with teachers and school counselors from across the district on how they can use facets of hip-hop culture to upset and invert the standard curriculum, one that is Anglonormative not only in terms of content but also modes of delivery and implementation (Macedo, 2006). This professional development resonated with me for several profound reasons. It was held on a Friday evening at 5:30 after an exhausting workday. Nearly 25 people attended, eager to engage in a discussion on critical pedagogy and how critical discourse (and not the typical banking approach to education) was the liberatory educational praxis that Black students deserved (Freire, 2002). This anecdote, though confined to a room of fewer than 30 educators, shattered the stock story and myth of the disinterested and disaffected urban teacher. Rather than bemoaning students and parents, these teachers started to interrogate their own praxis, to examine the ways in which they are complicit in punishing Black students, and to envision ambitious partnerships with others who were also seeking to teach in a way that centers the experiences of the most marginalized students. John and these teachers, many of whom live and teach in West Louisville, obliterate the hyperbolic stories I had heard about the people there being either uninterested or incapable of nurturing the cognitive, social development, and occupational aspirations of children in the community.

URBAN LEAGUE OF LOUISVILLE

My collaborations with the Urban League of Louisville have been some of the most rewarding experiences of my professional career. Under the visionary leadership of then-president and CEO, Sadiqa Reynolds, the Urban League of Louisville is generating considerable support and enthusiasm in West Louisville. Ironically, I met Dr. John Marshall and Sadiqa Reynolds the same night at the Urban League office near 18th and Broadway. I was also introduced to Lawrence Wilbon, then director of youth development and education.

In my conversations with Sadiqa and Lawrence, I learned about all of their exceptional year-round programming specifically for elementary and secondary students attending school across the city. For instance, the Street Academy was an academic and cultural enrichment program designed for elementary and middle school students in grades four through six. Students complete homework and have access to mentors and other educational resources to help academic promotion. Project Ready was a more comprehensive program for high school students that focuses on academic enrichment, career exploration (especially science, technology, engineering, and math [STEM] fields), social skills development, goal planning and attainment, and cultural knowledge/awareness. These are flourishing programs with consistent student participation. Presently, Project Ready had nearly 150 students from across the city participating in regularly scheduled activities.

In addition to these programs, the Urban League of Louisville routinely facilitates educational presentations and seminars and hosts workshops about intellectually stimulating extracurricular activities that young people might not normally be inclined to investigate. Since I have been in Louisville, the Urban League invited renowned researcher and lecturer Dr. Ivory Toldson to speak with parents, educators, district representatives, and community stakeholders about the disproportionate number of suspensions and expulsions for students of color in the district. Additionally, the Urban League hosted a family chess night where they invited a seasoned chess player to teach the game and to discuss why exposing their children to the game as early as possible would be a wise move. Both of these events were very well attended.

Communicating These Experiences to My Students

To fully appreciate the conversations I broach with my students regarding the intersections between race, class, gender and education, it is crucial to reiterate the demographic makeup of the school counseling profession. School counseling overwhelmingly comprising White, middle-class women who, through the indoctrination they receive from the dominant socializing institutions in this country, frequently operate from an ethnocentric and paternalistic perspective with regard to people of color (Mitcham-Smith, 2007). Holcomb-McCoy (2004) argued that school counseling programs exacerbate the ethnocentrism White students exude by not providing a more comprehensive, interdisciplinary curriculum to mitigate the blatant shortcomings inherent to K–12 and undergraduate education in this country. Not surprisingly, then, many of my White students, having been socialized and oriented toward Black communities from a racist perspective, aspire to enter schools hoping to "help 'disadvantaged' students whose race and class background has left them lacking necessary knowledge, social skills, abilities and cultural capital" (Yosso, 2005, p. 70). Confronting this malignant White savior complex (Hughey, 2010) is vital in shifting the focus away from the perceived flaws of Black people and onto the pervasive systemic racism that precipitates disparate educational outcomes between students that are often ascribed to Blackness.

During my interactions with students, I seize every opportunity to communicate these experiences and stories. I challenge my students to be self-reflexive so they can develop an antiracist perspective toward Black communities and an appreciation for community-based scholarship that is done through horizontal and not hierarchal relationships. I want my students to recognize racist and deficit-based characterizations of Black communities when they hear them in social, academic, and professional settings and to defiantly push back against these narratives. I believe it is my professional responsibility to always ask how the social and political utility of race and racism operate and appear at the intersection of race and education as "achievement gaps" that work to reproduce mischaracterizations about Black children (Ladson-Billings & Tate, 1995; Ladson-Billings, 1998). Further, challenging mostly burgeoning professionals to critically interrogate their Whiteness as they prepare to work in Black spaces is nonnegotiable. Again, because the profession is dominated numerically by White, middle-class women and ideologically by White American values (Bridgeland & Bruce, 2011), challenging these burgeoning professionals demands that they understand Whiteness and develop the fortitude to push past White racial guilt and fragility (Washington & Henfield, 2019). I hope they sense my passion for organic engagement and community-based scholarship because of how fulfilling it is and decide it is something they, too, would ultimately like to do. Not only because they find it rewarding but because this work is consonant with the ideals of social justice, social advocacy and social change that should, ideally, undergird and permeate every facet of our profession and every fiber of our being.

References

Akom, A. A. (2009). Critical hip hop pedagogy as a form of liberatory praxis. *Equity & Excellence in Education, 42*(1), 52–66.

Alexander, M. (2012). *The new Jim Crow: Mass incarceration in the age of colorblindness.* New Press.

American School Counselor Association. (ASCA). (2019). *ASCA National Model: A framework for school counseling programs* (4th ed.). Author.

Anderson, C. (2016). *White rage: The unspoken truth of our racial divide.* Bloomsbury USA.

Anderson, E. (2004). The cosmopolitan canopy. *The ANNALS of the American Academy of Political and Social Science, 595*, 14–31.

Anderson, E. (2015). "The White Space." *Sociology of Race and Ethnicity, 1*, 10–21.

Bell, D. A. (1992). *Faces at the bottom of the well: The permanence of racism.* Basic Books.

Bemak, F., & Chung, R. C. Y. (2008). New professional roles and advocacy strategies for school counselors: A multicultural/social justice perspective to move beyond the nice counselor syndrome. *Journal of Counseling & Development, 86*, 372–381.

Bemak, F., & Chung, R. C. Y. (2005). Advocacy as a critical role for urban school counselors: Working toward equity and social justice. *Professional School Counseling, 8,* 196–202.

Booth, J. & Washington, A. R. (2015). Individual counseling and Black males living in urban contexts. In M. S. Henfield & A. R. Washington (Eds.), *Black male student success in the 21st century urban schools: School counseling for equity, access and achievement.* Information Age.

Bridgeland, J., & Bruce, M. (2011). 2011 National survey of school counselors: Counseling at a crossroads. *College Board Advocacy & Policy Center.*

Brooks, M., & Steen, S. (2010). 'Brother Where Art Thou?' African American male instructors' perceptions of the counselor education profession. *Journal of Multicultural Counseling and Development, 38,* 142–153.

Brown, E. (2002). *The condemnation of Lil B: New age racism in America.* Beacon Press.

Bryan, J., & Henry, L. (2010). A model for building school-family-community partnerships: Principles and process. *Journal of Counseling & Development, 90,* 408–420.

Coates, T. (2015). *Between the world and me.* Spiegel & Grau.

Dale, S., & Daniel, J. H. (2013). Talking about the Trayvon Martin case in psychology and counseling training and psychotherapy. *Journal for Social Action in Counseling and Psychology, 5,* 37–49.

Day, J. K. (2014). *The Southern manifesto: Massive resistance and the fight to preserve segregation.* University Press of Mississippi.

Day-Vines, N. L., & Day-Hairston, B. O. (2005). Culturally congruent strategies for addressing the behavioral needs of urban, African American male adolescents. *Professional School Counseling, 8,* 236–243.

Dixon, A. L., Tucker, C., & Clark, M. A. (2010). Integrating social justice advocacy with national standards of practice: Implications for school counselor education. *Counselor Education and Supervision, 50,* 103–115.

Embrick, D. G. (2015). Two nations, revisited: The lynching of Black and Brown bodies, police brutality, and racial control in 'post-racial' Amerikka. *Critical Sociology, 41,* 835–843.

Farmer-Hinton, R. L., Lewis, J. D., Patton, L. D., & Rivers, I. D. (2013). Dear Mr. Kozol . . . Four African American women scholars and the re-authoring of Savage Inequalities. *Teachers College Record, 115,* 1–38.

Feagin, J. R. (1999). Excluding Blacks and others from housing: The foundation of White racism. *Cityscape: A Journal of Policy Development and Research, 4,* 79–91.

Forman, M. (2002). *The 'hood comes first: Race, space, and place in rap and hip-hop.* Wesleyan University Press.

Freire, P. (2000). *Pedagogy of the oppressed.* Bloomsbury.

Freire, P., & Macedo, D. (2005). *Literacy: Reading the word and the world.* Routledge.

Giroux, H. A. (1984). *Ideology, culture, and the process of schooling.* Temple University Press.

Griffin, D., & Steen, S. (2011). A social justice approach to school counseling. *Journal of Social Action in Counseling and Psychology, 3,* 74–85.

Hacker, A. (2003). *Two nations: Black & White, separate, hostile, unequal.* Scribner.

Hall, L. K. (1981). Support systems and coping patterns. In L. E. Gary (Ed.), *Black men.* Sage.

Hamer, J. F. (2001). *What it means to be daddy: Fatherhood for Black men living away from their children.* Columbia University Press.

Hancock, A-M. (2004). *The politics of disgust: The public identity of the welfare queen.* New York University Press.

Harding, V. (1974). The vocation of the Black scholar and the struggles of the Black community. In Institute of the Black World (Ed.), *Education and Black struggle: Notes from the colonized world* (pp. 3–29). Harvard Educational Review Monograph 2.

Harris, C. I. (1993). Whiteness as property. *Harvard Law Review,* 1707–1791.

Henfield, M., Washington, A. R., Bersevic, Z., & De La Rue, L. (2019). Introduction to trauma-informed practices for mental health and wellness in urban schools and communities. *The Urban Review, 51,* 537–539.

Henfield, M. S., Washington, A. R., Rue, L. D. L., & Byrd, J. A. (2017). Black male school counselor educator contextual explorations in leadership. *Professional School Counseling, 21*(1b), 1–10. https://doi.org/10.1177/2156759X18773591

Hill Collins, P. (2004). *Black sexual politics: African Americans, gender, and the new racism.* Routledge.

Hipolito-Delgado, C. P., & Lee, C. C. (2007). Empowerment theory for the professional school counselor: A manifesto for what really matters. *Professional School Counseling, 10,* 327–332.

Holcomb-McCoy, C. (2004). Assessing the multicultural competence of school counselors: A checklist. *Professional School Counseling, 7,* 178–186.

Hughey, M. W. (2010). The white savior film and reviewers' reception. *Symbolic Interaction, 33*(3), 475–496.

Kena, G., Musu-Gillette, L., Robinson, J., Wang, X., Rathbun, A., Zhang, J., Wilkinson-Flicker, S., Barmer, A., & Dunlop Velez, E. (2015). *The Condition of Education 2015* (NCES 2015-144). U.S. Department of Education, National Center for Education Statistics. http://nces.ed.gov/pubsearch.

Keisch, D. M., & Scott, T. (2015). US education reform and the maintenance of White supremacy through structural violence. *Landscapes of Violence, 3,* 1–44.

King Jr., M. L. (2010). *Where do we go from here: Chaos or community?* Vol. 2. Beacon Press.

Kozol, J. (1991). *Savage inequalities: Children in America's schools.* Harper Perennial.

Ladson-Billings, G. (1998). Just what is critical race theory and what's it doing in a nice field like education? *International Journal of Qualitative Studies in Education, 11,* 7–24.

Ladson-Billings, G., & Tate, W. F. (1995). Toward a critical race theory of education. *Teachers College Record, 97*, 47–68.

Lipman, P. (2004). *High stakes education: Inequality, globalization, and urban school reform.* RoutledgeFalmer.

Macedo, D. (2006). *Literacies of power.* Westview.

Massey, D. S., & Denton, N. A. (1993). *American apartheid: Segregation and the making of the underclass.* Harvard University Press.

Moynihan. D. (1965). *The Negro family: The case for national action.* Office of Policy Planning and Research, U.S. Department of Labor.

Nobles, W. W. (1998). Foreword. In A. G. Hilliard. *SBA: The reawakening of the African mind.* Makare.

Omi, M., & Winant, H. (2014). *Racial formation in the United States* (3rd ed.). Routledge.

Ratts, M. J., DeKruyf, L., & Chen-Hayes. S. F. (2007). The ACA advocacy competencies: A social justice advocacy framework for professional school counselors. *Professional School Counseling, 11*, 90–97.

Ratts, M. J., Singh, A. A., Nassar-McMillan, S., Butler, S. K., & McCullough, J. R. (2016). Multicultural and social justice counseling competencies: Guidelines for the counseling profession. *Journal of Multicultural Counseling and Development, 44*, 28–48.

Rose, T. (2008). *Hip hop wars.* Basic Civitas Books.

Rose, T. (1994). *Black noise: Rap music and black culture in contemporary America.* Wesleyan University Press.

Shakur, A. (1987). *Assata: An autobiography.* Zed.

Tibbs, D. F. (2012). From Black power to hip hop: Discussing race, policing, and the fourth amendment through the "War on" paradigm. *Journal of Gender, Race, & Peace, 15*, 47–79.

United States. National Advisory Commission on Civil Disorders, & Kerner, O. (1968). *Report of the National Advisory Commission on Civil Disorders, March 1, 1968.* US Government Printing Office.

Washington, A. R., Goings, R. B., & Henfield, M. S. (Eds.). (2020). *Creating and sustaining effective K-12 school partnerships: Firsthand accounts of promising practices.* IAP.

Washington, A. R. (2018). Integrating hip-hop culture and rap music into social justice counseling with Black males. *Journal of Counseling & Development, 96*(1), 97–105.

Washington, A. R. & Henfield, M. S. (2019). What do the AMCD Multicultural and Social Justice Competencies mean in the context of Black Lives Matter? *Journal of Multicultural Counseling & Development, 47*, 148–160.

Woodson, C. G. (2006). *The mis-education of the Negro.* Book Tree.

Yosso, T. J. (2005). Whose culture has capital? A critical race theory discussion of community cultural wealth. *Race Ethnicity and Education, 8*, 69–91.

Guest Commentary and Reflection

There's More to the Story: Counter-Narrating Urban Failure and Success

NOELLE W. ARNOLD

In educational literature, narratives related to educational "failures" or "successes" are largely attached to cause-and-effect relationships or treated as accountability-based outcomes, which are often only a portion of the equity story (Sleeter & Banks, 2007). Urban schools bear unique issues, but these issues are complex. In this volume, Benson et al., Bean-Folkes et al., and Washington remind us that urban schools and communities are also unique and positive places with distinct histories, cultures, and sociopolitical contexts (Lightfoot, 1983; Johanek & Puckett, 2007). Moreover, these education systems are filled with a rich array of excellence, intellect, and talent in those environments.

Counter-Narrating "Urban"

Researchers, theoreticians, policymakers, and practitioners in higher education do not necessarily possess a shared definition of urban education (Milner, 2012). "People across the U.S. classify schools in different parts of the country as urban because of characteristics associated with the school and the people in them, not only based on the larger social context where the schools and districts are located" (Milner, 2012, p. 557). It is true that urban education has some connections to the people who live and attend school in that context. However, the collection of essays in this section clearly illustrate that urban contexts are not "bad." The participants in these studies and authors who write about them problematize the "essentializing" or "typologizing" of these schools and the people in them. Urban education scholar Pedro Noguera (2003) noted that "the term urban is less likely to be employed as a geographic concept . . . than as a social or cultural construct used to describe certain people and places" and that the people the term described "are relatively poor and, in many cases, non-White" (p. 23). "Current discourse and practice in education regarding [urban schools and leadership] are often framed in deficit perspectives, . . . ineffective leadership, poor test scores, underfunded school districts, lack of parental involvement, . . . plight of Black males, poor-college-going rates, and high levels of dropout" (Tillman, 2009, p. xi). These perspectives tend to ignore more imaginative and productive elements of the urban narrative.

COUNTER-NARRATING DISCOURSES OF DEFICIT

One theme of these chapters is that counter-narratives disrupt taken-for-granted discourses and master narratives surrounding success or failure of urban schools and the value of those in them. For example, in this volume, Benson et al. describe characteristics of Camden High, a so-called failing school that bears striking resemblance to schools often typified as "good" or successful schools. Good or successful schools have been described as having caring teachers (Wynne, 1981); positive school culture (Dumay, 2009); and diversity of curriculum and enrichment (Miller & Gentry, 2010). According to the authors, Camden students "recognize the value of enrichment classes and service organizations within their schools-*diversity of curriculum* [emphasis added], possess emotional attachments to their schools-*positive school culture* [emphasis added], and appreciate the support they receive from teachers and support staff-*caring teachers* [emphasis added] (p. 1). The normalizing discourses that affirm or negate particular failure and success are upended. "Accountability language, practices, social relations, and ways of valuing and thinking" (Lipman, 2004, p. 171) becomes the discourse of schools that value the languages of accountability and efficiency.

SUBVERSION

As Bean-Folkes, Brown, and Rose show, counter-narration also includes unmasking how some things deemed "good" obscure systemic and historical inequities. For instance, the chapter unmasks the city's reputation for "revitalization" and high median income as smokescreens for unemployment, underfunded schools and communities, and lack of access to services. As the authors remind us, new initiatives, programs, or schemes do not, by themselves, negate issues of racism, otherness, privilege, or marginalization or the material and symbolic conditions within which education is embedded. The authors show that true change occurs when there is access, inclusion, and voice in learning contexts. In this way the authors subvert the master narrative of "all things are equal" and highlight all the ways they are not.

The telling of a more complete story includes creative and often subversive ways individuals and groups and the people who lead them find to work around systems of inequity (Witherspoon & Taylor, 2010; Khalifa, 2013; Khalifa, Arnold, & Newcomb, 2015). Another includes correct problem identification by analyzing historical and existing oppressions that serve as foundations of inequity (Arnold, 2020; Green, 2015; Marshall & Khalifa, 2018). Still others include interrogating existing structures of promoting and "measuring" success or failure that may be inadvertently grounded in deficit models or blame individuals or groups for their inequity (Braaton, et al., 2017; Green 2017; Khalifa, Douglas, & Chambers, 2017; Young & Arnold, 2020).

Strengths-Based Approaches for Teaching and Learning

Strengths-based approaches concentrate on the inherent strengths of individuals, families, groups and organizations, deploying personal strengths to aid recovery and empowerment. In essence, educational "success" must embrace an asset-based approach where the goal is to promote the positive. In community development, the term "asset-based" is used to describe communities as areas of potential rather than areas that are lacking (Kretzmann & McKnight, 1993). There is emerging evidence of the use of strengths-based approaches with children, young people, and families. The literature has identified an association between personal strengths in young people and academic success, self-determination, and life satisfaction (Park & Peterson, 2006). At the core of the strengths-based education is the underlying belief that there is much more potential for growth-building on strengths rather than fixing weaknesses. Our goal is to train educators and those who work with schools to become educators in and promoters of assets rather than deficiencies.

Dignity

Former secretary of education Arnie Duncan stated, "If we want to maintain the trust of parents and communities in our schools, we must start by treating our children with respect and human dignity." Dignity is an essential human condition, defined as self-respect, a sense of pride in oneself, and being worthy of respect by others. One concern for educators is how to work with communities where students learn and live in spaces and places where they experience multiple assaults to their sense of dignity (Witherspoon & Taylor, 2010).

Schools too often represent as exclusionary places with a wide gap between espoused values and goals of the school and actual values and goals that "act out" that mission (Howell, Kirk-Brown, & Cooper, 2012). Senge (2006) said that core values and missions are only helpful when translated into concrete behaviors. Irby et al. (2015) described dignity work as "a body or research, policy, and practice that centers on dignity as its guiding principle and as an indicator of success" (p. 6). Reflecting on this statement, we posit that inclusion is produced by treating others as human beings, no matter their state, condition, or behavior. Irby and colleagues say there must be "intentional efforts to understand and eliminate all subjective experiences and conditions of oppression, humiliation, and degradation" (p. 7). Irby reminds us that although inherent dignity is inviolable and cannot be stripped, a person's sense of dignity can. We must address dehumanization at personal, systemic, and institutional levels.

The Dignity in Schools Campaign (2013) published a revised *Model Code on Education and Dignity*. While their work was specifically in response to zero tolerance policies in schools, their principles have some important implications for inclusive leaders. The Model Code is organized into five major parts that include a commitment to (1) education, (2) participation, (3) dignity, (4) freedom from discrimination, and (5) monitoring and accountability. For educators this might include educating around marginalizing issues, incorporating dignity as an explicit value and goal, creating antidiscriminatory policies and practices, and monitoring progress on dignity and holding one another accountable when we fail to do so.

VOICE AND CONTEXT MATTERS

The heuristics we use to understand educational inequity will shape how we go about assessing or ameliorating inequity. Success or failure metrics are "not discourse-neutral and serve to entrap certain students and individuals in certain tracts, hierarchies and other hegemonic processes" (Arnold & Crawford, 2014, p. 257). "Accountability language, practices, social relations, and ways of valuing and thinking" (Lipman, 2004, p. 171) is the discourse of schools. It is important to understand when "efforts may exacerbate rather than ameliorate inequality if institutions have not modified policies and procedures nor prepared the institutional culture and climate to support them" (Arnold, Crawford, & Khalifa, 2016, p. 891). Dismantling inequity and its practices requires a different set of commitments by individual institutions and the broader collective. Organizations should collaborate with those faced with historical and existing inequities to construct policies, plans, and practices to imagine and create equity. Typically, the conversation concerning urban education is manipulated by those furthest removed from the experience. Those from primarily privileged positions pontificate on the matter, yet they too often neglect to authentically engage students (Friend & Caruthers, 2012). Policies, plans, and practices are created by those who are unaffected by inequitable practices (Bailey, Bailey, Green, & Johnson, 2015). However, Washington's essay reveals the promise of engaging with schools, communities, organizations, and leaders. He shares how such collaborations between these entities were particularly beneficial because he could incorporate these interactions into the university classroom to better prepare students to engage in partnerships.

If our schools are to be different, the preparation of those who work in them must also be different. Considering context in education can shed new light on existing and taken-for-granted practices in education (Ferrare & Apple, 2010). Those who prize education "need capacities for and skills in engaging others' voices with an intent to understand, to learn, and to use this knowledge to design more responsive educational systems for children and the families they serve" (Larson & Ovando, 2001, p. 215). They must be able to consider context as "both physical and metaphorical, as locations for inclusion, acceptance, and respect, or alternately as locations for marginalization, exclusion, and despair" (Shields & Sayani, 2005, p. 385).

Discussion Questions

1. How do current metrics of equity exacerbate inequities?
2. How can equity metrics be adapted (or embedded) in the future to enhance the development of equity-centered schools?
3. What are systemic and historical issues of inequity and how might these factor into school rankings?

Additional Readings

Dahill-Brown, S. E. (2019). *Education, equity, and the states: How variations in state governance make or break reform*. Harvard Education Press.
Grant, M. C. (2018). Equity, equality, and reform in contemporary public education: Equity, equality, and reform. In M. C. Grant (Ed.), *Equity, Equality, and Reform in Contemporary Public Education* (pp. 1–30). IGI Global.
Lewis, A. E., & Diamond, J. B. (2015). *Despite the best intentions: How racial inequality thrives in good schools*. Oxford University Press.
Ling, T., & Nasri, N. M. (2019). A systematic review: Issues on equity in education. *Creative Education, 10*(12), 2151–4755.
Rosiek, J., & Kinslow, K. (2016). *Resegregation as curriculum: The meaning of the new racial segregation in U.S. public schools*. Routledge.
The National Equity Project. https://nationalequityproject.org/
Woodson, A. N., & Love, B. L. (2019). Outstanding: Centering Black kids' enoughness in civic education research. *Multicultural Perspectives, 21*(2), 91–96.

References

Arnold, N. W. (2020). Place-based leadership. In R. Papa (Ed.), *Oxford research encyclopedia of education*. Oxford University Press.
Arnold, N. W., & Crawford, E. R. (2014). Metaphors of leadership and spatialized practice. *International Journal of Leadership in Education, 17*(3), 257–285.

Arnold, N. W., Crawford, E. R., & Khalifa, M. (2016). Psychological heuristics and faculty of color: Racial battle fatigue and tenure/promotion. *The Journal of Higher Education, 87*(6), 890–919.

Bailey, M., Bailey, V., Green, K., & Johnson, K. (2015). *Dismantling the ivory tower.* Allied Media Projects.

Braaten, M., Bradford, C., Kirchgasler, K. L. & Barocas, S. F. (2017). How data use for accountability undermines equitable science education. *Journal of Educational Administration, 55*(4), 427–446.

Burr, K. H. (2018). Separate but (un)equal: A review of re-segregation as curriculum: The meaning of the new racial segregation in US public schools. *The Qualitative Report, 23*(7), 1773–1776.

Dignity in Schools Campaign & United States of America. (2013). *Model code on education and dignity: Presenting a human rights framework for schools.* US Department of Justice Office of Justice Programs.

Dumay, X. (2009). Origins and consequences of schools' organizational culture for student achievement. *Educational Administration Quarterly, 45*(4), 523–555.

Ferrare, J. J., & Apple, M. W. (2010). Spatializing critical education: Progress and cautions. *Critical Studies in Education, 51*(2), 209–221.

Friend, J., & Caruthers, L. (2012). Reconstructing the cultural context of urban schools: Listening to the voices of high school students. *Educational Studies, 48*(4), 366–388.

Green, T. L. (2015). Places of inequality, places of possibility: Mapping 'opportunity in geography' across urban school-communities. *The Urban Review, 47*(4), 717–741.

Howell, A., Kirk-Brown, A., & Cooper, B. K. (2012). Does congruence between espoused and enacted organizational values predict affective commitment in Australian organizations? *The International Journal of Human Resource Management, 23*(4), 731–747.

Irby, D. (2015, June 30). Shaping a cooperative vision for boys and men of color. *Research Project Update Report Dignity-Based BMOC Work: What it is and why it matters for our boys and men of color.* University of Wisconsin–Milwaukee.

Johanek, M. C., & Puckett, J. L. (2007). *Leonard Covello and the making of Benjamin Franklin High School: Education as if citizenship mattered.* Temple University Press.

Khalifa, M. (2013). Promoting our students: Examining the role of school leadership in the self-advocacy of at-risk students. *Journal of School Leadership, 23*(5), 751–788.

Khalifa, M., Arnold, N. W., & Newcomb, W. (2015). Understand and advocate for communities first. *Phi Delta Kappan, 96*(7), 20–25.

Khalifa, M. A., Douglas, T. R. M., & Chambers, T. T. (2016). White gazes of black Detroit: *Milliken v. Bradley I*, postcolonial theory, and persistent inequalities. *Teachers College Record, 118*(3), 1–34.

Kretzmann, J. P., & McKnight, J. (1993). *Building communities from the inside out.* Center for Urban Affairs and Policy Research, Neighborhood Innovations Network.

Larson, C. L., & Ovando, C. J. (2001). *The color of bureaucracy: The politics of equity in multicultural school communities.* Taylor and Francis.

Lightfoot, S. l. (1983). *The good high school: Portraits of character and culture.* Basic Books.

Lipman, P. (2004). *High stakes education: Inequality, globalization, and urban school reform.* Psychology Press.

Miller, R., & Gentry, M. (2010). Developing talents among high-potential students from low-income families in an out-of-school enrichment program. *Journal of Advanced Academics, 21*(4), 594–627.

Milner, H. R. (2012). But what is urban education? *Urban Education, 47*(3), 556–561.

Noguera, P. (2003). *City schools and the American dream: Reclaiming the promise of public education.* Teachers College Press.

Noguera, J., & Noguera, P. (2018). Equity through mutual accountability. *The Learning Professional, 39*(5), 44–52.

Oztok, M. (2013). *The hidden curriculum of online learning: discourses of whiteness, social absence, and inequity* (Unpublished doctoral dissertation, University of Toronto).

Park, N., & Peterson, C. (2006). Moral competence and character strengths among adolescents: The development and validation of the Values in Action Inventory of Strengths for Youth. *Journal of Adolescence, 29*(6), 891–909.

Senge, P. M. (2006). *The fifth discipline: The art and practice of the learning organization* (Rev. ed.). Currency Doubleday.

Shields, C. M., & Sayani, A. (2005). Leading in the midst of diversity: The challenge of our times. In F. English (Ed.), *The SAGE handbook of educational leadership* (pp. 380–402). SAGE.

Sleeter, C. E., & Banks, J. A. (2007). *Facing accountability in education: Democracy and equity at risk.* Teachers College Press.

Tillman, L. C. (2009). African American principals and the legacy of Brown. In F. W. English (Ed.), *Educational Leadership and Administration, 4*(57), 1–48. SAGE.

Witherspoon, N., & Taylor, D. (2010). Spiritual W.E.A.P.O.N.S: Black female principals and religio-spirituality. *Journal of Educational Administration and History, 42*(2), 133–158.

Wynne, E. A. (1981). Looking at good schools. *The Phi Delta Kappan, 62*(5), 377–381.

Young, M., & Arnold, N. W. (2020). Inclusive leadership. In R. Papa (Ed.), *Oxford Encyclopedia of Educational Administration.* Oxford University Press.

Part 4

Reflections on Educator and Institutional Influences (Educators)

Chapter 10

Fictive Kin as Driving Forces for Academic Success in Detroit

Black Women's Narratives on
Successfully Navigating through College

DIANE FUSELIER-THOMPSON, EZELLA MCPHERSON,
AND CARLY BRAXTON

Introduction

In *Savage Inequalities: Children in America's Schools,* Kozol (1991) suggests students from inner cities (e.g., Detroit, East St. Louis, Chicago, San Antonio, New York, New Jersey) are less likely to succeed. He claims this is due to the public education system's lack of educational resources, which includes a paucity of teachers, updated facilities, financial resources, and books and materials comparable to the resources found in suburban schools. Analyzing our personal experiences through Yosso's (2005) community cultural wealth model and Fordham's (1988) fictive kin concept, we counter Kozol's assessment of urban education in Detroit, Michigan. In our predominantly minority communities, social and cultural capital, school-based fictive kin[1], and community members provide support for Black youth's academic foundations, including preparation for academic success at the country's top institutions of higher learning. Yet little is known about the informal networks, familial capital, or fictive kin who support the educational trajectory of success for Black students in Detroit's K–16 settings. Detroit residents demonstrate a love not only for their city but also for building strong neighborhoods and communities (Clark, 2014). According to Yosso (2005), "Familial capital engages a commitment to community well-being and expands the concepts of family to include a broader understanding of kinship. It is from these kinship ties that individuals learn the importance of maintaining a healthy connection to their community and resources" (p. 79). This concept of kinship extends to the sharing of educational resources through informal networks in the community. Similar to other urban and metropolitan cities, Detroit residents have a history of combining community resources to support each other in neighborhoods and community spaces. These resources extend to supporting college-going behavior and contribute to a successful educational trajectory for many first-generation minority college students.

Some educational research has focused on deficit factors (e.g., living in poverty and single-parent homes) that contribute to the academic failure of minority students from urban communities who pursue postsecondary aspirations and have low expectations (Kozol, 1991; Wyner, Bridgeland, & Dilulio, 2007). Other scholars have written about high-achieving students from urban areas who face financial, social, and/or academic challenges in K–16 settings (Trent & St. John, 2008; Wight, Chau, Thampi, & Aratani, 2010) who have few expectations for postsecondary education. However, some students from urban public K–12 schools exhibit personal resilience and perform well in school despite obstacles in their personal lives or community (McPherson, 2014a, 2017; Moore, 2014; Moore, 2010). Thus far, few studies have examined minority urban communities from a strengths-based perspective. One example is the identification of fictive kin who support Black women who pursue postsecondary education (McPherson, 2012; Tickles & McPherson, 2016). The purpose of this manuscript is to provide first-person counter-narratives centered on the lived experiences of three college-educated Black women from predominantly minority communities in the city of Detroit. Their experiences include their formal and informal networks of college preparation, access to fictive kin, and the familial and cultural capital that contributed to their educational successes.

Support Networks for Blacks

FAMILY SUPPORT

Many Black parents have historically advocated on behalf of their children pursuing both a high school education and a college education (Harris, 1970; Wilson & Allen, 1987). In this context, many Black families serve as the backbone of support for their college-aged children. Black families provide emotional (e.g., praise and encouragement), financial, and academic support for Black collegians, including those of the first generation (Guiffrida, 2005; Palmer, Davis, & Maramba, 2011). Black parents also teach their college-aged children to be resilient in order to facilitate completing college despite adversities they face on college campuses and/ or in their personal lives.

Few studies have disaggregated the data in order to better understand family support experiences among Black collegians based on race and gender. Palmer et al. (2011) examines the impact of family support on the college persistence of Black men from an urban area and found that Black men's families shared information about their college experiences. Their immediate families and extended families (e.g., grandparents) motivated them to succeed despite obstacles. Scholars who completed studies on the role of family support for Black women in college (Banks, 2009; McPherson, 2012; Watkins, 2009) found that Black parents provided financial and/ or academic support for their daughters. Moving beyond genetic family support, studies have examined the role of peer fictive kin in supporting Black female college students' retention and graduation (Banks, 2009; McPherson, 2012; Tickles & McPherson, 2016). These studies found that fictive kin who were peers, mother figures, and/or mentors supported the psychological, emotional, academic, and/or social successes or challenges that Black women faced during their college experiences.

PEER SUPPORT

Black peers influence each other's ability to graduate from high school and persist in college (Marsh, Chaney, & Jones, 2012; McPherson, 2014b; Palmer & Gasman, 2008; Tickles & McPherson, 2016). Black students who participated in informal social networks were more likely to be more engaged socially and academically in high school and/or college than peers who lacked those networks. Black female peers provided each other with the emotional support that encouraged them to pursue their educational goals, despite obstacles they encountered during their educational journeys. Thus, Black female peers become their sisters' keepers by ensuring they crossed the finish line and made it to graduation.

COMMUNITY RESOURCES

In addition to peer support, the use of community resources is important for understanding the success of Black collegians. In high school and college, Black students rely on community resources or fictive kin to provide them with information on college admissions and how to succeed academically. In high school, fictive kin comprises a broader community which could include neighbors, teachers, peer counselors, and/or school counselors who provide Black students with information about the college application process and how to fund college, including filling out college scholarship applications and the Free Application for Federal Student Aid (FAFSA) (Freeman, 1997; McPherson, 2012; Tierney & Venegas, 2006). In college, peer mentors, mentors, college counselors, faculty members, and/or administrators serve as fictive kin who provide information about how to become successful college students through use of campus resources, studying, and managing time (Tickles & McPherson, 2016). In the next section, we develop a model of the retention conceptual framework that merges fictive kin with social capital.

Retention Conceptual Framework

In the transition from high school to college, vital information gets passed along to students about college access, academic preparation, college success, and cultural norms (Tinto, 2012). This knowledge is also known as social capital. Social capital brings together people (e.g., community resources, peers, organizations) by providing resources through social networks inside and outside of organizations (Yosso, 2005). However, social capital in predominantly minority urban areas will differ from those of majority affluent communities. In urban areas, Black collegians have used social capital in the form of fictive kin, meaning pseudo-families that include mentors, peers, and community members (Banks, 2009; McPherson, 2012;

Fictive Kin as Driving Forces for Academic Success in Detroit | 175

Tickles & McPherson, 2016) to increase their knowledge of and about the college-going process.

Through mentorship that can originate through fictive kin ties, resilience also accounts for Black students being successful despite obstacles (McPherson, 2012; Tickles & McPherson, 2016). Walsh (1998) defines resilience as "the capacity to rebound from adversity strengthened and more resourceful" (p. 4). The framework of resiliency "is based on the conviction that both individual and family strength can be forged through collaborative efforts to deal with sudden crisis or prolonged adversity" (Walsh, 1998, p. 3). In order to better understand our educational successes, we developed a student retention framework that combines fictive kin support, peer support, and community resources that contributed to academic retention, persistence, and graduation from college (see Figure 10.1).

The conceptual framework shown in Figure 10.1 depicts the intersections of concepts that constitute the retention framework with the overlapping forms of support, including fictive kin, peers, and community resources. This chapter fills a gap in the literature by employing the retention framework to examine the authors' narratives, the narrative of the three Black women from Detroit, lived experiences of how fictive kin contributed to our educational trajectories, retention, and graduation from college.

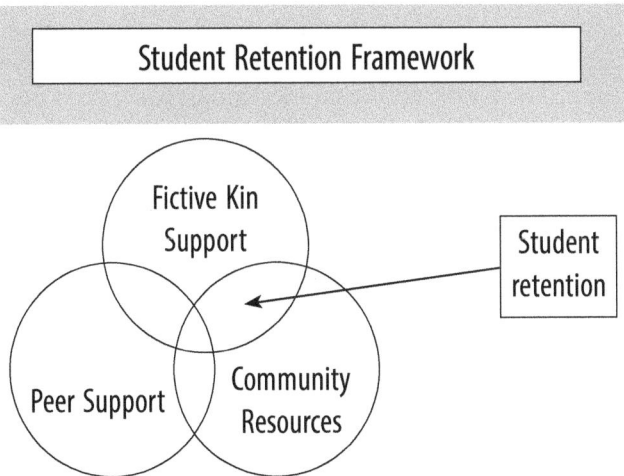

Figure 10.1. Retention Framework. Credit: Diane Fuselier-Thompson, Ezella McPherson, and Carly Braxton.

Research Methods

The purpose of this chapter is to provide first-person counter-narratives centered on the access the authors and the three Black women enjoyed by having fictive kin and social capital that contributed to their educational successes. By employing the retention framework, we share lived experiences about the role of our fictive kin in our academic successes, despite obstacles during college. This study answers the question: How did your fictive kin support your retention and graduation? In other words, how did your access to formal and informal networks in your predominantly minority community support you academically, financially, and socially in college? The narrative analysis research method was used to answer this question.

Criteria for participation. Participants had to identify as a Black woman from a predominantly minority community in the city of Detroit and college completion with at least a bachelor's degree.

Narrative analysis. Narrative analysis gathers data that is useful for "oral, first-person accounts of experience" (Riessman, 1993, p. 69). The main point of personal narratives does not involve generalization but rather obtaining a better understanding of a storyteller's lived experiences. Ellis and Bochner (2000) add that personal narratives usually center on a "single case" that may elicit an emotional response to a traumatic experience (p. 744).

Data collection methods. Personal narratives were used by the authors to share K–12 and postsecondary school experiences, also characterized as K–16. The stories are recollections of pivotal experiences in our educational histories from memories and/or journal entries.

Data analysis procedures. We utilized open coding as a data analysis technique in order to organize and interpret our data. Open coding allows us to examine recurrent themes from the written narratives (Ryan & Bernard, 2000). We placed the narratives in an analytic matrix in order to further analyze and interpret the data. The interpretive approach is appropriate for understanding the meaning of a storyteller's experiences (Riessman, 1993). The next section employs the retention framework to report the findings of the study.

Findings on Family Backgrounds and Neighborhood Contexts

Neighborhoods and communities provide the context for success or failure. In urban areas, some Black women encounter barriers when pursuing K–16 schooling due to their family backgrounds and neighborhood contexts. Remaining in our old neighborhoods would certainly have changed our K–16 and career trajectories. In this section, we briefly describe our family backgrounds and neighborhood contexts to help our readers understand how our backgrounds shaped our later college experiences and educational opportunities.

> **Diane:** My father came to Detroit at age seven and attended Detroit Public Schools throughout his education. He graduated from Cooley High School with a full scholarship to attend Wayne State University but declined the offer of admission to go into the U.S. Navy. My mother graduated from a small Catholic "Negro" high school in Opelousas, Louisiana. I was born and raised in Detroit and attended public school until seventh grade. I subsequently attended a Catholic grade school and all-girls Catholic high school in the City of Detroit. I completed high school at the top of my class and a semester earlier than my graduating class. While both of my parents graduated from high school, neither could advise me on the college application process, paying for college, and the challenges that awaited me in higher education. My maternal grandmother who could not read or write was my greatest inspiration to succeed in college. After second grade, my family moved to the University District area of Detroit, which was a very diverse mixture of well-educated residents. Interestingly enough, my old neighborhood was east of a university, and my new neighborhood was just west of the same university. Property values were distinctively different, and residents were much more affluent in the University District. My family's move created a much different fictive kin social network. The middle-class values and diversity of my neighborhood was the exposure that shaped my worldview and expectations for college. My neighbors were well educated and included a lawyer, a judge, a dentist, Ford and General Motors executives, and a Detroit City council member. The exposure to these people provided me [with] insights into the kind of education and experiences that were necessary to achieve their stature. In my new neighborhood, everyone spoke about college after high school as if it was an expectation not an option. This was new terrain for me because no one in my family had attended college. The expectations in social gatherings

in the University District were undoubtedly about the college you aspired to attend and identifying strategic neighborhood contacts to match your career aspirations. My new neighbors offered a wealth of resources about colleges and strategies for achieving college goals, including neighborhood alum, who could serve as social and cultural capital in my college quest.

Ezella: My paternal grandmother was born, lived, went to school, and died in Detroit in October of 2004. My father was born and raised in Detroit. He graduated from Frank Cody High School, which at the time had a predominantly White student population. He dropped out of Cuyahoga Community College in Cleveland, Ohio. My mother was born in Los Angeles, California. She was the first person in her immediate family to earn a high school diploma, graduating from Columbus, Ohio's Franklin Heights High School, which had a predominantly Black population. While our family lineage is rooted in the city, my sister and I are considered "city girls" who just happened to grow up in a working-class family in Norman, Oklahoma. We lived in low-income housing in Norman. When we first moved to Norman, we lived in Kings Gate, considered "the projects." We changed apartments several times throughout our K–12 education.

Carly: My mother and father were born and raised in Detroit and are products of the Detroit Public School system. My mother attended Cass Technical High School, and my father attended Southwestern High School. When my parents were tasked with deciding what school their children would attend, the decision was not as simple as choosing the closest neighborhood school. Our neighborhood was an area characterized by blight, poverty, drugs, and violence. However, due to my parents, grandparents, and aunts and uncles' sheltering, I wasn't fully exposed to the perils that seemed almost unavoidable for those who lacked family support or for those bound by the ignorance of their provinciality. At the risk of sounding cliché, it truly took a village to ensure that my sisters and I did not succumb to the environment around us.

These neighborhood and family contexts provide some insight into our backgrounds and could have served as barriers to our educational success. Under deficit models, such as those of Kozol (1991) or MacLeod (2009), our childhood neighborhoods and family backgrounds should have put us in a position of failure or dropping out because we were "never supposed to make it in school."

Findings on Fictive Kin and Social Capital

As a form of social capital, fictive kin in minority urban communities are instrumental in supporting the academic, social, and life issues for Black female college students. This section describes the role of fictive kin in supporting us academically, financially, and emotionally through college challenges.

ACADEMIC SUPPORT

Our fictive kin supported us academically by helping us find and use safe and positive spaces to pursue academics in a strict scholastic and family environment centered on using institutional resources.

> **Ezella:** In college, I always had an informal network of community support, including supervisors, coworkers, mentors, peers, and professors. However, I was intimidated during my first term at University of Michigan because I was involved with *smart* peers. I grew up in Norman, Oklahoma, which I like to call the South. Due to the racist views in the South, Blacks were deemed to be *less smart* than Whites. Since I had not taken any advanced placement or honors classes like many of my college peers, I relied on my sister-friends (or rather fictive kin) to teach me about how to be a successful college student with regard to reading texts, preparing for college exams, and even writing strong college papers with the support of professors. Luckily, my sisters embraced the use of campus resources such as the Sweetland Writing Center, tutoring, and attending professors' office hours. If we had questions about assignments, needed to review past exams, or needed support for our classes, the resources to help us were available. After our

freshmen year, we studied together inside the dorms or even in our apartments. Our motto was "friends who study together will graduate together." Needless to say, we all graduated from the University of Michigan with bachelor's degrees.

Carly: There were upper classmen serving as peer mentors who lived in the living-learning community I was housed in at Central Michigan University; they were also Multicultural Advancement/Cofer Scholars (MAC Scholars) who had been academically successful. I did not perform well my first semester in college; I received an overall GPA of 2.33, the lowest I had ever received in my life. Though I was academically prepared and didn't find my college work difficult, my issue was that I lacked self-management skills. Once I started to explore campus and find my place, I wanted to get involved in everything. My involvement was at the expense of my class attendance. In order to maintain my scholarship, I needed to keep a minimum 2.5 GPA. As fictive kin, my peer mentors called me into a meeting and reminded me that I could lose my scholarship if I didn't bring my grades up. They also provided me with tools and resources to ensure that I could get back on track academically. This was a pivotal moment in my college-going experience. I became focused, began to utilize campus resources (such as academic advisors), and became serious about learning how to manage my time and how to study. This moment of academic adversity and the admonishment I received from my peer mentors proved to be the catalyst for developing the foundation I needed to be successful and graduate.

Diane: My African American academic advisor recognized early that I was a first-generation student and the support I needed to navigate a large PWI. He guided my academic trajectory, even while pledging a sorority, and remained with me until graduation in four years with a double major.

Our narratives suggest we had family support through fictive kin in K–16 settings that helped us successfully navigate high school and college environments. Similar to prior research on the Black family structure (Banks, 2009; Guiffrida, 2005; Palmer, Davis, & Maramaba, 2005; Watkins, 2009), our fictive kin supported us by providing us with academic support and encouraged us to be resilient by holding us accountable.

FINANCIAL SUPPORT

In addition to academic support, our fictive kin provided us with financial support, which was crucial in helping us to afford college.

> **Diane:** Throughout junior high school, I was known throughout the neighborhood as a very responsible babysitter, providing services for three to five families while attending school. By the time I began attending high school, I was working every day after school at a daycare center and babysitting. Our neighbors knew that I was college bound, and I was able to pay all of my application and college exam fees using my earnings, as well as have savings for some college expenses. In addition, neighbors and family provided money to help with college costs before I left for school and periodically once I arrived in Ann Arbor. During college I looked forward to receiving $5 cash in the mail, an annual dinner at the Gandy Dancer, and receiving a $100 bill from a longtime family friend. While these occasional financial "hits" were great, my work-study position in the Office of Financial Aid provided the true insight into the network I needed for financial sustainability in college. It was great to have my fictive kin, which were known to me prior to college, provide periodic financial support and to expand my network of fictive kin within the context of the university environment. This provided the resources I needed to sustain the completion of my college education.

> **Ezella:** My informal mentoring relationships were important because during my trials and tragedies in college, I spoke with them, and they kept me grounded. My work family (Susan, Dan, Jackie) at the University of Michigan–Ann Arbor Office of Student Activities and Leadership understood when I had low energy, so they would not push me too hard during those times. They allowed me to work and study. They even gave us work-study students our own desks. That definitely made me feel like I had a place and a space at the university. So, it

contributed to my sense of belonging at the university as well. It was great they that also wanted to retain us (another Black woman and me) at work and school by funding us through work-study programs for all four years from our freshman year until we graduated.

During the spring before my senior year of college, I had a conversation with my pseudo-mama, U of M Vice President for Student Affairs E. Royster Harper regarding funding my education. I let her know that I struggled to pay for college; I was behind with credits due to life's issues. I was also missing a scholarship on my student account. With her political power at the university, she advocated for me, an out-of-state student, to continue to receive work-study funds during the summer between my junior and senior year. I needed the funding to attend summer school in order to graduate on time since I had withdrawn from a few classes for personal reasons. I successfully passed all of my summer classes and finished my bachelor's degree in four years all due to the financial support of my fictive kin.

As the narratives suggest, similar to that of prior research (Banks, 2009, McPherson, 2012, Watkins, 2009) on the Black family structure (meaning Black parents paying for college for their daughters), our fictive kin provided us with financial support that allowed us to pay for college and subsequently graduate.

Life Issues

When we experienced life issues, our fictive kin sisters were our *sisters' keepers* throughout our college experiences. We also held each other accountable so that we could walk across the graduation stage together. Below are some stories to show how we supported each other.

Diane: There were four classmates who joined me at the University of Michigan in the Fall term. I had already spent a Winter and Summer term on campus and gave them the campus tour to help with their adjustment. There was no summer bridge program; it was just me identifying the resources and sharing the informal knowledge of the campus. Some of my classmates had college-educated parents, but they couldn't assist them on this large campus with all of the systems needed to function in the first year. We initially studied together, and then as we entered different majors, we became a support group (although we didn't call it that at the time). There were tears, frustration, and opportunities to be heard by our peers, and we would return to our respective residence halls feeling better about the daily challenges we faced in college. These ladies were from my neighborhood schools and fictive kin network and provided the support to let me know *I was not alone* in this journey. Four years later, we would graduate together. Since I had arrived a semester early, I was able to complete a double major and graduate with these ladies, some of whom I had shared 8th grade, 12th grade, and now college graduation celebrations with.

Ezella: I was very comfortable with my college friends. We were our sisters' keepers during life's struggles, ranging from parental support, to peers and family members dropping out of college, roommate conflicts, sibling childbirths, deaths, and even academic failure during the college journey at the University of Michigan. We laughed together, cried together, prayed for each other, and experienced trials, triumphs, and even tragedies together. If a friend was in crisis, then we stayed up to the early hours of the morning (between 2 a.m. to 4 a.m.) to listen, soothe, comfort, and offer advice to our friends in-person or over the phone through a two- or three-way phone conversation. Without my sisters I would have never made it through college, let alone graduate school. We held each other accountable from new student convocation to graduation!

Carly: I found a strong sense of peer support among my best friends from high school. Even at a young age we had experienced so much together and had always been there for one another through personal crisis to celebratory occasions. Transitioning from high school to college, I was initially unsure if I would find my place on Central Michigan University's (CMU) campus. I was still very connected to the relationships I had with my best friends (we all went to separate institutions). I was unsure if I would make new friends.

Fortunately, I clicked with my college roommate and my next-door neighbor (both Black women) and we became inseparable. We referred to ourselves as the "Big Three." We were all housed in the same residence hall because we were a part of a living-learning community due to the scholarships we received: the Multicultural Advancement/Cofer Scholars (MAC Scholars). Beyond required scholarship activities, we studied together, hung out, joined student organizations, and met new people. It was through this relationship that I found my place at CMU, which ultimately made it easier to persist toward graduation. Though the "Big Three" didn't remain as close throughout our entire undergraduate experience, we all graduated from Central Michigan University within four years.

Community Support

Finally, our fictive kin provided us with community support that was crucial to providing us with information to obtain access to college and later succeed by navigating the college environment.

Diane: One of the ladies with whom I babysat told me she was starting a daycare center around the time I began high school and wanted me to work there. During my four years of high school, I managed a nursery school in the neighborhood, developing curricula, supervising children, and managing a budget. These experiences would later prepare me for my college experience and later my administrative role in higher education. At the time, my employer was working on her master's degree at the University of Michigan and took me along with her on the ride to Ann Arbor. While she was in class, she handed me a campus map with several offices to visit (admissions, financial aid, etc.), all of which were essential to the college-going process. I had never visited a college campus before that time and did not know about the admissions process. I was accepted into the University of Michigan in December, one semester before my high school graduation. The principal would later waive a religion requirement so that I could begin college in January. As I write this paper, I am reminded that I have friends on Facebook who attended my grade school, junior high, high school, and/or attended the University of Michigan with me. We have either remained in contact through social circles or reconnected after all of these years, returning to our hometown of Detroit. It was something about the sense of "community" within our neighborhood and school that kept us motivated and connected through the years. The irony is that within our community of fictive kin, many of my friends seek me out to understand the college-going process and college selection for their children.

Ezella: One of the first community resources that set me up for success was Black college students who attended the University of Oklahoma. They tutored my Black peers in English, math, and science at Irving Middle School. One day a friend mentioned that I should join the group to study for classes in seventh grade. I graciously accepted the offer. It was an amazing experience to see role models who were in a position I wanted to be in: a college student. They encouraged us to use resources in middle school, including going to their tutoring sessions after school or going to instructors' free periods during the lunch hour or after school. These resources significantly impacted my educational trajectory because I was never afraid to ask for help if it meant succeeding in my studies from middle school throughout undergraduate and even graduate school. We also obtained a small glimpse of college life as well. These experiences made me encourage my U of M peers to volunteer as tutors at Detroit's Salvation Army Community Center during our freshman year.

Carly: In transitioning to Central Michigan University, I was dealing with the culture shock of being a Black girl from Detroit, someone who had spent most of her life around Black people, to now attending this predominantly White institution and moving to a predominately White community. This was an intimidating change for me. Even with finding support within the friends I had acquired, I still had a difficult time navigating the "outside world." Beyond providing academic and financial support, I found a tremendous sense of community through the MAC Scholars program. MAC Scholars were encouraged to be advocates for diversity and inclusion on campus. I was able to participate in various events, lectures, discussions, and community-building activities that exposed me to not only people from diverse backgrounds, but I also gained a deeper understanding of the importance of diversity and appreciating the differences of others. I also developed a strong sense of self pride and appreciation for the various identities I possessed. Participating in the MAC Scholars program helped to ease the social anxiety I felt around being the "other." My MAC Scholar experience was instrumental to my acclimation to the campus environment, as well as my success as a student.

Consistent with past research on fictive kin (McPherson, 2012; Tickles & McPherson, 2016) and Black families' support of their daughters' college educations (Banks, 2009; Watkins, 2009), the authors' personal narratives suggest fictive kin are important in helping Black women understand college expectations regarding the use of campus resources (e.g., tutoring). Fictive kin also helped Black women obtain financial support to pay for college and taught them how to give back through community service participation.

Discussion, Conclusion, and Implications for Future Research

For each of us, the support of fictive kin provided us with academic, financial, social, campus, and community resources that helped us navigate barriers related to academic preparation, financial issues, and life issues (Banks, 2009; Guiffrida, 2005; Harris, 1970; Palmer et al., 2011; McPherson, 2012; Watkins, 2009). Using narrative experiences to understand how fictive kin contributes to academic success can provide useful information for K–20 practitioners for developing institutional programs identify formal and informal networks that support Black women's access to college and successful matriculation. Additional research in the area of resilience, social capital, social networks, and community cultural wealth may be helpful in order to explain the theoretical and practical strategies for reducing attrition and the "loss of talent" among Black women who plan to pursue college degrees. Some of these Black women lack adequate social and cultural support (Walsh, 1998) to overcome obstacles that hamper their academic or career aspirations. It is our hope that by sharing our personal experiences, it will encourage and support Black women in urban communities to pursue college and to utilize their fictive kin networks to gain the necessary resources to be successful in their academic pursuits.

Note

1. Fictive kin are family members who lack a genetic connection (Fordham, 1988). They may share commonalities, which constitute the foundation of their relationship, such as in the case of a mentor/mentee relationship.

References

Banks, C. A. (2009). *Black women undergraduates, cultural capital, and college success*. Peter Lang.

Clark, A. (2014). *A Detroit anthology*. Rust Belt Chic Press.

Ellis, C., & Bochner, A. P. (2000). Autoethnography, personal narrative, reflexivity: Research as subject. In N. K. Denzin & Y. S. Lincoln (Eds.), *Handbook of Qualitative Research* (pp. 733–768). SAGE.

Fordham, S. (1988). Racelessness a factor in Black students' school success: Pragmatic strategy or pyrrhic victory. *Harvard Educational Review, 58*(1), 54–84.

Freeman, K. (1997). Increasing African Americans' participation in higher education: African high-school students' perspectives. *The Journal of Higher Education, 68*(5), 523–550.

Guiffrida, D. (2005). To break away or strengthen ties to home: A complex issue for African American college students attending a predominantly white institution. *Equity Excellence in Education, 38*(1), 49–60.

Harris, E. E. (1970). Person and parental influences on college attendance: Some Negro-White differences. *The Journal of Negro Education, 39*(4), 305–313.

Kozol, J. (1991). *Savage inequalities: Children in America's schools*. Harper Perennial.

MacLeod, J. (2009). *Ain't no makin' it: Aspirations and attainment in a low-income neighborhood*. Westview Press.

Marsh, K., Chaney, C., & Jones, D. (2012). The strengths of high-achieving Black high school students in a racially diverse setting. *The Journal of Negro Education, 81*(1), 39–51.

McPherson, E. (2017). Oh you are smart: Young, gifted, African American women in STEM majors. *Journal of Women and Minorities in Science and Engineering, 23*(1), 1–14.

McPherson, E. (2014a). African American women's resilience in hard sciences. In J. Koch, B. Irby, & B. Polnick (Eds.), *Girls and women in STEM fields: A neverending story* (pp. 21–37). Information Age.

McPherson, E. (2014b). Informal learning in science, math, and engineering majors for African American undergraduates. *Global Education Review, 1*(4) 96–113.

McPherson, E. (2012). *Undergraduate African American women's narratives on persistence in science majors* [Unpublished doctoral dissertation]. University of Illinois.

Moore, C. (2014). *The resilience breakthrough: 27 tools for turning adversity into action.* Greenleaf.

Moore, W. (2010). *The other Wes Moore: One name, two fates.* Spiegel & Grau Trade.

Palmer, R. T., Davis, R. J., & Maramba, D. C. (2011). The impact of family support on the success of Black men at a Historically Black University: Affirming the revision of Tinto's theory. *Journal of College Student Development, 52*(5), 577–597.

Palmer, R., & Gasman, M. (2008). 'It takes a village to raise a child': The role of social capital in promoting academic success of African American Black men at a Black College. *Journal of College Student Development, 49*(1), 52–70.

Riessman, C. K. (1993). *Narrative analysis.* SAGE.

Ryan, G. W., & Bernard, H. R. (2000). Data management and analysis methods. In N. K. Denzin and Y. S. Lincoln (Eds.), *Handbook of qualitative research* (pp. 769–802). SAGE.

Tickles, V., & McPherson, E. (2016). Mentoring our own: African American women engineering. In K. E. Tassie & S. M. Brown Givens (Eds.), *Women of color navigating mentoring relationships: Critical examinations* (pp. 95–113). Lexington Books.

Tierney, W. G., & Venegas, K. M. (2006). Fictive kin and social capital: The role of peer groups in applying and paying for college. *American Behavioral Scientist, 49*(12), 1687–1702.

Tinto, V. (2012). *Completing college: Rethinking institution action.* University of Chicago Press.

Trent, W. T. & St. John, E. P. (2008). Resources, assets and strengths among successful diverse students: Understanding the contributions of the Gates millennium scholars program. *Readings on Equal Education, Vol. 23.* AMS Press.

Walsh, F. (1998). *Strengthening family resilience.* Guilford.

Watkins, A. P. (2009). *Sisters of hope, looking back, stepping forward: The educational experiences of African American women.* Peter Lang.

Wilson, K. R., & Allen, W. R. (1987). Explaining the educational attainment of young Black adults: Critical familial and extra-familial influences, *Journal of Negro Education, 56*(1), 64–76.

Wight, V., Chau, M., Thampi, K., & Aratani, Y. (2010). Examining the landscape of child poverty. *Current Problems in Pediatric and Adolescent Health Care, 40*(10), 263–266.

Wyner, J., Bridgeland, J. M., & Diiulio, J. (2007). *Achievement trap: How America is failing millions of high achieving students from low income families.* Jack Kent Cooke Foundation & Civic Enterprises.

Yosso, T. J. (2005). Whose culture has capital? A critical race theory discussion of community cultural wealth. *Race Ethnicity and Education, 8*(1), 69–91.

Chapter 11

"Old School" Urban Education

How Friends, Families, Communities, and Teachers Support Success in Early Childhood

THERESA J. CANADA

Introduction

Chapter 3 of Kozol's (1991) book is aptly titled "The Savage Inequalities of Public Education in New York." It appears his third chapter was the basis for the title of the entire book, which established the foundation for all urban school systems described in *Savage Inequalities*. The reason for this title likely stems from the inequalities in terms of educational disparity throughout New York City public schools. Kozol asserted that New York City public schools epitomized the denial of competition offered to poor children. Yet during the 1960s, New York City public schools offered many poor children the opportunity for a better life.

The purpose of this chapter is to restory the description of the New York City public school system as depicted by Kozol (1991). Although Kozol's focus in *Savage Inequalities* was on schools in the Bronx (a borough of New York City), this chapter focuses on another section of New York City: Harlem. During the early 1960s, schoolchildren in my Harlem neighborhood, were below grade level in reading and math (Pinkney & Woock, 1970), similar to the children in the South Bronx. As such the education received by the majority of Black children in this neighborhood resembled that of most Latino and Black children in the South Bronx.

Kozol (1991) also discussed the consequences of medical and early education denial. He mentioned that such denial during early childhood could destroy the learning skills of young children, so much so that by the time a child in New York City enters secondary school they no longer have the ability to learn. Somehow that was not an outcome for me or many of my elementary school classmates. It was the public schools and the later development of early childhood centers that offered access to educational opportunity to children in Harlem and other New York City boroughs. The focus of this chapter is based on my experience during the beginning of desegregation, the mid-1960s, in New York City public schools.

In 1954, the US Supreme Court ruled that segregation in public schools was unconstitutional and as such violated the Equal Protection Clause of the Fourteenth Amendment (*Brown v. Board of Education*—Case Brief Summary, n.d.). Although it had been almost a decade since the *Brown* decision, my school was similar to most urban schools and was still racially segregated due to residential segregation. As such, the *Brown* decision did not affect de facto segregation in schools. This chapter describes how classmates, family, the community in which we lived, and teachers supported the success of young children.

This chapter is situated within Yosso's (2005) community cultural wealth model (CCWM), which includes six types of capital (aspirational, linguistic, familial, social, navigational, and resistance) that Yosso states may be used to frame interactions with students of color in education. Yosso defines aspirational capital as "the ability to maintain hope and dreams despite educational barriers" (p. 77). Linguistic capital is defined as students' adeptness using communication skills. Familial capital is being able to skillfully use and recognize extended family and community members in their relationships with others. The definition of social capital is based on the network of students, including peers and others, to navigate social structures. Students' ability to navigate social institutions, specifically those that are unsupportive, defines the fourth form: navigational capital. Finally, resistance capital is defined as one's capability to persevere despite the presence of injustice, based on heritage, parents, and those in the community. Yosso's model is applied to young school-age children's experiences in New York City public schools. This chapter incorporates three forms of community cultural wealth—aspirational, familial, and social capital. These will be described as part of my experience within a local New York City school set against a counternarrative of Kozol's (1991) images of New York City's public schools.

Friends and Teachers

While Kozol portrayed families in the South Bronx as helpless and hopeless, the experiences described in this chapter are those of hope and perseverance. According to Yosso (2005) social capital includes networks of people and community resources. The ability to have these social connections provides "both instrumental and emotional support to navigate through society's institutions" (p. 79). There is much that can be said about the role of families and friends who encourage and support academic achievement in the early grades. The relationship with friends as a young child was important to my early success in school. These childhood relationships provide incentives to not only feel comfortable in the classroom but also to excel academically.

The relationship with family and friends provided support and encouragement both in and out of class. As a young child, I lived in a diverse yet majority Black neighborhood in New York City. The elementary school I attended from kindergarten until the third grade was located a few blocks from my home. Since the public school I attended was a local school, the majority of my classmates lived in the neighborhood. The fact that this neighborhood was still ethnically diverse meant that not all of my classmates were Black and included Caribbean students, an Asian American girl, and a Latina. The diversity that existed within this community school was not part of the discussion in Kozol (1991).

I had two types of friends while growing up in New York City—friends at school or classmates, and friends in the neighborhood. In a few situations, classmates were also neighborhood friends. In order for me to have friends, my mother had to know that person's parent(s). If my mother did not speak with those parents and clarify that they had similar values, then I was unable to visit that person's home. At this age, all of my friends were girls. I knew several of the boys, but of course in the third grade, there were no playdates between boys and girls. Friends in the community and in school were the basis of social capital (Yosso, 2005) that supported success in the early grades in this public school.

The friends in my third-grade class were all achievement oriented. We would read together, and if someone had a problem, we would volunteer to work with each other during lunch or briefly after school. Sometimes we would study at each other's homes. But that was rare, due to parents' work schedules. Regardless of what was going on outside of the classroom, classmates supported each other when it came to the specific subjects taught in school. All of the students wanted to excel in every subject. If someone did not receive a passing grade, we did not embarrass them. We would surround them to see if we could help them correct their mistakes. This was the most important aspect of the classroom friendships. We all were in there together to do well and to not leave anyone behind. This behavior substantiates Yosso's (2005) cultural community wealth identified as social capital.

Our class was the top third-grade classroom. We did not know that at the time, but we did know that we all either read well, wrote well, and/or performed well in math. Plus, we subconsciously knew that if one student did not pass, it meant that the same could happen to any one of us. So it was a great emotional feeling to be surrounded by classmates who wanted to achieve academically and who supported each other to achieve. Instead of negative competition there was an environment of healthy competitiveness that according to Graves (2011) encourages academic self-concept and achievement in third-grade African American children.

While school friends were the strongest ties to academic success, neighborhood friends were also connections to social activities. To have friends who served as social connections and friends in school for academic support made learning so much easier. Classmates and I were commended in our school and neighborhood for being excellent students. This was yet another confirmation of the importance of cultural community wealth (Yosso, 2005).

Teachers

The discussion of teachers in this chapter relates to those who worked in one particular New York City school community. Just as it was with students, many teachers of color were assigned to schools with majority Black and Latino students. This created a close bond between the teachers and parents within the community. The teachers knew parents well. Even if parents never visited the school, teachers reached out to parents through phone calls and letters. There was a strong bond between teachers and parents. Parents were made aware of our strengths by classroom teachers. Teachers not only sent notes home but if necessary visited our homes. This showed a commitment from teachers that made every child feel important. It also provided a level of trust between the teacher, child, and families. The bond between family and the local public schools was important to many families. It was the link to opportunity for their children. The family connection to early childhood programs and schools provided aspirational capital as defined by Yosso (2005). The public schools during the 1960s provided a support network where families were welcomed and the teachers knew each child, their siblings, and their parents.

According to Randolph (2004), it is Black teachers who are most instrumental in the success of young Black children in northern urban schools. The first Black teacher that taught me was during the third grade, and she was an icon. She was smart, savvy, and sensitive and had a command over the class so that any student could learn. She made me feel proud and special. To see her in the class each day provided encouragement that I too could succeed academically. If not for the Black teachers in this school, chances are I would not have received the quality education needed at that age and would not have necessarily pursued a career—period.

Families and Community

FAMILIES

I am the second child of four siblings. I have an older sister and a younger brother and sister. We were reared in a home with both parents, where both parents worked outside of the home and both parents contributed to the financial stability of the family. Yet, the major responsibility for taking care of children was left to our mother, which is most often the case in our society (Betz, 2005). Several values were instilled during the formative years between the ages of three to eight. This included basic home training activities. For example, keeping my clothes neat in the closet or dresser drawers and placing school shoes in a certain place in the bedroom. Making sure that we ate together as a family in the evenings was also an important activity. It was during these dinner meetings that my mother would share information about activities within the neighborhood with her extended family of siblings and inquire about our schoolwork.

The concept of familial capital (Yosso, 2005) was demonstrated at home and away from school. Completing one's homework was a requisite immediately after returning home from school. If I did not complete homework assignments before dinner, then I would follow up with the work immediately afterward. My older sister and I had chores. For example, taking out the garbage or sweeping the kitchen floor after dinner. Yet, if we had more homework to complete, my mother would allow us to skip our chores. She stated that she wanted us to make sure we did our best in school. For her, education was a priority. It was not just a matter of meeting the minimum standards: she wanted us to excel.

Parent involvement is a clear indicator for early school success (Graves, 2011; McWayne, Campos & Owsianik, 2008). McWayne, Campos, and Owsianik (2008) investigated parental involvement in Head Start programs and found there was a relationship between parent satisfaction and their involvement with their child's Head Start program. My mother was the parent most involved in my early education, which resulted in teachers having a better understanding of my family background and academic capabilities. This early educational success was a result of teachers, parents and young children participating in the early childhood educational setting.

COMMUNITIES

Unlike the depiction in Kozol (1991) regarding the South Bronx community, not all of those in my community were poor, Black, and uneducated. I suspect that areas of the South Bronx contained familial capital (Yosso, 2005) as did the area where I lived. My neighborhood was ethnically and economically diverse. There was a Black attorney, Black businessman, Black physician, Black preschool teacher, and Black city and government workers who either lived in my apartment building or nearby buildings. It was a vibrant environment where people worked and interacted with each other. This community consisted of families, neighborhood stores, a hospital, a post office, The YWCA, and various restaurants or diners. It was a fast-paced neighborhood where several public transportation routes were available. All types of people were constantly traveling in and out of the community at all times.

This early childhood experience was considered a time when the community watched out for the children who lived there. Many of the neighbors who did not work outside of the home would see you coming and going from school. There was a support network, where often these same individuals would chastise you as if they were your parents. There was a sense of protectiveness that the community provided for young children. Everyone knew each other: who your parents and siblings were and where you lived. Community members "looked out" for children back in the day. These community members encouraged children to attend school and get good grades. They only wanted the best from us and the schools we attended.

An extension of the local community was the church community. The Black church is known for encouraging education and supporting young children's educational opportunity (Barrett, 2010). Teachers in church school were just as supportive of your academic success as were teachers in the public schools. Education within the church community consisted of more than biblical teachings. Young children learned about social protocol and various forms of cultural socialization. Much of the heritage of one's ancestors was discussed and passed on in the oral traditions for which the Black church was known. Therefore, there was educational encouragement throughout the local community and the church community.

Recommendations and Implications

There are several recommendations that can be made for today's urban early childhood school environments. First and foremost, there must be more highly qualified and caring teachers. There especially needs to be more teachers of color to serve as role models for the diverse student body that exists in urban schools. Urban schools must reach out to the community in which they serve. Allow an open communication between what occurs in the community and provide open access to those individuals within the schools themselves. We must stop closing the doors to the schools as if they are fortresses. When the community knows they are welcomed in the schools, those community members will support programs within the school. The most important factor in the success of urban schools is parent involvement and parent engagement. Urban early childhood parents may not have all of the answers, but they know what is best for their children (Canada & Bland, 2014). As such, urban schools must create approaches to include parent voices to promote the learning environment for children.

The environment for children in today's urban early childhood settings is not much different from that of my generation. If urban schools could prepare students for success in the 1960s, they can certainly supply that same level of preparation in urban early childhood settings now and in the future. Despite the despair and hopelessness Kozol (1991) emphasized in

New York City Schools, certainly at least one urban school in New York City produced several well-educated Black girls. Therefore, this chapter suggests that in order to achieve current and continued success in urban early childhood settings, there must be the support of friends, families, communities, and teachers.

Conclusion

The title of this chapter is prefaced with "old school," a term reflecting the lingo used by many people when referring to an earlier era. In particular, the term is typically spoken by seasoned individuals from various urban communities within the United States. For the purpose of this narrative the term defined the urban school experience with respect and places urban schools in high regard. Therefore, the emphasis of this chapter was to substantiate the resourcefulness of urban schools within our society and the role these schools have played in educating young Black girls. Why the focus on Black girls? Co-ed socialization was not something that took place during early childhood. Thus, this was my experience as a young Black girl in the New York City public school system up until the third grade. After the third grade, I left the community school and transferred to a public school in another neighborhood.

When an urban city is mentioned in our society, the reaction from most observers is mostly negative. But there was a time when those who attended the New York City Public Schools (now called New York City Department of Education) were fortunate to receive one of the best educations in the country. I was one of them. The New York City public school experience provided more than education; it provided cultural and social opportunities as well. These experiences encompassed all that the City of New York had to offer and more. Just as these schools provided this exposure to students in the past, schools today can do the same.

The role of education has always served as a vehicle for opportunity to Black Americans in urban communities. Much of that comes from the Great Migration from the south to the north for Blacks (Wilkerson, 2010) and others from the various Caribbean islands to New York City. Based on my life experiences, the combination of friends, families, communities, and teachers provided the support network to excel as a young child in an urban school. Learning was enhanced by those around me who loved and cared about my well-being. As a young girl, I always felt I could achieve academically and was encouraged to do so. My counternarrative is that despite the negative description of the early childhood experiences of children in the South Bronx, there were pockets of excellence throughout many of the New York City public schools. These were places where individuals found ways to support the educational foundation that led to excellence for many young Black girls within the community. The early childhood period is crucial to the future success of students. Unless there is an intervention during this period of a child's life, the possibilities of future academic success are limited.

References

Barrett, B. D. (2010). Faith in the inner city: The urban Black church and students' educational outcomes. *Journal of Negro Education, 79*(3), 249–262.

Betz, N. E. (2005). Women's career development. In S. D. Brown & R. W. Lent (Eds.), *Career development and counseling: Putting theory and research to work* (pp. 253–277). John Wiley & Sons.

Brown v. Board of Education (n.d.). Case brief summary. http://www.lawnix.com/cases/brown-board-education.html

Canada, T. & Bland, K. (2014). *Parents of young children: Their perception of teacher quality and access to quality care*. http://wcgmf.org/application/files/5915/5130/4023/parents_of_young_children.pdf

Graves, S. (2011). School and child level predictors of academic success for African American children in third grade: Implications for No Child Left Behind. *Race Ethnicity and Education, 14*(5), 675–697. http://doi.org/10.1080/13613324.2010.547849

Kozol, J. (1991). *Savage Inequalities: Children in America's schools*. Harper Perennial.

McWayne, C., Campos, R., & Owsianik, M. (2008). A multidimensional, multilevel examination of mother and father involvement among culturally diverse Head Start families. *Journal of School Psychology, 46*(5), 551–573. http://doi.org/10.1016/j.jsp.2008.06.001

Pinkney, A., & Woock, R. R. (1970). *Poverty and politics in Harlem: Report on project uplift 1965*. College & University Press

Randolph, A. W. (2004). The memories of an all-Black northern urban school: Good memories of leadership, teachers, and the curriculum. *Urban Education, 39*(6), 596–620.

Wilkerson, I. (2010). *The warmth of other suns: The epic story of America's great migration*. Random House.

Yosso, T. J. (2005). Whose culture has capital? A critical race theory discussion of community cultural wealth. *Race Ethnicity and Education, 8*(1), 69–91. http://doi.org/ 10.1080/1361332052000341006

Chapter 12

"I Have Seen the Mountaintop"

Intersectionality and the Auto-ethnography of a Mediocre Student at a Gifted School

HEATHER MOORE ROBERSON

Introduction

Since the *Brown v. Board of Education* (1954) precedent and the federal mandate that public schools should be desegregated with all deliberate speed, the formal educational experiences of students of color have constantly been under surveillance. As educational researchers tried to understand the needs of students of color and those from low-income communities, they also analyzed the ways that schools themselves should adjust to better support the needs of students from different cultural backgrounds. However, even in the 21st century there is still a two-tiered system. On the one hand, wealthy White students tend to have more diverse educational opportunities. On the other hand, some Black and Brown low-income students attend schools that look very similar to the schools highlighted in Jonathan Kozol's *Savage Inequalities* (1991).

While most of the urban schools that Kozol described were under-resourced, my urban public high school was viewed as a space of privilege for gifted students and wealthy families. On the surface, I truly benefited from the formal educational experiences I had in high school. Each student enrolls in Advanced Placement (AP) and International Baccalaureate (IB) courses as early as their sophomore year of high school: these courses will push students' intellectual curiosity and advance critical thought ("School Profile"). Furthermore, each student at the high school has the option to pursue an IB diploma and even apply for sophomore status at the college of their choice. Despite all of these educational opportunities, I was still othered in this setting. My cultural capital did not match the dominant values of the school because I was a mediocre Black adolescent female in a predominately White gifted school. By mediocre, I mean the system treated me as an average student with little to no attention to what I could contribute or the gifts I possessed, beyond their dominant narrative of giftedness.

In this chapter, I consider, *what are the needs of mediocre students of color in gifted educational settings?* In academic scholarship on gifted education, there is limited discussion of mediocre students. Utilizing intersectionality while rethinking scholarly conceptualizations of giftedness and "at-risk" student identities, my research will consider the aforementioned question using an auto-ethnographic methodological framework. First, I contend that educators must have diverse understandings of gifted students. I situate my personal narrative inside a notable urban public school that has received national recognition for student achievement, transformative educational programming, and high graduation rates. Through my experiences, I learned that "'urban' as a descriptor does not simply refer to space and place but is also used to refer to the value designation of human beings, their status in the world, and their potential" (Gadsden & Dixon-Román, 2017, p. 437). As such, all gifted students are not always treated or educated equally. Secondly, I argue that academics who study gifted education should redirect their gaze upon the average students in gifted classrooms and ask what types of educational programming would benefit this distinct group. Lastly, I argue that mentoring students who have been pushed to the margins can radically shift their educational experiences. I conclude with a discussion of Tara J. Yosso's community cultural wealth as a theory that can help reframe my experiences as a "mediocre" gifted student. Overall, this narrative will encourage educators to rethink the experiences of urban public school students.

The Site: River Oak Academy

River Oak Academy[1] is an academically rigorous 5th- to 12th-grade magnet school that offers exceptional academic programs, exclusive extracurricular programming, and boasts a diverse student body from various socioeconomic backgrounds. In part, this public school would be considered an "urban emergent" school or school(s) "that are typically located in large cities but not as large as the major cities. They typically have some of the same characteristics and sometimes challenges as urban intensive schools" (Milner, 2012, p. 560). However, my alma mater is unlike other under-resourced, "majority-minority" urban schools in the city. It is one of the top public schools in the second-largest city in New York State. In 2006, the school was listed as one of the top schools in *Newsweek*'s list of America's Top Public High Schools. Students apply to River Oak and are selected using a "competitive assessment." Every academic year, River Oak receives more applications than the number of available seats. This medium-sized educational institution enrolls 5th to 12th graders and provides state-of-the-art programs for a "diverse" student body. River Oak also offers the "full IB program," which allows students to enroll in discussion-based, writing-intensive college preparatory courses. In addition, high school students who are interested in experiential learning opportunities can apply to shadow a local doctor at a leading Cancer Institute. Although this school has strong academic programs, there is a growing low-income student population. In past academic years, several students from each graduating class went on to Ivy League schools and other top postsecondary institutions across the United States. But my own experiences at this school add complexity to the one-dimensional narrative that dominates educational experiences at gifted schools.

The Narrative of a Mediocre Gifted Student

At River Oak, I was an outsider among the student population and among scholar athletes. In the United States, gifted education is not standardized across school districts or even between individual schools. Gifted students can be placed in specialized classrooms or attend a specialized school that explicitly serves gifted students. In some school districts nationwide, gifted classrooms may be part of a larger school setting. While a school may be considered low performing, there can be classrooms, a portion of the school day, or even entire floors devoted to a gifted population. Over the past 50 years, gifted education has been defined in various ways. For instance, the Marland Report defined gifted students as individuals who "by virtue of outstanding abilities are capable of high performance" and require "differentiated educational programs" separate from what is offered in most public school settings (Bonner, 2000, p. 644; Harris & Ford, 1991, p. 6). But by 1994, "one third of states had no mandate for gifted education programs which suggests that gifted students are not viewed as a population in need of special services" (Ford, 1998, p. 5). Even in the 21st century, youth who are classified as gifted are generally students with high grade point averages (especially in STEM-related subjects), an expansive vocabulary, and exceptional writing skills. But since a gifted designation for a student is largely determined by performance on standardized tests, IQ scores, and teacher recommendations, gifted student populations rarely include historically marginalized groups largely because of their inability to perform similarly to their White, Asian American, and wealthy counterparts (Harris & Ford, 1991, p. 5; Sullivan, 1973, p. 375).

While River Oak Academy was marketed as a culturally diverse school, the school's top students were generally White or from wealthy families. Many of these students at River Oak Academy breezed through the curriculum and were comfortable in their surroundings. The most confident gifted students were my peers enrolled in the IB program; some of them completed enough coursework to skip their freshman year of college. In addition, several of my peers were longtime students at River Oak and enrolled at the school in fifth grade. But as a new ninth grader at River Oak Academy, I was no longer placed in the top 5% of my class, and I struggled to keep up with the fast-paced nature of the curriculum. Furthermore, as a sophomore, I was not a confident student athlete. Before high school, I was a dance major at a popular performing arts junior and senior high school. But since my high school failed to offer any true dance programs or opportunities, I reluctantly joined the varsity volleyball team. I was tall, athletic, and enjoyed being in team environments where I could learn from others. But I was an outsider even in this environment. As a sensitive adolescent, I cried when I was reprimanded by coaches and was virtually unable to balance the rigorous academic course load with a competitive, traveling volleyball team.

I did not fit alongside the other members of the team who seamlessly balanced their identities as both students and athletes. One of the captains of the team (and the head coach's favorite player) went on to play volleyball at the University of Pennsylvania and graduated high school with above a 4.0 grade point average. Meanwhile, I struggled to maintain a C average in Advanced Placement European History, a required course for all sophomores. So at the end of my sophomore year, I quit the volleyball team and focused on my formal education. I knew that if

I wanted to attend a competitive college or university, I had to become a better student. But unfortunately, my classroom teachers, who still had to abide by state standards and public school restrictions, did not nurture my educational curiosities.

My identity as a Black working-class student and scholarly interests in Black popular culture indirectly challenged the dominant cultural capital inherent in gifted programs. Although cultural capital was a term coined by Pierre Bourdieu, sociologists of education like Prudence Carter have incorporated the concept into their discussions of formal and informal educational spaces. Cultural capital is defined as an "individual's access to certain cultural signals (such as attitudes, preferences, tastes, and styles) either enables or limits their entry into high status social groups, organizations, or institutions" (Carter, 2003, pp. 136–137). More importantly, Carter argued that cultural capital is "context-specific and its currency varies across different social spaces where struggles for legitimation and power exist" (Carter, 2003, p. 137). Like many students, I too saw the value in dominant and nondominant cultural capitals in my various "educational" spaces.

Throughout my adolescence, my mother determined which schools I attended and, in 2000, forced me to attend River Oak Academy. Prior to high school, I was enrolled in a predominately Black performing arts (junior) high school in a predominately Black working-class neighborhood school. Although I was gifted, I was anxious in various social settings. So when my mother pushed me to take the River Oak test, I was disappointed. I was comfortable at my previous educational institutions. I was in a predominately Black school with teachers who understood my nondominant cultural capital(s). But the dominant cultural capital was different at River Oak. Many of the school's top students were destined for the Ivy League and were the children of city judges, high-ranking politicians, and surgeons at local hospitals. Admittedly, my parents viewed it as a privilege to be considered a student at River Oak Academy while it was the norm (or even a below-average educational option) for my White, wealthy peers.

As a mediocre student, I was passionate about learning new concepts and studied history that was rarely taught in my predominately White high school social studies courses. But teachers at River Oak Academy did not nurture this gift. I only received one opportunity to explore my love for Black history: as a senior during an IB History of the Americas final project. This assignment asked students to investigate mainstream media responses to famous leaders in American history. I conducted a comparative analysis of the impact of Martin Luther King and Malcolm X in the civil rights and Black Power movements. But I also questioned which set of ideologies was deemed more acceptable by a White, middle-class politic. Even though I deeply enjoyed this assignment, I wondered why I was not allowed to conduct more self-designed research that spoke directly to my interest in Black history, social justice, and popular representations of Black masculinity. Although my scholarly interests in high school directly challenged the dominant cultural capital of this gifted space, if other history teachers pushed me to home in on these interests, I may have been more invested in my formal educational experiences in high school.

As a mediocre (gifted) student, I was treated as a refurbished model minority student. Stacey Lee's "model minority" concept was first used to describe the experiences of Asian and Asian American students in American classrooms. These students were defined as model minorities, or the "example" which all students from historically marginalized groups should follow. Lee described model minorities as students who were quiet, seemingly assimilated, and regularly overlooked by teachers because they are assumedly "hard workers" (Lee, 2001, p. 515). But the model minority rhetoric imposed upon students implies that these youth do not require additional support or assistance from school faculty or administrators. This model minority stereotype can be easily applied to the educational experiences of non-Asian or Asian American students. In my own experiences in high school, I contend that I was a "refurbished" model minority student because of my mediocre grade point average and my ability to master some dimensions of the dominant cultural capital in the school setting.

During my junior year, I struggled with the end-of-year standardized test that concluded my first IB English Language course. Throughout the academic year, we interrogated Ernest Gaines's *A Lesson Before Dying*, Edward Albee's *Who's Afraid of Virginia Woolf*, and other plays and short stories. As it was a discussion-based course, we were allowed to critique the author, ask pointed questions about the major characters, and situate the narrative in its proper historical context. I participated in some classroom debates but was certainly not the most vocal student in this English course. To my delight, I received Bs throughout the year. However, at the end of the academic year, students are asked to interrogate short passages and evaluate their use of specific literary techniques. This exercise was tape recorded and evaluated by members of the IB organization outside River Oak Academy. I knew how to prepare for New York State's Regents examinations and would spend weeks reading test-prep books that provided useful examples that may be used on the actual exam. However, the unknown IB model of standardized testing discouraged me. In this instance, I was treated as a model minority student because I failed to challenge the system and did not question the course structure *until* the final examination. I respected my teachers and did not challenge the course materials. I knew how to behave within the classroom: I was taught to be nonthreatening, to listen to the instructor, and to pretend as though I fully grasped the material. But this performance changed when I was unsure about the IB final examination process. Thus, educators must acknowledge the ways that mediocre gifted students present themselves as the model minority when they may truly be struggling in silence.

Conclusion: Rereading Mediocrity alongside Community Cultural Wealth

Tara J. Yosso's theory of community cultural wealth adds complexity to my experiences as a diverse, gifted student. While I did not graduate at the top of my class, I adopted aspirational capital (or "the ability to maintain hopes and dreams for the future, even in the face of real and perceived barriers") and navigational capital (or "the skills of maneuvering through social institutions") at River Oak Academy (Yosso, 2005, p. 77, 80). The aforementioned capital, in particular, prepared me for the rigors of a private liberal arts college. In essence, my formal and informal educational experiences taught me the power of other types of capital that can prepare students for life after elementary and secondary education.

My firsthand experiences at a diverse high school in a medium-sized city directly contrast with some of Jonathan Kozol's vignettes of urban education. My public high school had several resources that were provided to its students. But unfortunately the faculty and administrators at River Oak did not consider the diverse educational experiences of gifted students and the various kinds of capital that youth learn outside the classroom. Educators of gifted (mediocre) youth should encourage students to look past their experiences in K–12 classrooms. Just because a student is not the smartest in their class does not mean they cannot be destined for a competitive college, a fruitful career, or a fulfilling life. I propose two recommendations for faculty and administrations who work with gifted students (especially youth who are located in urban, public schools).

First, academically "average" students should be reminded that *mediocre does not automatically equal failure*. As a high school student at a gifted school, I constantly compared myself to other students. I questioned whether I was good enough to be a member of the school community, whether I was good enough to be part of specific organizations, and whether I would be good enough to attend a competitive liberal arts college. This self-imposed pressure, in particular, dominated my worldview so much so that I never had time to fully appreciate my overall high school experience. The constant surveillance and judgment made me question whether I would be one of the students who would damage River Oak's reputation. But this mindset could have easily shifted if faculty and administrators had shared their own personal narratives with their students. Often, youth may feel unsure of their future prospects if they fail to achieve perfection. If I had known that I could accomplish my goals even though I wasn't valedictorian of my high school class, I may have thought differently about my formal educational experiences. If my former teachers had encouraged me to look past my current frame of reference and consider all of my future possibilities, then I might have considered the possibility of "growing up" to be a college professor before the age of 30.

Second, educators who work closely with gifted students should construct *unofficial individualized educational programs for this group that include mentoring and extensive support for gifted students of color*. While the "individualized educational programs" are generally restricted to students with special needs, these valuable documents are not always created for gifted students. Once students are classified as gifted, they are believed to be independent, focused intently on their academic experiences, and no longer needing personalized relationships with faculty or administrators. They have been branded as the model students that the entire student body should mimic. But what happens when members of this group are struggling to keep up with their new academic curriculum? How do we make accommodations for the gifted students who were admitted into gifted programs later in their educational trajectories? In the latter case, students who have been designated as gifted in junior high or high school, for example, may need additional mentoring and guidance to complete their formal education. By pushing gifted students to look beyond their current educational experiences to consider future career options, they should be actively mentored by faculty and administrators to ensure that they can maximize their formal educational experiences. Only then will educators and scholars embrace the diversity inherent in contemporary gifted education.

Note

1. River Oak Academy is a pseudonym.

References

Bonner, F. (2000). African American giftedness: Our nation's dream deferred. *Journal of Black Studies, 30*(5), 643–663.
Carter, P. (2003). "Black" cultural capital, status positioning, and schooling conflicts for low-income African American youth. *Social Problems, 50*(1), 136–155.
Ford, D. Y. (1998). The under-representation of minority students in gifted education: Problems and promises in recruitment and retention. *The Journal of Special Education, 32*(1), 4–14.
Ford, D. Y. (2014). Segregation and the underrepresentation of Blacks and Hispanics in gifted education: Social inequalities and deficit paradigms. *Roeper Review, 36*, 143–153.
Gadsden, V., & Dixon-Román, E. (2017). "Urban" schooling and "urban" families: The role of context and place. *Urban Education, 52*(4), 431–459.
Harris III, J. J., & Ford, D. Y. (1991). Identifying and nurturing the promise of gifted Black students. *Journal of Negro Education, 60*(1), 3–18.
Kozol, J. (1991). *Savage inequalities: Children in America's schools*. Harper Perennial.
Lee, S. (2009). *Unraveling the model minority stereotype: Listening to African American youth*. Teachers College Press.
Milner, H. R. (2012). But what is urban education? *Urban Education, 47*(3), 556–561.
Sullivan, A. (1973). The identification of gifted and academically talented Black students: A hidden exceptionality. *The Journal of Special Education, 7*(4), 373–379.
Yosso, T. J. (2005). Whose culture has capital? A critical race theory discussion of community cultural wealth. *Race Ethnicity and Education, 8*(1), 69–91.

Chapter 13

Dispelling the Myth of Despair and Hopelessness

How Ethical Leadership Creates a Counter-Narrative to Kozol's Leadership Caricature

LONNIE R. MORRIS JR. AND MACEO A. COOPER-JENKINS

Critics labeled *Savage Inequalities* (Kozol 1991) deceitful, manipulative (Branch, 1992), and typical (Zorn, 1994) for underestimating the impact of poverty on children of all races and failing to address misperceptions that poor children of color cannot learn. In this chapter, we argue that Kozol's deceit and manipulation resulted in an ill-executed caricature of impoverished schools that suggests the educational leaders are weak and desperate. Throughout the individual city accounts, he depicts educators and educational leaders as accustomed to poverty as well as overextended and disenchanted with their career decisions, leading them to be tense, harsh, less than enthusiastic, unsure of themselves, and rebellious. He attacks their physical attributes. He speculates on their desensitization to crime. In *Savage Inequalities*, a 14-year veteran high school football coach in East St. Louis is described as growing up poor in Mississippi, aware of the limitations of poverty, and wondering what else he could have achieved in life. A physics teacher is noted as a balding, 58-year-old bachelor. A Chicago kindergarten teacher is depicted as cold and rigid as she prepares students for naptime and a subsequent nursery rhyme exercise. A New York City teacher's voice is described as "droning." These depictions support Kozol's overarching narrative of urban education despair and hopelessness for students of color living in poverty.

With *Savage Inequalities* as the backdrop, we approached the narratives with an understanding that the Kozol leadership caricature was not reflective of our personal experiences reflecting community cultural wealth (Yosso, 2005) nor did it align with scholarship exploring the impact of behavioral modeling in education settings. Educational research shows exposure to positive leader behaviors, such as ethical leadership (e.g., normatively appropriate conduct through personal actions, interpersonal relationships, two-way communication, reinforcement, and decision-making) (Brown, Trevino, & Harrison, 2005), can positively impact the student learning experience and student success factors such as academic performance, grade point average (Hughes & Jones, 2011), ascension to cocurricular leadership positions (Sternberg, 2013), and persistence (Williamson, Goosen, & Gonzalez Jr., 2014). The importance of leader-modeled behaviors is noted in student character development frameworks such as Bowers, Rosch, and Collier (2016). Leadership and management researchers (Resick et al., 2013; Steinbauer et al., 2014) also identified leader-modeled ethical behaviors as critical to follower capability and capacity building. However, this was missing from the Kozol leader caricature and led us to the central research question: how do ethical leaders model a counter-narrative to assumptions of urban education despair?

Methodology

Narrative in the Study of Leadership

Although an infrequent approach in leadership literature, narrative inquiry has been used to understand phenomena similar to this study including responsible leadership (Pless, 2007), leaders in educational settings (Hussain & Albarwani, 2015) and leadership ethics (Auvinen, Lamsa, Sintonen, & Takala, 2013). At the center of narrative analysis are stories with three fundamental assumptions. First, human experience is always narrated, and narrative research is focused on how meaning is assigned to these experiences. Second, these stories are dependent upon past experiences, present experiences, values, and audience. Third, narratives are constructed with consideration for time, place, and character (Klenke, 2008). Leadership narratives can be used as both an interpretive and constructive approach evidenced by Parry and Kempster's (2014) exploration of love and charismatic leadership. The *Savage Inequalities* leadership caricature is rooted in unethical manipulation, which is manifest in pseudo-participative tales (stories that give readers and participants the false impression that the author is sympathetic to his or her feelings and problems) and pseudo-empathetic tales (accounts in which the author pretends to empathize with readers and participants) (Auvinen et al., 2013). Hence, in this study we use our narratives to both interpret ethical leadership in practice and construct a collective narrative that accurately reflects our community cultural wealth, experiences, and values as urban educational leaders.

Participants

Both participants are African American males with combined experience of 30 years of service in urban education settings both at the high school and college levels. Both attended and graduated from urban public high schools and earned undergraduate and graduate degrees. Both spent at least 10 years working with urban public schools in the greater Baltimore and Washington, DC regions.

Methods

A narrative protocol was created using questions from Kalshoven et al.'s (2011) framework for ethical leadership at work. Each participant responded to questions and prompts regarding fairness, integrity, ethical guidance, people orientation, power sharing, and role clarification. Completed narratives were shared. Both participants engaged in iterations of reading and rereading the narratives, coding the narrative transcripts, categorization, summarizing and theme development in an effort to answer the central research question: how do ethical leaders model a counter-narrative to assumptions of urban educational despair?

Findings

Three themes emerged from the narrative analysis: (a) finding patterns of meaningful exchange, (b) chaperoning the journey, and (c) embodying moral fortitude. *Finding patterns of meaningful exchange* describes our experience regularly engaging followers to create lasting impressions. *Chaperoning the journey* describes our experience guiding students on a designated path. *Embodying moral fortitude* describes a leadership ethos that personifies upstanding character and commitment to the well-being of others.

FINDING PATTERNS OF MEANINGFUL EXCHANGE

This theme describes the leadership experience of regularly engaging followers to create lasting impressions. It manifests in two subthemes. The first is *fostering long-term engagement*. It includes codes such as conversation, one-on-one access, compelling personal stories, desire to inspire others, relationships, trust, rapport, and concern for life challenges. We shared common leadership experiences as educators that involved allowing students one-on-one access, using small talk to create safe conversation spaces, listening to students' personal stories, and inquiring about experiences outside of our domain. Both leaders shared experiences of repeat student visits to their respective school offices, providing students the means to contact them outside of school via cell phone, email, or social media. One of the leaders gave the following example of how direct access outside of school fostered long-term engagement and meaningful exchange: "Students often send a text [message] to inform me that they may miss a deadline due to doctor's appointment, or a student may send a text to request an extension on a project. Enforcing the importance of communication, and providing the proper avenues for such communication to occur, encourages students to be open about their needs in order for me to better address them." In building rapport and trust, we become key fixtures in the students' lives. Through long-term engagement, leader-student relationships develop beyond mentoring and camaraderie. Leaders regularly experienced standing in the trenches with students during life-altering situations. When students were pushed to the brink, the educational leaders stepped in to support students' overall well-being. In cases of post–life trauma, the leaders retreated into less active roles but maintained the relationships. For one of the leaders, long-term engagement allowed him to support a student during a health crisis. He explained it this way:

> The examples that come to mind is the year one of my students was diagnosed with cancer. At the time of his diagnosis he was in his third year as a student worker in our office. I was one of the first people with whom he shared the diagno-

sis. Together we decided how he wanted to share it with the rest of the office. With his permission, I shared the news at a standing staff meeting where he was not present. We collected cards and donations for him. I checked in with him regularly. He went through three months of chemotherapy. He is now cancer free. He and I are still close to this day. In fact, since he graduated I have visited him at his home in Baltimore twice.

Some aspects of meaningful exchange through long-term engagement are innate to the educational functions of these leaders. The leaders described the nature of their respective professions as dictating some level of interaction as part of a natural student development pipeline. Both described multiple checkpoints and academic milestones where they could gauge student progression.

The second subtheme is *creating mediums for open expression*. It described formal and informal ways leaders communicate with students. *Codes* included acknowledging student voice, understanding your role, attentiveness, structured communication, cocurricular engagement, and custom approach. Both leaders valued student voices. They described experiences of giving undivided attention, removing communication barriers, and listening attentively. They also acknowledged times in which students faced emotionally charged situations that required acute sensitivity. One leader described it as his priority. "No matter what transpired, no matter if the student was right or wrong, I am always careful to acknowledge their feelings. No matter how you feel, you have a right to feel that way and express it . . . I am always open to listening. I think that's part of the rapport I have with students is because I always listen. No matter what the issue they know they will at least get a platform to share their stories with me." The leaders understood different communication strengths and preferences. When necessary leaders were willing to create custom communication channels for students. Leaders tailored communication and feedback to students' specific needs, which built the students' confidence. One of the leaders described his experience working with a talented student who feared speaking up in class. He recognized potential danger in her fear that might permanently mute her self-expression. He suggested she journal her thoughts as if she were in a conversation with him. He replied to her thoughts in writing. After a short time with the journaling exercise he noted growth in her confidence and openness. Her participation in class increased.

Creating patterns of meaningful exchange through communication mediums also taught leaders the value of silence. They understood that when working with students, leadership roles did not always require leadership input. At times the best form of leadership was listening and providing support. Both conceded this as a delicate slope requiring well-developed leadership acumen. One of the leaders commented, "I understand sometimes you don't want to hear what someone else thinks. You just want to vent. I'm okay playing that role. I offer my opinion if solicited. Then I try to help the student decide the best course of action for the desired results."

Chaperoning the Journey

This theme described the leaders' dual responsibilities of building student confidence and holding students accountable while guiding them on designated paths. Leaders recounted their chaperoning experiences through two subthemes. The first subtheme is *mentorship*. Meaning units included exposure, positive reinforcement, goal setting, and coaching. The leaders invested time and resources into helping students gain access to practical information and experience to guide their life choices. As student goals changed, the leaders modified their advice and coaching to support the new goals. Leaders were proud to connect students with meaningful experiences that helped develop their aptitudes and interests. When opportunities were not readily available, leaders created experiences for students to ensure they were exposed to practical application of important life skills. At times this meant incorporating student shadowing, internship, or apprenticeship experiences into operations they managed. The leaders trusted student mentees to assume responsibility for real issues that affected areas for which leaders had domain control. One of the leaders described his experience creating a paid student fellowship program at his school:

> We designed a summer-long program that gave them the opportunity to have candid conversations with various unit leaders from across the organization. We exposed them to industry publications. We engaged them in moderated, critical analysis discussions about contemporary issues in the industry. We gave them case studies focused on salient issues. We paired them with professional mentors from our unit with whom they could discuss their ideas. At the end of the fellowship we selected elements from their case recommendations to implement into our office.

Chaperoning through mentorship also included positive reinforcement, goal setting, expectations of success, and optimism. Leaders used positive reinforcement as part of deliberate feedback loops. They regularly revisited prior conversations with students to acknowledge progress made in key areas. Leaders valued the effect accolades could have on student efficacy. One of the leaders noted, "A simple 'I am proud of you' or 'keep up the good work' goes a long way to confirm to a student that I notice the difference and care to see more progress." Leader mentorship included engaging students early and often in goal setting. They expressed a desire to help students maximize opportunities and see beyond the here and now. Leaders understood the interconnectedness of student exposure, relationships, actions, and decisions. Leaders used standard prompts to engage students in thinking about their futures with the understanding that there is a basic trajectory of success that is informed by similar thought patterns. One leader described his goal-setting reinforcement strategy, "All conversations about goal setting are rooted in any combinations of 'what do you want to do after high school?' 'where do you see yourself in [5 to 10] years?' and 'what are you good at?'" The other leader described countless discussions with students about priorities, noting that "discussing priorities helps them weigh options with some sense of clarity."

The second subtheme that emerged for chaperoning the journey was *accountability*, which described the leaders' attempts to empower students with critical, ethical feedback. Meaning units included ethical counseling, explaining consequences, shared responsibility, and reflection. Leaders described experiences communicating expectations about integrity directly to students. Leaders provided clear behavioral guidelines with the expectation that students behaved with integrity. Leaders immediately addressed student infractions and explained present and future consequences. One leader described a student's use of inappropriate language on a college application. "I invited him and his father to meet with me. I then explained to him that the college application is a formal document and becomes a permanent part of your record with the institution. I explained to him how it impacted the review of his application in a negative way. I further explained his role in making better decisions and his responsibility in the admissions process." Leaders counseled students but also engaged them in a discussion considering all possible reactions to their actions. Leaders encouraged students to think beyond the current situation. One leader explained, "My goal is to get them to understand that they must think before acting. I want them to know they should consider consequences, both positive and negative because upon graduating from high school the accountability systems are much different than what exists in the high school setting."

Embodying Moral Fortitude

This theme described a personal leadership ethos that personified upstanding character and commitment to well-being of others. Two subthemes emerged as part of this theme: *personal investment* and *virtue routine*. Personal investment described leader behavior that supported expansion of the leader-student dynamic beyond the formal school-based relationship. Meaning units included urgency, role beyond position, and immediate concerns. Leaders recounted experiences in which they felt so invested in student personal development they were willing to alter conventional practices to accommodate student needs. The leaders understood supporting student development did not always fall into neat roles and responsibilities. Leaders were willing to deviate from norms to support students. One leader described there being "several situations in which I had to remove students from the classroom to have immediate conversations. While I recognize abandoning the rest of students in the classroom is not ideal nor a best practice, there are times that require a decision based solely on the urgency of the need."

The second subtheme, *virtue routine*, described the personal traits that demonstrate character and leadership strengths. Meaning units included modeling the way, transparency, authenticity, ethical assumptions, and humanity. Modeling the way was a key leadership function and informal method of communicating expectations. Leaders used modeling to translate multiple leadership lessons including integrity and transparency. One of the leaders described his experience: "The first thing with integrity is always lead by example. I work hard at being transparent with students. I try to show them through my own words and actions a great example of how to lead your life with integrity."

The embodiment of moral fortitude through virtue routines described the leaders as optimists who naturally see good in others. Leaders exhibited characteristics of integrity and ethics and expected others to do the same, even if those expectations were unspoken. Leaders assumed students operated under the basic human understanding of right and wrong. Leaders assumed students knew actions deemed as wrong were met with consequences. One of the leaders conceded the following: "At this age students understand what it means to carry [yourself] with integrity. The most effective method of instilling this principle is to provide examples of this behavior so students have a model to consider whenever faced with determining the best way to respond. Students are very much aware of the consequences of unethical behavior." Leaders stressed the significance of the common thread of humanity to students. Leaders encouraged students to see themselves as flawed humans. Leaders used this frame to help students alleviate some level of self-imposed pressure for perfection and life without challenges. Leaders communicated the human nature of facing challenges and overcoming adversity. It was described as "modeling behavior" that helps students see leaders as "people first" who understand that "problems and challenges are part of life's natural progression."

Discussion and Conclusion

Our narratives illustrate a significant departure from the leadership caricature Kozol offers in *Savage Inequalities* that depicts educational leaders situated in impoverished urban schools as weak, desperate, and diminished. Our narratives reinforce previous research that demonstrates how community cultural wealth is used in *creating patterns of meaningful exchange* in how educational leaders support student engagement and retention (Williamson, Goosen, & Gonzalez Jr., 2014; Yosso, 2005). Our findings align with previous narrative analysis research regarding responsible leadership behaviors (Pless, 2007), such as ethical leadership, which characterized this style of leader as a visionary, servant, networker, and change agent. Meaningful exchanges are critical components of ethical leadership behavior confirmed by Aronson (2001) and De Hoogh & Den Hartog (2009). These exchanges denote leader proclivity for developing strong relationships as an important component of the ethical leader-follower paradigm (Hollander, 2004). These traits are muted by Kozol's pseudo-participative and pseudo-empathetic manipulative depictions of the education leaders as impoverished, unsure, and tense characters who are unable to ably serve students or even take care of themselves.

Our narratives reaffirm how, in chaperoning the journey, educational leaders who may simultaneously serve high-poverty and low-academic-performing schools, move away from Kozol's manipulated tales of despair and hopelessness (Welton & Williams, 2014). The dual responsibility captured with this theme (building confidence and maintaining accountability) reflects elements of transactional behaviors found to be associated with ethical leadership (Trevino, Brown, & Hartman, 2003). Building confidence simultaneously demonstrates ethical leadership (Ciulla, 2004) and mitigates against follower unethical decision-making (Stenmark & Mumford, 2011). Leader examples of chaperoning the college admissions journey are significant to the counter-narrative because research shows colleges and universities are building ethical character assessment into the college admissions process (Sternberg, 2013). Although challenges plaguing urban student transition to college are documented, we recognize Kozol's manipulative narratives and leadership caricatures give a false impression that administrative pressures (Welton & Williams, 2014) and hopelessness permanently divert leaders from assisting students on this journey. The ethical leadership behavior captured in these narratives exemplifies the impetus for researchers (e.g., Cranston & Kusanovick, 2014) designing experiments that assist school leaders in developing personal ethical capacities.

Through *embodying moral fortitude* these narratives show how in modeling ethical leadership educational leaders create a counter-narrative to Kozol's leadership caricature. The behaviors in these narratives mimic positive ethical leadership experiences found in previous research. Brown and Trevino (2006) as well as Mayer et al. (2009) found leader ethical behaviors were catalysts for similar behaviors in followers. Leadership behaviors associated with moral fortitude have been shown in research and practice to predict student success and reduce achievement disparities between ethnic groups (Sternberg, 2013). Leader moral fortitude here refutes theorists (e.g., Poff, 2010) who suggest a collective failure of educational leaders to expose students to integrity, honesty, trustworthiness, and virtue competencies in a meaningful way. Multiple researchers (Brown et al., 2005; Kalshoven et al., 2011; Rubin, Dierdorff, & Brown, 2010) have categorized traits such as trust and integrity as critical components of ethical leadership. These findings reflect behaviors found in other values-based leadership narrative research including concern for defining moments in followers' lives, multifaceted connection to stakeholders, and basic desire to serve others (Pless, 2007).

References

Adelman, C. (2005). Executive summary: The toolbox revisited: Paths to degree completion from high school through college. *Journal for Vocational Special Needs Education, 1*(28), 23–30.

Aronson, E. (2001). Integrating leadership styles and ethical perspectives. *Canadian Journal of Administrative Sciences, 18,* 244–257.

Auvinen, T. P., Lamsa, A., Sintonen, T., & Takala, T. (2013). Leadership manipulation and ethics in storytelling. *Journal of Business Ethics, 116,* 415–431. http://doi.org/10.1007/s10551-012-1454-8

Bowers, J., Rosch, D. M., & Collier, D. A. (2016). Examining the relationship between role models and leadership growth during the transition to adulthood. *Journal of Adolescent Research, 31*(1), 96–118.

Branch, E. (1992). Lessons in inequality. *Black Enterprise, 22*(10), 14.

Brown, M. E., Trevino, L. K., & Harrison, D. (2005). Ethical leadership: A social learning perspective for construct development and testing. *Organizational Behavior and Human Decision Processes, 97,* 117–134.

Ciulla, J. B. (2004). Leadership and the problem of bogus empowerment. In J. B. Ciulla (Ed.), *Ethics, the heart of leadership* (2nd ed., pp. 59–82). Praeger.

Cranston, J., & Kusanovick, K. (2014). More drama in school leadership: Developing creative and ethical capacities in the next generation of school leaders. *Canadian Journal of Educational Administration and Policy, 151,* 1–33.

De Hoogh, A. H., & Den Hartog, D. N. (2009). Ethical and despotic leadership, relationships with leaders' social responsibility, top management team effectiveness and subordinates' optimism: A multi-method study. *The Leadership Quarterly, 19,* 297–311. http://doi.org/10.1016/j.leaqua.2008.03.002

Hollander, E. P. (2004). Ethical challenges in the leader-follower relationship. In J. B. Ciulla (Ed.), *Ethics, the heart of leadership* (2nd ed., pp. 47–58). Praeger.

Hughes, C., & Jones, D. (2011). A relationship among public school leadership, ethics, and student achievement. *National Forum of Educational, Administration and Supervision Journal, 27*(2), 50–73.

Hussain, S., & Albarwani, T. (2015). Leadership for sustainability perceptions in higher education institutions in Oman. *Management in Education, 29*(4), 151–157. doi:10.1177/0892020615593788

Kalshoven, K., Den Hartog, D. N., & De Hoogh, A. B. (2011). Ethical leadership at work questionnaire (ELW): Development of a multidimensional measure. *The Leadership Quarterly, 22,* 51–60.

Klenke, K. (2008). *Qualitative research in the study of leadership.* Emerald.

Kozol, J. (1991). *Savage inequalities.* Harper Perennial.

Martinez, M. (2014). College information, support and opportunities for all? *Journal of Cases in Educational Leadership, 17*(2), 94–107.

Parry, K., & Kempster, S. (2014). Love and leadership: Constructing follower narrative identities of charismatic leadership. *Management Learning, 45*(1), 21–38. http://doi.org/10.1177/1350507612470602

Pless, N. (2007). Understanding responsible leadership: Role identity and motivational drivers. *Journal of Business Ethics, 74*(4), 437–456.

Poff, D. (2010). Ethical leadership and global citizenship: Consideration and sustainable future. *Journal of Business Ethics, 1*(93), 9–14.

Resick, C., Hargis, M. B., Shao, P., & Dust, S. B. (2013). Ethical leadership, moral equity judgments, and discretionary workplace behavior. *Human Relations, 66*(7), 951–972.

Rubin, R. S., Dierdorff, E. C., & Brown, M. E. (2010). Do ethical leaders get ahead? Exploring ethical leadership and promotability. *Business Ethics Quarterly, 20*(2), 215–236.

Steinbauer, R., Renn, R., Taylor, R., & Njoroge, P. (2014). Ethical leadership and followers' moral judgement: The role of follower perceived accountability and self-leadership. *Journal of Business Ethics, 120*(3), 381–392.

Stenmark, C. K., & Mumford, M. D. (2011). Situational impacts of leader ethical decision-making. *The Leadership Quarterly, 22,* 942–955. http://doi.org/10.1016/j.leadqua.2011.07.13

Sternberg, R. (2013). Character development: Putting in into practice in admission and instruction. *Journal of College Character, 14*(3), 253–258.

Trevino, L. K., Brown, M., & Hartman, L. P. (2003). A qualitative investigation of perceived executive ethical leadership: Perceptions from inside and outside the executive suite. *Human Relations, 55,* 5–37.

Welton, A., & Williams, M. (2014). Accountability strain, college readiness drain: Sociopolitical tensions involved in maintaining a college-going culture in a high minority, high poverty, Texas high school. *The High School Journal,* 171–204.

Williamson, L., Goosen, R. A., & Gonzalez, G. F., Jr. (2014). Faculty advising to support student learning. *Journal of Developmental Education, 38*(1), 20–24.

Yosso, T. J. (2005). Whose culture has capital? A critical race theory discussion of community cultural wealth. *Race Ethnicity and Education, 8*(1), 69–91.

Zorn, J. (1994). Victimology updated: Kozol's 'Savage Inequalities.' *Academic Questions, 7*(3), 72.

Guest Commentary and Reflection
Same Place, Different Race

H. RICHARD MILNER IV

This is an extraordinarily important book that provides a compelling collective counter-narrative to Jonathan Kozol's widely read and cited work, *Savage Inequalities*. Kozol's work has been read in courses, book clubs, and professional development series inside and outside of the United States and has served as a *particular kind of* window into experiences of Black people who live below the poverty line in what I call "urban intensive" (Milner, 2012) environments across the United States. From this book, we learn that our interpretations of human experience are deeply rooted in, influenced by, and shaped through our varied, complex, and dynamic identities. In other words, authors in this volume stress how our identities, paradigmatic ways of knowing, worldviews, and positionality are powerful determinants of how we see, understand, interpret, name, and explain the worlds we experience and observe.

Researchers have questioned who can and *should* conduct research with and about people and communities of color: those who live below the poverty line (Banks, 1998; Milner, 2007; Scheurich & Young, 1997; Tillman, 2002) as well as other minoritized communities. Scholarship has considered what it means for journalists and researchers alike to construct stories about themselves and others, both from an emic perspective (insider's view) as well as through the etic perspective (outsider's view). For instance, what values, beliefs, perspectives, and paradigms should be attended to when Kozol (and others) study and construct a story of other people's lived experiences? To what degree are Kozol's storylines co-constructed with others? Moreover, from a broader perspective, how do those inside a community make sense of their experiences in ways that attend to their own biases in knowledge construction and knowledge dissemination? And perhaps most importantly for this interconnected analysis, what do we learn when those indigenous to a community disrupt, nuance, counter, and protest a way of knowing that has been constructed from an outsider to their experiences?

Indeed, this book challenges readers and researchers to engage the obvious and that which may be implicit, taken for granted, or not overt. People of Color, for example, have diverse experiences sometimes based on their embodied difference, and authors in this volume stress how Kozol fails to demonstrate nuanced accounts of what he observes, hears, and reads about in the context under study. Centralizing the diversity among people, in her essay, "'I Have Seen the Mountaintop': Intersectionality and the Auto-ethnography of a Mediocre Student at a Gifted School," Heather Moore Roberson explained how students' diverse experiences in gifted education must be considered. People who share similar labels and characteristics are not monolithic. Even as Black students are labeled and viewed as "gifted," their experiences will vary, and educators must develop the skillset to respond to them in order to maximize students' learning, development, and sense of belonging.

Even as Kozol may have good intentions, the authors in this book nuance, counter, and shed light on issues, perspectives, and experiences that Kozol did not necessarily consider or share because his life experiences and lenses are likely limited by who he is as a raced, gendered, sexualized, classed, and politicized being. Drawing from assets of community, Theresa J. Canada, in the essay "'Old School' Urban Education: How Friends, Families, Communities and Teachers Support Success in Early Childhood" debunks the value of an ethos of competition and stressed how classmates supported each other in school. Contrary to the notion that Black students do not care about education or that they are not interested in academic success, students in Canada's community wanted to excel in every subject, and they supported each other to succeed. In Canada's words: "If someone did not receive a passing grade, we did not embarrass them. We would surround them to see if we could help them correct their mistakes . . . We all were in there together to do well and to not leave anyone behind" (this volume). Stressing the value of friendships and community, Canada reminds readers that those in their community had a strong value of education and worked together to support each other for academic success. Like Canada, the essay "Urban Social Capital: Three African American Women from Detroit Share Stories of Academic Success" by Diane Fuselier-Thompson, Ezella McPherson, and Carly Braxton highlights the centrality of fictive kin through social networks they created and social capital they cultivated. The authors share how the social capital gleaned from fictive kin not only guided their early schooling education and experience but also traversed their community contexts, positively shaping their collegiate experiences to equip them with valuable life lessons as Black women. The authors demonstrate how minoritized people have been historically and contemporarily misrepresented, exploited, silenced, and taken for granted when those outside of a community construct stories about them (Dillard, 2000; Stanfield, 1995).

In the essay "Dispelling the Myth of Despair and Hopelessness: How Ethical Leadership Creates a Counter Narrative to Kozol's Leadership Caricature," Lonnie R. Morris Jr. and Maceo A. Cooper-Jenkins challenge Kozol's account of leaders and leadership in *Savage Inequalities* that depict educational leaders situated in "impoverished urban schools as weak, desperate and diminished" (this volume). Moreover, these authors disrupt and counter pervasive narratives in Kozol's work that present education leaders as impoverished and unsure how to support and cultivate student success. These authors draw from empirical research to substantiate the many assets and strengths educational leaders demonstrated in their work. What happens, however, when people privilege Kozol's voice and view over others such as those in this book? What happens more generally when dominant White male voices, beliefs, ideologies, views, and practices are privileged, valued, and validated over the voices, experiences, and practices of those who live them? This book addresses these interrelated questions and pushes the field closer to building a knowledge base that more responsively and responsibly advances the field.

In conclusion, this book should be read as a companion text with (or perhaps in place of) Kozol's work, particularly *Savage Inequalities*. For people who do not have a deep understanding of complexities related to people, places, and institutions of this community, this book will provide much-needed nuance, content, and context. Fundamentally, the essays in this book shed light on what happens when people from different races (and identities and systems of knowing), understand, read, interpret, and write about the same place. The authors in this book have provided a powerful resource for those of us interested in disrupting and dismantling consistent and pervasive negative narratives about minoritized communities. *Bravo!*

Discussion Questions

1. What potential value, if any, does Kozol's analysis offer in shedding light on inequity in urban contexts?

2. If you could address Kozol directly, what would you encourage him to consider in revising his work, particularly his book *Savage Inequalities*?

3. What are some recommendations and implications from the essays that will help influence your future research and/or practices in communities inside of and outside of your own?

Additional Readings

Boutte, G. S. (2015). *Educating African American students: And how are the children?* Routledge.

Howard, T. C., Camangian, P. Edwards, E. J., Howard, M., Minkoff, A. C., Orange, T. Tunstall, J. D., & Watson, K. T. (2019). *All students must thrive: Transforming schools to combat toxic stressors and cultivate critical wellness.* International Center for Leadership in Education.

Love, B. L. (2019). *We want to do more than survive: Abolitionist teaching and the pursuit of educational freedom.* Beacon.

Milner, H. R. (2015). *Rac(e)ing to class: Confronting poverty and race in schools and classrooms.* Harvard Education Press.

Winn, M. T. (2018). *Justice on both sides: Transforming education through restorative justice.* Harvard Education Press.

References

Banks, J. A. (1998). The lives and values of researchers: Implications for educating citizens in a multicultural society. *Educational Researcher, 27*(7), 4–17.

Dillard, C. B. (2000). The substance of things hoped for, the evidence of things not seen: Examining an endarkened feminist epistemology in educational research and leadership. *International Journal of Qualitative Studies in Education, 13*(6), 661–681.

Milner, H. R. (2012). But what is urban education. *Urban Education, 47*(3), 556–561.

Milner, H. R. (2007). Race, culture, and researcher positionality: Working through dangers seen, unseen, and unforeseen. *Educational Researcher 36*(7), 388–400.

Scheurich, J. J., & Young, M. D. (1997). Coloring epistemologies: Are our research epistemologies racially biased? *Educational Researcher, 26*(4), 4–16.

Stanfield, J. H. (1995). The myth of race and the human sciences. *Journal of Negro Education, 64,* 218–231.

Tillman, L. C. (2002). Culturally sensitive research approaches: An African-American perspective. *Educational Researcher, 31*(9), 3–12.

Part 5

Renarrativizing "Home" (Place)

Chapter 14

And Still We Made It

Counter-Narratives of Success, Educational Attainment, and Opportunity in Atlanta

BRITTANY M. WILLIAMS AND LYNTORIA NEWTON

The belief that education functions as a meritocracy rests at the core of the American dream. The American dream posits that any American, including those from low income and otherwise disadvantaged beginnings, can "make it" if they study and work diligently (Karabel, 2005, Chapter 18; Meyer, 2010 in Sadovnik, 2010; Tierney, 2007). As a result, the American Dream is inextricably linked to public education. Meritocracy, like the American dream, rests upon the assumption that individual action dictates life outcomes. Accordingly, the existence of a meritorious education system "requires an American institution to teach it, sustain it, and provide the tools children need to pursue it" (Hochschild & Scovronick, 2004, p. 110; Karabel, 2005). But what exactly does a meritocratic educational system look like? Traditional academic success, as defined by grades and testing, is just one of many factors that can impact a student's overall wellness and well-being. Yet this success is often tied to White middle-class norms of success (Apple, 2010; Collins, 2010; Meyer, 2010). Thus, there is a widely held perception of educational success that is often judged by how quickly Students of Color *become White* (as socially and behaviorally constructed) and how fast low-income students mirror upper-middle-class actions.

In his analysis of inner-city schools in East St. Louis, Jonathan Kozol (1991) paints a picture of hopelessness, loss, and despair without explicitly acknowledging the systems of oppression that created these conditions. "There are four computers in the school, which holds almost 600 children" he similarly writes of students in a *failing* San Antonio school (Kozol, 1991, p. 231). This statement, like others in the text, fails to acknowledge the nuances of underfunded public schooling as well as the inherent inequity in a school funding system based on taxes when Black U.S. nationals work double time to gain forms of capital equal to those of their White counterparts only to lag behind due to generations of inequity.

Ultimately, Kozol fails to acknowledge the sociocultural structures that allow students to perform and develop in spite of the obstacles outlined in his text, thus ignoring the fact that while White and Black students function in *similar* educational systems, they do so from very different planes (Farmer-Hinton, Lewis, Patton, & Rivers, 2013; Albert, Barnes, Greenleaf, & Williams, 2014). "In a fair game," Michael Schwalbe writes, "no one gets special advantages" (Schwalbe, 2008, p. 53). "When a game is rigged," he continues, "some people get advantages that others don't; not surprisingly, the people who rig a game in their favor usually win" (Schwalbe, 2008, p. 53). Schwalbe and Kozol both make astute observations regarding inner-city schools: they often suffer from a severe lack of funding yet face comparison with communities whose students perform on a high level due to nepotism and long histories of discrimination that lead to wealth for some and generational poverty for others. Kozol's framing of urban education leaves us with a significant question and a defining point of departure for this text: what happens when structures of success do not reflect mainstream conceptualizations of educational attainment yet facilitate successful outcomes for students?

Toward a More Holistic Narrative

As Black women who came of age in the City of Atlanta, we know that the narratives about inner-city public schools fail to paint the full picture of our educational journeys. We also know this perception continues for students like us when reaching the higher education landscape (Harper, 2010; Harper, Patton, & Wooden, 2009; Patton, 2009). The dominant narrative on Atlanta Public Schools, in particular, is that they are plagued by a cheating scandal and rampant victimization, while failing to acknowledge how community support, teacher advocacy, and other forms of learning contribute to understandings and experiences of educational growth. High GPAs and test scores are typical indicators of student accomplishment, yet our status as high-achieving students was not defined by these constraints. More specifically, our educational journeys embraced alternative frameworks for learning and success such as community teaching, critical pedagogical practices, and the ability to engage with methods of nontraditional education, all of which contributed to our liberated understanding of success. As we excelled within and beyond the Atlanta Public School system, particularly through the 21st Century Atlanta Scholars program, we came to understand that success extends beyond diploma completion and must also include the ability to contribute to our communities. We also learned that knowledge transfer functions beyond teacher-to-student exchanges and can simultaneously include lessons learned from neighbors, community leaders, and peer relationships.

To date, there is little conversation about how our experiences have led us to *make lemons out of lemonade* as the elders in our families describe. Further, we often find ourselves combating preconceived perceptions of success and knowledge (Harper, 2010) when we inform people that we identify as proud products of Atlanta Public Schools. Where the words of those who learn of our Atlanta Public Schools pride fail to express negative sentiments, their facial expressions often say much more. Rather than viewing our backgrounds as sites of resistance building and character development, we are instead viewed as representations of educational deficits as compared to our White middle-class peers and colleagues (Harper, 2010; Yosso, 2005). We reframe this misconception by operationalizing Yosso's (2005) community cultural wealth (CCW) model as a standard by which we resist deficit perceptions of urban education (Yosso, 2005).

CCW provides a framework that represents how we walk through the world; it contextualizes our experiences with graduate study and gives voice to the issues and concerns we seek to illuminate around urban student success narratives. Yosso posits that we upend the notion that the forms of cultural capital predominantly available in resource-poor communities represent as being without and instead provides an antideficit outlook from which to view the skills and knowledge of students of color (Yosso, 2005). Yosso's model pushes against negative cultural assumptions that rest upon old stereotypes of families of color and success while highlighting the positive forms of capital students of color bring to the classroom, namely aspirational capital (Yosso, 2005). Both of us bring to educational spaces a level of determination, grit, and commitment to being better each day, a quality that our faculty has commended and that many of our peers have been envied for. While many would call it *overachieving*, we position our ambition as the driving force behind our obligation to doing and being twice as good as our colleagues. Accordingly, this reflective, integrated analysis positions urban public schools as places where alternative education and definitions of success are critical in navigating poverty and injustice and where new definitions of academic success might be imagined.

Brittany's Story

My current stance on educational attainment, academic success, and communal prosperity are relatively new. I came of age during the Bush era of the early 2000s, at a time when the City of Atlanta was home to what I can only describe as several thriving Black, middle-class, working-class, and *privileged poor* communities (Jack, 2016). My family was of the "privileged poor" sect, meaning those who lack socioeconomic capital but often mitigate this through resource-rich programs and other once-in-a-lifetime opportunities (Jack, 2016). For years, I viewed college (and education more broadly) as a means to a job rather than a space for inquiry, but I always knew higher education was a requirement. In my mind, education was a way I could come to afford the homes, cars, and ultimately livelihood that I would watch from afar and consume through media and popular culture narratives.

The desire to attain a lifestyle grander than my own ignited my passion for excelling. It was not enough to *do well* in school: I had to outperform and outshine each and every single student, then do it all again when in out-of-school-spaces. I now understand this as grit and determination, parts of my identity that are inextricably tied to a privileged poor upbringing I vow to never forget (Harper, 2010; Jack, 2016; Yosso, 2005). I have come to see my West Atlanta childhood as providing the experiences that gave root to my curiosity (Yosso, 2005). The "sketchy" people and places around me ("sketchy" being a coded term I often hear to mean "poor") did not stifle my upbringing but enhanced it. When I reflect on the academic structures that supported me outside of my school, I know that the Adamsville Library, Atlanta Urban Debate League, and 21st Century Atlanta Scholars programs were pivotal in my development because they created opportunities for enhancing my worldview.

The Adamsville branch of the Atlanta Public Library system is not an adequate representation of resources across the city, but it was home. I often found myself requesting texts that were available in wealthier neighborhoods with larger libraries but always reading them in my childhood apartment or at my local branch. The differences in library quality became especially salient to me in middle school when I realized how much Atlanta neighborhoods like Inman Park were carefully stocked in comparison to my Westside branch. Nevertheless, the homey feeling I got when my Black librarian reinforced that I could grow up to become anyone I wanted was part of why I often returned throughout elementary and middle school. Where many would see my library as useless due to the lack of funding and resources, I saw a place to complete homework assignments and to ask for help. This was especially true when I needed to gather data from encyclopedias and other resources prior to my parents' computer purchase.

The local library became not only a place of refuge but also where my librarian would double and triple check my assignments, quiz me to make sure I was up-to-date in my areas of study, and prove that I would always remember the research skills she helped me to develop. My experiences there were just some examples of where I gained support and accountability from those around me. Though I visited my local library less often once my parents purchased our first computer, it still held and continues to hold a special place in my heart. There was a sense of care in these experiences that contributed to my development, but they remain part of a narrative that rarely, if ever, makes it to the mainstream. This was not unique to me, and they certainly were not isolated situations. Many of my peers have taken to social media to write about the indispensable ways in which our coaches, librarians, teachers, and district leaders who considered us one of their own influenced our achievement—my story is a tribute and commitment to doing the same. Despite growing up as a poor Black girl, I did not truly understand the impact of power, privilege, and oppression on educational attainment and outcomes. It wasn't until I began to take Africana studies and sociology courses in college that I came to realize the role(s) of systemic oppression in my life and the lives of others. In my home, we were often able to connect the ways in which racism affected us on a micro level in terms of job placement and home loans but not on macro levels through redlining and other forms of systemic oppression. This is because many of these disadvantages were counteracted by my engagement with the Atlanta Public School 21st Century Atlanta Scholars program—a program supported and developed by then superintendent Dr. Beverly L. Hall.

During my 21st Century tenure, I learned standard dining etiquette for day-long interviews and formal occasions, came to know how to name the concept of "code switching," began to acquire knowledge on navigating academic and social landscapes, and was often reminded that I was more than a test score. Many of the leaders and primary facilitators of the program would help us to develop and craft narratives that would become the cornerstone of our college entrance essays and enabled us to familiarize ourselves with multiple cultural literacies that would allow us to not only enter college but to excel in what would ultimately be a foreign environment. When I would come home late from 21st Century programs, extra study sessions provided by my English literature teachers, or marching band practice, many of the drug dealers and people otherwise deemed "bad" by the larger society would greet me at the bus stop and watch until I made it to my parents' apartment safely. "You gotta [sic] make it, for all of us," I remember one of them telling me. These experiences are representative of a larger culture of caring for one another and creating support and opportunity where they may not otherwise exist. These were the moments that shifted my concept of education, schooling, and ultimately learning, and they were never a direct result of state-mandated curricula. Instead, they were a result of the labor of my teachers, community leaders, and even local drug dealers: all of whom desired to see *some of us make it.*

Lyntoria's Story

I spent most of my formative years living and attending racially diverse public schools in Battle Creek, Michigan. In middle school, I attended classes with many of the same teachers who taught my mother, aunts, uncle, and cousins, and my teachers would often remind me of this. Upon entering Battle Creek Central High School as a freshman, I was prepared to graduate from the same high school my family attended for generations. However, the summer after finishing my freshman year at Battle Creek Central High School, my parents decided to move to Atlanta, Georgia, thus changing the trajectory of my academic career. I did not attend the same high school from freshman to senior year, so my parents knew that much of my success would depend on my own self-advocacy and the interventions of teachers of color who would work well beyond their job descriptions to ensure my success.

Upon moving to Atlanta, my parents and I quickly learned that Atlanta schools abided by extremely strict zoning and district boundaries. I was required to attend a high school in my zoning district, which at that time was in a transitional phase. In addition to transitioning into a school of multiple "small learning communities," my new high school was also in the midst of a major renovation. This meant that I, along with hundreds of other students, would have to be bused an hour across town to a dilapidated former middle school building. During my short time at South Atlanta High School, I was confronted with what Kozol (1991) would refer to as "savage inequalities." My school was more than 90% African American, and most of us came from socioeconomically challenged backgrounds. My personal transition to a new high school during a simultaneously transitional moment for South Atlanta High School was the first time that I felt forgotten as a student, invisible, and completely ill-equipped to thrive in my learning environment. I was reminded of these inequalities each and every day when I had to share worn textbooks with missing pages with my fellow classmates and adjust to the presence of long-term, ill-qualified substitute teachers and overcrowded classrooms.

After the first semester of my sophomore year, my parents noticed that my schooling situation was having a negative impact on my mental health and academic success, and we agreed that it would be best for me to return to Michigan and stay with relatives for the duration of the school year. Upon my return the summer of my junior year, my parents moved to a new neighborhood that shared split zoning with both South Atlanta High School and George Washington Carver High School of Arts, a performing arts high school just minutes away from South Atlanta High School on the southeast side of Atlanta. This is important to me because prior to moving to Atlanta, I had participated in my school orchestra as a violinist. While Carver High School did not have a string orchestra, they did have a harp ensemble, which I was interested in joining. Carver High School was at a much later stage of the "smaller learning communities" implementation, which had already been in place for two years. By the time I enrolled at Carver, the small classroom renovations had taken hold with the student-to-teacher ratio around 23:1. Here, the environment was starkly different from anything I had experienced at my other schools. I saw my principal and guidance counselor on a daily basis; they knew each student by name. Most of our teachers were sincere in their care for us, not through Kozol's approach of White guilt but rather a personal investment in our community. At Carver School of the Arts, most of our student body consisted of African American and Latinx students, and our teachers were predominantly African American. In a school system where the district's southwestern schools were disproportionately affected by standardized testing, we excelled all thanks to the dedication of teachers of color who took on a "save ourselves" attitude in approaching the curriculum. In preparation for state-mandated standardized tests that would determine our academic futures, as passing was required for our diplomas, many of my teachers of color effectively bridged our state curriculum with an Afrocentric curriculum and optional Saturday school sessions. This meant integrating historical and contemporary African American figures of prominence into our lessons. Our high school student and teacher body knew that we did not have all the resources that many high schools on the North Side of town had. But what we lacked in resources, we excelled at in community and peer support. My teachers constantly reminded me that higher education would be my 'ticket out' of poverty and provided me with the tools to access college applications and free SAT/ACT tutoring. Though most of my classmates and myself were from low-income backgrounds, when we walked through those doors each morning we were a family of students, teachers, and administrators who understood the power and necessity of saving ourselves.

Discussion

We take issue with the narrative Kozol (1991) and his supporters have fashioned. He paints urban communities as spaces associated with dilapidated structures, communities with lack of parental support rather than working adults, and where victimization functions multigenerationally, making learning nearly impossible, while failing to show counter-narratives of success (Farmer-Hinton et al., 2013). Accordingly, Kozol and his sympathizers fail to mention the communal sense of responsibility and belonging those charged with educating and supporting youth in low-income urban communities held for us and the ways in which this often enabled our success despite the "savage inequalities" that exist in urban schools (Farmer-Hinton et al., 2013; Tyson, 2003; Williams & Bryan, 2012; Williams et al., 2014). Accordingly, our issue is not with the totality of Kozol's text, as there is certainly truth to the claims and analyses made on urban education. Like Black scholars before us, however, we take issue with the lack of holistic care associated with narratives on urban education and how standardized education and sociocultural capital impact our experiences (Farmer-Hinton et al., 2013; Yosso, 2005). The care and support we received at our local libraries and other learning-centered spaces were not ours alone and remain hidden in narratives on urban education.

At school, students become accustomed to and learn cultural norms and standards, and the same can be said of the reproduction of social boundaries (Brint, 2006; Collins in Sadovnik, 2010, 2007; Pallas, 1999; Tyson, 2003; Wells, 2009). This means school, for many students, can be a site for positive and negative reinforcement, thereby making educational environments critical to how students come to understand themselves and those around them. In a schooling structure that bases success mostly on test scores and middle-class behavior, inner-city students like us are automatically disadvantaged because the barometer by which our experiences become measured are often the opposite—as in middle class and White—of who we are. This leaves little room for discussing the personal and sociocultural skills that students gain from their teachers and community leaders, which may not always show up on tests but are arguably equally important in student success and educational acquisition beyond the K–12 level, thereby reinforcing a deficit perspective from which we understand students (Harper, 2010; Yosso, 2005).

This very negative and one-sided perception is evidenced throughout Kozol's text. It becomes especially visible in the ways he discusses how wealthy Texans perceived urban education (Kozol, 1991). Kozol paints a narrative that wealthy Texans understand urban education insofar as it allows poor people the competence to vote but rarely in their own interests—thereby suggesting a lack of agency among Black Texans (Kozol, 1991, p. 216). Kozol, like other researchers, misses the mark here when he fails to unveil how cultural and social resistance manifests in urban communities and provides a type of educational awareness that leads to conditions no one should ever have to live in. Farmer-Hinton, Lewis, Patton, and Rivers (2013) connect experiences like these to those highlighted in Yosso's CCW model (Yosso, 2005). Even though schools reward students who fall within an accepted set of cultural norms, meaning teachers react favorably toward students who display elitism—we know that the life skills we attained in urban public schooling are forms of knowledge one can only acquire through experience (Kingston, 2001). Kingston

(2001) declares, "Whether schools merely certify the elite culture or also actually cultivate it is unclear, but in any case, the cultural resources of the elite significantly account for their academic success and hence, their later success in careers" (p. 89). While this is true of our peers who grew up in socioeconomically rich communities, we know it fails to represent the alternative educational structures and new definitions of success to which we ascribe.

For each of us, being a part of an educational system where our teachers and programs took seriously our development meant internalizing its importance to us. With regard to the 21st Century Atlanta Scholars program with which we are both formerly affiliated, we were able to spend time with high-performing Atlanta students across the district, obtain more personalized and targeted assistance with college admissions, and discuss navigating the world beyond our home communities. As many of us would be first-generation college students, learning to navigate across social classes and cultural environments was extremely crucial to our academic development and precollegiate preparation. This mentorship and guidance in the face of prevailing assumptions of failure helped equip us for postsecondary education in ways many of our middle-class peers were not. Rather than entering higher education as starry-eyed, bushy-tailed, first-year students with eyes wide shut, we entered the educational environment aware of the obstacles we needed to overcome and did so.

Many scholars have repeatedly highlighted the significance of mentorship and one-on-one development in Black student growth and academic success, opportunities we were afforded well before acquiring the language to write about them (Carter, 2005; Carter, 2010; Harris, 2008; Patton, 2009; Williams & Bryan 2012; Williams et al., 2014). Similarly, researchers (Carter, 2005; Carter, 2010; Harris, 2008; Williams & Bryan, 2012; Williams, 2014) have drawn attention to the significance of minoritized student pride in their heritage and communities as critical in school success. When Black students, more specifically, take greater pride in who they are, they fare better not only academically but also socially in educational and professional settings (Carter, 2005; Carter, 2010; Harris, 2008; Williams & Bryan, 2012; Williams, 2014). Educational leaders invested in teaching us how to express pride in our home communities propelled us to become more resilient—or display grit that many of our peers struggle to develop in postsecondary education. Where higher education professionals find themselves questioning the lack of grit in middle-class students, we find our experiences and those of other students like us to be evidence to the contrary. We have become, then, the model for students who need to learn how to accept feedback and use it to propel and inform their growth and continuing education.

The life-altering moments and opportunities we grew accustomed to were not limited to the two of us. Yet, when we discuss the institutions and educational systems from which we've come, we are often met with confusion or perplexity—a burning desire to figure out how we managed to thrive in postsecondary spaces that many have come to believe are solely meant for the academically and economically privileged. This is especially true as Atlanta Public Schools (APS), viewed through media sensationalism, has come to solely represent failure, disappointment, and mediocrity. What society fails to acknowledge is the significance of how APS students, and in our case younger family members and one another, may internalize these perspectives. These are experiences that can lead to additional stressors and struggles beyond those that inner-city youths are already tasked with overcoming. Given this, as well as our commitment to viewing urban education beyond deficit perspectives, we have come to understand success and education as the ability to thrive academically rather than being thwarted by unhealthy comparisons to socioeconomically advantaged students using scales that were not designed with our realities in mind (Farmer-Hinton et al., 2013; Harper, 2010; Yosso, 2005).

The skills we came to learn, particularly those beyond standardized testing measures, continue to contribute to our academic success. Collectively, we hold bachelor's degrees from an elite liberal arts institution, a master's degree from an Ivy League, and recently completed degrees in top-tier Ph.D. and MFA programs. We are both proud of our accomplishments but reject the idea that they alone represent our success. In fact, it was never our academic study alone that prepared us for postsecondary education. Instead, it was learning coping strategies to survive in a systemically oppressive Western society and navigating academic spaces prided on defining success as exclusive practices that has undeniably shaped our ability to function both within and outside of elite academic circles. Though the process of attaining success is ongoing and we expect to continue learning for the rest of our lives, the resiliency and belief of self that was honed during our tenure in Atlanta Public Schools lives on inside us forever. What were once perceived to be unrealistic demands, especially those set by the Black women tasked with teaching us, became the tools and techniques that allow us to share this story and to contribute to the larger urban education literary canon. It is also the strength that compels us to pay it forward to future generations of urban public school students.

Conclusion

By painting urban education with a broad brush of despair, researchers and scholars fail to acknowledge the communal structures and systems in place that facilitate growth despite the spatial constructs that students exist within. Until Black students, and students of color broadly, are considered part of the norming standards of education, the classroom will remain a space where previously acclimated social and cultural capital, White privilege, power, and dominance manifest with and without the presence of White people. Students of color do not resist learning, we contend, but instead resist the idea that one must become closer to "Whiteness" and embody the elite's cultural practices to attain success and reflect educational attainment (Harris, 2010; Kingston, 2001). Accordingly, we argue in favor of educational success models that consider the sociocultural capital minoritized students possess (Harper, 2010; Yosso, 2005).

By narrating these experiences, we pay homage to local educators, activists, and parents who enabled us to become the women we are today and to thank those no longer with us, such as the late Eyatta Fischer—formerly of Atlanta Public Schools who introduced us to the very call for the present book. As we illuminate, it is time for a more holistic picture of urban schooling (Farmer-Hinton et al., 2013). Inner-city schools and communities could greatly benefit from increased understanding, greater compassion, and deconstruction of systemic oppression should we wish to stop students from exiting formal educational structures well before they have had the chance to start. Moreover, we maintain that urban schools do not need more reductionist and hackneyed narratives suggesting the impossibility of triumph in urban communities as inner-city schools do not simply produce victims. Instead, we need educational structures that understand the totality of student experiences and those that encourage resiliency and promote multiple standards of student success. We stand before you as active agents who have sculpted our own narratives despite limited resources and a lack of systematic support. Moreover, we stand as representations of agency and wherewithal: able to do a lot despite being given very little. We challenge every educator, parent, and student reading this narrative to unlearn single-sided descriptions of urban education. We challenge you to then take on the task of writing them, thereby contributing to a larger culture with more holistic views of urban education.

References

Apple, M. W. (2010). Whose markets, whose knowledge? In A. R. Sadovnik (Ed.), *Sociology of education: A critical reader* (2nd ed., pp. 195–211). Routledge.

Bischoff, K. (2008). School district fragmentation and racial residential segregation: How do boundaries matter? *Urban Affairs Review, 44*(2), 182–217. http://doi.org/10.1177/1078087408320651

Brint, S. (2006). *Schools and societies* (2nd ed.). Stanford University Press.

Carter, P. L. (2010). Race and cultural flexibility among students in different multiracial schools. *Teachers College Record, 112*(6), 1529–74. https://doi.org/10.1177/016146811011200605

Collins, R. (2010). Functional and conflict theories of educational stratification. In A. R. Sadovnik (Ed.), *Sociology of education: A critical reader* (2nd ed., pp. 37–52). Routledge.

Farmer-Hinton, R. L., Lewis, J. D., Patton, L. D., & Rivers, I. D. (2013). Dear Mr. Kozol . . . Four African American women scholars and the re-authoring of *Savage Inequalities*. *Teachers College Record, 115*(5), 1–38. https://doi.org/10.1177/016146811311500501

Harper, S. R. (2010). An anti-deficit framework for research on students of color in STEM. In S. R. Harper & C. B. Newman (Eds.), *New directions for institutional research: Vol. 148. Students of color in STEM: Engineering a new research agenda* (pp. 63–74). Jossey-Bass.

Harper, S. R., Patton, L. D., & Wooden, O. S. (2009). Access and equity for African American students in higher education: A critical race historical analysis of policy efforts. *Journal of Higher Education, 80*(4), 389–414. https://doi.org/10.1080/00221546.2009.11779022

Harris, A. L. (2008). Optimism in the face of despair: Black-white differences in beliefs about school as a means for upward social mobility. *Social Science Quarterly, 89*, 608–630. http://doi.org/10.1111/j.1540-6237.2008.00551.x

Jack, A. A. (2016). (No) harm in asking: Class, acquired cultural capital, and academic engagement at an elite university. *Sociology of Education, 89*(1), 1–19. https://doi.org/10.1177/0038040715614913

Karabel, J. (2005). *The chosen: The hidden history of admission and exclusion at Harvard, Yale, and Princeton*. Houghton Mifflin.

Kingston, Paul. (2001). The unfulfilled promise of cultural capital theory. *Sociology of Education, 74*, 88–99. https://doi.org/10.2307/2673255

Kozol, J. (1991). *Savage inequalities: Children in America's schools.* Harper Perennial.

Meyer, J. W. (2010). The effects of education as an institution. In A. R. Sadovnik (Ed.), *Sociology of education: A critical reader,* 2nd edition (pp. 133–148). Routledge.

Pallas, A. M. (Ed.). (1999). James S. Coleman and the purposes of schooling. In *Research in sociology of education and socialization* (Vol. 19, pp. 9–34). JAI Press.

Patton, L. D. (2009). My sister's keeper: A qualitative examination of significant mentoring relationships among African American women in graduate and professional schools. *Journal of Higher Education, 80*(5), 510–537.

Schwalbe, M. (2008). *Rigging the game: How inequality is reproduced in everyday life.* Oxford University Press.

Tierney, W. G. (2007). Merit and affirmative action in education: Promulgating a democratic public culture. *Urban Education, 42,* 385–402. http://doi.org/10.1177/0042085907304911

Tyson, K. (2003). Notes from the back of the room: Problems and paradoxes in the schooling of young Black students. *Sociology of Education, 76,* 326–343. http://doi.org/10.2307/1519869

Wells, A. S. (2009). *Why boundaries matter: A study of five separate and unequal Long Island school districts.* Teachers College Press.

Williams, J. M., & Bryan, J. (2013). Overcoming adversity: High-achieving African American youth's perspectives on educational resilience. *Journal of Counseling & Development, 91,* 291–300. http://doi.org/10.1002/j.1556-6676.2013.00097.x

Williams, J. M., Greenleaf, A. T., Albert, T., & Barnes, E. F. (2014). Promoting educational resilience among African American students at risk of school failure: The role of school counselors. *Journal of School Counseling, 12*(9), 1–34. https://files.eric.ed.gov/fulltext/EJ1034726.pdf

Yosso, T. J. (2005). Whose culture has capital? A critical race theory discussion of community cultural wealth. *Race Ethnicity and Education, 8*(1), 69–91. https://doi.org/10.1080/13613

Chapter 15

In Search of Oz

Culture, Education, and Counter-Narratives of Inequity in Southern Black Schools

TOBY S. JENKINS

Introduction

In the classic story, *The Wizard of Oz* (Baum, 1900) Dorothy is swept up in a storm and taken away to a foreign and sometimes frightening land. Dorothy spends the length of the movie searching for a sense of belonging, searching for home. Along the way, she meets other abandoned souls: those that have a shortcoming here or there and who are also looking for someone to patch them up. As a collective, they are in search of a wizard to work his magic and meet their unique needs. They are searching for Oz. In many ways, this story mirrors the educational experience for many traditionally marginalized students. Students are searching for educational leaders who are willing to take bold transformative action in order to provide them a truly impactful education. And educators are still searching for effective ways to engage, educate, and serve these communities of students (Rendón, Jalomo, & Nora, 2004; Lopez, 1993; Lambert, Terenzini, & Lattuca, 2007; Hurtado, 1992; Harper, Patton, & Wooden, 2009). Part of the problem is that in our attempt to "transform" education, we stand still. We continue to focus on faults and problems rather than taking a creative and inspiring journey (the yellow brick road) toward fresh perspectives. We focus on pathology rather than possibility.

We focus on pathology when we repeatedly describe the long list of problems and failures within "urban" schools, resulting in a national image of "urban" schools as educational dead-lands and "urban" communities as scary wastelands. Even now as the city is trendy and downtown is the rave, "urban" is still code for the bad parts of town. Fifteen years ago, the code was "inner city" ("8 Sneaky Racial Codes," 2014). This type of oppressive geographic labeling is not new to any historically disenfranchised group of people. In the 1950s, the poor Black neighborhoods in any major city were known as the "Black Bottoms" ("The Black Bottom," 2016). These were the communities with no view, difficult access out, and where scores of African Americans were packed onto the worst land in the city. They lived there because that's what they could afford. They lived there because segregation didn't allow much else. They still live there because that's what economic oppression looks like. The Black Bottom is not just a part of history: it is very much a part of our current social norm. In 2005 the Black Bottom was the Lower Ninth Ward in New Orleans. I share this to acknowledge that the intersecting powers of economic and racial oppression are real. But as deficient and difficult as life might be, the Black Bottom is not a hopeless place. Especially when it comes to education. The view of education from the bottom is that of a sunrise—of opportunity, of hope. And so, this aligning of economics, education, hope, and optimism literally becomes a part of the cultural experience for many communities of students.

In 2007, I began a long-term research study examining the ways that college students from ethnically diverse backgrounds define culture and explain its utility in their lives (Jenkins, 2013). After five years of engaging in individual and group dialogues and reading self-authored cultural life stories of over 150 students (across various ethnicities: African diaspora, Asian Pacific American, Latino, and European American), I came to better understand what culture means to young adults in contemporary society. Of course, there were the usual suspects—family, spirituality, art, community, and food. But there were two particularly interesting elements that all students seemed to discuss when describing their culture. First, they saw their culture as being valuable because it taught them important politics of survival. According to these students, your cultural community teaches you how to navigate the tough terrain of racism, classism, sexism, and oppression (Jenkins, 2013). Rather than viewing the very difficult circumstances their family might have been facing as a deficit, they viewed these struggles as important spaces to learn life lessons of tenacity and resilience. The other surprising descriptive was that almost all of the students discuss education as defining their culture. I wasn't surprised about education being valued by their home community or family. But I did find it interesting that when asked broad questions like, "What is one major thing that defines your culture?," the student response was, "education" (Jenkins, 2013). The sense of hope and optimism in education was still present within their families and the dedication to making sure their children were educated was also very much alive. But also students often felt that even if their parents had limited abilities to teach them the complicated intricacies of college success, their parents had still given them a firm foundation to help them be successful (Jenkins, 2013). Essentially, the major questions I sought answers to were the following: Do contemporary college students have a sense of cultural efficacy? And do they believe that their culture is a valuable and useful tool to help them navigate life?

Cultural efficacy is ultimately about valuing the cultural capital that marginalized communities have to offer. Centered on the cultural experience of ethnically diverse communities, Yosso (2005) shares six forms of cultural capital that provide a representative voice for the cultural inheritance that is often deemed valuable by the cultural group regardless of their value to the larger society. These include (1) aspirational capital or the ability to achieve hopes and dreams; (2) linguistic capital or multiple language skills; (3) familial capital or family history and memory; (4) social capital or support systems in the form of friendship and community networks; (5) navigational capital or the skill to navigate through various institutions; and (6) resistant capital or the skills developed through behavior that work in opposition to oppression. In light of these factors, Yosso (2005) describes community cultural wealth as the total inheritance of the skills present in these six forms of cultural capital. In my studies of both the contemporary meaning of culture to college students and the historical cultural experiences within southern Black schools, I have used Yosso's cultural capital framework to ground my research. To understand the rich cultural heritage with which students enter any educational environment is to truly understand the benefits and personal impact of culture.

In this chapter, I will specifically examine African American education from a "within the history" and "inside the culture" perspective. I can best explain the value of this "inside the culture" approach by sharing a bit of my personal life. As a busy working couple and parents to a two-year-old, my husband and I often struggle to keep up with life. At the end of the day, many things are not accomplished. And if someone were to come into our home with their outsider stranger's eye, they might immediately see all of the chaos—the toys on the floor, dishes in the sink, appliances that need to be fixed, and the general truth that the house is too small, too old, and too worn for us. What they wouldn't see is the hard work, struggles, and sacrifices that I made years ago as a young single woman to buy a second home in my childhood community as a way to invest in the declining neighborhood. They wouldn't see the community of neighbors who now pitch in to help us—the teenage boys who take our garbage cans to the street for a dollar, not because they need the money but simply because it's a good thing to help your neighbors. They wouldn't see the old family friend, J.R., who does yardwork for us because he can't find other employment. So though we could probably get those same boys to cut the grass for less money, we save that task for J. R. to help him pay his bills. They wouldn't see the family dinners every night, story time every evening, and porch time every summer. And most importantly, they wouldn't see the history there. The home is next door to my parents' house where I was born, raised, walked, and played. Now my child is playing and walking on that same land, making his way over to Nanny and Papa's house each day for a visit. We are family. We are home. I am a college professor. My husband is a retired veteran working in his second career. We can afford much more than this. But right now, I'm not sure that living elsewhere is worth the cultural price that we might pay. And this has always been the case with our schools. My critique of Kozol's *Savage Inequalities* is more of a caution against observing, analyzing, and labeling communities through the eye of a "cultural stranger."

After working so many years in education, one thing I know for sure is that there are no perfect schools. There is always something missing. Overcrowded schools are not okay. Understaffed schools can't adequately serve students. Any underfunded organization cannot produce at its full capacity. I make no positive case for the underfunding and under-resourcing of schools. But what I am suggesting is that many communities of people (and the institutions that they populate) have been historically labeled as "deficient," "problematic," and "difficult" without seeing the full picture of their cultural life. One of the critical pieces of learning about truly transformative education is that it really has very little to do with resources, structures, and numbers and much more to do with cultures, communities, and love.

A few years ago, I decided to begin a multiyear project collecting the oral histories of African American elders who attended Black schools in the South. I am a higher education scholar concerned with issues of cultural inclusion and cultural practice on college campuses. I have come to realize that to truly understand how cultural inclusion should look in practice, you need to get off the campus and go into community environments where cultural engagement is done so well it's almost organic. A conversation with my mother sparked the idea about the Black school project. She spent about 19 years serving as a teaching assistant in one of the worst middle schools in our city. She taught learning-disabled students, which was another code for students with behavioral problems. She may have only had one or two students with true developmental delays. The rest were just rowdy. The class was so difficult it required two instructors to lead the classroom. In nineteen years, my mother had seven lead teachers. Each teacher lasted less than three years. A few left after one year. All of the lead teachers were White. All of the students were Black. I share this information on race because after years of hearing my mother's crazy stories about the students chasing teachers out of the classroom, I have come to understand that her ability to stay was rooted in a sort of cultural love. My mother used absolutely no formal training in her work with those kids. She actually didn't have any: her teaching assistant role didn't require a college degree. She referred to no theories. She had very few resources. But I cannot help but think that maybe my mother was able to teach a group of poor kids who were a little rough around the edges because she was one of them. She was raised on a farm in South Carolina and was used to having very little. As a teacher, she used the resources that Black folks have used for centuries to make it through tough situations: imagination, creativity, sternness, and love. She taught them with a pedagogical approach I call "mama love." She engaged them in cultural art projects that had these students, who were supposedly the most learning disabled in the school, winning state awards that no other class in the school was winning. She completely ignored the school's reading lists and brought African American historical fiction to read aloud to them (most of them could not read). They so anticipated story hour that many of them began to ask her for extra help to learn to read themselves.

Of course, I think she's great because she's my mom. But as an educator, researcher, and evaluator, I also had this gut feeling that the key to her success lay in her ability to boost a cultural sense of self in those students. Students loved school because they saw themselves in it. This brings me to the work of Black schools. Many Black teachers have been doing this for years—loving students, believing in them, culturally affirming them, and seeing their work as educators as a way to contribute to the upliftment of their racial community. Perhaps then, looking at the cultural genius of Black schools is a way to better understand what truly culturally inclusive education looks like. Hearing the cultural stories of Black school alumni might help us to grasp how a school might be resource deficient yet still culturally rich. In this chapter, I will first reflect on the critical importance of culturally centered education and ethnographic research by revisiting two important scholars, W. E. B. Du Bois and Carter G. Woodson. Finally, I will share the snippets of the oral stories collected from African American alumni of Black schools in South Carolina. The memories shared by the African American alumni of these schools help to paint a picture of the rich cultural community that often lies beneath the surface of inequity.

Background

The Wonderful Wizard: W. E. B. Du Bois

The introduction to this chapter was framed by the story of the Wizard of Oz. As the story goes, when the characters finally reach the Emerald City they find that the wizard is just a regular guy. He has no magical abilities, no answers, no superpowers. He simply had a title that made others believe in him. Because his initials, O.Z., were etched on his hot air balloon when he arrived in the land of Oz, the residents assumed he was the grand wizard sent to rule over the land (Baum, 1900). Two simple letters gave him authority. Within the arena of educational research we can sometimes make this same mistake of over-privileging research that has been highly publicized as the premier authority. With the groundbreaking fieldwork of Jonathan Kozol (1991), there has been a tendency through the years for educational leaders and scholars to "read" his work through a one-dimensional lens: one voice of authority on urban inequity; one lens through which to view urban schools; one scathing denouncement of poverty and inequality in education. One of the problems that comes with this form of group thinking among educators is that we don't take time to encounter new perspectives, evaluations, and readings of what life in an urban school is actually like in a contemporary world. We generally agree that there hasn't been much gain or change over the years, and so we must continue to take up the cause of fighting the deprivation in urban schools. And we continue to reach back to the work of experts like Kozol to champion this cause. I actually don't challenge the authenticity of Kozol's read of the urban schools that he visited. His work reflects how he truly saw it—his lens, his view. I am simply suggesting that his gaze wasn't culturally deep enough. There is value in looking to the views and perspectives of other "wizards" or ethnographic scholars. In fact, there is a classic ethnographic educational scholar who did the work of visiting with and working for poor, primarily African American schools in rural settings long before Kozol's work examining urban schools.

Revisiting the work of W. E. B. Du Bois is critical to this conversation because his work is an example of the "within the culture" lens that I mentioned earlier. He actually worked as a teacher in the communities about which he eventually wrote. He lived in these communities (often with the families of his students). In fact, his Harvard credentials don't make a work like *The Souls of Black Folk* (1903) an endearing and critical piece of cultural ethnography. The time that Du Bois actually spent living with and among southern Black folk is what makes his research valid. He did more than observe school life: he visited the families, slept in homes, and walked out to the farms to truly understand the lives of his students. He came away from his work in rural Black schools understanding more than the practice of educating African Americans, rather he understood education as one critical component of African American life.

As a young educator, Du Bois admittedly spent a lot of time being genuinely frustrated and struggling to educate communities who were living in real poverty, facing dire social oppression, and barely able to commit to attending school because of the labor demands of farming. Yet he writes a text that ultimately expresses an appreciation, admiration, and love for the souls of Black folk. His words don't paint their lives as perfect, but he expresses an appreciation for the way they encounter this struggle on a daily basis. He doesn't condemn the school, the student, or the parent. He simply paints for us a rich and full story of what the struggle to be educated looks like among this community of poor people.

The Wonderful Wizard: Carter G. Woodson

Before overcrowded urban schools, metal detectors, and zero-tolerance policies—and before the narrative of equating anything "urban" with poor, deadly, Black, or Latino—elegantly built southern White missionary schools were doing the savage work of educating culture, race, and identity out of African Americans. Many of the early Freedman schools constructed throughout the South originally sought to acculturate African Americans to European cultural norms. What is important to note here is that in many cases, these schools were a stark contrast to the modern image of the "urban" school in the "hood." Set in the South, with a vast amount of land and beautiful landscape many of these schools were aesthetically appealing. The Penn School, on St Helena Island, South Carolina, was a beautiful campus with several classroom buildings, a carpentry workshop, a chapel, a cafeteria, and several dormitories to house students during the week. The school had significant resources to provide a comprehensive learning program so that when students graduated, they would be prepared for college and also able to build their own homes, sew their own clothes, and grow their own food (http://www.penncenter.com). This is undoubtedly impressive. But it is not without its own cultural limitations.

Though at the most basic level, the intent of the missionaries was a worthy one, the school curriculum was most often Eurocentric and forced a suppression of existing African American language and culture (Lynn, 2006). Students had to be "taught" culture because they were assumed to not have any. The ways that education policies and curricula within schools funded by the wealthy and White can be used to culturally strip students of cultural efficacy do as much injustice to students as the unequal resources that are often found in schools segregated by class.

The importance of a school's ability to build cultural efficacy cannot be understated. But this argument is admittedly not new. In 1933, Carter G. Woodson stated, "To handicap a student by teaching him that his black face is a curse and that his struggle to change his condition is hopeless is the worst sort of lynching . . . it is strange, then, that the friends of truth and the promoters of freedom have not risen against the present propaganda in schools" (p. 7). I argue that this statement still holds much weight in our contemporary world. *The Mis-Education of the Negro* (1933) has been lauded as one of the most important books on education ever written. Yet, like Du Bois, Woodson is another scholar studied often in African American studies and rarely mentioned in the study of education. In his explanation of the insights shared within his book, Woodson (1933) explains that the project was a result of over 40 years of participation in the education of the "black, brown, yellow and white races . . . with students in all grades from kindergarten to the university" (p. i). In other words, his conclusions and reflections were based on decades of professional experience, engagement, and ethnographic study of educational environments. In Woodson's assessment, the very idea that educational institutions will create the next great leader, visionary or change agent among impoverished ethnically diverse populations is virtually impossible because in many ways, school has educated the agency out of this population. Woodson was one of the first proponents of culturally responsive pedagogy. To him, African Americans did not simply need the same education as White Americans; they needed an education that would fully include their history, heritage, social conditions, and culture from a serious and appreciative point of inquiry. In other words, a poor kid in an urban school doesn't need the same education her peers are receiving in an affluent suburban school; she needs an education that matters in her life and that privileges her cultural experience. She needs an education that helps her to navigate her world: to move within it, beyond it, and come back to it in order to transform it. But too often, educational systems crush this sense of agency and optimism for social change. "The same educational process, which inspires and stimulates the oppressor with the thought that he is everything . . . depresses and crushes at the same time the spark of genius in the Negro by making him feel that his race does not amount to much" (Woodson, 1933, p. iii.). According to Woodson (1933), any person receiving this type of education is more culturally damaged than the person who might attend the less affluent but culturally richer school. He warned against the tendency to compare educational institutions without the full context of all that is being taught in these school systems. Woodson (1933) stated, "Negroes who have been so long denied opportunities . . . are anxious to have everything the white man has even if it is harmful" (p. 5). Even if it is harmful, I am not sure that the answer to the inequality between an "urban" and "suburban" school is simply to give poor kids the same education that rich kids receive. What we need is truly transformative education. Students need learning that is relevant to their lives and that places their world (community, family, personal experiences) in the center of the learning circle.

We must see the circumstances of their neighborhood, not as a strike against the students but as an important venue for students to study and to build the skills necessary to raise up the community that raised them. How do we engage students themselves in helping to solve the social problems surrounding them? Resistant and liberatory education has long been taught in schoolhouse shacks, one-room praise houses, and shotgun homes. To see this type of possibility for alternative learning, educators must move beyond deficit-based research practices that assume certain kinds of schools couldn't possibly offer a quality education.

A Visit to Emerald City:
The Cultural Stories of Black Schools

We learn to love stories at a very early age. Stories teach moral lessons, share knowledge, and pass on values. They provide us with a context to better understand complex issues or broad concepts. Stories help us to make sense of the meanings of life experiences. According to Banks-Wallace (2002), story telling, the interactive process of sharing stories, is a vehicle for preserving culture and passing it on to future generations.

The practice of storytelling as a form of documentation and education has been around since the ancient world. However, in more recent ethnographic practice, the work produced years ago by Zora Neale Hurston is viewed as one of the foundations for African American studies (Gates, 1990). The stories that Hurston collected in the South in the early 1930s offer a glimpse into the lives of African Americans during that period and the culture that was created out of their lived experiences. These stories sustain legacies by providing verbal pictures of the past that put the present more clearly into focus. But most importantly, because a read of Hurston's stories is now an essential part of the African American studies literary canon, she helped to cement the intellectual importance of narrative inquiry. It is in the spirit of Zora Neale Hurston that I began the work of sitting with southern folk and hearing their stories of culture, life, and colored schools.

Before the attack on urban schools, southern Black schools were some of the first institutions that educated a massive population of African Americans and that were eventually labeled as deficient. Much of what has been discussed about colored schools has involved the unequal quality of educational resources. However, very little has been done to explore the cultural environment within these schools (https://www2.ed.gov/pubs/EdReformStudies/EdReforms/chap1b.html). What did cultural education look like in Black schools? Were the schools able to engineer an environment of cultural love and pride despite inadequate resources? Though these schools were found largely in the rural South, their ability to develop strong feelings of cultural and self-efficacy in students and to brilliantly integrate family, community, and cultural life into the educational experience offers insight into urban school settings today. Ultimately, the history of Black schools teaches us how to make the community and culture relevant in education.

In this ongoing project, I am collecting the oral histories of African American alumni of Black schools in the South. So far, there have been four schools visited and 24 stories collected. All participants have requested that their real names be used and their identity be disclosed in all written and media publications of this project. It is important to note here the sense of ownership, belonging, and credit that is sought by participants in projects of this nature. The participants made very clear that these are their stories, their lives, their community, and their history. Because of the recent public interest, particularly in Gullah culture, it was important for us to create a mutual agreement of partnership to prevent this from becoming another instance where an external other is given credit for simply reporting an experience that they lived. The Gullah culture represents Black communities in south Atlantic regions who despite enslavement retained many of the traditions of the African countries from which they were stolen. Here, I offer two short stories from alumni of the Penn School and the Rosenwald School on St. Helena Island, South Carolina. These stories are written in the words of the interviewees in order to honor their voice and to share their stories in the truest form (Banks Wallace, 2002; Barnes, 1990; Degaldo, 1990; Ladson-Billings & Tate, 1995).

The Penn School

Founded in 1862
St Helena Island, SC
Alumnus Name: Ms. Gardenia Simmons-White, 78 years old

I grew up during the time of segregation, but being here on St Helena Island I can't say we even really knew what segregation was. You see there really weren't too many white people on the island. You had a handful that owned the local stores but they were okay. They lived among us. And at the Penn School it was started by white missionaries—Laura Townes was a white woman. And they only had white teachers until 1948. But we interacted with those people—we ate with them, we went to their houses. So we didn't really know this idea of white being separated from black until we went away and came back home.

I attended the Penn School from the first through the 12th grade. I started when I was five years old. And I graduated in 1952 so I had both sides of it. I was there when it was a private school and I was there for four years when it became Penn High School. In 1948, it was deemed that there must be education for all children on St Helena Island. Before, there was the Penn School, which was private and not everyone could go. And the rest of the children went to the Rosenwald School, which was in an area where most children could walk to it. These were mainly one-room schools and they only went to the sixth grade. So once a child hit the sixth grade there was no more education. Whereas the Penn School provided a high school education and was really prepping students to go to college. So, the Penn School was turned into a county school. In 1948, this was when we had our first black principal at Penn School. The school became open to more students and the name changed. It actually went through three name changes. First it was Penn School and the premise was to get an education. You see if you got an education you could do more because as slaves you couldn't read or anything. Then in the early 1900s the name changed because this is when you had the debate between Booker T Washington and Du Bois on what the purpose of education should be. This is when they incorporated the trade into the Penn curriculum and the name changed to Penn Normal, Industrial and Agricultural School. When students got to high school they had to select a trade. It didn't negate their academics but not everyone was going to go to college. In the very beginning the purpose of the Penn School was teacher training. But everyone didn't go to college so with the trades you could do more. We had carpentry, blacksmiths, shoe making—all of that was a part of the curriculum. They had home economics—how to cook, sew, and entertain. So when they graduated they would be self-sufficient—they could build their house, fix their cars, make their own clothes. They had self-sufficiency and independence.

The other important part of the Penn School was it had boarding options. Students came from Bluffton, Hilton Head, Hartsville because there were no high schools for African Americans in those places so they came to the Penn School. You had dormitories, teacher houses, cafeteria, classrooms, labs, auditorium, and so forth. And when all students got to the eleventh grade they were required to board at the school. They were training us to go to college. They made us have that experience so that when you did go to college you knew how to behave, how to be independent and take care of yourself, and how to be responsible.

I learned everything there. Our curriculum was based on English, math, science, physical education. It was good to have home ec for me because my father raised us and I didn't have a mother for a long time, so having home economics and having a female teacher helped me to grow as a young girl. In those days we took the bags that rice and flour were sold in and we made our skirts from those bags in class. They had a hygiene class and taught us to take care of ourselves—to clean our hair, to wear our clothes neatly.

All of the teachers stood out. We had a music and English teacher that I loved. Those teachers were strict. I remember the home economics teacher Ms. Dalton had just come out of college. They expected us to be respectful. They cared about us learning. They taught us not to settle. They taught us not to compromise our integrity. They taught us to be proud of ourselves. The teachers knew our parents—they lived in the community. So if you misbehaved the teacher would just come home and tell your parents. They loved us and we loved them. They were all interested in teaching and for us to get an education. We read a lot. Church was our foundation. It was fun going to school. Today it seems there is no respect across the board—students don't respect teachers and teachers don't respect students—you can't learn in that type of environment. We also didn't have all of the distractions. What entertained us was our culture.

I'm invested in the Penn School because I graduated from there and it never left me. When I graduated, I spent 40 years working in New York. But I came back home every year. When they had dances and community service projects we all still participated. We got a great education. When I got to college I never had to take any remedial courses. I'm a nurse—I earned my bachelor's degree and I got my master's degree. We did well. But we never forgot about home. Our education at Penn taught us to love our community. It gave us roots here. And so that's why you see so many of us have returned to live on St Helena after having lived many other places. We love it here. We understand that we can get exposure by going out in the world and experiencing different things but this place is always home. At Penn we really learned how important it is to help people. That some people aren't as fortunate and that we needed to get an education to help others. So many people that didn't get the education we got didn't understand this power and responsibility of education. You see when you aren't educated you don't know any better—you don't realize that you can stand your ground. Our education at Penn taught us to be confident and to know that we didn't have to settle for less.

If you could describe the Penn School in just one word, what would it be?

I would say Penn School can be summed up in three words: history, education, and culture. It was a beacon to this community. It made us aware of our heritage—where we've been and where we're going. It was about maintaining our culture and not allowing anyone to take it away from you—it's about being proud of who we are.

Rosenwald School

St Helena, SC
Queen Brown Porridge, 70 years old

I attended the Rosenwald school from first grade to sixth grade. It was a two-room house. Our teachers were Ms. Janie Dudley and Ms. Jenny Gardner, and Ms. Lucille Manigold was our cook. We would get there about seven in the morning. First thing was devotional service, then health check, then we would have a snack and those that were assigned to help in the kitchen they would go with the cook, and the rest of us would do our lessons. We had two teachers so each teacher would teach like two subjects. We helped a lot in the kitchen. We were assigned duties to help prepare the meals, help serve and help clean up. And we also were exposed to cleanliness because each morning we had health check—to check our nails, check our hair, and make sure our clothes were neat on us. And we had a religious program each morning. We would have devotional service we would sing hymns and have prayer and that's how we started our school day. Most days we would get to school very early before the teachers. Our older brothers and sisters attended the Penn School for high school and so we would just stand out with them as they were waiting on their bus and the high school bus driver would just let us ride and drop us off at the elementary school. But the Rosenwald school didn't have a bus. We would walk about two miles home after school but we would get a ride in the morning. So when we hitched a ride on the Penn bus we would get to school way too early. So we would go collect the wood and the chips for the wood stove and start the fire to heat the building. So the school was warm by the time the teachers came. Then we would have so much time on our hands that we would go to the old man's house across the street from the school and get wood and start the fire for him in his house. Some mornings we would pick blackberries until the teachers came and then we would take them in once school started and we would make preserves from the blackberries when we helped in the kitchen. We did a lot of things. There was a candy store by the school and the teachers didn't allow us to go there until school was over. And even when we got there before the teachers the man that owned the store, Mr. George Austin, he wouldn't sell us the candy because the teachers at the school had given him instructions.

Most of the parents didn't have a car to get to the school so there were often days when the school was closed and the teachers would go to each home and visit the parents and talk about our progress and just keep them up to date with what was happening at school. And we were required to have a little garden at home and when the teachers came for their home visit they would go out back and look at our little garden to make sure we were doing it right. They made us do the garden at home instead of school because they were teaching us to help our family. Our family could benefit from the food we grew. We also had to make our beds every morning and make sure our room was clean because if we got sick the teachers would bring us home or they would just stop by sometimes and our parents didn't want to be embarrassed.

Our learning experience was very good. During the school day we learned English, writing, reading, and arithmetic. And we enjoyed it. I mean maybe we didn't have all of the best books and supplies that they have today but we really learned a lot from what we had. And those teachers really loved us and made sure we learned. All of them were so loving and patient. They were just like a mother to us. After we left that school in sixth grade we would still give them a hug whenever we saw them around town. I think Ms. Janie Dudley was the last to die—she just died this year. But all of us stayed in touch with her and even helped her as an old lady.

But it wasn't until the Rosenwald schools closed down and the big state-run school was built that we had fancier things like a cafeteria. At the Rosenwald school we ate a lot of soups and sandwiches and they were served right there in the classroom. Ms. Dudley was a very strong person telling us about life. She traveled a lot and she would tell us about life and what to expect—not just to read and write. One of the most important things I learned was how to carry myself as a lady—how to act with respect, how to take care of your body, and how to interact with boys. We did a lot of crocheting and basket making. You know basket making is important culturally here in St Helena so they taught us how to do it—a lot of arts and crafts. Education meant a lot to my generation. Today kids are going to school because they have to. It's not a place they really want to be. But we loved our school. It was such a loving environment. We were never bored. They would let us pick berries during recess to take home to our families. The teachers would always go outside and play with us so we were never alone. Our parents didn't go very high in school so they wanted their children to get an education. They were farmers and did odd jobs. And they were really involved to make sure the children got an education. So the Rosenwald School is very dear to me—it was important to the community. They refurbished it several years ago and it's now a daycare for the Penn

Center. A lot of us went to the rededication and supported it as much as we could. We had wonderful memories there.

If you could describe the Rosenwald School in just one word, what would it be?

Exciting.

Conclusion: There's No Place Like Home

Metaphorically, Oz is a space of belonging. It is welcoming—a place where the outsiders can call home—munchkins and fairies are treated like kings and queens. It is different and a bit unorthodox, but it works. We should all be searching for Oz, for places of possibility, creative imagining, and cultural inclusion. In many southern Black schools, parents, dedicated neighbors, and teachers were able to engineer an experience that many educators in affluent schools today struggle to achieve. I have found several key characteristics shared among all of the narratives that I have collected. First, teachers were essentially neighbors and community members. A different relationship is developed between teacher and student or teacher and parent when we share the same community space. In the past, even when parents could not physically make it to school, the school came to them. Even when parents couldn't read themselves, the school still updated them verbally on their child's progress. To make learning more relevant, the curriculum was tied to real family issues—putting food on the table. When parents were poor and couldn't afford new clothes—students were taught to make clothes at school that they could wear the next day ("Separate and Unequal," 1994). Teachers understood the special needs of their students and wove these needs into the learning process.

Essentially the second characteristic of these schools was the value of educating for life. One of the many observations that I have made when reviewing these videos and discussing this work with colleagues, is simply how incredibly good these elders look. My oldest participant was 95 years old. She physically looked about 80. She was coherent and active—she offered me food to eat and walked me to my car when I left. But one of the critical tools she and many others learned in school was agriculture. She spent her entire life growing and eating her own food. In today's world of fast food, fast conveniences, frozen meals, and chemical-based diets, I'm not sure if most of us will even live to her age much less be that healthy. Because children were growing up in a society that excluded and discriminated against them, school was a space where they could learn to survive: to develop self-confidence and learn practical life skills like growing food or building a home. This type of education provided disenfranchised folks with a sense of agency to live and survive.

The third theme that surfaced from these schools is a value for culture and a commitment to the community. Across 24 interviews, time and again, elders discussed how they were taught to value and appreciate Blackness at school. They were repeatedly taught the many achievements of their race. And they were taught to see their folkways as valuable practices—basket weaving, sea island cooking, boat making, and farming. In the two interviews previously shared, it is clear that the education that the two women received endeared them to their community—it rooted them in St. Helena. So today, if as my research suggests, family, culture, and community are still so important to students, why do so many seek to get away from their community when they graduate? I argue that society is teaching young people that success resides outside of their community—that their success depends upon how far away they can get from their home community.

In recent years, it seems that one of the most popular mantras for young people whose families and communities have been socially oppressed has been the phrase, "Making it Out." The idea of making it out of the housing project or the impoverished community communicates the larger desire to avoid getting caught up in a cycle of oppression—to experience a new opportunity through school or work and to ultimately elevate oneself up and away from the bottom of society. Making it out represents both physical and philosophical mobility. On a Facebook group page titled, "Making It Out of the Ghetto," the following post was on the wall for the description of the group:

> For those of us who: Were brought down by societies prejudices; Were seen as a waste; Grew up around gang violence; Seen, been in or, lost someone to gun violence; Went to a poorly funded grammar and high school; Lived day by day; Used food stamps; Grew up on welfare; Know what "getting jumped" means; were victims of racial profiling; In grammar school would run to get the book with a front cover & all the pages; know what a RIP shirt is; who seen a mother cry for her murdered son/daughter; survived this war zone and through all this managed to make it farther than what was ever expected from us. (http://www.facebook.com/group.php?gid=2390551946)

Getting away from the oppression that is pervasive in "ghetto" communities (any place where poverty is concentrated) has been a part of our cultural landscape for decades. We have heard many success stories of young adults that "make it out" through sports, entertainment, and college. As I prepared this chapter, I posted the following on my Facebook page: "Making It Out of the Ghetto. What does it mean? Should that be the dream?" I wanted to get a sense of whether young people are being taught to have the same level of cultural and community commitment as was seen in Black schools. Below I share a few public responses:

> I think it's telling that everyone is trying to get out of the ghetto, and no one is trying to eliminate the ghetto. When people talk of "escaping" they are saying they have left the poverty . . . and subsequent ignorance and violence of the ghetto. Very rarely do they say, "I want to pull everyone out of the poverty." Trust me, I understand that's a daunting task. But at some point we have to start saying that it's unacceptable for anyone to live that way, and that just certain individuals being blessed or chosen to escape that circumstance isn't enough.
>
> —Bomani Armah, African American man

> I've always struggled with the idea of my "making it out the ghetto." Many people talk about where I come from in a way that separates me from where I come from. . . . that I am only here because I am smart, amicable, and resourceful. That is not necessarily true. We all have those family members that are very smart but just didn't get the same opportunities we were given. So many good things happened to me during my lifetime, whether it's the teachers I had, the friends I met along the way, or just chances that have allowed me to be where I am today. Perhaps making it "out" should come with less elitism than it carries these days . . . not that we are one of the "special" blacks, but that we are a member of the community given life-changing opportunities. Opportunities that we, who "made it out," should extend to others as well?
>
> —Dayo, African woman

The need persists to explore the role, responsibility, and social impact of educated children from so-called ghetto communities. Are students really aspiring to use their education to raise up the community that raised them? Or is success seen as their ability to navigate their way away from that community? And more importantly, what role do schools play in encouraging students to view their communities as worthless places from which they should seek to escape? The students from the oppressed communities that we often write off as hopeless might be the only hope that their community has—if they are educated in a culturally intentional way. And so it is important that those of us that evaluate, research, lead, and teach in these communities don't do so from a place of deficiency and disdain.

In the field of education wizards do exist. Many educators like my mom were magical wizards who created a sense of hope in environments that seemed hopeless to the naked eye. This is what southern Black schools were able to do. The ways that these nontraditional spaces of education often two-room houses and one-room shacks—were able to instill in students a love of their cultural community is impressive ("Separate and Unequal," 1994). They developed the future educators, business owners, farmers, doctors, and carpenters who would take care of their communities. And the teachers, who lived in the community, genuinely loved the local families; they were appreciatively patient with the culture of poverty among their students and modeled an important form of cultural leadership. These poor shacklike schools were good enough for a brilliant mind like Du Bois to do his work. In these modest spaces was a sense of hope, a determination to succeed, and an educational practice rooted in possibility.

In the Wizard of Oz, Dorothy's main objective was never to "make it out" or to get away from Kansas. She was determined to get back home. Many critics of Kozol's work have pointed out the creative approach that he takes with storytelling results in obvious exaggerations (Farmer-Hinton, Lewis, Patton, & Rivers, 2013; Winters, 2006). As Goslee (1999) notes, it is difficult to discern whether he is telling the complete story of what he has seen, or if he has chosen to only include examples that make his point. Even when communities are economically lacking, cultural goodness can still be present. We must paint an authentic portrait of the cultures of oppressed communities.

There is also danger in positioning economically wealthy schools as the Emerald City. The system of busing that followed Kozol's work in

Boston turned out to be problematic in a variety of ways (O'Brien, 2016). When considering the context of this discussion on community cultural wealth, one of the primary issues with busing was physically taking talented students out of their communities. Education is very much about place making. Students tend to feel connected or rooted in the local area in which they are schooled. This is true throughout the educational experience from preschool to college. I was bussed as a child because my neighborhood school did not have academically advanced programs. To this day, when I ride on the other side of town where my middle school and high school were located, I feel more connected to that community than the neighborhood where my parents' house is physically located. Why? Because I hung out at my friends' homes over there. After school, I grabbed food with my friends at the restaurants there. I went to the movies with my friends there. We have a physical relationship with the area where we attend school. Even at the college level, alumni feel a sense of connection to their college town. It is a second home. So, the solution to inequity is not to remove students from their neighborhood so that they can attend the great rich school. Rather, the goal is to help their home school become great and to provide students with the skills to develop their home communities from a grassroots level. Regardless of how fantastic, glittery, and flashy Oz seemed, Dorothy never wanted to stay there because Oz simply did not have the real magic of Uncle Henry and Auntie Em. It lacked the authentic and genuine love of family. With all of its faults, there is truly no place like home. My mom's classrooms felt like home. Many southern Black schools felt like home. It is because of this homegrown, culturally rich, and love-based educational practice that many of the most impoverished African American students were able to ease on down the road to new and brighter futures.

References

Banks-Wallace, J. (2002). Talk that talk: Storytelling and analysis rooted in African-American oral tradition. *Qualitative Health Research, 12*(3), 410–426.

Barnes, R. D. (1990). Race consciousness: The thematic content of racial distinctiveness in critical race scholarship. *Harvard Law Review, 103*(8), 1864–1871.

Baum, L. F. (1900). *The wonderful wizard of oz* (100th Anniversary Edition). George M. Hill.

Black Bottom Wordpress. (2009, March). *History: Black Bottom* (web page). https://theblackbottom.wordpress.com/communities/blackbottom/history/

Du Bois, W. E. B (1903). *The souls of Black folk.* University Press John Wilson and Son.

Delgado, R. (1990). When a story is just a story: Does voice really matter? *Virginia Law Review, 76*(1), 95–111.

Detroit Historical Society. (2016). *Black Bottom Neighborhood* (web page). http://detroithistorical.org/learn/encyclopedia-of-detroit/black-bottom-neighborhood

Department of Education. (1994). *Education reforms and students at risk: A review of the current state of the art.* https://www2.ed.gov/pubs/EdReformStudies/EdReforms/chap1b.html

Farmer-Hinton, R., Lewis, J. D., Patton, L. D., & Rivers, I. D. (2013). Dear Mr. Kozol . . . Four African American women scholars and the re-authoring of Savage Inequalities." *Teachers College Record, 115*(5), 1–38.

Gates, H. (1989). Introduction: Narration and cultural memory in the African American tradition. In L. Goss & M. Barnes (Eds.), *Talk that talk: An anthology of African American storytelling* (pp. 15–19). Simon & Schuster.

Goslee, A. (1999). Response to Savage Inequalities by Jonathon Kozol. *Rouge Forum Newsletter.* http://www.rougeforum.org/newspaper/fall1999/savage.htm

Harper, S. R., Patton, L. D., & Wooden, O. S. (2009). Access and equity for African American students in higher education: A critical race historical analysis of policy efforts. *Journal of Higher Education, 80*(4), 389–414.

hooks, b. (2001). *Salvation: Black people and love.* Harper Perennial.

hooks, b. (2003) *Teaching community: A pedagogy of hope.* Routledge.

Hurtado, S. (1992). The campus racial climate. *The Journal of Higher Education, 63*(5), 539–569.

Jenkins, T. (2013) *My color, my culture, myself: Heritage, resilience, and community in the lives of young adults.* Temple University Press.

Ladson-Billings, G. & Tate, W. (1995). Toward a critical race theory of education. *Teachers College Record, 97*(1) 48–68.

Lambert, A. D., Terenzini, P. T., & Lattuca, L. R. (2007). More than meets the eye: Curricular and programmatic effects on student learning. *Research in Higher Education, 48*(2), 141–168.

Lopez, G. E. (1993). The effect of group contact and curriculum on White, Asian American, and African American students' attitudes. [Unpublished dissertation]. University of Michigan.

Lynn, M. (2006). Education for the community: Exploring the culturally relevant practices of black male teachers. *Teachers College Press, 108*(12), 2497–2822.

Making It Out the Hood. (2008). http://www.facebook.com/group.php?gid=2390551946

O'Brien, K. (2016). In defense of busing. *Jacobin.* https://www.jacobinmag.com/2016/07/busing-boston-desegregation-schools-gentrification-civil-rights/

Rendón, L., Jalomo, R., & Nora, A. (2004). Theoretical considerations in the study of minority student retention in higher education. In J. M. Braxton (Ed.), *Reworking the student departure puzzle*. Vanderbilt University Press.

The Root Staff. (2014). 8 sneaky racial code words and why politicians love them. *The Root.* http://www.theroot.com/8-sneaky-racial-code-words-and-why-politicians-love-the-1790874941

Winters, M. (2006). Savage exaggerations. *Education Next Journal,* 6(2), 71–75.

Woodson, C. G. (1977). *The mis-education of the Negro*. Associated Publishers.

Yosso, T. J. (2005). Whose culture has capital? A critical race theory discussion of community cultural wealth. *Race Ethnicity and Education,* 8(1) 69–91.

Chapter 16

Bringing the Love Back Home
An Ode to the Wiz

JODI L. JORDAN, DEBORAH J. PATTON, AND LORI D. PATTON

As children growing up in East St. Louis, IL, love of home, family, education, and community were the bedrock of our formative years. Although each of these components in their own right represent for us what it meant to be born and raised in East St. Louis, collectively they were the forces that allowed us to thrive in a place so often forgotten and forsaken in larger narratives of schooling and of Black girlhood. In this essay, we, three sisters (Jodi, Lori, and Debbie) from East St. Louis share parts of our journey, deeply rooted in community cultural wealth, to illuminate why our city matters despite the one-note narratives that drive mainstream discourses surrounding East St. Louis.

The opportunity to respond to Kozol's *Savage Inequalities* allows us to lift up our memories of East St. Louis and to bring meaning to them. Though we do not physically live in the city anymore, returning to our neighborhood is a ritual that allows us to revisit the past and to pay homage to those who indelibly impacted our lives. In the article "Whose Culture Has Capital? A Critical Race Theory Discussion of Community Cultural Wealth," Yosso (2005) discusses the phenomenon experienced by individuals who have been "injured by racism and other forms of oppression." Yosso states that these individuals "discover that they are not alone and moreover are part of a legacy of resistance" such that "they become empowered participants, hearing their own victims of racism can often find their voice . . . hearing their own stories and the stories of others, listening to how the arguments against them are framed and learning to make the arguments to defend themselves" (p. 75). With this understanding this thinking that the following reflections are shared in an effort to provide a greater sense of the cultural capital we possess as former residents of East St. Louis. We contend that our upbringing brought forth at least four types of capital that were not reflected in Kozol's writings. Couched in Yosso's research on cultural capital, we can ascribe to the definition of culture that states, "Culture refers to behaviors and values that are learned, shared, and exhibited by a group of people" (p. 75) As we consider our familial, social, academic, and experiential associations, we can connect them to aspirational, familial, social, navigational, and resistant capital—all of which are connected to cultural capital. Yosso (2005) defines cultural capital as "dynamic processes that build on one another as part of community cultural wealth," which is demonstrated through an array of knowledge, skills, abilities, and contacts possessed and utilized by Communities of Color to survive and resist macro and micro forms of oppression (p. 75).

We situate our joint narrative in *The Wiz* (Lumet, 1978). This 1978 film was meaningful for us because it was one of the first times we had viewed a film that featured an all-Black cast, included soulful music, and featured Black actors who would ultimately become icons of our culture. As young girls, we experienced *The Wiz* in a way that transformed our lives and showed us images of Black people in the arts. The showmanship, the music, and the themes of hope, persistence, determination, and internal capacity (Jordan, 2017) would become an important part of our sociocultural educational journeys. *The Wiz* represented the type of reimagining that would be necessary to grapple with and at times resist the narratives of our city, East St. Louis. Each section of our reflections references a song from the production and brings further meaning and connection to the sharing of our experiences.

I Was Born on the Day Before Yesterday
(Lori/Familial Capital)

We were born at Scott Air Force Base and raised in East St. Louis to two amazing parents. Our mom, originally from St. Louis, was a nurse; my dad, originally from Brooklyn, New York, was retired from the Air Force. Both worked for the Veterans Administration Hospital in St. Louis. I will always be reminded of the stories that my parents shared with my sisters and I regarding how they ended up in East St. Louis. When my parents got married, they had initially lived in Hawaii. However, when my father was stationed at Scott, my parents wanted to find a "nice" neighborhood in which to settle. That neighborhood at the time was 100% white, and my parents had secured the finances to purchase a home on 45th Street in East St. Louis. This all-white neighborhood would soon consider itself tainted, given that the first Black family had moved in. The term "white flight" became the understatement of the century. These White people not only fled—they disappeared. And in their place entered a host of families with children who ultimately became the friends with whom we spent our formative years.

We grew up on 45th Street with two loving parents who laid much of the groundwork for me and secured my role as "baby of the family." In our family, Sunday dinners were always special. What made them special was the routinized way that our mother woke us up to go to church. We had ironed our clothes the night before, so Sunday mornings were typically quite smooth. We were to get dressed, comb our hair, and sit down for a breakfast prepared by our father. Our Sunday morning routine unfolded to the soundtrack of Reverend James Cleveland and the Mississippi Mass Choir, the Clark Sisters, Andre Crouch, and a host of other gospel artists whose sound literally filled our home and filled our bodies in preparation for church. Their music fostered an education for us that we would come to learn about as we moved from girlhood to womanhood. We could not fully understand why our mother would blast "I Don't Feel No Ways Tired." Yet we subliminally learned the importance of persevering in the face of adversity and doing so grounded in unyielding faith.

The Feeling We Once Had (Debbie/Social Capital)

Thinking about 45th Street always brings back wonderful memories and was maybe typical for coming of age in the 1970s and 1980s. We recall driving down the treelined street of our neighborhood and relishing the beauty of the well-maintained lawns and the stately brick homes on each side. Our house was beautiful, with its huge porch and arched windows. The children in the neighborhood loved to gather on our porch to play games, jump off the sides, or just hang out. All the homes on our street were nice, and our neighbors took pride in keeping their properties well groomed. "Picturesque" is a good word to describe the landscape. But each home had its own story, and its residents lent their unique view to how things functioned. Overall, life was "typical" for us as children, each with our own set of friends. We played outside all day, and it was safe. We were under the watchful eyes of our parents and the neighbors. We all understood what was acceptable. We had a core group of friends. We played but were taught to never go inside anyone's house. We actually lived in the time when you might get in trouble with your neighbor and then with your parents, too. We had to go in when the streetlights came on though many of our friends could stay outside. At night, there would be large group games, and we would watch from the porch or from the window. Our neighborhoods linked us together and there was no difference when we played together.

Poppy's Girls (Jodi/Familial Capital)

In the early days, we left our dad at home to prepare Sunday dinner while we walked with neighborhood friends to St. Mark's Church, which was just two streets over. There, at this church comprising local families, we were again introduced to life lessons. Not only were we taught the Bible during Sunday school and regular service, but we were also exposed to lessons about how to behave, how to respect our elders, the importance of being active and involved in community, and a host of other lessons that shaped our collective understanding and desire to serve and be in community with others. As we grew older, we would eventually transition to Union Tabernacle Church in St. Louis. This transition made sense as membership at St. Mark declined, and leadership began to shift. Church in St. Louis was important for us because our mother was from St. Louis, and our cousins and aunts attended this church. Now, our routine would change as our father would transport us to and from church as my mother remained behind in an effort to support St. Mark. Sometime later she would transport us to this space that became our second church home.

Throughout these years, my father *always* prepared Sunday dinners. He *always* prepared fresh greens and cornbread. There was *always* a protein and a delicious dessert. We were always loved, fed, and cared for. Most important is that these Sunday dinners did not just include us. Every

Sunday was its own little family reunion where extended family would drive all the way from St. Louis to East St. Louis to have dinner at our house on 45th Street in Washington Park. These moments revealed the value of family. They taught us to love unconditionally, and we experienced tremendous happiness. Our story is not particularly unique in that Sunday is a common day for church and family gatherings. What makes our experience unique is that we were doing Sunday dinners in a place that was not treated like family by the state. Our city of East St. Louis was in decline because it was not provided with the resources of other towns. East St. Louis, a place rich with families and the legacies of those families, has never been deemed worthy and ultimately suffers at the hands of policymakers and legislators who have fundamentally forgotten our city. While all of these challenges were unfolding, we were protected and shielded. We were taught to love ourselves and our community. Sunday dinners became the routine that set us up for success during the week.

Ease On Down the Road (Debbie/Resistant Capital)

An interesting facet of our great neighborhood is that we lived just down the street from the Roosevelt Project Homes. The projects looked like connected apartment buildings. We could not go far down the street without noticing clear class distinctions, although we did not articulate them as young people. We understood you didn't go into the projects, and you didn't play with the kids in the projects. We really didn't get to know many of the children from that area because we didn't go to the same schools.

However, generally speaking, we were perceived differently because we did not attend the neighborhood schools. Each year, one of us was asking our parents to let us go to the local elementary school, Wilson Elementary. They seemed to have more fun at Wilson. My friends walked to and from school together and really didn't ever seem to have homework. On the other hand, we went to St. Joseph's Catholic school. It was on the other side of town. We were driven each day by my parents; thus we never rode the bus. When we were girls, we loved St. Joseph's. Back then, the nuns, from the order of SSND-School Sisters of Notre Dame, wore their full habits. They looked so formidable in those long black dresses. However, they were loving and understanding and White.

Our mother was a nurse at Christian Welfare Hospital, which was next door to St. Joseph's. On reflection, we did not fully understand sacrifices our parents made for us to attend parochial school. We went to work with Mom and had to wait in the lobby after school until she got off to go home. In the mornings, we would sit in the lobby until it was time to leave and walk next door to the school. We were always aware that Mom was right next door: she reminded us often. We stayed out of trouble because it was far too easy for her to come to the school if there was a problem. We were fortunate that we had both of our parents living with us, raising us, and providing for us. Our responsibilities included chores and getting good grades. It was expected. There was no room for failure, and my parents did not suffer disappointment. They were strict, but we understood that they loved us and only wanted the best for us.

(S)He's The Wizard . . . Sister Carmen?
Jodi (Navigational Capital)

In grade school, and throughout much of high school, we remained with the same cohort of students. There was only one classroom per grade in my school. The population was 100% African American, while the nuns were all White during Debbie's and Jodi's years. The teaching population had changed by the time Lori attended where the teaching staff reflected the student demographic.

When Sis. Carmen Marie came to St. Joseph's as principal in the 1970s, she was a force to be reckoned with. Sis. Carmen was a Black woman and a nun. She had an Afro and wore a habit. We loved that she was the principal. She established a culture of high expectations and stressed proper speech and dress—no shirts hanging out and no slouching. She was a formidable school leader. But during that time, it was not only her role as principal that captivated us. It was efforts to teach us the importance of Black history. Sis. Carmen taught us about Juneteenth and slavery. While still in grade school, we learned the principles of Nguzo-Saba. We can still hear her saying "Umoja stands for Unity" and creating songs to teach us the importance of the colors red, black, and green. Red was for the blood that was shed for our ancestors who died during the transatlantic slave trade and those who continued to put their lives on the line. Black was for honoring and celebrating Blackness and Black culture. Green was for the earth and the land that our ancestors cultivated to build this nation despite receiving no credit for our contributions. Sis. Carmen took the Broadway show "The Wiz" and built a whole unit on each character and their attributes and taught us as young students about functioning in society and being aware of our ethnicity.

This education was most valuable, and it has paid dividends late in life for many of the students with whom she interacted. We were gifted with an opportunity to understand the world at a young age. Racism was defined for us, and having a sense of history was drilled into our experiences. Yosso refers to this type of training as "resistant." Because of what we learned, we knew how to create the desired experiences for ourselves when we went to college. In addition to this wonderful cultural experience, we received a great education. Our educational experience was grounded in culture, morality, and integrity. These experiences definitely shaped my life and my career as an educator. One lesson that I have always valued was believing in my students and never giving up on them. This is because my teachers never gave up on me. My favorite teacher to this day is Sister John Lalande. She was the best teacher. But what I remember is the day she pulled me aside and asked me if I was ready. I replied, "Ready for what?" She then moved me from the middle group (we did that kind of ability tracking back then) to the high group and said that I was ready. This was important because it defied what others thought about me and what I thought about myself. I would go on to remain in the top tier of my classes academically.

If You Believe (Lori/Navigational Capital)

More important than the academic achievement was the eventual foundation of confidence and cultural understanding gained from our school experiences. St. Joseph's and later Assumption High School were not schools for entitled students; rather, they were faith-based schools designed to provide students with vital links to characteristics such as integrity, compassion for others, and community pride. Our education was a catalyst to building up young adults who could travel diverse lanes in life but still have the ability to draw from lessons learned in order to forge skillfully into new areas. When I think back on all of these things, I am consistently reminded of good times and learning moments. I always think about Assumption and the great meals that the women would cook. I ate lunch there almost every day. The pizza and the spaghetti were favorites. We ate from real plates and used real silverware. Again, Black women like Miss Hogg (Spanish) and Miss Cotton (Algebra) were role modeling for me as they had for my sisters. I also had White teachers who never treated me as less than. I learned a great deal in class. I was on the softball team, in the gospel choir, on student government for my class, assisted with homecoming floats, etc.—the type of involvement that would shape my graduate education and career in higher education. I had roots at St. Joseph's and Assumption because my sisters preceded me. Therefore when I got to these schools the teachers and principals already knew me and made me feel at home. Community was established and maintained on the premise of academic excellence and high expectations that often started at home

Ya'll Got It (Debbie/Aspirational Capital)

Not going to college was never an option for me or my sisters. It was an expectation. After high school, there was no "I want to work first" or "I want to explore." According to my parents, college was the only option, and we each followed that option. My mom attended Homer G. Phillips, McKendree College (bachelor's) and St. Louis University (master's). I attended St. Mary's University in San Antonio, Texas, heavily influenced by the instructors at Assumption. Jodi attended Washington University for undergrad and St. Louis University for both a master's in counseling and a doctorate in educational leadership. Lori was originally slated to attend St. Louis University but ended up attending SIU-Edwardsville. She then attended Bowling Green State University to pursue a master's and later attained a doctorate in higher education at Indiana University. We are all proud of our accomplishments, yet we have an even greater sense of pride as products of East St. Louis.

Don't Nobody Bring Me No Bad News (Lori/Resistant Capital)

I often talk to my partner about East St. Louis. I share with him how the parochial schools were a great foundation. However, St. Joseph's would ultimately become a middle school and later close. Assumption closed as well and became a minimum-security prison. In both cases there were concerns about asbestos and the fact that neither school had enough finances to correct the situation leading to closure. Whereas some of my friends went to Althoff Catholic in Belleville, Illinois, many of us attended the local public schools. I attended Lincoln High School from 11th to 12th grade. As I transitioned from an Assumption pioneer to a Lincoln Tiger(ette), I faced a very different reality. When I recount my experiences at Lincoln Senior High, I reflect on the positive experiences as well as the negative ones. I think about the condition of Lincoln Senior High School where, due to overcrowding, my homeroom was in the gym, and I had to share my locker. Most times for PE there was very little physical activity. I never ate lunch at school because the facilities did not seem clean. It was during my time at Lincoln where I realized the stark differences between private schools and public schools in East St. Louis. I also realized that my sisters and I experienced economic privilege in ways that some of my classmates had not. Lincoln became the space where I would come to know some of the realities of savage inequalities.

Conversely, Lincoln was the space where I learned to counter the hegemonic assumptions about East St. Louis. Despite the physical conditions of the building, I had teachers who genuinely cared about students. They came prepared to teach, and I was there to learn. Lincoln also became the place where my understanding of school "spirit" was elevated beyond what I understood it to mean. The "spirit" was infectious and overshadowed much of what would typically be considered negative in my mind. I learned to resist these things and grasp tightly to remarkable experiences that shaped my life, my educational trajectory, and my unwavering love for East St. Louis. I took every opportunity to attend winning basketball games and watch the pom-pom squad perform, listen to the stellar jazz band, engage in career exploration, visit college campuses, engage with teachers, and marvel at Black excellence: it was all available to me. Black excellence still thrives in East St. Louis beyond the stories of a rundown, poverty-stricken city as characterized in a book chapter and hyper-stigmatized in the media. The community cultural wealth of East St. Louis is what always resonates in our love of this city.

References

Lumet, S. (1978). *The Wiz* [Film]. Motown.
Yosso, T. J. (2005). Whose culture has capital? A critical race theory discussion of community cultural wealth. *Race Ethnicity and Education, 8*(1) 69–91.

Guest Commentary and Reflection

Emerald City, Oz, and *Savage Inequalities* in Education: Centering the Ruby Slippers

THEODOREA REGINA BERRY

There's no place like home.

—Dorothy in *The Wizard of Oz*

Near the end of the musical *The Wiz*, based on the book and the movie entitled *The Wizard of Oz*, Dorothy sings a song that begins, "When I think of home, I think of a place where there is love overflowing." The authors of the chapters "In Search of Oz," "And Still We Made It," and "Bringing the Love Back Home" eloquently speak of Yosso's (2005) notions of community cultural wealth as a means of building and solidifying the knowledge deemed most worth knowing for Black/African American students toward cultural efficacy. In these chapters, outsiders may have viewed the learning/educational spaces as deficient, including Jonathan Kozol, author of *Savage Inequalities*.

Kozol shines a bright light on the disparities faced by Black/African American public school students attending schools in large metropolitan areas. He focuses on the ways in which these schools are underfunded and under-resourced. But, as Williams and Newton point out, "Kozol fails to acknowledge the social and cultural structures that allow students to perform and develop in spite of the obstacles." In turn, Jordan, Patton, and Patton, illuminate and name the structures of family, teachers, and community that operate to disrupt these obstacles. The chapters do not speak directly to how such structures can also be useful to those of us who attended well-resourced, well-funded public schools where the very knowledge we carried into the classrooms from our communities was completely disregarded.

As a public school educator in the city of Philadelphia, my mother was keenly aware of the schools with the best teachers, programs, and funding and that is where she enrolled me and my siblings. My community cultural wealth (Yosso, 2005)—familial and aspirational capital came primarily from fellow congregants at my mother's home church; most were college educated and shared information with one another about educational opportunities for their children. Through my mother's research as well as advice and recommendations from folks at church, she sent me to a middle school in a mostly White, affluent community in the northwest part of the city. The bad news was that they educated us without any regard for our interests, experiences, or prior knowledge. The good news was that I carried my cultural efficacy, my ruby slippers, into this space. There were a couple of wizards through my journey of middle school. These were teachers who recognized my use of cultural efficacy and provided me with ways to polish my ruby slippers. They were my "Glenda." You see, Glenda didn't use her power to get Dorothy home; she recognized the power that Dorothy had within herself to get home. In middle school, I was searching for Oz, hoping to gain a sense of belonging in this particular place. But what I really wanted was home, not just someplace where I "fit" in but somewhere I could be seen and understood. The participants of the study highlighted in the chapter *In Search of Oz* described their schools as places that not only valued who they were but also understood the value their families placed on education. These educators were wizards, like Jenkins's mother, who understood their abilities and desires and empowered them to perform academically.

As a critical race feminist curriculum theorist, implications of this work for research are centered on the ways in which autoethnography, ethnography, and personal narrative (lived experiences) contribute to knowledge deemed most worth knowing in the scholarship on public schools for the education of Black/African American students. Black women education scholars wear the ruby slippers that empower us for this work as we engage in a multiplicative praxis (Berry, 2014; Wing, 1997). Such praxis merges the complexities of our marginalized and oppressed identities into our everyday practices. The scholars in these chapters have clearly articulated the ways in which families, communities, neighbors, and friends were important to the ability of Black/African American students to be successful in school. Implications of this work for policy and practice in urban schools start with teacher education. Many scholars discuss the significance of preparing transformative educators for schools. What practices are teacher educators employing that are deemed worthy of emulation by these future teachers and suitable for urban schools? In short, in what ways are teacher educators demonstrating the true value of the ruby slippers Black/African American students wear to school every day? Cultural efficacy via community cultural wealth must be central to the preparation of truly transformative educators. Curriculum and pedagogy must value the sources of strength and knowledge that bring our students to these classrooms. Finally, educational policies in schools, school districts, and higher education must reflect the significance of community cultural wealth (Yosso, 2005). Policies must move away from knowledge transference emulating Freire's (2000) notion of the banking system. Williams and Newton state, "Knowledge transfer functions beyond teacher to student exchanges, and can simultaneously include lessons from neighbors, community leaders and peer relationships." Policies tend to focus on how students will be assessed and evaluated rather than on what students have learned and can apply. If we truly value what students have learned, then education must include information garnered from such knowledge transfers that build cultural efficacy.

My K–12 schooling and educational experiences were good only because I possessed such community cultural wealth and was taught how to apply it in traditional school settings. And, in a few cases, I had the honor of being in the presence of wizards who could see my ruby slippers. In those moments, I felt like I was home. Love was overflowing.

Discussion Questions

1. Is Kozol's work still relevant today? If so, why? If not, why not and how might we make it more relevant?

2. In what ways are Black women's voices important to Yosso's (2005) notions of community cultural wealth?

3. Autoethnography, ethnography, and personal narrative were used to address the significance of cultural efficacy

and community cultural wealth in the education of Black/African American students? In what ways might we be able to employ a quantitative depiction of the significance of cultural efficacy and community cultural wealth through the voices of Black women scholars?

4. What recent key policies appear to work for/against the value of community cultural wealth in education for Black/African American students? In what ways might these chapters support/thwart the efforts to de/value such constructs?

Additional Readings

Berry, T. R. (2018). *States of grace: Counterstories of a Black woman in the academy.* Peter Lang.

Berry, T. R., & Candis, M. R. (2013). Cultural identity and education: A critical race perspective. *Educational Foundations, 27*(34), 43–64.

Brown, K. D. (2014). Teaching in color: A critical race theory in education analysis of the literature on preservice teachers of color and teacher education in the US. *Race Ethnicity and Education, 17*(3), 326–345.

Dixson, A. D., Clayton, D. M., Peoples, L. Q., & Reynolds, R. (2016). The impact of racism on education and the educational experiences of students of color. In A. N. Alvarez, C. T. H. Liang, & H. A. Neville (Eds.), *Cultural, racial, and ethnic psychology book series. The cost of racism for people of color: Contextualizing experiences of discrimination* (pp. 189–201). American Psychological Association. https://doi.org/10.1037/14852-009

Johnson, S. C. (2020). U.S. education and the persistence of slavery. *Journal of Curriculum and Pedagogy, 17*(1), 5–24.

References

Berry, T. R. (2014). Internationalization, internalization and intersectionality of identity: A critical race feminist re-images curriculum. *Journal of Curriculum Theorizing, 30*(1), 4–14.

Freire, P. (2004). *Pedagogy of the oppressed.* Continuum.

Wing, A. K. (1997). Brief reflections toward a multiplicative theory and praxis of being. In A. K. Wing (Ed.), *Critical race feminism: A reader* (pp. 27–34). New York University Press.

Yosso, T. J. (2005). Whose culture has capital? A critical race theory discussion of community cultural wealth. *Race Ethnicity and Education, 8*(1) 69–91.

Part 6

Sunday Dinners with Love

Chapter 17

The Meaning of Sunday Dinners

RAQUEL L. FARMER-HINTON

My family home is my grandparents' home. I consider myself lucky to have moved there after my parents' divorce. We had mature trees, manicured bushes, and a garden. I had my own room, next to the only bathroom (which my grandfather installed by himself in the late 1950s). My uncle lived downstairs in the basement, which my grandfather helped to construct. My mom's room was the "middle" bedroom and my grandparents' room was nearer to the front door. If Kozol were to drive by, this home would be located in a poor neighborhood, and it would look like it had no real value. It is a small, white house with a chain-link, gated fence. There are no hallways nor walk-in closets. It is located in the middle of low-rise public housing to the front and back. Yet like clockwork every Sunday and each holiday, this home was more than where I grew up. It was a convening. We clamored to get inside, eat well, and enjoy the company of family. What Kozol would not see is the cultural wealth being reproduced and what we would not show are the complexities of benefitting from such cultural wealth. In this chapter, I explore my grandparents' home as the site where we partook in cultural wealth as well as how the adults (grandparents, elders, aunts, and uncles) established norms and aspirations. Lastly, I include what we would never reveal to anyone: the challenges of meeting expectations, bending to norms, and whether to reproduce our family's cultural ways of knowing and doing.

Making Pearl Street

When people convene for a meeting, there is a purpose or an objective. In my grandparents' home on Pearl Street, we convened for food and fellowship. The purpose or intention was in the ether. The adults wanted to know about school and our futures. Simply put, the adults wanted to know that you were alright.

The tradition of Sunday meals and holiday gatherings started when the Collins family was a young family (my grandparents and their seven children). My grandmother was known for her hospitality. She would flinch at the thought of not having enough food even though folks knew they never had to RSVP for a meal. The doors were literally always open (including the countless times when grandchildren called or came over for grandparents to fill parental duties). My grandmother was also a master chef. She could turn a little into a lot, and the genius of it all is that she cooked from memory and intuition. Three-layer cakes and delicious pies—no problem. Hog head cheese—no worries. Hearty beef stew—like the back of her hand. I delighted in my grandmother. She played cards with me. We watched *Dallas* (a popular 1980s television show) together. I watched her make many a meal and dessert. My most loving memory would be the smell of tea cakes after school.

My grandfather was a steady force. He could tinker with and fix just about anything. If we were sick, he picked us up from school and brought us to Pearl Street. If we needed a ride, no problem. If the alarm at the church went off, the alarm company called him, as the deacon, to turn it off. The best parts were my grandfather's wise and unexpected contributions to conversations he did not appear to be participating in. His wisdom came from a place deep within like he had learned many lessons so long ago. My grandfather left Mississippi for the promises of jobs and opportunities in the St. Louis metropolitan area. Part of family lore is that my grandfather had a round-trip ticket to St. Louis from his hometown in Mississippi; he gave away the return ticket because he knew he could not continue to be a sharecropper in Mississippi. My grandfather was quiet yet giant in spirit. Giving away the ticket was his quiet-yet-giant way of rejecting oppressive living and working conditions. His shared wisdom was also quiet yet loomed large. Since he was not particularly talkative, we knew his commentaries would be priceless.

With seven children to prepare for adulthood, they had to be cognizant about their kids' education and their religious values. Their children had to look presentable and behave above reproach. Their children's intelligence was not a question except when adults or peers (think the 1950s) mistreated or overlooked them due to race or gender. Yet, their children were also reared in the practical ways and norms of the time. My grandmother believed that girls needed to know how to sew, cook, and take care of a home. My grandfather believed that only boys would ever need to go to college.

Except that they all went to college and graduated—all seven (four girls and three boys). My mom is not the oldest, but she attended college first. She, along with her siblings, attended college at a time when there were other economic opportunities in factories or as maids/janitors. After graduating, these children pursued teaching, counseling, community development, engineering, and medical careers. They married, bought their own homes, and raised their children: all of whom convened on Pearl Street for family gatherings.

Learning on Pearl Street

When I started to compose this essay, I reached out to the cousins closest to my age; these were the cousins with whom I shared my formative years on Pearl Street. I really wanted to better understand our family gatherings but also was curious to know how my cousins saw these gatherings. What Kozol would not see is the cultural wealth being reproduced; without seeing the wealth, there is no way to see the complexities and nuances that it consists of.

As cousins, our thoughts and experiences were not necessarily uniform. The biggest advantages named were the benefits of being members of a successful family. One cousin described it as a SUCCESS THIS WAY banner marking the pathways carved out for us. Unlike our K–12 peers who matriculated in local schools in the 1980s, we were not first-generation college students. We would become second-generation college students. We would be beneficiaries of parents who could not afford to go away to college. We pursued opportunities to attend college both within the state, in neighboring states, and at HBCUs in the South. As adults, we are now educators, medical professionals, artists, writers, business owners, and journalists. We have married, purchased homes, and are raising the fourth generation of our grandparents' lineage. The disadvantages named were that the same norms that sustained older generations were, at times, the same norms that bore conservatism and the need to please our elders.

What Kozol would not see is the cultural wealth being reproduced. High expectations and edifying praises were as available as granules of sugar—and just as sweet. If we made good grades, *that's wonderful* and *I'm so proud of you* filled the room like a chorus. If we bounced back from bad grades, our parents and grandparents seemed to already know we had potential based upon the resounding *I knew you could do it* echoing within our home on Pearl Street. Even when we accomplished things in ways that were unfamiliar to their professional backgrounds and experiences, they were so impressed and collectively said *oohs and aahs*. Imparting this sort of cultural wealth was very informal and unstructured, yet it served a purpose of reinforcing our potentials and abilities.

In addition to the high expectations on Pearl Street, we also learned, as one cousin said, that "we can be anything." Our elders did not hold seminars on what to do and when to do it. They modeled it. They did not reveal any tips or tools on how to find a college. They just reiterated that finishing college was not difficult; if they graduated, then we could graduate, too. They did not tell us how to find a partner to marry. They just modeled how to make marriages last or how to leave marriages with dignity. They did not tell us how to purchase a home. They just provided examples of the kind of real estate that adults with careers could purchase. As one of my cousins would share about our family's cultural wealth, we had a "dope" family that has served as a "standard bearer" for younger generations.

Our family set a "foundation" for what was possible as a cousin shared. As adults, we can now understand that we are living my grandparents' legacy. My grandparents did not have the benefits of college degrees. My grandfather only completed the eighth grade, and my grandmother went to night school to receive her high school diploma when we were all very young children. My grandfather worked in a packing house slaughtering animals that were consumed or sold. My grandmother did *day work* where she worked as a maid during the day while her children were in school. In that external world, they were laborers. In our community, they were granted the respect of Mr. and Mrs. Collins, and they carried that respect everywhere they went.

In reflecting on how my family modeled success and shared familial wisdom as cultural wealth, my scholarly interest is to move beyond documenting the cultural wealth of families of color so that we can better explore the complexities of this wealth. As an adult in this family, I am wondering about nuances such as why my elders were never specific. They could have shared the specific financial, social, or academic difficulties of navigating college. They could have revealed the specific ways they survived both the good and the bad in their personal relationships. They could have revealed their professional and financial struggles with intention such as walking us through the process of home affordability or guiding us through meeting professional benchmarks. As a family, our elders' aspirations and pride are/were abundant; yet there was a dearth of specifics. Perhaps those times were simpler. For example, adults stayed at one job most of their lives and retired with pensions; they lived near their support systems for the rearing of children. Additionally, college tuition and house prices were relatively more affordable then (see Martin, 2017), particularly considering the inequalities and affordability issues that have grown over time.

Additionally, as scholars move beyond documenting the cultural wealth of families of color, we also have to explore critiques of how cultural wealth is reproduced. As an adult family member, I wonder about the extent to which our cultural wealth is consistently applicable moving forward. I have concerns that our norms are steeped in religious traditions that are conservative and narrow. I worry that strong messaging and norms limit creativity and risk taking for the changing economy. And I am concerned that strong voices create vulnerabilities in others. As the third generation of this family, my cousins reproduced what our elders carved out for us. And we bore the pressure of knowing we could not let our family down. We essentially bended to family norms. This is the nuance and complexity of cultural wealth: without such critiques, how can our cultural wealth begin to operate in more personalized, intentional ways?

In sum, the literature on Black students and their families is beset with deficit language and narratives even when the intention was to frame conversations about new policies and practices (see Kozol, 1991). The literature has expanded to document community cultural wealth, and that literature offers us a lens to dismantle deficit frameworks (see Yosso, 2005). With this volume and other works, we can offer a more nuanced view of how cultural wealth is reproduced, including the example of how after several generations, family members continue to reiterate, or even revise, the lessons learned from homes like ours on Pearl Street.

References

Kozol, J. (1991). *Savage inequalities: Children in America's schools.* Harper Perennial.

Martin, E. (2017). *Here's how much more expensive life is for you than it was for your parents.* https://www.cnbc.com/2017/06/21/life-is-much-more-expensive-for-you-than-it-was-for-your-parents.html

Yosso, T. J. (2005). Whose culture has capital? A critical race theory discussion of community cultural wealth. *Race Ethnicity and Education, 8*(1), 69–91.

Chapter 18

East St. Louis

Where Our Black Lives Always Mattered

DALLAS JEWELL WATSON AND JOI D. LEWIS

We are from East St. Louis . . .

We are from three generations in District 189, South End, train tracks, teachers who grew up with our parents, news flashes on Thursdays from the *Monitor*
From church every Sunday and prayers every night
From the America they didn't used to show on TV . . . the descendants of slavery
From forgotten places and once unknown faces, like George Floyd and Breonna Taylor, before #justiceforgeorgefloyd and #sayhername
From poetry, spoken word, and hip hop as pedagogy.
We are from *The Miseducation of Lauryn Hill*, Marvin Sapp's *Never Would Have Made It*, and Doug E. Fresh and Slick Rick's *The Show*
From a family that cares and teachers who went the extra mile.
We are from advising student scholars and building resistance movements
From stepping up as Generation Next and becoming a movement for Black excellence

From late nights and early morning scholarship sessions with our dad and grandad about the constitution and the few civil liberties we had left and how it was our duty to fight for more from knowing that our wealth was not located in the bank, but in our brains and in the books on the shelves in the study, and in church, at the barber and beauty shop.
We are from the NAACP banquet and its annual scholarship named after our dad and grandad
From living and holding contradictions
From a grandmother who served on the food line at the University of Kentucky, to a granddaughter who would become a dean
From being tracked in special education classes to a straight A honors student
From a 13 on the ACT to a doctorate from an Ivy League institution
From where there are no big I's and little you's, where everybody is somebody
From your address does not determine your success.
We are from long meetings, advocating for students, and navigating bureaucracy in the academy.
We are from student protests, loud cheers for the "I got an A" on my paper and quiet compassion for the failed test
From affirmative action, tokenism, and every administrative committee possible.
We are from being the only one in a room full of White people
From being overworked, underpaid, early mornings, late nights and not enough left for merit pay.
We are from impossibilities, stereotypes, we shall overcome, and the revolution must be televised.
We are from #blacklivesmatter, #sayhername
Unnamed mothers, the women who birthed a movement,
Who nurture the dreams, who wipe the tears, who heal the wounds.
We are from a grandmother who said, "Get your education, something no one can take from you."

We are from being told that higher education is not for people who look like us to knowing that we are what the future of higher education looks like.

◆ ◆ ◆

My (Dr. Joi's) grandmother, Ms. Trudy B. Lewis, had a fourth-grade education and a PhD in wisdom. When she passed away in 1992, she had 33 grandchildren and 44 great-grandchildren. At least 30 of her grandchildren went to college; that's what we did. She would often say, "Get your education, it's something no one can take from you." Every day we would go to her house after school. She would say, "Don't you turn on that TV until you've done at least an hour of homework." "Grandmama," I would say, "I don't have any homework." "Then make some up . . . do some kind of school work for an hour." At the end of the hour, Grandmama would ask my older cousin KeiKei, who was a teacher in East St. Louis, to check on our work.

My grandmother's house on Gay Avenue in East St. Louis was the family gathering place, my idea of a village. Not only was my grandmother's house on Gay Avenue, but my Aunt Mossie and two of her three children lived next door, and my Aunt Lillie and Uncle Carl lived across the street with five of their eight children. My Aunt Big Sister lived one block over. At the core of our family connections was the belief in education, both formal and familial. Yosso (2005) lifts up the priceless value of community cultural wealth. Familial and aspirational wealth was our inheritance. My dad used to say that he did not have much of a 401k, but he had a great deal invested in 401 Kids. When he passed away in May of 2018 after retiring from a hugely successful career as a public servant, he had very little money to leave his children, but he left an abundance of riches to not only his family but also to his community of East St. Louis.

In this chapter, my niece Dallas Jewell Watson (the only one of my grandmother's 33 grandchildren and 44 great-grandchildren who shares her birthday) and I share reflections on growing up in East St. Louis, three decades apart. I lived there my entire childhood; Dallas lived there for two years, from third to fifth grade, before she and my sister moved to the next town over. The inheritance of familial and aspirational capital (Yosso, 2005) that we received from having parents, grandparents, great-grandparents, aunts, uncles, and cousins who lived in East St. Louis and attended school in District 189 transcends the boundaries of geography and generation and greatly expands the notion of cultural capital. When scholars like Kozol and others use only the terrain of boarded-up buildings, inadequate educational materials, and compromised school facilities to assess the "failure" of urban schools, so much of this inheritance is missed. Our stories are organized around three phrases Grandmama Trudy B. always used to say: "None of us is as smart as all of us"; "It's the small foxes that destroy the vine"; and "Many hands make light work." We use our stories, grounded in these sayings, to demonstrate the dividends of the inheritance we have received from the generations before us, and the responsibility we have to ensure that the interest is compounded and shared.

I think it is important to name our social location in this moment, less than two months after Mr. George Floyd was brutally murdered in Minneapolis at the hands of police. I live less than 15 miles from that scene. In Kentucky, my mother's home state, we are still waiting on justice for Breonna Taylor who was murdered in her home by police in Louisville. What does this proximity to death mean, as we contemplate freedom? What does equitable education mean, as we witness the deep contradictions—and even sometimes the promises—of segregated school districts? The irony is that Minnesota is touted as having one of the best educational systems in the country, and East St. Louis is labeled as one of the worst. However, the "best" of Minnesota is really reserved for White people. Indeed, Dallas literally had to leave Minnesota and go to East St. Louis to find her voice and begin to see herself as a scholar. East St. Louis is the place where three generations of Black excellence were nurtured.

"None of Us Is as Smart as All of Us" (Grandmama Trudy B.): Freedom School

Dallas

My name is Dallas Jewell Watson. I was born in Saint Paul, Minnesota, in 2004, and moved to East St. Louis, Illinois, when I was in the third grade. Today I attend a mixed-race high school in Belleville, Illinois. My story will give you the perspective of a young Black woman on the rise. I will include stories from my time in Saint Paul, East St. Louis, and Belleville.

Being a young Black kid in Minnesota was a struggle. I lacked a sense of Black identity and culture. Until I moved to Illinois, rap music and hip-hop were lacking in my life. Of course, my father and mother played those genres of music, but in everyday life, I didn't hear them very often. The summer before we ended up moving to East St. Louis, my mother put me into a program called Freedom School. Freedom School, a program sponsored by the Children's Defense Fund, was a place for young Black students to get together and have fun. I now know its purpose was much more than that; it is designed to promote culturally affirming activities and field trips, with an emphasis on literacy, math, and leadership development, run by well-trained, caring Black staff. We would make up chants like *boom chicka boom* and dance to Soulja Boy's "Superman" song. Freedom School made me feel a part of Black culture and allowed me to interact with more Black people. I loved Freedom School. If the directors chose not to make Freedom School available in Saint Paul, I would not have had those critical early childhood connections with Black culture. Freedom school launched my journey with Black people, and if I had not had that experience, I may not have learned so much about my culture at such a young age.

When I was in third grade, I moved to East St. Louis with my mother. In my new school, there was maybe one White person. This was an anomaly for me because I had always been in somewhat of a mixed school. My family knew my third grade and fourth grade teachers personally. This allowed me to establish an immediate connection with both. During that period, my foundation for becoming a scholar and an intellectual developed, and it was unequivocally the influence of seeing more Black people and having more Black teachers than I ever had in Minnesota. In Minnesota, I was not reaching my full potential, but in East St. Louis I launched my journey to becoming a scholar. Having two Black teachers helped me learn that I am smart. I believe that young Black students need a Black teacher in their early lives to help establish a strong foundation and belief in their brilliance.

Those influential Black teachers helped me on my journey, but today I am in a mixed high school where White people are in the majority. African Americans are the next largest section on the diversity pie chart. Personally, I tend to like a mix of Black people and White people in my school. In corporate America, there may be a "boy's club," or Black women and Black men may be the minority in their company. My friends and I cofounded a club called the Next Generation, at our school. Our mission is to provide a safe space for young students of color in honors classes to support each other around challenges of being one of a small number of students of color in those classes and also identify opportunities for us to thrive. We created this club to include students of color with varied aspirations: including higher education, entrepreneurship, community organizing, and leadership. We just recently got word that our club was approved; this is great news in the middle of such a challenging year, with COVID-19 and the murders of numerous Black people across the country by police. I am also excited about sharing the information that we are learning about how to navigate predominately White educational spaces with students of color who are younger than us. By having a space for us we are free to express ourselves without judgment or microaggressions.

Dr. Joi

There is no shortage of challenges in the world, most of which will require lots of people's minds to address. One would be hard pressed to find a learning environment that does not require you to do group projects. My entire childhood growing up in East St. Louis was a group project. Growing up with more than 30 first cousins, I had to learn how to work together and listen to the elders in our community, both our blood family and our fictive kin.

I always knew East St. Louis was a special place, and I will tell anyone who will listen that it is my happy place. I went to college at Southern Illinois University at Edwardsville. I did not fully understand the value of the community cultural wealth (Yosso, 2005) that was so present in our everyday life until I went to SIU, 45 minutes away, which felt like another world. It meant something to go to school in District 189, in East St. Louis. Our teachers, administrators, and maintenance workers all took great pride in our schools. They had extremely high expectations of every child in the school. It was in District 189 where I discovered Broadway musicals and developed my love for opera. I can thank Ms. Parsons, the choral director, for letting me join the choir when I was only six years old. That opportunity laid the foundation for my training with Mrs. Joan Brown, who coached me to become the highest-ranked First Soprano in opera in the state of Illinois.

Although we were rich in human and cultural resources in East St. Louis, my peers and I knew that we lacked certain material resources and would sometimes try to get out of doing work because some of the books were missing pages. Our teachers would firmly say, "That is a reason not an excuse; you still need to get your homework done and it must be excellent." We were expected to ask for help, to work with our peers, and to talk with our parents, grandparents, and extended family about the work we were doing. In fact, many of our assignments required us to do this. We simply could not do things on our own. It was in East St. Louis that I learned that true freedom is not about individualism but about the collective. It is critical to be connected to others. Our humanity depends on it.

I moved from East St. Louis when I was 18 and have lived in the upper Midwest for most of my adult life. I now live in Saint Paul, Minnesota, where my niece Dallas (and her mom, my sister, Jennifer), also lived for several years. When they decided to move back home to East St. Louis, Dallas was eight years old. It was the end of August. Dallas was excited about moving there to be with so many cousins and to get to be close to my dad. But she had one request: could she come back and stay with me next summer so she could go to Freedom School? I said of course. I checked in with her again in November and asked if she still wanted to come and stay with us in the summer so she could go to Freedom School. Dallas replied without pausing, "Aunt Joi I can come and visit for a week or something, but now I go to Freedom School every day." I immediately got it and am eternally grateful to have grown up in Freedom School. There I learned what it meant to be part of a community in which "none of us is as smart as all of us."

"It's the Small Foxes That Destroy the Vine" (Grandmama Trudy B.): Encouragement and Integrity

Dallas

My journey of growing into a scholar started at an early age. It all began in Minnesota around kindergarten. Like many young Black kids who go to a predominantly White school, with White teachers, I was at a disadvantage because the teachers had assumptions about our abilities. For instance, my teacher suggested that I should be in special education. Although I didn't learn about this until I was older, I now realize that if I had been in special education, my life would have been very different. From kindergarten until the fourth grade, my reading level was not the best. When I was in fourth grade, my mother put me in a program to help me improve my reading. The program is called the Network for the

Development of Children of African Descent (NDCAD). Over time, my reading improved dramatically. Today, I am a straight A student, I take three honors classes, and will add in some AP classes in the Fall semester. If my parents had accepted my kindergarten teacher's suggestion, I very likely would not be where I am today. An individual who may not really see you or have your best interests at heart can easily ruin the direction of your journey. There is so much at stake when you are not at a culturally competent school.

Although I developed a sense of myself as an academically accomplished student in grade school, especially after moving to East St. Louis, I can now see that the absence of affirming Black teachers in middle school had an impact on me. As a freshman in high school, I was scared to take any challenging classes because I felt that those classes would be too rigorous. Also I was scared because I believed that White people were smarter than me. I think this comes from not being in a culturally affirming environment. For example, in my middle school, there was an algebra class that had only six Black kids, but the class had 30 kids in total. At first, I hated this class because I felt that it was too extreme. My one saving grace is that I continually worked at my schoolwork. I would go in and ask for tutoring with my teacher after school, and although she was not Black she was very helpful and encouraging. Ultimately, I earned an A in the class. In my middle and high schools, seeing a significant number of Black students in honors classes is a rare occurrence. There may be six maximum in a class. As one of so few black honors students in predominantly White classrooms, at first I felt brainwashed about race and academics, believing the White students had an intellectual advantage over me. Once I was in the class, however, I realized that White people are not more intelligent than I am. They may have more resources, but even then some do not take advantage of these. It's not a matter of intelligence; it is a matter of opportunity.

Many Black kids are taught at an early age that if you want to change your socioeconomic status then you need to play sports. Although I really love watching the NBA, I realized that academics was my way to change the circumstances around socioeconomic status that I care so much about. So, one night I couldn't take being bored in class anymore and knew I had to be challenged even more, so I switched to an honors class during my freshman year. That class launched me into the honors track that I am now on, and I am really loving it.

Dr. Joi

When I was growing up, I did not really understand what my grandmother meant when she said, "It's the small foxes that destroy the vine." But she would often repeat it, usually after she had given me some instructions to go into her room and bring some object back. It never failed that when I would get to the room, I could not remember what the object was. My grandmother would get up to get the object, but before she did, she would say, "It's the small foxes that destroy the vine." I would kind of shrug my shoulders and go on with my day.

During my senior year at Lincoln Senior High School, this saying was often repeated. Mrs. Massenburg, our Honors English teacher, gave us an assignment to look up some extremely difficult words, many of which I had never heard of. We were working on etymology. The relative lack of supplemental resources available at our school did not impact Ms. Massenburg's commitment to making sure we were being challenged as much as possible in her class. In order to look up the definition of those words, we had to catch the bus over the river to the "big city," St. Louis, to use the giant dictionaries in the public library. I had never seen such big books. They were intimidating, sure; but Ms. Massenburg was even more intimidating if you did not have your work done.

I worked hard and looked up as many words as I could. I left a couple of them blank, with the intention of trying to find them at home. My dad had a variety of dictionaries available for our use at home. Unfortunately, when I used those dictionaries to try to find the somewhat arcane words, they were not there. I panicked a little bit, but then I just let it go. It was the weekend, and I wanted to just relax. I had already given up a big portion of my Saturday to work on this assignment. I got to school early on Monday morning (an extremely rare occurrence, because my dad ran chronically late). Many folks were gathered before class, scrambling to get those last definitions done. I asked Ian Buchanan, arguably the smartest boy in our class, if he had the two definitions I was looking for. Ian handed me his paper and I copied the definition down, word for word. I finished just before the bell rang to start class. I turned in my assignment with the help of Ian for those last two definitions and I thought I was good to go.

The next day everyone got their assignment back except me. Ms. Massenburg told me to stay after class. I could not figure out what the problem was. She then told me that she noticed that Ian and I had the same exact definition for two words. She asked if I had copied the definition from Ian. I copped an attitude and said, "Why didn't you ask Ian if he had copied from me?" Ms. Massenburg shared that there were a couple of misspelled words, and they were consistent with words that Ian had misspelled in the same way in other parts of the assignment. Busted. To make matters worse, Ms. Massenburg said that I would be expelled unless I went home and told my dad directly what I had done and have him sign off on the assignment. This was worse than the assignment. My dad's biggest value was integrity. Ms. Massenburg knew this, which is why she charged me with giving him the news. After school I went to my grandmother's house as usual and told her what had happened. She said, "It's the small foxes that destroy the vine." I asked her what that had to do with anything. My grandmother explained that you have to pay attention to the small things. They are the things that can really do you in.

Life is a compilation of many small decisions. For those of us who grew up in places that others discount or ignore, those small decisions can be the difference between opportunities or dead-ends, and in some cases between life and death.

"Many Hands Make Light Work" (Grandmama Trudy B.): Role Models and Mentors

Dallas

My favorite subject in school is history. Unfortunately many of my fellow students strongly dislike the subject and believe that it is boring. My passion for history developed when my mother and I moved to East St. Louis and moved in with my grandfather. My late grandad, James Lewis Sr., was a history buff. He was the executive director for the board of elections in East St. Louis for thirty-five years. He was very respected for his work. Personally, I'm more interested in bills and laws than I am in the political system itself. In so many ways, my grandad encouraged me to have an interest in history and political science. For example, during the 2012 presidential election, my grandad asked me to write an essay about the debate between former President Barack Obama and Republican candidate Mitt Romney. I will always remember writing this paper and feeling at the time that the debate was "so boring." Now I'm actively listening to presidential candidates' policies and views and remembering the things my granddad told me about why this is all so important. It took my grandfather showing me the world of politics for me to eventually have an interest in history.

In my sophomore year of high school, I took an Honors English class. I was nervous about taking the class because I had never taken an honors English class before. Early in the year, I had to give a speech about what my name means. I knew that I had to do a great job because my teacher is a speech coach. I wanted to demonstrate to the class and the teacher that I was the bomb even if I had not yet internalized it. I decided to ask my Uncle Jay for help with the speech because I knew that he was a "beast" at public speaking. I practiced and I practiced, over and over again. I received an A, and the class said I had the best speech, which resulted in extra credit points. This led me to try out for the speech team. I was able to capture my voice, and my uncle's help launched me into being on the speech team, where I have already placed second in numerous tournaments. That decision to try out for speech changed my life. I have been more outgoing, and I now have space to talk about aspects of pop culture that I love including such as: Colin Kaepernick, the Exonerated Five, and D. Smoke. The speech team is considered "nerdy" and maybe that is partially true, but speech gives me an avenue to talk about so many different topics. I am grateful that my uncle kept pushing me to try out for the team; that decision was a game-changer.

I am also fortunate enough to have an aunt who is very successful. With her support, I am able to get so many opportunities that other individuals can only dream of. I have been able to visit many places in the United States. My aunt has taken me on college tours on the East Coast, and she has also taken me to see several NBA games. Seeing a Black woman be able to live a great life in a world that was not built for us helps me work toward achieving that goal for myself. In life, we all need someone we can depend on. For me, it's my aunt. She continually shows me that I can do anything. She is my shoulder to cry on, my uplifter, and my friend. My aunt is there to give me guidance in life and it's very helpful. I am the person I am today because of her help, and that of many others.

For me to reach my goals I have to have support in my journey. No one—and I mean no one—can do it by themselves.

Dr. Joi

I did my first speech when I was three years old at my family's church in East St. Louis. Thanks to church and the Dunbar Elementary School Chorale, I was a soloist by the time I was five years old. Those speaking and singing debuts were affirmed by standing ovations and many rounds of applause. That is what it meant to grow up in an all-Black city that believed in you and your family and your peers.

I went on to be a member of the Talkative Tigers Speech Team at Lincoln Senior High, proudly following behind my brother James Lewis Jr. who was the captain of the speech team. I now make my living as a speaker on issues of Healing Justice (Radical Self-Care + Social Justice). You can imagine my excitement when Dallas joined the speech team at her school.

When she moved to East St. Louis, from Saint Paul, Minnesota, at eight years old, Dallas was a quiet, reserved child who did not say much. Within a few months at Katie Wright Elementary School located in East St. Louis, Dallas was encouraged to learn the speech, "Hey Black Child." She began reciting it all over the city and was asked to be the opener for many programs. Dallas's third and fourth grade teachers were Mrs. Shannon Brooks and Mrs. Vera Edwards, both of whom were classmates of my brother's from elementary school through high school. Dallas had the benefit of not only being encouraged by them, but being expected to show up in excellence. Her fifth grade teacher was not from East St. Louis, and she was White. Dallas was not doing well in her class, and she often felt misunderstood. I reached out to my sixth grade teacher, Dr. Carpenter, who had retired as the deputy superintendent of East St. Louis Public Schools. I asked her to check on Dallas. Not only did Dr. Carpenter check on her, but she sat in on Dallas's class for almost two weeks straight. Her assessment was that Dallas was bored and was not being challenged. Dr. Carpenter developed an intervention and worked with the teacher to support Dallas.

That is the East St. Louis I know and love. The one where I could call my sixth grade teacher some 30-plus years later, and she would go and check on my niece.

Conclusion

Our time in East St. Louis spans more than three generations. Although we each have a different relationship to the place, we've inherited some key core values from East St. Louis: there is always enough to share, say good morning, Black excellence, always be proud of East St. Louis and our people. We belong to a community of people who will forever root for us. We never doubted the deep conviction that Black lives have always mattered. Generations of brilliance and wisdom, like that of our (great) grandmother can be found in so many likely and unlikely places. If, like Kozol, you only see what is broken, then it is impossible to recognize, capture, or understand the vast reserve of community cultural wealth that is East St. Louis. #weareEastStLouis

Chapter 19

We Were Always a Community

Cooking, Eating, and Living in the
John DeShields Housing Project

ISHWANZYA D. RIVERS

As a single mother of six children who worked two jobs (one full-time and one part-time), we rarely saw my mother for meals throughout the week. While my mom left dinner warming on the stove, we were responsible for feeding ourselves. The necessity of working and providing for her family meant that my mom sacrificed interaction and bonding with us over meals; however, Sundays and Sunday dinners were the opposite: my mom had time and energy to plan and cook Sunday dinner, which was vastly different from our weekday dinner. Sunday dinners involved a ritual of planning, shopping, cooking, and eating where we were unknowingly exposed to and benefited from what Yosso (2005) calls community cultural wealth (CCW) (familial, aspirational, resistant, navigational, and social capital). "Community cultural wealth is an array of knowledge, skills, abilities, and contacts possessed and utilized by Communities of Color to survive and resist macro and micro forms of oppression" (Yosso, 2005, p. 77). With Sunday dinner, my mother not only nourished our bodies but armed us with meaningful skills needed to survive in the world.

Planning Sunday Dinner—(Familial and Aspirational Capital)

Sunday dinner began with menu planning, where my mom would wake up early, sit at the kitchen table, and write out the day's menu along with the accompanying grocery list. As an early morning riser, I could catch my mom alone, where we would have conversations about our family. For instance, my family ended up in East St. Louis because my maternal great-great-grandmother migrated to East St. Louis with my great-grandmother, who was an only child. It was from my great-grandmother that our family grew when she had eleven children who would become my grandmother, two great aunts, and eight great uncles. In speaking about family, the conversation centered on our larger family and family lore and gossip. For instance, my great-uncle Edward lived in so many different cities and states that we never knew his exact address. However, the family lore went that whenever my grandmother (his sister) was facing a health issue, he knew about it, and that is when he would appear in town without notifying anyone or receiving word from anyone. Now, many would call this a coincidence, but it often seemed my great-uncle would appear at the exact moment my grandmother was sick. For me, my uncle's mysterious comings and goings portrayed that it was okay to "leave" the family to make a new life for yourself in the city and state of your choosing; but that you could always "return" home to family. Leaving home didn't mean that love between one another disappeared or you couldn't be close by. His visits, but more so his departures, planted the idea that I could move away for college, a career, and start a new family and still carry love and home in my heart, as evidenced by the fact I "moved" away for college in 1997 and haven't lived at home since.

During the meal planning, we also talked about our neighbors, the neighborhood—the John DeShields Housing Project, and the city of East St. Louis. We dreamed of what it would mean to move out of the projects, what it would take to move into a house, and how it would feel to own a home (aspirational capital—the ability to maintain hopes and dreams for the future, even in the face of real and perceived barriers). How could we afford a home that would provide enough space, considering we lived in a four-bedroom apartment with a kitchen, living room, and two bathrooms? And while the neighborhood would be better, how would it compare to the closeness we felt with our current neighbors in the nearby buildings? How would we replace our friends (both adults and children)?

How would we replace the fact that we all looked out for one another? In what other neighborhood would you know if an entire family was sick or if someone in the family had died and what help they needed, or if the family had fallen on hard economic times and was having a difficult time? In many ways, we supported each other by sharing food, other material items like clothes and shoes, childcare duties, and even a place to stay if needed. While the neighborhood was our home, our neighbors were family whom we cared for and interacted with in ways that allowed us to be an extended family (familial capital).

Shopping for Sunday Dinner—(Social Capital)

My mother often encountered people she knew in the grocery store where we shopped for Sunday dinner. These interactions led to conversations that ran from extremely brief to quite long and were dependent on the individual's identity, who might be a casual acquaintance, old school classmate, or longtime close friend. These conversations also varied from quick catching up to gossip or in-depth debates—but also informing one another about financial and social opportunities. For instance, during these conversations, adults would talk about East St. Louis economics and politics and what that meant for the larger city regarding services and opportunities. They would often talk about opportunities and openings for their children in sports, academics, and other extracurriculars. If it were summer, these conversations would move to camps, summer jobs, or ways of getting kids involved and out of the house. The grocery store encounters were a time of networking and accessing people and community resources (social capital).

With limited access to grocery stores, East St. Louis residents shopped at the same stores, including educators, clergy, and politicians, so in coming across friends, we also encountered individuals who provided access to additional resources in their professional roles. They would often ask about school or our next steps regarding graduation and college. They also provided information about enhancement and enrichment programs and activities that were beneficial in helping us achieve our next steps. These individuals knew where we should apply and whom we should talk to about these programs and often offered to put in a word for us. The grocery store was more than a place to gather tangible items of nourishment and sustenance; the store also provided us with intangible commodities that nourished our development, skills, and access (navigational capital—refers to maneuvering skills through social institutions).

Cooking Sunday Dinner—(Resistant and Navigational Capital)

While planning and shopping for Sunday dinner was an event between my mom and me, cooking was a family event and involved my siblings (three sisters and two brothers) helping to prepare the meal. During these tasks, we all discussed school and our futures in terms of dream careers, families, where we would live as adults, and places we wanted to travel. My mother, listening to our conversations, talked of how we needed to make choices that steered us clear of the gangs, violence, drugs (addicts and sellers), and teenage pregnancy present in our neighborhood (resistant capital—knowledge, and skills fostered through oppositional behavior that challenges inequality). Personally, this included my involvement in school events and programs such as the National Honor Society, Saturday Scholars Program, Upward Bound, and other afterschool programs. As a gifted and honors student, I took advantage of every academic and enrichment program offered by our local school district and the community. These programs were the resources and tools I used to succeed in college (navigational capital refers to skills of maneuvering through social institutions). Sunday dinner gave us the time and space to think about what and who we wanted to be that went beyond the physicality of the government projects (aspirational capital).

Conclusion

As adults scattered across the United States, we have not lost the concept of gathering for Sunday dinner. Assembled in the same city, the ritual of planning, shopping, cooking, and eating Sunday dinner remains a time of reverence for my family. As we plan the meal, it now includes our nieces and nephews as we regale them with conversations about our ancestry and family lore. Now we encounter our casual acquaintances, close friends, and classmates in the grocery store and exchange the same city and personal gossip while giving each other details on opportunities related to jobs and enhancements and enrichments for their children. Cooking is still a family affair with everyone engaged in their favored task as we ask the next generation about their goals, plans, and wishes. Sunday dinners represent the opportunity for us to cherish family and spend time with one another that we often did not and still do not have.

Reference

Yosso, T. J. (2005). Whose culture has capital? A critical race theory discussion of community cultural wealth. *Race Ethnicity and Education, 8*(1), 69–91.

Guest Commentary and Reflection
"You Can't Keep Telling Us What We Already Know": A Fugitive End to Educational Narratives of Tragedy

DAVID STOVALL

With the blessings of the authors of this edited volume, I will start my comments with an attempt to clear the air about Kozol's *Savage Inequalities*. When we get down to the bare-bones reality of the situation, we must tell a sometimes unwelcome but necessary truth: *Kozol decided to tell White people what Black folks have known for centuries—the system of US schooling was never intended to do right by us.* Even worse is the idea that many feel that the primary duty of educators and people working adjacent to education is to center our analysis solely in the longitudinal suffering of Black people. When this happens, the ability to ignore the fugitive efforts to educate our people in the face of extreme hate becomes even harder to envision. Ironically, the fugitive efforts of Black educators remain the critical component in sustaining the capacity of Black youth to identify the issues and concerns that affect their lives while working with others to change their collective realities.

For these reasons, it is important to move away from the idea that someone external to our situation (in this case a White journalist) has to operate as the source of validity to justify our struggle. Where I am in full support of White people who operate as race traitors and coconspirators against White supremacy, I also know that their work *looks and feels* different from the pages of *Savage Inequalities*. David Gillborn, Andy Clarno,

John Rogers, and Sherry Marx are intentional in their work when naming White supremacy, their own privilege, and the commitment that White people must make to combat White supremacy internally and externally.

At the same time, I also agree that we have to understand the realities of what it is that we're in (a moment that exposes the perpetual commitment to anti-Blackness, late-stage capitalism, totalitarian regimes, climate disaster, persistent global health crises, etc.), there is also the responsibility to engage in practices that refuse the grip of White supremacy and racial capitalism. Although it is a road less traveled, the editors and authors in this volume remind us of its necessity for the foreseeable future.

Returning to Kozol, it is important to note that he is not the sole culprit in creating tragedy porn for White audiences. Instead, we should understand his 1992 intervention as one that is credited to a long line of work that has "revealed" the realities of urban schooling to the (White) world. Where the "heartstrings" approach has the potential to pull people into the fray to potentially get involved, it remains deeply limited in its scope. In some instances, charitable efforts may increase momentarily, but the impetus to engage in longitudinal efforts to address the conditions faced by students of color remain scant and overlooked.

As a critical race theorist, I try my best to remain connected to the realities of young people and families that are willing to resist racial capitalism and White supremacy because at any given moment I could fall prey to its grasp. Drs. Ishwanzya Rivers, Lori Patton, Raquel Farmer-Hinton, and Joi Lewis (2021), in offering a necessary challenge to the accepted narrative of *Savage Inequalities*, remind us that no matter the situation, Black people have resisted and continue to create spaces for people to thrive. It is difficult work but also rooted in love and understanding, something that is not always offered in traditional school spaces. Like this section highlights, much of this work happens outside of traditional school spaces (homes, churches, community centers, playgrounds, etc.). I have always considered these spaces to be fugitive ones, where we decide where rules don't necessarily work, and a collective decision is made to do something else. Instead of running from something, we are running to the places that allow us to maintain and build on our own terms. It is in these places where educators are able talk with families about what can be done to navigate school spaces. Young people are able to talk with each other, figuring out how to support each other in challenging spaces. These fugitive spaces are where planning takes place about what needs to be done and how to do it. They are invaluable spaces—ones that Kozol did not care to capture.

I am happy that this edited volume is daring enough to push back on deficit narratives while invoking Tara Yosso's notion of a community cultural wealth. The ability to navigate our situations while speaking in the language that assures us comfort and love is what's missed when we don't think of education beyond the K–12 classroom. If we understand education as a broader, community-based exercise rooted in history to remind us of the work to be done in the present moving toward the future, it takes us to a different place. This destination is deeply rooted in the responsibilities of abolition, where the things that are unacceptable must be destroyed while we build something else in its place. The hope is that this commitment is never forgotten as we prepare for the enemy's next move.

Discussion Questions

1. If we know that schooling (order, compliance, and rewards for regurgitating the rules of White supremacy) is unacceptable, what must we do to work with others to create spaces where we can educate ourselves?

2. Can education (the ability to think, create, and work with others to change our collective conditions) happen in the places we call schools?

3. What strategies should we utilize to train ourselves to maintain the commitment to actively interrupt the policies and practices that continue to harm students of color in K–12 schools?

Additional Readings

Givens, J. (2021). *Fugitive pedagogy: Carter G. Woodson and the art of Black teaching.* Harvard Education Press.

Purnell, D. (2021). *Becoming abolitionists: Police, protests and the pursuit of freedom.* Penguin Random House

Watson, K., & Marie, T. (2022). Somewhere between a rock and an outer space: Apocalyptic education. *Journal of Futures Studies, 26*(3), 25–44.

References

Kozol, J. (1992) *Savage inequalities: Children in America's schools.* Harper Perennial.

Rivers, I. D., Patton, L. D., Farmer-Hinton, R. L., & Lewis, J. D. (2021). That wasn't my reality: Counter-narratives of educational success as East St. Louis' educators 'reimagine' Savage Inequalities. *Urban Education,* https://doi.org/10.1177/0042085920987283

Afterword

Reflections on Community Cultural Wealth

TARA J. YOSSO

When I started to conceptualize and write "Whose Culture Has Capital?" (Yosso, 2005), I was focused on a myriad of details, like making sure I referenced the multiple articles, books, and discussions swirling in my head and strewn across my desk. I used a flowchart to visually show some of the scholarly traditions that informed critical race theory and an expanded Venn diagram with two-directional arrows to show community cultural wealth in relationship to and distinct from Pierre Bourdieu's concept of cultural capital (Bourdieu & Passeron, 1977). Bourdieu identified cultural capital as knowledge deemed valuable by dominant groups (elite Whites) and then kept as exclusive to those who had already positioned themselves at the top of the social hierarchy. The initial community cultural wealth model was inspired by traditions in Mexican immigrant and Chicana/o communities of passing on cultural knowledges to facilitate critical navigation through society's institutions (see Yosso, 2006). I felt it was important to frame the model broadly and to use the panethnic term People of Color, despite its impreciseness, because it is undeniable that across time and place, and amidst the horrors of colonization and slavery, Communities of Color have possessed and utilized an array of cultural knowledges, skills, abilities, and networks. Sharing and passing on these knowledges, in ceremonial, creative, defiant, and clandestine ways, has been crucial for our collective survival (Delgado, 1989). It was challenging to define the model's six forms of "capital" and point readers to their attendant robust bodies of research while also capturing how each was dynamic, multifaceted, and interdependent on the others (see kaleidoscope visual in Yosso & García, 2007). I included additional details in the endnotes for the ideas I was still working out, for example, about how emotional, moral, and educational consciousness and a hard work ethic were modeled by kin, and about the ways cultural knowledges have been co-opted and commodified. I also tried to anticipate some of the critiques.

Reflecting on the trajectory of this model as it has been taken up by scholars and practitioners across the United States and around the world, I am truly excited about how it has been taken in this collection of narratives as a tool of reclamation. For too long, the story told through Jonathan Kozol's (1991) work, though relevant, has crystallized a view of the cities these authors called home and the schools they attended as sites indelibly marked by "savage inequality." The authors here present counternarratives that question whose interests are served by circulating only one story about Black families in segregated neighborhoods and schools. Positioning their individual and shared experiences in conversation with critical literatures and traditions, their reflections carry forward stories of Black neighborhoods as spaces of affirmation (Irvine, 2002), of Black families "raising resisters" (Robinson & Ward, 1991; Ward, 1996), and of the ongoing efforts of Black school communities sustaining "communal bonds" (Morris, 1994, 1999) across generations. Uplifting these voices, they create a beautiful counter-narrative map of predominantly Black urban cities indelibly marked by community cultural wealth.

As Derrick A. Bell (1992) reminds those engaged in this work of counter-storytelling, "For us, this writing is not some idle vogue. Nor are we willingly confrontational. Rather we feel we must understand so as better to oppose the dire forces that are literally destroying the many people who share our racial heritage" (p. 145). Despite extensive scholarship analyzing the landmark *Brown v. Board of Education* decision to end school segregation over seventy-five years ago, there are many stories yet to be told about the parents, students, teachers, principals, counselors, school staff, and community organizers carrying forward their ancestors' dreams in the struggle for more equal educational opportunities (e.g., Yosso & García, 2021; McNeil, 1983; Siddle Walker, 1996, 2000, 2018; Tillman, 2004; White, 2002). The personal narratives told herein add much to our understanding of the details and dimensions of growing up in segregated neighborhoods and attending segregated schools. If I felt a great responsibility to account for the details in writing and visually conceptualizing sixteen years ago, today, as a mother of two school-age children, the weight of challenging deficit thinking and passing on knowledges to the next generation feels even more profound. There are indeed "dire forces" that continue to resurrect racial myths that pathologize our families and frame our stories in one-dimensional terms. It is urgent that we expose such stories as incomplete and recover the layers of humanity that have been misrepresented and misunderstood in their wake (e.g., Valencia, 2010). Intentionally bringing a more complete picture of enduring, evolving forms of community cultural wealth into our frame, we express our collective hope for a more just future.

References

Bell, D. A. (1992). *Faces at the bottom of the well: The permanence of racism.* Basic Books.
Bourdieu, P., & Passeron, J. C. (1977). *Reproduction in education, society, and culture.* SAGE.
Delgado, R. (1989). Storytelling for oppositionists and others: A plea for narrative. *Michigan Law Review, 87,* 2411–2441.
Irvine, J. J. (2002). *In search of wholeness: African American teachers and their culturally specific classroom practices.* Palgrave/St. Martin's Press.
Kozol, J. (1991). *Savage inequalities: Children in America's schools.* Crown.
McNeil, G. R. *Groundwork: Charles Hamilton Houston and the struggle for civil rights.* University of Pennsylvania Press.
Morris, J. (1999). A pillar of strength: An African-American school's communal bonds with families and community since *Brown. Urban Education, 33*(5), 584–605.
Morris, J. (2004). Can anything good come from Nazareth? Race, class, and African American schooling and community in the urban south and Midwest. *American Educational Research Journal, 41*(1), 69–112.
Robinson, T. & Ward, J. (1991). 'A belief in self far greater than anyone's belief': Cultivating resistance among African American female adolescents. In C. Gilligan, A. Rogers, & D. Tolman (Eds.), *Women, girls, and psychotherapy: Reframing resistance* (pp. 87–103). Haworth.
Siddle Walker, V. (1996). *Their highest potential: An African American school community in the segregated South.* University of North Carolina Press.
Siddle Walker, V. (2000). Valued segregated schools for African American children in the South, 1935–1969: A review of common themes and characteristics. *Review of Educational Research, 70*(3), 253–286.
Siddle Walker, V. (2018). *The lost education of Horace Tate.* New Press.

Tillman, L. C. (2004). African American principals and the legacy of *Brown*. *Review of Research in Education, 28*, 101–146.

Ward, J. (1996). Raising resisters: The role of truth telling in the psychological development of African American girls. In B. Leadbetter & N. Way (Eds.), *Urban girls: Resisting stereotypes, creating identities* (pp. 85–99). New York University Press.

White, M. A. (2002, Spring). Paradise lost? Teachers' perspectives on the use of cultural capital in the segregated schools of New Orleans, Louisiana. *Journal of African American History*, 269–281.

Valencia, R. R. (2010). *Dismantling contemporary deficit thinking: Educational thought and practice.* Routledge.

Yosso, T. J. (2005). Whose culture has capital? A critical race theory discussion of community cultural wealth. *Race Ethnicity and Education, 8*(1), 71–93.

Yosso, T. J. (2006). *Critical race counterstories along the Chicana/Chicano educational pipeline.* Routledge.

Yosso, T. J., & García, D. G. (2007). 'This is no slum!': A critical race theory analysis of community cultural wealth in Culture Clash's *Chavez Ravine*. *Aztlan: A Journal of Chicano Studies, 32*(1), 145–179.

Yosso, T. J., & García, D. G. (2021). Carving out a legal narrative from *Galarza* to *Soria*: Accounting for the complexities of history, race, and place in educational research. *International Journal of Qualitative Studies in Education*, DOI: 10.1080/09518398.2021.1930267

Contributors

Dr. Noelle Arnold
Noelle Arnold is the senior associate dean and professor of educational administration in the College of Education and Human Ecology at The Ohio State University. In addition to other units, Arnold oversees the EHE Office of Equity, Diversity and Global Engagement. Arnold has written and presented extensively and has nine books published or in press and more than 70 publications. A former administrator at the district and state level, Arnold also serves as a consultant throughout the United States, advising districts on diversity and inclusion, crisis leadership, and teaching and leading in urban and rural contexts.

Dr. Jane Bean-Folkes
Jane Bean-Folkes is an avid reader of children's literature. She is a K–12 ELA supervisor in New Jersey. Her research interests involve multilingual classrooms, written academic language, African American language, sociocultural and sociolinguistic perspectives of education for nondominant language speakers as they learn the academic language in urban settings. She serves on the national committees of the National Council of Teacher of English, the Literacy Research Association, and the American Educational Research Association. Her publications include edited chapters in publications from Peter Lang, NCTE/Routledge; her journal articles include *Handbook of Reading Research*, *The Educational Form*, *The Reading Teacher*, as well as National Council of Teachers of Education and International Literacy Association journals.

Dr. Keith E. Benson
Keith E. Benson is the author of *Education Reform and Gentrification in the Age of #CamdenRising: Public Education and Urban Redevelopment in*

Camden, NJ (2019) and currently the president of the Camden Education Association. He has taught in Camden City public schools for fourteen years prior to being elected to the CEA presidency.

Dr. Theodorea Regina Berry
Theodorea Regina Berry is vice provost and dean, College of Undergraduate Studies with a tenured faculty appointment as professor of curriculum studies, Department of Learning Sciences and Research, College of Community Innovation and Education at the University of Central Florida. Dr. Berry centers her work in curriculum theory/curriculum studies, critical race theory/critical race feminism, and qualitative research methodology (archival/historical, autoethnography, ethnography, narrative). Dr. Berry is a vice president for Division B (Curriculum) of the American Education Research Association for the 2023-2026 term.

Mrs. Carly Braxton
Carly Braxton is a native Detroiter who earned her bachelor's degree in public relations from Central Michigan University. She received her master's degree in higher education from the University of Michigan-Ann Arbor. Carly is currently pursuing her doctorate in English, with a concentration in rhetoric and writing studies at Wayne State University. Her current research is focused on antiracist pedagogy and linguistic justice, primarily related to teaching and writing.

Dr. Susan Browne
Susan Browne is an associate professor in the Department of Language, Literacy and Sociocultural Education at Rowan University, where she teaches undergraduate and graduate reading courses. She serves as a research advisor to master's and Ed.D. candidates and teaches in the College of Education Center for Access, Equity and Success PhD program. Dr. Browne co-directs the Rowan University Writing Project. Her research interests and publications are in the areas of critical pedagogies, urban education, multicultural literature, and reader response. Most recently, she is the co-editor of *Reconceptualizing Social Justice in Teacher Education: Moving to Anti-racist Pedagogy* published by Palgrave Macmillan.

Dr. Amber Bryant
Amber Bryant is a research scientist in the field of education and studies the intersections of economics, education, and policy. Dr. Bryant has

published articles in *Urban Review, Education Law and Policy Review,* and *Education Policy Analysis Archives*. She coauthored a book in 2019 entitled, *Global Issues and Urban Schools: Strategies to Effectively Teach Students in Urban Environments around the World* while at the University of North Carolina at Charlotte. Currently, Dr. Bryant works as a project manager at the Inter-university Consortium for Political and Social Research at the University of Michigan.

Dr. Theresa J. Canada

Theresa J. Canada is a professor of education and educational psychology department at Western Connecticut State University. Research interests include cultural diversity in education, early childhood, equity, and urban education. Her most recent book chapter is "Development and Implementation of an Early Childhood Parenting Curriculum for Preschool Teachers" in L. N. Roberts (Ed.), *Redesigning Teaching Leadership, and Indigenous Education in the 21st Century*. She is also author of the 2018 book *Desegregation of the New York City Schools: A Story of The Silk Stocking Sisters*.

Dr. Dorinda J. Carter Andrews

Dorinda J. Carter Andrews is a professor and chairperson of the Department of Teacher Education at Michigan State University. Her research is focused on Black education and racial equity and justice in P-20 learning environments. She utilizes critical racial and Black feminist/womanist frameworks and methodologies to examine issues of race, culture, and power in schools. She has given two TEDx talks on education, and her scholarship has been published in *Harvard Educational Review, Urban Education, Journal of Teacher Education, American Educational Research Journal,* among others.

Mr. Maceo A. Cooper-Jenkins

Maceo A. Cooper-Jenkins is a secondary education teacher leader currently serving as an instructional coach, new teacher mentor, and racial equity professional development facilitator. Cooper-Jenkins is recognized as a leader among his peers and revered for his unique ability to motivate students and teachers of all levels in their pursuit of excellence. As a teacher leader, he plays a vital role in the training and development of teachers across the district. Cooper-Jenkins earned his certificate in administration and leadership from Loyola University, his M.Ed. in secondary education from Towson University, and his bachelor's in biology from Morgan State University.

Dr. Raquel Farmer-Hinton

Raquel Farmer-Hinton is an associate professor in the Department of Educational Policy and Community Studies at the University of Wisconsin-Milwaukee. Raised and educated in East St. Louis, Illinois, her research, teaching, and service commitments focus on urban communities and remedying educational inequities, particularly college access and readiness. She received undergraduate and graduate degrees from the University of Illinois at Urbana-Champaign. Dr. Raquel Farmer-Hinton previously held positions as a Spencer Postdoctoral Research Fellow at the University of Chicago, a postdoctoral research fellow at the Educational Testing Service in Princeton, New Jersey, and a research associate at Westat in Rockville, Maryland.

Dr. Diane R. Fuselier-Thompson

Diane Fuselier-Thompson is an Assistant Professor in the School of Social Work at Wayne State University in Detroit, Michigan. She received both her bachelor's degree and master of social work from the University of Michigan. Her research interests include higher education access among minority women who pursue science, technology, engineering and mathematics (STEM) fields of study and the influence of an urban context on their college preparation and career pathway. Dr. Fuselier-Thompson examines social and cultural networks in urban communities that contribute to college access and success in STEM and how understanding cultural capital in communities of color can contribute to the development of support programs in postsecondary education.

Dr. Chayla Haynes

Chayla Haynes is associate professor of higher education administration in the Educational Administration and Human Resource Development Department at Texas A&M University, College Station. Her scholarship centers on critical and inclusive pedagogies, Black women in higher education, and the methodological capacities of intersectionality and critical race theory. Dr. Haynes is also coeditor of *Interrogating Whiteness and Relinquishing Power: White Faculty's Commitment to Racial Consciousness in STEM Classrooms*.

Dr. Omari Jackson

Omari Jackson is a sociologist who serves as an associate professor of Urban Educational Leadership in the Department of Advanced Studies, Leadership and Policy at Morgan State University. He is the director of the Urban Educational Leadership doctoral program. He has more than 15 years of experience in higher education, as a precollege advisor, learning specialist, instructional coach, and faculty member. His research interests include lived experiences of middle-class blacks as well as the recruitment, retention, and postsecondary success of underrepresented students. He is from Detroit, lives in Baltimore, and has a deep appreciation for urban cities.

Dr. Toby S. Jenkins
Toby S. Jenkins is an associate professor in educational leadership and policy studies and interim associate dean of Diversity, Equity, and Inclusion in the Graduate School at the University of South Carolina. Jenkins has authored five books focused on culture, diversity, and inclusion in education. *My Culture, My Color, My Self: Heritage, Resilience and Community in the Lives of Young Adults* (2013) was named by the Association of American University Presses to the list of "Top 100 Books for Understanding Race Relations in the US." Her sixth book is *The Hip-Hop Mindset: Air-Walking and Trash-Talking* (2023).

Dr. Jodi L. Jordan
Jodi L. Jordan's career spans three decades as an educational leader, consultant, university administrator, child advocate, and community servant. She has provided intensive training and technical support to educators, focusing primarily on early childhood education instruction and teacher interaction with children 0 to 5 years old. With significant leadership as director of several childcare facilities and as a school founder and administrator, she is a staunch advocate for children from the most divested areas. She is a member on multiple community and university boards and has consistently worked to enhance early childhood care and education instruction.

Dr. Jada Renee Koushik
Jada Renee Koushik is a postdoctoral fellow at the Wilfrid Laurier in the Faculty of Social Work where she examines the impact of race and racism on the mental health of racialized faculty, staff, and students on campus. Dr. Koushik teaches environmental justice and racism in Canada and beyond course at the University of Waterloo. She earned her PhD from the University of Saskatchewan and both graduate and undergraduate degrees from the University of Michigan, Ann Arbor. Her scholarship has been published in *Urban Environmental Education Review, Journal of Environmental Education, Journal of Sustainability Education*, among others.

Dr. Joi D. Lewis

Joi D. Lewis is a community healer and facilitator of Black liberation. As a speaker, scholar, author, CEO of Joi Unlimited, and president of the Healing Justice Foundation, she's on a mission to put healing in the hands of anyone, anywhere. Dr. Joi's book, *Healing: The Act of Radical Self-Care*, educates individuals about the "Orange Method" of healing justice. She is the co-founder of Auntie & Z. She spent 20-plus years in higher education leadership as a dean, vice president, and chief diversity officer. While she resides in Saint Paul, Minnesota, her work is deeply informed by growing up in East St. Louis, Illinois. She's an unapologetic joy instigator, radical self-care evangelist, and food prep pro. She offers this meditation to all who believe in liberation: *May the revolution be healing!*

Dr. Marvin Lynn

Marvin Lynn serves as professor and dean in the School of Education and Human Development at the University of Colorado at Denver. He conducts research on race, education, the work and lives of Black male educators, and best practices for advancing teacher diversity in the United States. His coedited book (currently in its second edition) with Adrienne Dixson, *The Handbook of Critical Race Theory in Education*, features the scholarship of the most prolific scholars in the fields of education and the law and is regarded as one of the most important resources in the area of race and education. Dr. Lynn has been a featured commentator on major news outlets, including the *New York Times*, the British Broadcasting Corporation, *Christian Science Monitor*, and others.

Dr. Ezella McPherson

Ezella McPherson is the CEO/founder of Dr. McPherson Coaching, a college student retention company. Her research expertise centers on college student persistence and retention, Black girls and women's education, STEM education, and qualitative research. Her scholarship is published in edited books and journals, including *Education and Urban Society, Journal of Women and Minorities in Science and Engineering, Urban Education,* and *Women, Gender, and Families of Color*. She has published two books, *Dream On! Supporting and Graduating African American Girls and Women in STEM* (2021) and *Real Outreach: A Practical Guide to Retaining and Graduating College Students* (2021). She is a member of the University of Michigan's Diversity Scholars Network and earned her master's and PhD from the University of Illinois at Urbana-Champaign.

Dr. H. Richard Milner IV

H. Richard Milner IV (also known as Rich) is Cornelius Vanderbilt Chair of Education and Professor of Education in the Department of Teaching and Learning at Peabody College of Vanderbilt University. His research examines practices and policies that support teacher effectiveness in urban schools. Professor Milner is president of the American Educational Research Association, the largest educational research organization in the world. He is an elected member of the National Academy of Education and a Fellow of the American Educational Research Association.

Dr. Steve D. Mobley Jr.

Steve D. Mobley Jr. is associate professor of higher education and student affairs in the Department of Advanced Studies, Leadership, and Policy in the School of Education and Urban Studies at Morgan State University. His scholarship focuses on the contemporary placement of historically Black colleges and universities (HBCUs). Particularly, Dr. Mobley Jr's research underscores the understudied facets of HBCU communities including issues surrounding race, social class, and student sexuality. He earned his bachelor's in communication and culture from Howard University. Upon graduating from Howard he completed his master's in higher education management from the University of Pennsylvania, and earned his PhD in higher education from the University of Maryland.

Dr. Heather Moore Roberson

Heather Moore Roberson is an award-winning teacher and published scholar in the fields of critical race theory, childhood studies, and social justice. Moore Roberson has authored articles in the *Radical Teacher* and *Professing Education* journals and has written numerous book chapters for various interdisciplinary edited collections. She is an associate professor of community and justice studies and Black studies and Dean of Diversity, Equity, & Inclusion at Allegheny College.

Dr. Lonnie R. Morris Jr.

Lonnie R. Morris Jr. is assistant professor of organizational leadership at the Chicago School of Professional Psychology. He is scholar-practitioner with 20-plus years of leadership in higher education as an executive, administrator, consultant, and professor. He is a two-time national award winner for innovation in online instruction. He is the coeditor of *When Leadership Fails: Individual, Group and Organizational Lessons from the*

Worst Workplace Experiences (2021) and *Handbook of Research on Instructional Systems and Educational Technology* (2017).

Ms. Lyntoria Newton
Lyntoria Newton is a documentarian and impact producer based in Chicago, Illinois. She is devoted to exploring the stories that relate to Black history and Black liberation. She is currently associate producer on the forthcoming film *Life After* with director Reid Davenport. She is also producer for the forthcoming feature film *Hangtown* with director Stuart Harmon. She has taught documentary filmmaking courses at Bay Area Video Coalition Media, San Francisco Film School, and Northwestern University. Lyntoria holds a BA from Hampshire College and an MFA in documentary film and video from Stanford University.

Ms. Deborah J. Patton
Deborah J. Patton is a board-certified psychiatric nurse practitioner. She completed her master's degree at St. Louis University and has been in the psychiatric nursing field for over 20 years. She has experience treating depression, bipolar illness, anxiety disorders, schizophrenia, and co-occurring substance use disorders. She is a mental health expert within the metropolitan St. Louis area and provides advocacy and services to numerous communities in need of mental health and wellness support.

Dr. Lori D. Patton
Lori D. Patton is one of the most accomplished and influential scholars in the field of higher education. She is a tenured full professor of higher education and student affairs at The Ohio State University and chair of the Department of Educational Studies. Patton Davis is also past president of the Association for the Study of Higher Education. Patton Davis is best known for her important cross-cutting scholarship on race in higher education, diversity initiatives on college campuses, Black girls and women in educational and social contexts, and college student development. She has advised university presidents and other senior administrators, philanthropic foundation executives, culture center directors, and educators in urban K–12 schools.

Dr. Ishwanzya D. Rivers
Ishwanzya D. Rivers is assistant clinical professor at the University of Louisville in higher education administration. Dr. Rivers's research and

teaching interests are college access, college choice, recruitment, and retention for minoritized students, with an emphasis on the community college. Raised and educated in East St. Louis, her research centers on urban communities and urban residents and their agency in educating and developing educational institutions. She is the coauthor of *"Dear Mr. Kozol . . ." Four African American Women Reauthoring Savage Inequalities* (2013) and *That Wasn't My Reality: Counter-Narratives of Educational Success as East St. Louis' Educators "Reimagine"* Savage Inequalities. She received her MEd and PhD from the University of Illinois at Urbana-Champaign.

Dr. Chanelle N. Rose

Chanelle N. Rose, is associate professor of history and coordinator of the Africana Studies program at Rowan University. Her areas of research and teaching include modern American history, specializing in African American history, civil rights–Black Power movements, the African diaspora, conservatism, tourism, and urban history. Her first book, *The Struggle for Black Freedom in Miami: Civil Rights and America's Tourist Paradise, 1896-1968* (2015) examines the long struggle for racial equality in the country's most popular tourist destinations. It complicates the Black/White binary and offers a new way of understanding the complexity of racial traditions and White supremacy in southern metropolises like Miami. Her current book project, tentatively entitled *Reimagining Black Conservatism: Black Democrats and Grassroots Organizing during the Post-WWII Urban Crisis (1975-1995)*, explores modern Black conservatism in local communities by looking at how the post-WWII urban crisis of the 1970s and 1980s made this political ideology more attractive to a wider swathe of the African American community that voted Democrat.

Dr. David Stovall

David Stovall is professor in the Department of Black Studies and in the Department of Criminology, Law, and Justice at the University of Illinois at Chicago. His scholarship investigates critical race theory, the relationship between housing and education, and the intersection of race, place, and school. Bringing theory to action, he works with community organizations and schools to address issues of equity, justice, and abolishing the school/prison nexus. He is also involved with the People's Education Movement, a collection of classroom teachers, community members, students, and university professors in Chicago, Los Angeles, and the San Francisco Bay Area who engage in collaborative community projects centered on creating relevant curricula. In addition to his duties and responsibilities as a professor at UIC, he also served as a volunteer social studies teacher at the Greater Lawndale/Little Village School for Social Justice from 2005 to 2018.

Dr. William T. Trent

William T. Trent is professor of education policy, organization, and leadership at the University of Illinois Urbana-Champaign. He has held research appointments at the Center for Education Policy at Duke University and the Center for the Social Organization of Schools at Johns Hopkins University. Trent has served as an associate chancellor at the University of Illinois, director of the Educational Opportunity Program at George Washington University, and director of Project OPEN, a TRIO Talent Search program in Washington, DC. His research focuses primarily on issues of educational inequality.

Dr. Mirelsie Velázquez

Mirelsie Velázquez is Associate Professor of Latina/o Studies at the University of Illinois at Urbana-Champaign. As a historian of education, her work centers conversation on race, gender, and Latina/o/x communities. Her book, *Puerto Rican Chicago: Schooling the City, 1940–1977*, chronicles the Puerto Rican community's response to the urban decay in which they were forced to live, work, and especially learn. Her work has most recently appeared in the journals *Latino Studies*, *Centro*, and *Gender and Education*.

Dr. Ahmad R. Washington

Ahmad R. Washington Ph.D., is an Associate Professor at the University of Louisville, with dual appointments in the department of Pan-African studies and the department of Counseling and Human Development. He currently serves as the school counseling program coordinator, where he works with pre-service school counseling students as they prepare to transition into the profession. Dr. Washington received his B.S. in psychology from Francis Marion University, his M.A. in clinical counseling from Webster University, and his Ph.D. in counselor education and supervision from the University of Iowa in 2013. Dr. Washington's primary research and pedagogical interests within school counseling explore how hip-hop culture, as texts, discourses and practices, represent salient and constructive sites of fugitivity and refusal, particularly for black students confronting and negotiating structural anti-Blackness.

Ms. Dallas Jewell Watson

Dallas Jewell Watson is a first-year student at Macalester College in Saint Paul, Minnesota. She is a member of the Improv Team and a mentor for Upward Bound and Trio students. She is the cofounder of Auntie & Z. Her current scholarly interests are: African studies, American studies and Spanish. Dallas is the recipient of her Belleville, Illinois high school's Mighty Maroon Award and the East St. Louis NAACP Oratory competition awards. She is also a Questbridge National Match Recipient. In her free time, she likes to read, exercise, and listen to music. Her dream is to create a scholarship for low-income Black students.

Dr. Brittany M. Williams

Brittany M. Williams is assistant professor of higher education and student affairs administration at the University of Vermont. Her research explores higher education finance, specifically social class; workplace retention and human resource concerns anchored in an analysis of structural inequities and (in)effective supervision; and campus and community public health policy, outcomes, and disparities. Williams has been featured in and by the White House Initiative on HBCUs, National Public Radio (NPR), the National Black Women's Health Imperative (BWHI), Teach for America, the National Minority Aids Council (NMAC), and in a host of academic journals. She is a 2022 National Academy of Education (NAEd)/Spencer Postdoctoral Scholar.

Dr. Tara J. Yosso

Tara J. Yosso is professor in the School of Education at the University of California, Riverside. Her research examines access to educational opportunities for Students of Color at critical transition points in their schooling trajectories (e.g., high school to college, baccalaureate to doctorate). Her extensively cited publications and award-winning book *Critical Race Counterstories along the Chicana/Chicano Educational Pipeline* (2006) recover counternarratives of race, schooling, inequality, and the law. Her work specifically highlights the array of knowledges, skills, abilities, and networks (community cultural wealth) Students of Color bring to school. Yosso regularly advises educational practitioners and leaders about how her community cultural wealth approach can guide efforts to end structures and practices of discrimination and foster a critical historical perspective of the communities we aim to serve.

Index

*Page numbers in italics refer to images;
page numbers followed by* (t) *refer to tables.*

21st Century Atlanta Scholars
  programs, 234, 236, 238, 240
Abbot districts, 122
Abbot Rulings (NJSC), 122
Abbot v. Burke (1985), 121
academic success: "asset-based"
  approaches, 164–65; Black-White
  comparisons, 85–86; community/
  school contributions, 116, 233; and
  familial capital/kinship ties, 62,
  107, 112, 126, 129, 148, 172, 175,
  182–83, 192, 195, 196, 224, 247;
  family role models, 197, 286–87;
  metrics, 107, 108, 165, 166; as
  personal and sociocultural skills,
  239; race and class norms, 124, 156,
  174, 231, 239, 252, 283, 285, 286,
  287; redefinition of, 234, 239–40;
  "success" or "failure" narratives,
  114, 161, 162, 163. *See also* fictive
  kin; higher education success;
  life lessons/skills; strength-based
  approaches; teachers
accountability discourse, 162, 164,
  165, 217–19
Achebe, Chinua, 19

activism. *See* school-centered activism
Adamsville Public Library (Atlanta),
  234–35
Adichie, Chimamanda Ngozi, 69
AERA (American Educational
  Research Association), xiii
African American community. *See*
  Black community; *individual
  communities*
African American male counselor
  educators (AAMCE), 150
African American studies, 252, 254
African American teachers. *See* Black
  teachers
Afrocentric curriculum, 149–50, 238.
  See also Black history
after-school education. *See* enrichment
  programs
agency, 94, 95, 123, 239, 242. *See also*
  cultural efficacy; resistant capital/
  resistance
Albee, Edward, 206
American Dream, 31, 231. *See also*
  meritocracy myth
American Educational Research
  Association (AERA), xiii
Anacostia (Washington), 11–12

Andrews, Dorinda J. Carter: bio, 319; chapter by, 49–53
Angelou, Maya, 44
Anglonormative precepts, 148, 153
antiracist education, 32, 147–48, 155–56. *See also* critical pedagogy
Anyon, Jean, 96
Armah, Bomani (social media respondent), 262
Arnold, Noelle W.: bio, 317; chapter by, 161–68
Aronson, E., 219
arts and craft education, 74, 135, 259, 261. *See also* performing arts programs
Asian American students, 206
aspirational capital: Black teachers and, 132; defined, 12, 126, 192, 247; neighborhood community, 71, 196–97, 304–5; parents/grandparents, 12, 14, 15, 291; school-family relationships, 195; student optimism/"grit," 111, 247. *See also* fictive kin
assimilation, 42, 252
Assumption High School (East St. Louis), 273–74
Atlanta Public Schools, 232, 233, 241, 242
Atlanta Urban Debate League, 234
autoethnography, 52, 80, 83, 202, 278. *See also* counter-storytelling; ethnography; standpoint theory
automobile industry, 36, 37, 80, 96. *See also* deindustrialization

Baker, Tina Q. (student), 110, 111
Baltimore (MD), 119, 213, 215
basket making, and folkways, 259
Battie, Naima (student), 113
Battle Creek Central High School (MI), 236
Bean-Folkes, Jane: bio, 317; chapter by, 119–39; comments on, 161, 163
Bell, Derrick A., 72, 98, 99, 314. *See also* counter-storytelling
Belleville (IL), 292
Benson, Keith: bio, 317–18; chapter by, 103–17; comments on, 161, 162
Berry, Theodorea Regina: bio, 318; chapter by, 277–80
Black Boy (Wright), 73
Black community: economic isolation, 81; ethnic diversity, 193–94; middle class, 80; school-centered activism, 62, 64, 148; as spaces of affirmation and resistance, 314. *See also* fictive kin; *individual communities; specific forms of cultural capital*
Black history, 28, 272
Black Power/Liberation, 206
Black schools, rural Southern, 249, 251, 254, 258, 259–61
Black teachers: critical pedagogy, 20; investment in students, 237–38; parent-community bonds, 196–97; as role models, 199; and student confidence, 294–95. *See also* aspirational capital; fictive kin
Black women's collegiate experiences, xiii–xiv, 225, 130(t), 234–35. *See also specific spaces; neighborhoods*
Blackness: and Black culture, 272; and excellence, 263, 292, 301; and pathology discourse, 71, 149, 153; used to justify inequality, 157–58
"blame the victim," 70, 143, 163
Bluffton (SC), 256
Board of Education (1954), *Brown v.* (*See also* Brown vs. Board of Education).
boarding schools, Southern, 251, 254, 256, 260, 263, 264

Bochner, A. P., 176
Bourdieu, Pierre, 10, 11, 313. *See also* cultural capital
Bowers, J., 212
Bowling Green State University, 9
Bradley, Milliken v., 87
Bradshaw, Ms. (teacher), 73
Braxton, Carly: bio, 318; chapter by, 171–89; comments on, 225
Brooks, M., 150
Brown, M. E., 220
Brown v. Board of Education (1954), 87, 119, 123, 201, 314
Browne, Susan: bio, 318; chapter by, 119–39; comments on, 161, 163
Bryant, Amber C.: bio, 318–19; chapter by, 79–91; comments on, 95–96
Burke, Abbot v. (1985), 121
Bush administration, 85, 234. *See also* No Child Left Behind program (2001)
businesses/stores, local, 131–32, 305–6. *See also* social capital
busing, mandatory, 16, 237, 263–64
Byrne, Jane, 58

Camden (NJ), neighborhood community, 121, 132, 128(t), 119–20, 126–27, 131–32
Camden Advisory School Board, 108–9
Camden City Police Force, 121
Camden City School District (CCSD): state takeover, 120, 134. *See also* charter schools
Camden County Municipal Utilities Authority, 121
Camden High School (CHS), 130. *See also* resistant capital/resistance
Camden Public Schools (CPS): experiences, student, 135, 128(t),

134–35; research study protocol, 126, 127(t); stigma, 113, 115
Campos, R., 196
Canada, Theresa J.: bio, 319; chapter by, 191–99; comments on, 224–25
career training education (CTE), 104. *See also* school tracking
Caribbean students, 193, 198
Carmen Marie, Sister (teacher), 272
Cartens Elementary School (Detroit), 30
Carter, Prudence, 205, 240
Carter Andrews, Dorinda J.: bio, 319; chapter by, 49–53
Casteel, C. A., 86
CCWM. *See* community cultural wealth model (CCWM)
centering marginalized voices. *See* autoethnography; community cultural wealth model (CCWM)
Central Michigan University (CMU) peer support, 183
chaperoning, 214–16. *See also* mentorship
charter schools: growth of, 32, 104, 109, 123, 133, 136; neighborhood school closures and, 122; and outside teachers, 134–35
Chekhov, Anton, 83
Cherry Hill (NJ) suburb, 119, 122
Chevere, Joselyn (student), 111, 113
Chicago Board of Education, 63, 64
Chicago Near North Side, 57–68. *See also* Puerto Rican community
Chicago Public Schools, and educational experiences, 64, 96
Children's Defense Fund, 293
Christie, Chris, 105, 113, 122
church, 83, 197, 269, 270, 300. *See also* Sunday dinners
civil rights, education, 62, 64
Clarno, Andy, 309

Class Act (movie), 18. *See also* school tracking
Clemente High School (Chicago), community activism, 61
"code switching," 25, 31, 236
Cohen, George (principal), 40
Coleman, James, xiv
collectivism, 13, 224, 295. *See also* social capital
college admissions process, 110, 114, 177, 220. *See also* higher education success
Collier, D. A., 212
Common Core State Standards, 32
communication strategies. *See* linguistic capital
community cultural wealth model (CCWM): about, 10, 120, 233, 313; core values, 236, 301; cultural capital, six forms defined, 12, 126, 192, 247; goals, 10, 120; sense of belonging, 50, 301; teacher and family relationships, 83, 129, 260
community responsibility, 107, 134, 261, 262–63; relational, 20–21. *See also* resistant capital/resistance
community-engaged research, 151, 154
compensatory justice. *See* busing, mandatory
Consent Degree in Chicago (1980), 59
Cooley High School (Detroit West Side), 84, 87, 177
Cooper Hospital (Camden, NJ), and neighborhood revitalization, 121
Cooper-Jenkins, Maceo A.: bio, 319; chapter by, 211–22; comments on, 225
Cortez, Gabriel, 64
The Cosby Show, 17, 19
counter-storytelling: challenging class and racial myths, 10, 13, 95, 314–15; defined, xv, 61, 70, 98, 124, 314; as self-preservation, 76; and social change, 63, 65. *See also* critical pedagogy; critical race theory (CRT); standpoint theory
Cream, Mrs. (teacher), 130, 131
critical pedagogy: about, 82, 279, 310–11; culturally relevant, 28, 124, 135, 272; hip-hop and spoken word, 153, 289–91; identity and praxis, Black women scholars', 20, 278–79; love-based, 213, 251, 257, 264, 310; "pedagogies of the home," 12–13. *See also* liberatory education
critical race theory (CRT): about, 10, 11, 98, 310, 313; in education, 106, 123–24, 126–27; and feminism, 106, 278–79. *See also* counter-storytelling
Crooklyn (film), 129
cultural capital: Bourdieusian conception of, 10, 11, 313; context-specific, 202, 205; sociocultural, minoritized students, 242, 247; White middle-class values, 10, 11, 125. *See also* community cultural wealth model (CCWM); cultural efficacy; Yosso, Tara J.
cultural competency, school, 155, 296
cultural efficacy: defined, 247; as liberatory education, 277, 278–80; southern schools, Black, 261; and student success, 240–42; value of folkways, 261
cultural enrichment programs, 293, 295. *See also individual programs*
culturally relevant pedagogy: and curriculum, 9, 28, 253, 260, 272; framework, 124, 135, 272
culturally responsive pedagogy: goals of, 120, 153, 165–66; teaching practices, 51, 52, 95, 300. *See also* liberatory education

Index | 333

culture of poverty framework, 96, 125
Cutler, D. M., 37

Dana (student), 129, 130, 128(t), 131–32
dangerous cities, label: anti-Black state and federal policies, 143–44; criminality imagery, 121; Detroit, 81–82; Philadelphia, 129, 128(t); urban uprisings, 142; Washington, DC, and refuge, 95
Dangerous Minds (film), 103
Danns, Dionne, 59, 60
Davila, Erica, 64
Dayo (social media respondent), 262
DCPS. *See* Washington (DC) public school system
De Hoogh, A. H., 219
deficit narratives: dominant framework, 1–2; conflation of people with buildings, 29, 105, 113, 161–62; critiques of, 29, 137, 145, 248; culture of poverty framework, 96, 125; devaluation of Blackness/Brownness, xiv, 10–12; in education research, 162, 253; outsider perspectives and, 103; as pathologizing, 103, 162, 246, 315; success metrics, 109, 110. *See also* community cultural wealth model (CCWM); cultural capital; Kozol, Jonathon
dehumanization, 11, 70, 113, 164
deindustrialization, 37, 38, 142. *See also* Detroit (MI)
Delgado, Richard, 98
Den Hartog, D. N., 219
desegregation, 26, 60, 63, 314. See also *Brown v. Board of Education* (1954); meritocracy myth; segregation

Detroit (MI), neighborhood communities: deindustrialization, 37, 79, 80–82; economic and racial demographics, 96, 80(t), 81(t); stock stories, 28, 29; student experiences, 30, 32, 83, 178; University District, 177–78; water shut-off crisis, 79
Detroit Board of Education, 26
Detroit Public School system: conditions, 27, 80, 88; cultural wealth within, 40, 84, 172, 177, 178
Detroit's Salvation Army Community Center, 185
DeVos, Betsy, 32
A Different World (television show), 19
Dignity in Schools Campaign (2013), 164
disaster relief parallels, 79, 82
displacement, student and worker, 61, 272
dominant ideology. *See* deficit narratives; meritocracy myth; stock stories
Donaldson, M., 98
double consciousness, 107
Douglass, Frederick, 29
Du Bois, W. E. B., 75, 107, 153, 250, 251, 256, 263
Dudley, Ms. Janie (teacher), 259
Dunbar Elementary School Chorale, 300
Duncan, Arnie, 164

early childhood education, 192, 196, 197, 198
East St. Louis (IL), neighborhood community: Black excellence, 275, 292; cultural pride, 267–68, 289–91; economic decline, 37, 271; outsider views, 10, 211, 232, 292; school district, 187, 294–95; student experiences, 29, 267, 268; Sunday dinners, 304–6

"ecological fallacy," xv
education: business-model, 104–5; civil rights, 62, 64; community-based, 310–11; formal and informal, 205, 207; and housing policy, 144. *See also* experiential learning; social capital; sociocultural education; standardization and testing
educational equity: Black educators on, 310–11; contradictory pedagogies, 123; course/curricular access, 275; discourse, 10, 30, 191–92; metrics, 122, 163, 165–66. *See also* Abbot Rulings (NJSC); critical pedagogy
educational inequalities: course/curricular access, 146, 275; overcrowding, 67, 121, 237, 251, 275; property tax funding model, 144, 232; school disciplinary practices, racialized, 146, 153, 155; staff quality/experience, 86, 104, 115, 146, 237; under-funding, 27, 88, 163, 277; under-resourcing, 87, 115, 237. See also *individual neighborhood communities*
educational justice: legal fight for, 87, 121–22; school-centered activism, 60, 62, 64, 148. See also *Brown v. Board of Education* (1954); critical pedagogy; liberatory education
Educational Leadership programs, 129, 128(t)
educational system: contradictory pedagogies, 123; and disinvestment, 3, 60, 62; gifted education, 73, 224; magnet schools, 31, 40, 202–3; and meritocracy ideal, 231; and social mobility, 198, 234; systemic barriers, teachers on, 89; White privilege and norms, 19, 85, 232, 242. *See also* charter schools; church; life lessons/skills; school tracking

Elliot, Te'mon'et (student), 113, 114, 115
Ellis, C., 176
Elon College (NC), 19
emancipatory discourses. *See* counter-storytelling; critical pedagogy; critical race theory (CRT); oral histories
Emerald City, imagery of wealthy schools, 263–64
enrichment programs, 293, 306
enslavement, history of, 150, 152, 256, 272
environmental racism, 32
equality of opportunity myth, 191–92. *See also* meritocracy myth
essentialism, 10, 11, 49, 151, 162; "good school" vs. "bad school" stereotypes, 23, 68, 162. *See also* stock stories
ethical leadership models, 220, 225, 263
ethnocentrism/Eurocentrism, 155, 251–52
ethnography: autoethnography, 50, 80, 83, 202, 278; cultural, 254, 263, 278
experiential learning, 84, 241, 247. *See also* counter-storytelling; life lessons/skills
extra-curricular activities, 31, 40, 294, 299

familial capital/kinship ties: and academic success, 172, 175, 182–83, 224–25; defined, 41, 62, 107, 192, 247; formal and informal learning, 30–31; work ethic, 17, 18, 44, 314. *See also* mentorship; Sunday dinners
family. *See* familial capital/kinship ties; fictive kin

Farmer-Hinton, Raquel L.: bio, 320; chapter by, 283–88; referenced, 10, 94, 98, 239, 310
feminist theory, critical race, 106, 278–79. See also critical race theory (CRT)
Ferguson, Plessy v., 87
fictive kin: and academic success, 224–25; college mentorship, 41, 74, 75, 111, 174, 175; community members, 174, 235; defined, 72, 75, 76n1; neighbors, 174, 304–5; peer support, 173–74, 179–80, 182–84; student retention framework and, 174, 175; teacher-student relationships, 63, 129, 134, 214–15; work-study programs, 186. See also mentorship; social capital
fine arts education, 135
first generation college students, 177, 180, 184, 185, 240. See also mentorship
Fischer, Eyatta, 242
Floyd, George, 292
Forbes, 81
Ford Motor Company, hiring practices, 37. See also automobile industry
Fordham, S., 171
Forman, M., 143
Frank Cody High School (Detroit), 178
Franklin Heights High School (Columbus, Ohio), 178
Freedman schools, Southern, 251–52
Freedom School, and Black identity/culture, 293, 295
friends/friendships, 193, 194, 198. See also fictive kin
Freire, P., 279
From Neurons to Neighborhoods (2000), xiv

fugitive spaces, Black educators', 310–11
funding, school: inequitable, 16, 87; property tax model, 144, 232; state inequities, 122. See also Abbot Rulings (NJSC); educational inequalities
Fuselier-Thompson, Diane: bio, 320; chapter by, 171–89

Gaines, Ernest, 206
Gandhi, Mahatma, 79
Garcia, D. G., 135
Gay, G., 120
gender, and caregiving roles, 195, 270
George Washington Carver High School of Arts, 237–38
gifted education, 73, 224
Gillborn, David, 309
Glaeser, E. L., 37
"good school" vs. "bad school" stereotypes: essentialism of, 23, 68, 162; and failure as racially coded, 114; as racially coded, 114. See also stock stories
"goodness" narratives, 93, 98, 110, 263
Goslee, A., 263
Gould, Stephen Jay *(The Mismeasurement of Man)*, xiv
graduation rates, 108, 110
Graves, S., 193–94
The Great Migration, 198, 287
Grosse Pointe Farms, Michigan (suburb), 24, 25, 26, 27
guidance counselors. See school counseling profession
Gullah culture, 255

Hall, Beverly L., 236
Harlem (NY), 1960s experiences, 196–97. See also New York City public schools

Harlem Renaissance, 44, 73
Harper, E. Royster, 181–82
Hauser Committee Report (1964), 64
Hawkins, Coral (fictional teacher), 63, 135
Haynes, Chayla: bio, 320; chapter by, 9–21; comments on, 49, 51
HBCUs (Historically Black Colleges or Universities), 42, 75, 285, 46n4
Head Start programs, 196
health and education discrepancies, 61
Hespe, David, 133
higher education success: campus resources, 179–80; community support, 184–87; consciousness-raising, 235–36; family and kin support, 173, 175, 182–83; and social mobility, 234, 238. *See also* fictive kin
high school students, and systemic barriers: dropout rates, 121; math scores by race/ethnicity, 87; reading scores by race/ethnicity, 86
Hilbert, Ms. (teacher), 73
Hilton Head (SC), 256
Historically Black Colleges or Universities (HBCUs), 42, 75, 285, 46n4
Holcomb-McCoy, C., 155
home, meanings of: family and kin, 249, 283–87; neighborhood as, 235, 304–5; school-home communities, 257, 264, 274; sense of belonging, 69, 260, 278, 279. *See also* Sunday dinners
home economics, 256–57
hope vs. despair, 45, 95, 246, 247, 262–63. *See also* community cultural wealth model (CCWM); ethical leadership models; resistant capital/resistance

housing projects, low-income, 178, 271, 304, 128(t), 261–63
housing segregation, 59, 246, 269
Howard University, experiences of, 19, 75
Howard University Hospital, 73
Hughes, Ms. (teacher), 73
Hughes, S., 96
humanizing approaches, 50, 52, 97
Hurston, Zora Neale, 254

I Know Why the Caged Bird Sings (Angelou), 44
identity: academic-athletic balance, 204–5; community vs. work, 286, 287; neighborhood and school, 112–13; place and displacement, 23–26; and praxis, Black women scholars, 20, 278–79. *See also* intersectionality
ideologies, dominant. *See* counter-storytelling; deficit narratives
individualism. *See* meritocracy myth
industry. *See* deindustrialization
Inman Park (Atlanta) library, 235
"inner city" and "urban": conflation with individuals, 202; "good school-bad school" stereotypes, 23, 49, 68, 114, 162; as racial and class coding, 234, 246, 251; in White American psyche, 143. *See also* stock stories
insider vs. outsider perspectives, 35, 223–24, 225–26, 247–48, 249–50
integrity, 257, 292, 297–298
International Baccalaureate (IB) programs, 202, 203, 206
International Journal of Qualitative Studies in Education, 97
intersectionality, 26, 202, 224
Irby, D., 164

"it's the small foxes that destroy the vine," 292, 297–298. *See also* familial capital/kinship ties
Ivy League schools, 203, 205, 241

Jackson, Omari: bio, 320–21; chapter by, 35–47; comments on, 49, 51
Jefferson County Public School District, 152–53
Jenkins, Mr. (teacher), 130, 131
Jenkins, Toby S.: bio, 321; chapter by, 245–66; comments on, 278
Jennings, M. E., 98
Jobs for America's Graduates program, 111
John DeShields Housing Project (East St. Louis), 304
Jordan, Jodi L.: bio, 321; chapter by, 267 75

Kalshoven, K., 213
Katie Wright Elementary School (East St. Louis), 299–300
Keisch, D. M., 144
Kempster, S., 213
Kentucky police violence, 292
King, Martin Luther, 206
Kingston, Paul, 239–40
Koushik, Jada Renee: bio, 321; chapter by, 23–32; comments on, 49, 51
Kozol, Jonathon: as "cultural stranger," 27, 95, 263; on equal opportunity myth, 60, 119, 144–45, 191–92; "good school" vs. "bad school" story, 23, 68; hopelessness imagery, 232; leadership caricatures in, 219, 220, 225; on racialized class reproduction, 30, 89; on students and communities, 29, 59, 63, 70, 179; on urban school inequities, 58, 89, 232. *See also* community cultural wealth model (CCWM); deficit narratives; *Savage Inequalities*; Yosso, Tara J.
Kricun, Andy, 121

labor market shifts, 35, 37. *See also* Detroit (MI); East St. Louis (IL)
Ladson-Billings, G., 123, 124, 136
Lalonde, Sister John, 273
Laticia (student), 128(t)
Latimer, Lewis, 44
Latina/o/x, 62, 64, 238
Lawrence-Lightfoot, Sara, 93, 98
leadership models, ethical, 220, 225, 263
Lean on Me (film), 103
LEAP Academy (charter school), 122–23
learning conditions, unequal, 43, 89. *See also* educational inequalities
learning-disability label, 249
Lee, Spike, 129
Lee, Stacey, 206
Lenaami (student), 112–13
A Lesson Before Dying (Gaines), 206
Leticia (student), 129, 130, 134
Lewis, James Jr. (brother of Joi), 300
Lewis, James Sr. (grandfather of Joi), 298
Lewis, Joi D.: bio, 322; chapters by, 1–5, 289–301; referenced, 94, 310
Lewis, Trudy B. (grandmother), 291, 292
liberatory education, 63, 311. *See also* critical pedagogy
libraries, public, 235, 239, 297
life lessons/skills: practical and sociocultural, 4, 68, 75, 287; and survival, 246–47, 259–61, 297–298, 303–4

338 | Index

Lincoln Senior High School (East St. Louis), 275, 297, 300
linguistic capital: and "code switching," 25, 31, 236; defined, 12, 107, 192, 247; oral histories, 249, 258–60; and Whiteness, 18
Lipman, P., 144
lived experience. *See* experiential learning
Lorde, Audre, 70
Louisville Urban League, 154–55
Louisville West End (KY) student experiences, 151, 152, 153–55
love-based pedagogy, 213, 251, 257, 264, 310. *See also* Sunday dinners
low-income urban youth experiences, 110, 111–13
Lynn, Marvin: bio, 322; chapter by, 93–100

MacLeod, J., 179
Madden, Mr. (teacher), 131
magnet schools, 31, 40, 202–3. *See also* River Oak Academy (NY)
"Making It Out of the Ghetto," 261–63
Malcolm X, 206
Mandela, Nelson, 19
Marland Report, 203–4
Marshall, John, 152–54
Martin, Ijshanna (student), 112
Marx, Sherry, 310
Maryland public schools, 16–17
Massenburg, Mrs. (teacher), 297–298
master narratives, deficit-driven, xiv, 10, 69, 71–72. *See also* deficit narratives
Mayer, D. M., 220
McGee, Mrs. (teacher), 155
McPherson, Ezella: bio, 322; chapter by, 171–89; comments on, 225
McWayne, C., 196

media narratives, 40, 115, 143, 151, 241. *See also* deficit narratives; stereotypes
mediocrity, 12, 205, 241. *See also* academic success; gifted education
mentorship: college, 41, 74, 75, 111, 174, 175; family members, 291, 298–99; paid fellowships, 216; peer, 240; work-study programs, 181–82. *See also* 21st Century Atlanta Scholars programs; fictive kin
meritocracy myth, 10, 31, 231
methods/methodology: autoethnography, 80, 82, 83, 202, 278; Camden study questionnaire, 127(t); critical race theory and counter-storytelling, 126–27; ethnography, 254, 263, 278; narrative analysis, 3, 94, 176, 254
Mexican American community, 60, 64
migration: economic, 80, 96, 198, 287; family stories, 284, 304; student experiences, 57–58, 185–86
Milliken v. Bradley, 87
Milner, H. Richard IV: bio, 323; chapter by, 323–27
Minnesota, student experience in, 295
The Mis-Education of the Negro (Woodson), 252–53
The Mis-measurement of Man (Gould), xiv
Mobley, Steve D. Jr.: chapter by, 67–78; comments on, 95
Model Code on Education and Dignity, 164–65
model minority stereotypes, 206, 208
Moore Roberson, Heather: bio, 323; chapter by, 201–9; comments on, 224
Morris Jr., Lonnie R.: bio, 323–24; chapter by, 211–22; comments on, 225

Mount Union College (Ohio), 14
Moynihan, Patrick *(Negro Family)*, xiv
Multicultural Advancement/Cofer Scholars (MAC Scholars), 180, 186
music education, 135, 268, 300. *See also* church

narrative inquiry, described, 2–3, 212–13. *See also* autoethnography; counter-storytelling
National Honor Society (school program), 306
national identity and schools, 64
Navarro, Rosa (teacher), 63
navigational capital: Black teachers and, 16, 130; defined, 13, 130, 192; life skills, 241, 246–47; local businesses/stores, 305–6; non-traditional learning spaces, 310–11; and resilience, 42, 43, 65, 46n5; student experiences, 64–65
Negro Family (Moynihan), xiv
neighborhood schools: charter schools vs., 32, 104, 109, 123, 136; community bonds and, 129, 131, 133; physical conditions and closures, 122, 274–75
Network for the Development of Children of African Descent (NDCAD), 295–96
New England, Black faculty experience, 41–42
New Jersey Department of Education (NJDOE), 108, 122, 133
New Jersey Legislature, 122
New Jersey public schools, 96, 119, 134. *See also* Camden City School District (CCSD)
New Jersey Supreme Court, 121–22
New Orleans, 82, 246
New York City Department of Education, 198
New York City public schools, 196, 199
New York State, 203
New York State Regents examinations, 206–7. *See also* standardization and testing
Newark (NJ), 121
Newsweek school rankings, 203
Newton, Lyntoria, 278–79; bio, 324; chapter by, 231–44; comments on, 277–78
Next Generation (school club), 293–94
Nguzo-Saba principles, Kwanzaa, 272
Nichols, Samir (student), 120
NJDOE Quality Single Accountability Continuum assessment, 108
No Child Left Behind program (2001), 85, 115
Nobles, Wade, 149–50
Noddings, N., 131
Noguera, Pedro, 162
"none of us is as smart as all of us," 292–95
Norcross, George, 105, 122
North Carolina colleges, 18, 19

Omi, M., 151
oral histories, 249, 258–59, 254–60
origin stories, urban, 94
overcrowding, 67, 121, 237, 251, 275
Owsianik, M., 196
Oz (image/concept), 260

Palmer, R. T., 173
"paradigm of the personal," 110
parents/parental: aspirations, 287; community bonds with Black teachers, 194–95; encouragement and support, 12, 14; expectations, academic, 272, 274; involvement, 197; sacrifices, 271–73; styles, 73,

parents/parental *(continued)*
  287. *See also* aspirational capital; familial capital/kinship ties
Parkside (Camden) neighborhood, 129, 128(t). *See also* Camden Public Schools (CPS)
parochial schools, 274
Parry, K., 213
Paterson, NJ, 121
Patton, Deborah J.: bio, 324; chapter by, 267–75
Patton, Lori D.: bio, 324; chapters by, 1–5, 267–75; referenced, 94, 239, 310
peer support, 174, 180, 183. *See also* fictive kin; mentorship
The Penn School (SC), oral history, 252, 255, 256, 258
performing arts programs, 204, 294, 205, 237–38
personal narratives, value of, 97, 314. *See also* autoethnography; counter-storytelling; experiential learning
Philadelphia, student experiences, 278, 128(t)
pink-collar roles, women's, 37, 46n1
place and belonging, 27, 28. See also *individual cities*
Plessy v. Ferguson, 87
poetry as pedagogy, 289–91
police/policing: in housing projects, 94; racialized violence/brutality, 81, 142, 292, 294; school-community relations, 88, 121
pop-cultural icons, 17, 268, 299
"portraiture," educational tool, 98
positive school culture concept, 162
poverty, systemic, 81, 121, 232, 262–63
predominantly White institutions, 19, 180, 185, 293–94, 295–96
press forward toward the goal, 20–21

pride: cultural education and self, 186, 257, 301; *positive school culture,* 162; relationship between school and community, 273–74; students, urban, 240; teachers' role, Black, 130, 131, 195, 294. *See also* community cultural wealth model (CCWM)
Prince George's County, Maryland, 16
privileged poor communities concept, 234
Project Ready (Louisville), 154
public libraries, 235, 239, 297
public-private partnerships, 122. *See also* charter schools
Puerto Rican community, 63, 64

Qualitative Inquiry, 98
Queen Brown Porridge (Rosenwald School alumna), 258–60. *See also* Black schools, rural Southern

race and racism: biological discourses, 151; emplaced, and privilege, 28–32; institutional, 40, 123, 142; internalized, 32; redlining, 27, 235; school disciplinary practices, 146, 153, 155; school tracking, 10, 30, 131; student experiences of White academic spaces, 19, 42–43. *See also* culture of poverty framework; segregation; structural racism; Whiteness/White normalcy
Race to the Top (2008), 115
race traitor, 309–10
racial capitalism, 310
racial demographic shifts, 80, 80(t)
Randolph, A. W., 195
redlining, 27, 235
Reed, Dana (mayor), 108, 121, 122
rescue narratives, White, 136, 147, 155

resilience/resilience systems, 75, 76, 115, 175; navigational capital and, 42, 65, 42n5. *See also* fictive kin
resistant capital/resistance: Black educators and, 309–10; community advocacy and, 153; defined, 13, 16, 44, 107, 192; self-determination and, 126, 310–11; of students, 113, 120, 123, 275; work ethic, 17, 18, 44, 314. *See also* culturally relevant pedagogy; school-centered activism
re-storying. *See* counter-storytelling
retention, student, 134, 173, 240
"revitalization" discourse, 161
Reynolds, Sadiqa, 154
River Oak Academy (NY), 202–7, 209n1. *See also* magnet schools
Rivera, Angelica, 64
Rivers, Ishwanzya D.: bio, 324–25; chapter by, 303–7; referenced, 92, 237, 308
Robin (student), 127, 129, 133, 126(t)
Rogers, John, 308
role models: Black teachers as, 130; classroom leadership and, 212–17, 295–96; family members as, 289, 296–97; model minority stereotypes, 204, 205, 206; pop-cultural icons as, 17, 266; students within "ghetto" as, 261. *See also* mentorship; school counseling profession; teachers
Rosch, D. M., 212
Rose, Chanelle: bio, 325; chapter by, 119–39; comments on, 161, 163
Rosenwald School (SC) oral history, 255–56, 258–59
Ryan, Paul, 141, 143

Saturday Scholars Program, 306
Savage Inequalities (Kozol): about, 1–2; teacher education canon, 9, 115, 145, 223, 250–51; and White audience, 309, 310. *See also Brown v. Board of Education* (1954); deficit narratives; Kozol, Jonathon; urban education studies
scholarship awards, college, 14, 177, 180, 184
School Based Youth Services (Camden), 110
school board participation, 108, 109. *See also* state takeover
school conditions: dilapidated structures/physical, 67, 274–75; overcrowding, 67, 251, 275; underfunding, 27, 88, 163, 277
school counseling profession, 147; Black consciousness and professional identity, 149–50; counselors as fictive kin, 18, 110, 174, 237; critical pedagogy, 153; multicultural competency and reflexivity, 155–56; school-community collaboration frameworks, 146–48; social justice advocacy, 145–46, 149–50; unpacking racial myths, 151–52; White middle-class homogeneity, 146, 147, 151, 155–56. *See also* community-engaged research; strength-based approaches
school funding: per-pupil, 122; property tax financing, 144, 232; students protests over cuts, 120
School Sisters of Notre Dame (SSND), 271
school tracking, 10, 30, 131
school-centered activism, 62, 64, 123, 148
schools/schooling: closures, 122, 274–75; clubs as safe spaces, 293–94; community collaborations, 152; contradictory values and

schools/schooling *(continued)*
goals, 164; disciplinary practices, racialized, 146, 153, 155; family history and connections in, 236–37; naming and heritage, 61; physical conditions, 84; student-to-teacher ratios, smaller, 237; zoning, 16. *See also* charter schools; educational inequalities; magnet schools
Schwalbe, Michael, 232
Scott, T., 144
Scott Air Force Base, 268–69
Scott-Montgomery Elementary School (DC) Gifted and Talented program, 73. *See also* enrichment programs
second-generation college students, 285–86
segregation: class, 37, 252; educational/school, 59, 119, 152, 255; legal, 150; racial and ethnic, 62, 64; residential, 59, 246, 269; school-centered activism, 62, 64. See also *Brown v. Board of Education* (1954); desegregation; meritocracy myth; white flight
self-determination and resistance, 126, 310–11
self-efficacy, 254, 256, 258, 260–61
Senge, P. M., 164
Signature Partnerships, school-community, 152
Simmons-White, Ms. Gardenia (student), 255–57
social capital: defined, 13, 41, 107, 194; neighborhood, 75, 132, 177–78, 193–94, 305–6; Bourdieusian definition, 125; school staff and, 111, 130, 133. *See also* collectivism; fictive kin; life lessons/skills; Sunday dinners
social mobility, 125, 234, 297
social networks. *See* social capital

socialization process, 143, 296. *See also* cultural capital
sociocultural education, 197, 257, 269, 293. *See also* church; life lessons/skills
sociology of education, 204, 235. *See also* Bourdieu, Pierre; Carter, Prudence
Solórzano, D., 2, 72, 98, 124
The Souls of Black Folk (Du Bois), 251
South Atlanta High School, 237
South Bronx (NY), 193, 196, 199
South Carolina, 250, 256
speech teams, 299–300
sports/athletics, 131, 203, 296
St. Helena Island (SC), 252, 261
St. Joseph's Catholic school (East St. Louis), 271, 272–74
St. Mark's Church (St. Louis), 270
St. Paul (MN), 293, 295
standardization and testing: and accountability discourse, 115; IB and gifted programs, 204, 206–7; vs. life skills, 241; and success indicators, 39, 134
standpoint theory, 106
state takeover, school district 122, 134
Steen, S., 150
stereotypes: Black communities, 28, 150, 151–52; Black male, 72–73; in education research, 67–68; student resistance to, 113, 114, 115. *See also* deficit narratives
stock stories, 49, 93, 95, 153–54. *See also* deficit narratives
storytelling, 254, 292. *See also* autoethnography; counter-storytelling
Stovall, David: bio, 325–26; chapter by, 309–11
The Street Academy (Louisville), 154

strength-based approaches, 68, 147, 163, 225
structural racism: as resource redistribution, 29, 244; and systemic inequality, 10, 79, 95, 161, 233, 240. *See also* segregation
student loans, teacher, 132–33
student retention framework, 172, 173, 174
suburban school districts: affluence, 24, 25, 26, *27*; as Emerald City, 261–62; as racialized and classed spaces, 49; school-board participation, 102
Sunday dinners: as family reunions, 270–71, 283–84; informal learning and storytelling, 303–4; shopping and social networks, 305–6; significance of, 4, 14, 269. *See also* familial capital/kinship ties; social capital
Sweetland Writing Center (UofM), 179

Talkative Tigers Speech Team, 300
talking back. *See* counter-storytelling
Tarte, Joel (student), 114, 115
Tate, W., 98, 124
Taylor, Breonna, 292
Teach for America, 109
teacher education: Black educators on, 124; class and race insularity, 135–36; cultural competency, 95, 124, 205–6; culturally responsive pedagogy, 120, 153, 165–66; deficit narratives, 86, 97, 145; humanizing approaches, 50, 52, 97; lessons from students, 84–85; philosophies/ ethics, 84, 85, 87, 90; portraiture as tool, 98; rescue narratives, White, 136, 147, 155. *See also* community cultural wealth model (CCWM); critical pedagogy

teachers: care ethic, 63, 162; classroom communication, 215–16; and culturally responsive practices, 51, 52, 95, 300; as fictive kin, 132, 172, 174, 259, 260; and hiring practices, 62; impact/support, 132, 133, 238, 296; and navigational capital, 42–43; parent-teacher relationships in community, 257; and retention, 88, 249; and staff quality/experience, 86, 104, 115, 146, 237; on systemic barriers and conditions, 88, 89; and White racial biases, 86. *See also* Black teachers; church; *individual teachers*
Teachers College Record, 1
Things Fall Apart (Achebe), 19
third-world living conditions, 79. *See also* Detroit (MI)
thriving, 241, 267, 310
To whom much is given, much is required, 45
Toldson, Ivory, 155
Townes, Laura, 255
tracking/streaming. *See* school tracking
trade school. *See* vocational training
transformative education. *See* liberatory education
Trent, William, xiii–xv, 3–4; bio, 326
Trenton, NJ, 121
Trevino, L. K., 220
Troutman, Brene (student), 112
Truesdell Elementary (northwest Washington), 15–16
Tubman, Harriet, 29
Tuley High School (Chicago), 61
Turrick (student mentor), 75
Tyack, David, 64

under-funding, school, 27, 88, 163, 277

Union Tabernacle Church (St. Louis), 270
United Nations (UN) on living conditions, 79
United Way, on income inequality, 81
University District (Detroit), 177–78
University of Illinois (Urbana-Champaign), 59
University of Louisville (Kentucky), 152
University of Michigan, 39, 84, 96, 179–80
University of Michigan–Ann Arbor Office of Student Activities and Leadership, 181–82
University of Oklahoma, 185
University of Pennsylvania, 204
University of Saskatchewan, 25, 32
Upward bound, after-school program, 306
"urban" as term. See "inner city" and "urban"
Urban Education, 1
urban education studies: white gaze, 49–51, 309–11. See also community cultural wealth model (CCWM); insider vs outsider perspectives; Kozol, Jonathon
"Urban Hope Act" (2012) (NJ), 122
US Bureau of Labor Statistics, 121
US Supreme Court, 194. See also *Brown v. Board of Education* (1954)
USA Today, 108

Valencia, Richard, 98
values and ethics, community: collectivism, 13, 294–95; community responsibility, 107, 134, 261, 262–63; dignity/dignity work, 164–65; graduation, college, 180; integrity, 257, 273, 292, 297–98; love-based pedagogy, 213, 251, 257, 264, 310; work ethic, 17, 18, 44, 314. See also familial capital/kinship ties
Velázquez, Mirelsie: chapter by, 57–66; comments on, 94–95
victim-blaming ideology, 70, 143, 163
victimization discourse, 68
village. See familial capital/kinship ties; fictive kin
violence: gang, 83, 261–62; police, racialized, 81, 142, 292, 294
vocational training, 104, 256

Waiting for Superman, 103
Wall Street Journal, 122
Walsh, F., 175
Washington, Ahmad R.: bio, 326; chapter by, 141–60; comments on, 161, 165
Washington, Booker T., 256
Washington, Harold, 58
Washington (DC), public school system: environmental conditions, 69, 70–71; neighborhood characterization of, 10, 11, 15, 16; student experiences, 71, 75, 95; teacher experiences, 213
Washington Park (St. Louis), 271
Watson, Dallas Jewell: bio, 327; chapter by, 289–301
Wayne State University (WSU), 41
#weareEastStLouis, 301
West Atlanta, 234–35
Whetstone, Deliyah, 110, 111
white flight, 59, 64, 80, 269
white gaze, 49–51, 309–11. See also deficit narratives; Kozol, Jonathon; urban education studies
White institutions, predominantly (PWIs), 57, 185, 202, 205
White missionary schools, 255
White privilege, 19, 85, 130, 242, 310

Index | 345

White rescue narratives, 136, 147, 155
White supremacy, 50, 52, 97, 144, 311
Whiteness/White normalcy: alienation discourse, 143; equity discourse, 10, 30; and identity, 25; linguistic capital, 18, 25, 31; material advantage, 152; middle-class educational norms, 231, 238, 242; and racial myths about Blackness, 86, 151, 156, 295–96. *See also* school counseling profession
Who's Afraid of Virginia Woolf (Albee), 206
Wilbon, Lawrence, 154
Williams, Brittany M.: bio, 327; chapter by, 231–44; comments on, 279
Wilson, W. J., 81
Wilson Elementary (East St. Louis), 271
Winant, H., 151
Winter, Steven, 61
"within the history/inside the culture," 247–48. *See also* insider vs. outsider perspectives

The Wiz (film), 268, 272, 277, 278
The Wizard of Oz (film), 245, 277, 278
Women of the Dream (Camden, NJ), 111
women-headed households, 15, 83
Woodson, Carter G., 150, 153, 250, 252
work ethic, 17, 18, 44, 314
work-study programs, 181–82
Wright, Richard *(Black Boy)*, 73

Yasmine (student), 129, 128(t), 130–31, 134–35
Yosso, Tara J.: bio, 327; Black cultural capital overview, 2, 4, 125, 233; chapter by, 313–16; on counter-storytelling method, 72, 98, 124, 267–68. *See also* community cultural wealth model (CCWM); counter-storytelling

zero tolerance policies, 164, 251
zoning policies, 16, 237

www.ingramcontent.com/pod-product-compliance
Ingram Content Group UK Ltd.
Pitfield, Milton Keynes, MK11 3LW, UK
UKHW040843010225
454384UK00009B/113